Situated astride the trade routes of the western Mediterranean, the Catalan kingdom of Majorca has long deserved attention. It was established under the will of King James I of Aragon, who conquered Majorca in 1229, but was ruled from 1276 to 1343 by a cadet dynasty. In addition to the Balearic islands the kingdom included the key business centres of Montpellier and Perpignan, and other lands in what is now southern France. It was also home to important Jewish and Muslim communities, and was the focus of immigration from Catalonia, Provence and Italy.

This book emphasises the major transformations in the trade of the Balearic islands from the eve of the Catalan conquest to the Black Death, and the effect of the kingdom's creation and demise on the economy of the region. Links between the island and mainland territories, and as far afield as England and the Canaries, are analysed in depth.

A MEDITERRANEAN EMPORIUM

A MEDITERRANEAN EMPORIUM

The Catalan kingdom of Majorca

DAVID ABULAFIA

Reader in Mediterranean History, University of Cambridge,
and Fellow of Gonville and Caius College

PUBLISHED BY THE PRESS SYNDICATE OF THE UNIVERSITY OF CAMBRIDGE
The Pitt Building, Trumpington Street, Cambridge, United Kingdom

CAMBRIDGE UNIVERSITY PRESS
The Edinburgh Building, Cambridge CB2 2RU, UK
40 West 20th Street, New York NY 10011–4211, USA
477 Williamstown Road, Port Melbourne, VIC 3207, Australia
Ruiz de Alarcón 13, 28014 Madrid, Spain
Dock House, The Waterfront, Cape Town 8001, South Africa

http://www.cambridge.org

First published 1994
First paperback edition 2002

A catalogue record for this book is available from the British Library

Library of Congress Cataloguing in Publication data
Abulafia, David.
A Mediterranean emporium: the Catalan kingdom of Majorca / David Abulafia.
p.   cm.
ISBN 0 521 32244 8
1. Majorca (Spain) – History.   2. Balearic Islands (Spain) –
Commerce – History – 13th century.   I. Title.
DP302.B27A28   1994
946'.754–dc20   93-1700   CIP

ISBN 0 521 32244 8 hardback
ISBN 0 521 89405 0 paperback

Transferred to digital printing 2005

for Philip Grierson
'tu se'lo mio maestro e'l mio autore'

E poblà la dita ciutat e illa ab majors franquees e llibertats que ciutat sia e'l món; per què és vui una de les bones ciutats que sia e'l món, e noble e ab majors riquees e poblada tota de catalans, tots d'honrats llocs e de bo, per què en són eixits hereus qui són vui la pus covinent gent e mills nodrida que ciutat qui e'l món sia.

And he [King James I] resettled the said city and island, offering more privileges and liberties than in any other city in the world; as a result it is now one of the finest cities in the world, a noble city, wealthier than others, and wholly inhabited by Catalans, all from honourable places and of good standing, from whom have descended heirs who are now the most fortunate and best favoured people of any city in the world.

Ramón Muntaner on the City of Mallorca, c. 1325,
Crònica, cap. 8.

Contents

Preface

I

The Catalan kingdom of Majorca is a perplexing entity. It stood in the middle of an emergent association of kingdoms and principalities that historians have, with an excess of zeal, labelled the 'Aragonese–Catalan Empire', whereas in fact the various rulers of this 'empire' seem to have been almost as often at war with one another as at peace. Majorca's brief period of independence, from 1276 to 1343, was marked by constant attempts by the neighbouring kings of Aragon to assert their authority over its own rulers; indeed, for several years, from 1285 to 1298, the kingdom of Majorca to all intents ceased to exist, as a result of the hostile Aragonese invasion of the Balearics. The kingdom is perplexing, too, in its combination of territories strung out across a considerable distance, from the island of Formentera in the far south to the small enclave of Carlat on the edge of Auvergne; its three principal cities, Ciutat de Mallorca (now generally known as Palma), Perpignan and Montpellier, were very different in character, though all serviced the trade routes linking northern Europe, southern France and Mediterranean Spain to Africa and Italy. It is easy to dismiss the kingdom as a motley assortment of territories, awkwardly placed, lacking any viability as an autonomous state.

The aim of this book is to see how coherently this kingdom functioned, particularly as a commercial crossroads between Europe and Africa. This is, then, a study of the kingdom's external connections, its 'international status', both in trade and politics, rather than an attempt to describe its internal features: its agrarian development, its administration, both lay and ecclesiastical, its social relations. Nor does the career of the Mallorcan mystic and missionary Ramón Llull, who has justifiably attracted so much attention, feature

xi

significantly in this book, except briefly in chapter 1, where events in his life are used to set the wider scene. The heroes of the book are in the first instance the kings themselves, James II of Majorca (1276–85 and 1298–1311), Sanç or Sancho (1311–24) and James III (1324–43); in the second instance they are the merchants of the kingdom, Jews, Christians and (in rarer cases) Muslims. Attempts by King James II to create an integrated economy, tying the Balearics to the mainland territories, are thus an important theme of the book. So too trade between the constituent parts of the kingdom has been analysed closely; a complete outline of the commerce of Montpellier and Perpignan is therefore not offered, and the emphasis in discussing their trade links is firmly on trade links to one another and, above all, to Mallorca and Menorca.

Closely related to the question of the effect that the creation of the new kingdom had on the trade of its constituent parts is the question of the emergence of Mallorca as a major centre of trade in the western Mediterranean in the thirteenth century, and its long-term performance within the trading networks of the region. Thus it is essential to begin the history of Balearic trade well before 1276, even before the conquest by the Catalans in 1229, and to continue it beyond the reincorporation of Mallorca into the Aragonese patrimony in 1343. Only then can the impact of the creation of a special Majorcan kingdom be measured. Put simply, the question is this. Did it serve the interests of Mallorcan merchants better to be members of an Aragonese–Catalan–Valencian–Sardinian conglomerate of states under a single ruler, or to be subjects of a local king who was keen to prosecute their interests as far afield as north Africa and even England, but whose motives were in part mercenary?

There are further advantages in looking at the commercial documentation either side of 1276 and 1343. The period from 1229 to 1276, when the Balearics formed part of James I's Aragonese–Catalan federation, sees the transformation of a Muslim territory into a Christian one, not just in respect of the political structures, but also in a demographic sense: Catalan merchants, mainly Christian, alongside Italians and Provençaux, create a business community with remarkable speed, and so references to Mallorcans soon come thick and fast in the commercial documentation; the Muslims disappear from view; the Jewish community, flourishing at first, is increasingly exposed to royal persecution, especially under King Sanç. This was a settler society, different in character from, say,

Valencia, where a majority of Muslims can still be observed in the late thirteenth century, and where Islam was not officially suppressed till 1525. The Balearics formed a Christian forward position perched almost on the edge of Africa. Their entry into Spain was a gradual process, completed only by the conquest at the hands of Peter IV and the suppression of an independent kingdom that had tried to determine its own relations with Muslim Africa and with the kingdom of France.

The shape of this book reflects these concerns. The first chapter offers a rapid survey of the political history of the Balearics, with an emphasis on the period of the independent kingdom; the aim is to set the scene, and many points are taken up at greater length in later chapters. But, in view of the omission of the region from most histories of Spain and even of Aragon–Catalonia, such a survey seemed essential. In the second chapter, the historiography of the kingdom is examined, with particular attention to the problem of relating the mainland territories to the island part of the kingdom. In the third chapter, an attempt is made to answer the question of what constituted this kingdom: its relations with Aragon and the make-up of its constituent territories are analysed; this is constitutional history in a strict sense. The discussion at this point tries to take on board Jocelyn Hillgarth's important reassessment of how the Catalan–Aragonese commonwealth in the western Mediterranean functioned. This material is also essential for an understanding of the framework in which the kingdom's trade was conducted. The next two chapters address the religious minorities in the kingdom: any attempt to define what this kingdom was must confront the problem of the status of Jews and Muslims in the midst of the Christian settler population; a particularly important issue is the violent incorporation of Muslim Menorca into the Christian Balearics in 1287, after over half a century of internal autonomy. Moreover, the economic activities of the Jews and Muslims, as well as the indigenous Christians or Mozarabs, were of some importance to the economy of both the Balearics and Roussillon.

In the second and larger part of this book the emphasis shifts to trade: the antecedents, in Italian trade with Muslim Mayurqa; the growth of Catalan and foreign commercial communities after the conquest by James I; the crisis of the Vespers, when Majorca took opposite sides to Aragon–Catalonia; the attempts, from 1298 or thereabouts, to make the kingdom autonomous in its economic affairs; the evidence in the last two decades of Majorcan independence for intra-Majorcan trade between the mainland territories and the islands; and, finally, and more briefly, the changes in the character of Mallorcan trade after two events that need to be weighed up side by side: the fall of the Majorcan kingdom in 1343 and the arrival of the Black Death, five years later. The history of Mallorcan trade after 1343 is treated here in relation to what has been observed before that date; significant changes in the character of its exports, mirroring a wider tendency to economic specialisation in late medieval Europe, are analysed, with the particular help of the famous Datini archive in the Tuscan town of Prato.

A separate chapter is devoted to the problem of the Atlantic trade routes, which, it is suggested, remained very much alive throughout the lifetime of the independent kingdom; this chapter also addresses the Majorcan claim to the Canary islands, and the evidence from the magnificent Mallorcan portolan charts which still survive in many European museums and libraries. In appendix 1, the question of Mallorcan–Sardinian relations is examined; while links to southern France, Spain and north Africa have been discussed by earlier writers who have had occasion to mention Mallorcan merchants, the ties to Sardinia, the eastern neighbour of the Balearics, have been neglected; this is especially regrettable, since evidence from 1267 indicates the existence of a plan to unite Sardinia with the nascent Majorcan kingdom.

A difficulty has been the balance between coverage of the island and mainland sectors of the kingdom. The prime focus of the book is the Balearics, but every attempt has been made to take on board relevant commercial documentation from Perpignan and Montpellier, and the book has been written in the conviction that even treatment of the islands must show an understanding of their position within a larger kingdom. Thus policy towards the Jews was similar in Mallorca and in Perpignan; this was no mere coincidence. Plans to boost the economy affected mainland and islands, and were based precisely on the assumption that a common economic area could be created linking Roussillon, if not necessarily Montpellier, to the Balearics. In dealing with longer term developments, however, it has not generally seemed so useful to bring Roussillon and Montpellier on board, with the exception of occasional evidence for trade through Collioure in Roussillon, and some evidence concerning the Jews of

Perpignan which slightly antedates the formation of the Majorcan kingdom.

To reinforce this idea that all the territories of the Majorcan crown need to be borne in mind, I have based this book on primary sources, quite a few of which remain unpublished, in the archives of the three principal cities of the Majorcan state, Palma de Mallorca, Perpignan and Montpellier. It is there, rather than in Barcelona, that I have sought material; but I could not have written the book without the marvellous assistance provided by published texts from Barcelona. I have also made use of the Majorcan archives in Paris, which do most to illuminate the kingdom's constitutional position. Archive material from Genoa, Prato and London has also been laid under contribution. In those areas where modern scholars have already published significant contributions, I have tried to re-examine the documentation and to place it in the context of my wider argument about the viability of the Majorcan kingdom.

This book considerably extends the argument and subject matter of a series of articles by me that have appeared in journals and acts of congresses over the last few years; these are listed in the bibliography. Every attempt has been made to work this material into a coherent whole; but it has not been possible to avoid a certain amount of repetition when, for instance, dealing with the political, religious and economic aspects of the Majorcan kings' attempts to assert their own independence. In view of the novelty of the subject matter of this book to those who are not intimately involved in the history of the Crown of Aragon, and in view of the importance of the kingdom as a crossroads of trade in the late Middle Ages, occasional emphatic repetition has seemed desirable. Where issues addressed briefly in one chapter are taken much further in another, full cross-references have been supplied.

II

Spanish history is in my family's blood, at least until 1492 when my own ancestors joined the enforced exodus of the Sephardim. Even so, it may seem the height of folly, in days of increasing specialisation, for a historian who has spent some years engaged on research on the merchants and kingdoms of Italy to immerse himself in the rarefied world of Spanish history. But if, to outside observers, there is an obvious complaint about the writing of medieval Spanish history, it is the tendency to treat Iberia as a world unto itself; maybe, indeed, it is the openness of the Balearics to French, African and Italian contacts that has deterred some Spanish historians from paying attention to them. After all, they are not part of the Iberian peninsula; they are not, perhaps, automatically 'Spanish', though the arrival of the Catalan settlers in the thirteenth century drew them more and more into Spain to which they are now tied (though as an autonomous government within a federal kingdom). My initial approach to the lands of the Crown of Aragon was thus from Sicily through Sardinia to the Balearics, from the edges inwards, and this has perhaps dictated my emphasis on what held the Catalan–Aragonese commonwealth apart as well as what held it together. Catalonia–Aragon must be considered in the setting of the entire western Mediterranean, through which its merchants traded and over much of which its kings (often more than one at once) ruled. Within this space, the Majorcan kingdom formed an enclave, of ambiguous status, suspended in the midst of Catalonia, France, Genoa, Pisa, Sardinia, Naples, Sicily, Tunis, Tlemcen, Morocco, Castile, Granada, Murcia and Valencia.

At a time of increased interest in the concept of a federal Europe, possibly even a 'Europe of the regions', the history of the Catalan–Aragonese commonwealth, and of the ambiguous autonomy of the Majorcan kingdom, acquires an extra dimension. Nothing here is intended to suggest a political message for modern Europeans, still less for Spaniards, Italians and French people who inhabit the former lands of the Crown of Aragon. Yet it is also difficult to escape the conclusion that the drive to full independence in the Majorcan kingdom failed to take into account the region's existing economic and political relationships with the surrounding areas of the Mediterranean. There were limits to the extent to which what was in part an island kingdom could isolate itself from Europe. Inhabitants of an island kingdom on the other side of France might today draw a moral from these thirteenth-century experiences. Untrammelled control of Majorcan affairs by a local dynasty of Majorcan kings was an unrealistic, indeed impossible, objective. But, in an age when monarchs were seeking to exercise an unprecedented degree of authority, in which the 'state' itself was emerging in a recognisable form, even the rulers of a small and extenuated kingdom such as Majorca shared the objectives of their neighbours in France, Castile, Naples and elsewhere.

The original idea behind this book arose from discussions with Jocelyn Hillgarth, then spending a sabbatical at Clare Hall in Cambridge, to whom I had asked the simple question why so many Mallorcans appeared in the commercial documentation of the thirteenth-century Mediterranean, including Sicily, which was at that time the focus of much of my research. His answer was equally simple: go and look at the notarial acts in Mallorca istelf. Subsequently the scope of this book was enlarged, but my thoughts on the emergence of a mercantile élite in Ciutat de Mallorca will be found in chapter 6. His encouragement made this book possible; I am deeply grateful. As the character of the book altered, his arguments about the nature of the Catalan–Aragonese 'Empire' became of great importance to the direction of my research. Moreover, his willingness to help, particularly in the provision of microfilm material from the Archivo Capitular in Mallorca, made it possible for me to pursue work on this book while based in Cambridge. Fr Robert Burns has been another source of great encouragement and stimulation; his good company and sound advice at the Congresses of the History of the Crown of Aragon, and more recently on a visit to the University of California, Los Angeles, have been very greatly valued. His former pupil Larry Simon has been extremely generous in sharing microfilms; in this book, I have tried to steer away from his own special area of the internal religious history of post-conquest Mallorca. My colleague Anthony Pagden suggested I might like to publish this book under his auspices as we were sitting together awaiting the start of a Tripos examiners' meeting in the extraordinary edifice of the History Faculty at Cambridge. Blanca Garí of the Universitat de Barcelona did me the great kindness of reading the manuscript of the entire book, and I am grateful for her expert comments and her encouragement. Antoni Riera i Melis of the Universitat de Barcelona was kind enough to share his thoughts with me, and I have benefited greatly from his excellent study of the tariff war between Majorca and Aragon in the years from about 1299 to about 1311, and from his other fine publications. Antoni Mut i Calafell, archivist of the Arxiu del Regne de Mallorca, offered every facility; Alvaro Santamaría Arández extended a kind invitation to an important congress in Palma, my paper at which forms the core of chapter 10. Among many others who have provided invaluable help and advice at various stages are Henri Bresc (Paris), Paul Freedman (Vanderbilt University), T. N. Bisson (Harvard University), Kathryn Reyerson

(University of Minnesota), Silvia Orvietani Busch and Christopher Michael Davis (University of California, Los Angeles), Pau Cateura Bennàsser (University of the Balearic Islands), Anthony Bonner (Mallorca), Marco Tangheroni (University of Pisa), Elena Lourie (Ben Gurion University of the Negev), Yomtov Assis (Hebrew University of Jerusalem), Stephan Epstein (London School of Economics), Chris Wickham (University of Birmingham), Felipe Fernández-Armesto (St Antony's College, Oxford), Joan-Pau Rubiés i Mirabet (Queens' College, Cambridge), and last but by no means least Gary Doxey (Utah), who has worked in Cambridge under my direction on the Christian attempts to reconquer the Balearic islands before 1229. The British Academy and Gonville and Caius College generously covered research expenses in France, Spain and Italy. A special word of thanks is due to all those who have followed my course on 'Conquerors and conquered in the lands of the Crown of Aragon' in the History Faculty at Cambridge between 1989 and 1993; this is not the 'book of the film', but without their questions and comments I would not have been able to develop my ideas here.

Still less would I have been able to complete this book without the intellectual, practical and moral support of Anna Sapir Abulafia, and indeed of Bianca Susanna Abulafia and Rosa Alexandra Abulafia, who, apart from everything else, have all been delightful travelling companions in the lands of the Crown of Aragon.

Gonville and Caius College, Cambridge

D.S.H.A.

Note on nomenclature

In order to distinguish the island of *Mallorca* from the kingdom of *Majorca*, which included Menorca, Ibiza, Roussillon, Cerdagne, Vallespir, Carlat and the lordship of the greater part of Montpellier, advantage has been taken of the existence of two spellings in English: *Majorca* refers here to the entire kingdom, *Majorcan* to subjects of the king of *Majorca* from any of his territories; *Mallorca* and *Mallorcan* refer only to the island of that name. The Catalan form *Menorca* has been employed in lieu of *Minorca* for consistency, but it has not seemed appropriate to use *Eivissa* for *Ibiza*, in the light of general usage. Other place names have been kept in a recognisable form, with a preference for Catalan forms (*Lleida* and *Girona* for *Lerida* and *Gerona*, *Maó* for *Mahón*); but it seems affected to write *Catalunya*, still more so *Perpinya*. *Madina Mayurqa*, *Ciutat de Mallorca* or *Mallorca City*, *Palma de Mallorca* are all versions of the name of the capital of the Balearics, in Islamic, medieval and modern times.

The names of the rulers of Aragon–Catalonia are a perennial problem. I have used the Aragonese, rather than the Catalonian, numbering, on the grounds that the higher numbers tend to give rise to less confusion. *Peter IV of Aragon* is thus the same person as *Peter III of Catalonia*. It is often least ambiguous to use the sobriquet attached to these names, such as (in this case) *Peter the Ceremonious*. I have also used the English form of the royal names: *James*, not *Jaume*, *Jaime*, *Jacme*, *Chaime*, *Giacomo*, all of which have been tried by others; *Peter*, not *Pere* or *Pedro*. There is no obvious solution to the contemporary existence of a *James II of Majorca* and a *James II of Aragon*, and every attempt has been made to indicate which one is under discussion. With *Alfonso* or *Alfons* and *Sancho*, *Sanç* or *Sanxo*, which are less familiar in English, I have been less consistent: *Alfonso* appears here, as does *Sanç*. For lesser figures, Catalan or other appropriate forms have been used when they can be adequately reconstructed from

Latin versions, or from often very inconsistent Catalan versions. The Catalan and Mallorcan merchants trading to England have been allowed to retain the distorted forms used in the English documents. An attempt has been made where it seemed useful to do so to suggest the original Hebrew or Arabic form of some Jewish and Muslim names, using for Hebrew a system of transliteration based on modern Sephardi Hebrew pronunciation.

The kings of Majorca, 1229–1343

James I the Conqueror, king of Aragon, 1229–76

James II of Majorca, 1276–1285

(Alfonso III the Liberal of Aragon, 1285–91)

(James II of Aragon, 1291–8)

James II of Majorca (restored), 1298–1311

Sanç, 1311–24

James III, 1324–43

Note on the coinage of the kingdom of Majorca

There was no unified system of coinage in the Majorcan kingdom. Within the Catalan world, coinages based on the *denarius* or *diner* predominated, such as the *diner de tern* of Barcelona (12d = 1 *solidus*; 20s = £1). In Montpellier, the *denier* of Melgueil, minted nearby, circulated, though there was competition from French mints at Sommières, and, after 1293, in Montpelliéret, and attempts to limit the Melgorian currency to a small area began in 1282. In the Balearics, Valencian *diners*, struck from 1247, were widely used; in that year £1 Valencian was worth about 30 *solidi* of Barcelona, but 26s 6d of Melgueil, according to exchange rates recorded in Valencia itself. Accounts were often drawn up in Mallorca in *dirhams* or *millarenses* of north Africa, ten of which constituted a *besant*. By 1268 mints in Mallorca appear to have been manufacturing imitation *millarenses* for the use of merchants trading to north Africa; this practice was already established in Montpellier. In 1300 a Balearic coinage began to be minted, though it was not supposed to circulate in the mainland territories of the Majorcan kingdom. It consisted essentially of a base silver *diner* known variously as the *menut* and the *real senar*, sixteen of which constituted the fine silver *royal*. After 1343 a beautiful gold coinage eventually joined the ranks of the kingdom's coinage, which continued to be minted separately from that of the mainland for several centuries; Perpignan also became a centre for the production of gold coinage very soon after its conquest by Peter IV. In 1334–42 £1 of Barcelona was exchanged for about 30 *solidi* of Majorca in Barcelona.

See on these coinages P. Spufford, W. Wilkinson, S. Tolley, *Handbook of medieval exchange* (Royal Historical Society Guides and Handbooks, London, 1987), 137, 146–7, 153; P. Spufford, *Money and its use in medieval Europe* (Cambridge, 1988), 175, 288.

Map 1. The kingdom of Majorca.

Note: Carlat does not appear on the map; it is situated on the edge of Auvergne.

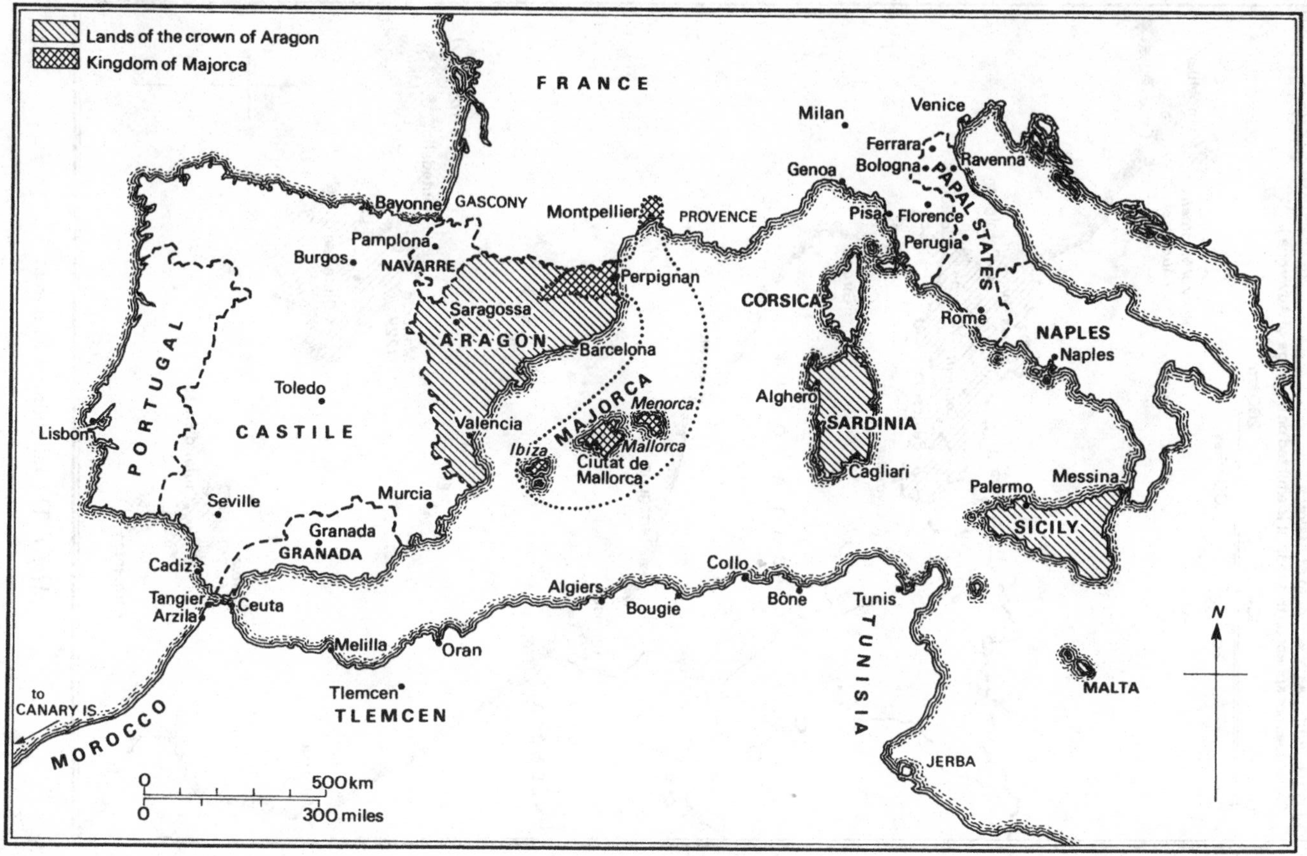

Map 2. The western Mediterranean.

PART I

Unity and diversity

CHAPTER I

The Balearic setting

I

Mallorca, Menorca and Ibiza (or Eivissa) are now quite prosperous islands whose income is largely derived from the vast number of summer visitors who flock to the Mediterranean in search of the sun and the sea. Yet the islands have attracted visitors and settlers dating back millennia; visible reminders of the links between the Balearic islands and the world beyond include the talayot and other prehistoric remains of Menorca, the fine Gothic churches of Palma de Mallorca, and the stately city of Maó or Mahón in Menorca, situated alongside what is said to be the world's largest natural harbour after Pearl Harbor in Hawaii. In fact, the Balearic islands have long functioned as a crossroads on the trade routes linking Africa to continental Europe, and, in the later Middle Ages, linking the Mediterranean to the Atlantic: for Mallorca lies 175 kilometres off the coast of Spain, and the distance between the Balearics and Algeria is not much greater.[1] Between 1276 and 1343 the most important of the islands gave its name to a small but wealthy kingdom, that of Majorca, which remains perhaps the most neglected of all the medieval Spanish kingdoms.

The battle for control of the Balearic islands epitomises the struggle between Islam and Christianity for domination in the western

[1] The surface area of Mallorca is 3,640 square kilometres; the island is about 100 kilometres broad at its greatest width, from east to west, and its dimensions north to south reach a maximum of about 75 kilometres. Menorca is half the width and less than one fifth of the area of Mallorca (700 square kilometres); it is much flatter and more barren. Ibiza, on the other hand, is quite rocky and has sheer coasts. Its measurements are a greatest length of 30 kilometres and an area of 575 square kilometres. It lies twice the distance of Menorca from Mallorca – 70 kilometres, in the case of Ibiza. The fourth island, 5 kilometres off Ibiza, is Formentera, of about 100 square kilometres; it is quite low-lying, and, like Ibiza, has good natural salt-pans.

Mediterranean; possession of the islands meant control of an advance
position from which it was possible to patrol the seas between what
are now southern France, eastern Spain and Algeria.[2] Following the
Moorish invasion of Spain, in 711, the Balearic islands remained
loosely attached to the Byzantine world, along with Sardinia; but the
inability of the Byzantines to protect Roman citizens in the western
Mediterranean stimulated contact with the new Roman Empire of
the Franks.[3] In 798–9 it was Charlemagne's ships that defeated
Moorish pirates who were raiding the Balearic islands. The battle
standards of the Muslim foe were brought to Aachen as a present for
the Frankish king. Only in 813 did the Moors again dare to attack the
islands, and only in 902 did they finally conquer them. Mallorca was
thus the last part of Spain to fall to the Moors.[4] A recent reassessment
of Frankish naval power points out that 'possession of the Balearics
gave the Frankish defence important strategic benefits as they lay
across the sea routes from Spain to Corsica, Sardinia, Italy and
Provence, providing a base from which Muslim shipping could be
harassed, so limiting the freedom of movement of pirates operating in
the western Mediterranean'.[5] This was as true in the thirteenth and
fourteenth centuries as in the eighth. Even before their belated
Muslim conquest, the islands were raided by the Vikings (859), who
returned as late as 1110 when King Sigurð Jorsalafari raided
Formentera on his way by sea from Norway through Gibraltar to the
Latin Kingdom of Jerusalem. Raider or crusader, Sigurð recognised
the strategic position of the Balearic islands on the route from the
Atlantic to the Mediterranean.

In the early eleventh century, they were a Moorish base with a
predominantly Muslim population from which the corsair Mujahid,
who also controlled Denia on the Spanish coast opposite Ibiza, could
raid into Christian territory. His attacks on Sardinia in the years up
to 1016 elicited a decisive response from the Pisans and the Genoese,
whose victory over Mujahid marks the start of their own naval
duopoly in the seas either side of Sardinia. A century later, in
1113–15, the Pisan navy joined the count of Barcelona, the most
powerful Christian warlord on the Spanish coast, in a successful

---

[2] J. Haywood, *Dark Age naval power* (London, 1991), 113.
[3] For the early medieval history of the Balearics, see now Josep Amengual i Batle, *Els orígens del Cristianisme a les Balears*, 2 vols. (Palma de Mallorca, 1991–2).
[4] Haywood, *Dark Age naval power*, 113–14, 196.
[5] Haywood, *Dark Age naval power*, 113.

attack on Mallorca and Ibiza. The presence in the fleet of prominent Sards confirms the supposition that Muslim control of the Balearics endangered Sardinia; while the presence on the international slave markets of Sard slaves may indicate what effect Muslim raiding parties could have on Mallorca's nearest neighbours. The pope, Paschal II, appears to have blessed the Pisan campaign of 1113, and almost certainly offered participants crusade privileges; this may be the first occasion on which the pope extended privileges devised for the First Crusade, and rapidly offered to the Catalan defenders of *Hispania Tarraconensis* (the ancient ecclesiastical province of Tarragona), to cover the conquest of an area away from the current Spanish land frontier.[6] However, the Pisans and Catalans proved unable to hold the islands, even though they returned home covered in glory; the Pisans commissioned a lengthy neo-classical victory poem, the *Liber Maiolichinus*, to remind the world of their heroism.

The Muslim rulers of the Balearics, for their part, became increasingly isolated even from the Muslim world. They were Almoravids, supporters of a popular Islamic movement that had swept out of west Africa into Spain during the late eleventh century; but by the mid-twelfth century a powerful new fundamentalist force, the Almohad movement, had established itself in north Africa and southern Spain. By the 1180s, the Balearics constituted the tiny rump of a once great Almoravid empire.[7] The islands were more than ever exposed to the danger of conquest. In 1162 the Genoese agreed to aid the German Emperor Frederick I should he attack the Balearics, a project which must reflect Genoese ambitions rather than imperial ones. Indeed, the context in which this promise is made is revealing: the Genoese had just been lured into a treaty with Barbarossa against their erstwhile friend King William I of Sicily, and were already bound by a short-term truce to the emir of Mallorca. While they were prepared summarily to break their agreement with the Norman king of Sicily, they were careful to stipulate that no action would be taken against Mallorca until the

---

[6] *Liber Maiolichinus de gestis Pisanorum illustribus*, ed. C. Calisse (Fonti per la Storia d'Italia, Rome, 1904), 9, lines 74–5. There is some difficulty knowing exactly what this passage signifies: *Pontifex tribuendo crucem, romanaque signa militi ducibusque* ... For a fuller analysis of these events, see G. B. Doxey, 'Christian attempts to reconquer the Balearic islands before 1229' (Ph.D. thesis, Cambridge University, 1991), which is being prepared for publication.
[7] A. Bel, *Les Benou Ghânya, derniers représentants de l'empire almoravide et leur lutte contre l'empire almohade* (Paris/Algiers, 1903), which is, however, no longer satisfactory.

truce had expired; the reason was that trade through Mallorca to north Africa could only gain in importance once trade to Sicily and beyond was rendered dangerous by their new alliance.[8] To lose the trade of one island was a misfortune; to lose that of both would be carelessness. Later, it was the Sicilians themselves who saw the Balearics as an easy target: King William II of Sicily harboured ambitious plans which culminated in a naval assault in 1181; the campaign was a disaster, not least because the Genoese refused to join in; but Christian schemes to capture the islands were not abandoned.[9]

By the late twelfth century the Italians had realised the advantages of trade via the Balearics. Access to the port of what is now called Palma, and was then called Madina Mayurqa, was valuable not so much for the produce of the Balearics, which was mainly insignificant, but for the strategic position en route to north Africa. Rather than join the Sicilian expedition of 1181, the Genoese had actually chosen to enter into a closer alliance with the emir of Mallorca, and for a time trade by way of the Balearics experienced an upsurge.[10] Along the coast of the Muslim Maghrib, the Genoese and Pisans sought wool, leather and also gold, which arrived by caravan from the southern Sahara, and could be ferried via Mallorca to Europe. Ibiza itself was a good source of salt, and probably grew substantially in importance over time. As the shippers of Catalonia broke into the trade of the western Mediterranean around 1200, they too, not surprisingly, saw that access to Mallorca would provide a jumping-off point into Africa. Unfortunately, the finer details of the early commercial history of Barcelona are hard to see clearly. Links with southern France, especially the Aragonese lordship of Montpellier and the Aragonese county of Provence, brought northern cloths to Catalonia for redistribution towards Sicily, the Maghrib and al-Andalus. Balearic pirates could impede the trade routes linking Barcelona to its Mediterranean markets.[11]

---

[8] David Abulafia, *The two Italies. Economic relations between the Norman kingdom of Sicily and the northern communes* (Cambridge, 1977), 129.

[9] David Abulafia, 'The Norman kingdom of Africa and the Norman expeditions to Majorca and the Muslim Mediterranean', *Anglo-Norman Studies*, 7 (1985), 44–5, repr. with additional note in David Abulafia, *Italy, Sicily and the Mediterranean, 1100–1400* (London, 1987).

[10] Abulafia, *Two Italies*, 156–8.

[11] David Abulafia, 'Catalan merchants and the western Mediterranean, 1236–1300: studies in the notarial acts of Barcelona and Sicily', *Viator*, 16 (1985), 209–42, repr. in David Abulafia, *Italy, Sicily and the Mediterranean, 1100–1400* (London, 1987), essay VIII.

Whether it was the Catalan merchants or their rulers, the kings of Aragon and counts of Barcelona, who initiated schemes to reconquer the Balearics in the early thirteenth century has been much debated.[12] Around 1204 Peter II of Aragon, who was shortly to become embroiled in the Albigensian crusade, conceived a plan to attack Mallorca with papal approval. For his son, James I (1213–76), a Catalan assault on Mallorca would not just be a holy war, but also an opportunity to show his unruly vassals in Catalonia that he was a decisive and capable war-leader. Yet he appears to have taken advice from a prominent Barcelona merchant, Pere Martell, when planning his war. According to his own account, reported in what is generally regarded as James' autobiography, James raised the topic of the conquest of Mallorca at a dinner party in Tarragona late in 1228, though other evidence suggests that the project was already in his mind beforehand.[13] This in itself would hardly occasion surprise, because the idea of attacking Mallorca was so well established as a long-term policy aim of the counts of Barcelona.

In 1229 the Catalan fleet, strongly backed by allied fleets from southern France and Provence, where Aragonese influence and lordship was extensive, swooped on the island; troops advanced to Madina Mayurqa and, after a short siege, captured the city.[14] Although Muslim irredentists held out for a time in the mountains, James the Conqueror had little difficulty in asserting his authority throughout the lowlands of Mallorca. Madina Mayurqa became Ciutat de Mallorca; the lands on the island were divided up among the conquering armies, and groups that had given significant help, such as the merchants of Marseilles and Montpellier, were amply rewarded with houses in the city and lands outside. Even the Italian merchants, who were strongly suspected of plotting with the Muslim ruler to keep the Catalans out, were wisely given lands and privileges. According to the late thirteenth century chronicler Bernat Desclot:

these men of Genoa and Pisa gave to the [Muslim] king of Mallorca evil counsel for their own ends. And they did this with no other purpose than

---

[12] J. N. Hillgarth, *The Problem of a Catalan Mediterranean Empire, 1229–1323* (English Historical Review, supplement no. 8, London, 1975), is the best introduction to the issue. Catalan edn: *El problema d'un imperi català* (Palma de Mallorca, 1984).

[13] James I, *Crònica o Llibre des Feits*, in *Les quatre grans cròniques*, ed. F. Soldevila (Barcelona, 1971), cap. 47.

[14] A useful account of the conquest of Mallorca is that of F. Fernández-Armesto, *Before Columbus. Exploration and colonisation from the Mediterranean to the Atlantic, 1229–1492* (London, 1987), 13–22.

that they might the better buy and sell and barter their wares and that the Catalans should not dare venture on the sea.[15]

The Catalans, as yet a naval power of quite limited capacity, were not in a position to challenge the Genoese and Pisans, and the Aragonese king was afraid that the Italians would ally with the irredentists if he did not treat them well. It must be stressed that the conquest was as much Provençal and Languedocien work as it was Catalan; a romantic tradition even staffs James' army with refugee Cathar noblemen from southern French lands now permeated by the oppressive atmosphere of the Inquisition.

The fate of Mallorca's Muslim population is not entirely clear, and is discussed at greater length in a later chapter. There were many enslaved, and some free, Muslims on the island in the late thirteenth century, though some of these Muslims were brought from the mainland by landlords such as the Knights of the Temple to till the soil. It has to be presumed that a large number were sold into slavery in 1229–31. If the Muslim population assimilated into the Christian settler population, it did so almost noiselessly.[16] The nearest parallel is perhaps Sicily, where Islam was almost completely eroded over a period of about 150 years, rather than Valencia, James' other great conquest, where it was still publicly avowed by large communities as late as 1525.[17] On the other hand, James I gave some encouragement to the Jews, who comprised an indigenous population as well as new migrants from Catalonia, Provence and north Africa. The monarchy saw the Jews as politically less troublesome than the Muslims, since they were unable to look across the sea to Africa to powerful rulers who might come and redeem them. The change in royal mood, pushing the Jews from privileged status to marginalisation and persecution, is documented elsewhere in this book.[18]

The conquest of Mallorca left the lesser islands untouched. James I waited till a second visit before he tackled the problem of Menorca, a windswept island mainly famous for its livestock and dairy goods, then as now. In 1231 he deceived the Muslims of Menorca into believing they were facing a massive invasion; the distant sight of the fires burning at the easternmost tip of Mallorca, at Capdepera, was

[15] Bernat Desclot, *Llibre del rey en Pere* in *Les quatre grans cròniques*, ed. F. Soldevila (Barcelona, 1971), cap. 14.   [16] See chapter 4.
[17] David Abulafia, 'The end of Muslim Sicily' and R.I. Burns, 'Muslims in the thirteenth-century realms of Aragon: interaction and reaction', in *Muslims under Latin rule, 1100–1300*, ed. J.M. Powell (Princeton, NJ, 1990), 103–33 and 57–102.   [18] See chapter 5.

thought by the Menorcans to herald an attack by a vast army.[19] To escape their supposed fate, the Menorcans entered into a treaty of submission that preserved their autonomy as a Muslim society, but that also obliged them to recognise the overlordship of the king of Aragon. They were obliged to pay a handsome tribute, partly in livestock, but they were also guaranteed the free practice of Islam. Menorca became a Muslim enclave in Catalan waters.

In 1235 it was the turn of Ibiza. The assault on the island has been described as 'the last private act of reconquista' in Spain. It was the work of the sacristan of Girona cathedral, Guillem de Montgrí, working under the patronage of the archbishop of Tarragona.[20] The king of Aragon insisted on his ultimate sovereignty, but was content to leave the island, and its neighbour Formentera, under the administration of its conquerors. In fact, the monarchy made little attempt at first to capitalise on its conquests. The grants of land to soldiers and other supporters, tax exemptions for foreign merchants and other privileges meant that the conquest of the Balearics brought the crown glory rather than substantial financial rewards. The government of Mallorca was actually ceded in 1231 to an Iberian condottiere, Prince Pedro of Portugal, who himself spent rather little time on the island, and there were other powerful interests, notably the count of Roussillon, Nunyo Sanç, who had been a supporter of James I back in Catalonia.[21]

It was in the 1250s and 1260s that James I began to formulate a distinctive policy in the Balearics. His concern lay in providing for his sons, of whom, by 1262, two legitimate ones remained, Peter and James. At this stage, James the Conqueror ruled four major entities, each technically distinct from one another: highland Aragon, as king, Catalonia, as count of Barcelona, newly conquered Valencia, as king, and the Balearics, as king of Majorca. Like many Spanish rulers before him, he decided to divide his lands between his children, offering Peter Aragon, Valencia and those parts of Catalonia that lay to the west of the Pyrenees. James would have the Balearics, the lordship of Montpellier, a prized possession in Languedoc, and those parts of the Catalan lands that lay mainly to the east of the Pyrenees: Roussillon, earlier held by one of the conquerors of Mallorca,

---

[19] James I, *Crònica*, caps. 119–24.

[20] James I, *Crònica*, caps. 124–5; Fernández-Armesto, *Before Columbus*, 31–3.

[21] Fernández-Armesto, *Before Columbus*, 29–30. See chapter 6 for the lands of Nunyo Sanç in the Mallorcan capital.

Cerdagne and adjacent lands. These territories were to constitute a
separate realm after James I's death; the king of Majorca, count of
Roussillon and lord of Montpellier was to hold none of his territories
from his elder brother, but was to be fully independent of him.[22]
James I even hoped to add Sardinia to the kingdom of Majorca,
expressing confidence (in 1267) that the pope was about to grant him
the troubled island. But in fact Aragonese interest in Sardinia only
precipitated an attempt by the king of Sicily and count of Provence,
Charles of Anjou, an inveterate rival of James I, to intrude his own
son as king of Sardinia.[23]

The later kings of Aragon had a different view of the kingdom of
Majorca. Peter of Aragon sought almost immediately to cajole James
II of Majorca (as his brother is usually called) into accepting
Aragonese overlordship. He was even to attend meetings of the
Catalan *Corts*, an obligation that points to the heart of the paradox:
the king of Majorca was to attend the parliaments of the count of
Barcelona, while he was also a vassal of the king of Aragon. Now, the
fact that the king of Aragon was exactly the same person as the count
of Barcelona did not resolve the confusion. Was the Majorcan state a
dependency of Catalonia or of Aragon? The question does not admit
of an answer. The constitutional picture, as will be seen, was confused
and contradictory. In addition, the Majorcan king also engaged not
to mint his own money in Roussillon, though he was free to do so in
the Balearics (in fact, he refrained from so doing till 1300). Within
three years of James I's death, Peter had his way; and, at a meeting
in Perpignan in 1279, James II of Majorca accepted that he was little
more than a great baron who possessed a very grand title, and
extensive rights of jurisdiction within his lands.

Dependence on Aragon remained, nonetheless, a live issue. Peter's
humiliation of the king of Majorca, in 1279, backfired; when in 1285
the king of France launched an attack on Aragon, as vengeance for
the seizure of Sicily by Peter the Great of Aragon, the Majorcan ruler
gave his support to France against his own bullying brother. James'
decision was crucial, since he thus permitted the French armies
eventually to march through his own county of Roussillon on their
way into Catalonia proper. His mainland capital at Perpignan
(where a handsome Palace of the Kings of Majorca can still be seen)
was attacked by Peter; James only evaded Peter's clutches by

---

[22] The constitutional position is analysed in chapter 3.   [23] See appendix 1.

feigning illness and refusing to emerge from his bedchamber to meet his brother, while his men heaved aside the flagstones in the room and opened up a drainage channel through which he escaped into open country.[24]

James was quite incapable of defending the Balearics from Peter. Indeed, it is generally thought doubtful whether the inhabitants of the islands had much sense of loyalty to the Majorcan kingdom, (though Jocelyn Hillgarth has argued for greater reserves of loyalty to James II than others have supposed). The Catalan population may well have seen the links with Catalonia as a secure means to prosperity: at the height of the quarrel with Peter, in 1284, trade out of Mallorca hardly touched the Catalan coast, and had to be directed mainly to north Africa; this may have caused some inconvenience.[25] But Mallorca flourished most successfully if lines of communication to all neighbouring coasts were kept open. In any case, the government of the kingdom was mainly based in Perpignan, and Mallorca was governed by a royal lieutenant. Ciutat de Mallorca was a ceremonial capital above all.

Aragonese wrath at Majorcan treachery knew no bounds. Peter's son Alfonso III recaptured Mallorca for Aragon in 1285, at the time of his father's death; and it was made plain that the islands were henceforth to be treated as an integral part of the Aragonese king's realms.[26] James II was to be dispossessed for all time. The king of Aragon resumed the use of the additional title *rex Maioricarum* in his acts. In 1287, Alfonso returned to Mallorca to launch a further attack on Menorca, which had continued to pay tribute to the rulers of Majorca, but which was suspected of attempting to betray Aragonese war plans to the Muslims of north Africa. The seizure of this island was also justified by the fear that the French and their allies might use its excellent harbour facilities as a base from which to raid Catalonia. What was striking was the severity with which the Aragonese treated the indigenous population. Perhaps as many as 40,000 Menorcan Muslims were taken into slavery and sold, though a chance was

---

[24] Bernat Desclot, *Crònica*, caps. 134–6.

[25] See chapter 7 for links to north Africa. On the loyalty of the Mallorcans to James II, see J.N. Hillgarth, 'Un nuevo documento sobre la resistencia de los mallorquines a la ocupación de Mallorca por Alfonso III de Aragón (1285–91)', *Estudios en honor de A. Mut i Calafell* (Palma de Mallorca, 1993).

[26] Ramón Muntaner, *Crònica*, caps. 141–51. But Muntaner tried to paper over the differences between the Aragonese and the Majorcans, even indicating that the invasion of the Balearics in 1285 formed part of a wider scheme to outwit the French king, to which James II of Majorca was supposedly a willing party: see chapter 4.

offered to pay the king a ransom instead. A few Muslims were left behind to cultivate the soil, but in effect the island was totally depopulated. Its relatively bleak conditions never made it an attractive place for new Christian colonists.[27]

It was only in 1298, when terms for a regional settlement of the conflict in the western Mediterranean were being pressed by the papacy, that James II of Majorca won back his kingdom, though he remained a vassal of the king of Aragon (also, confusingly, by now called James II). However, other means were at his disposal to disentangle him from Aragonese control. A vigorous economic policy was initiated, with attempts to impose tariff barriers against merchants from Catalonia who traded through the ports of the kingdom of Majorca, such as Ciutat de Mallorca and Collioure in Roussillon. A fine Balearic coinage was at last initiated. Autonomous consulates, offering protection and warehouse facilities to Mallorcan merchants, were established in major north African ports such as Bougie, which has been described as a virtual protectorate of Majorca. The Catalans, who had earlier provided consular facilities for Majorcan as well as Catalan merchants, were strongly opposed, since revenues from consulates were a substantial source of income to the tax farmers who ran them and above all to the Aragonese crown.[28] In Mallorca and Menorca there were quite successful attempts to create a series of small, well-planned agricultural towns that would increase efficiency of production; the surviving square street plan of Felanitx, Sa Pobla and Petra is testimony to James II's efforts.[29] A later ruler, Sanç or Sancho (1311–24) also had grandiose plans for the creation of a galley fleet able to rival those of Genoa and Venice; this idea came to nothing, but the special expertise of the Mallorcans as cartographers and as mariners was widely recognised. Jewish map-makers on the island had access to the geographical knowledge both of the west and of the Islamic world.[30]

[27] Ramón Muntaner, *Crònica* 172; C. Parpal, *La conquista de Menorca en 1287 por Alfonso III de Aragón* (Barcelona, 1901; Catalan edn, Barcelona, 1964); M. Mata, *Conquests and reconquests of Menorca* (Barcelona, 1984), 9–62. For the fate of the Muslims, see chapter 4.

[28] See A. Riera Melis, *La Corona de Aragón y el reino de Mallorca en el primer cuarto del siglo XIV*, vol. I, *Las repercussiones arancelarias de la autonomía balear (1298–1311)* (Barcelona, 1986), and chapter 8.

[29] G. Alomar, *Urbanismo regional en la edad media: las 'Ordinacions' de Jaime II (1300) en el reino de Mallorca* (Barcelona, 1976), and chapter 8.

[30] For the cartographers, see chapter 10.

II

As a cultural centre, Mallorca did not compare with contemporary Toledo or Barcelona; this was perhaps because the major source of patronage, the monarchy, was based in the mainland possessions, at Perpignan. Setting aside the cartographers, by far the most important cultural figure in Mallorca's history was the mystic and missionary Ramón Llull, who was born on the island in 1232 to a prosperous family of new Catalan settlers and who claimed to have experienced a vision on Mallorca which revealed to him a complex algebra for the description of the universe and for the demonstration of the truth of Christianity:

After this, Ramón went up a certain mountain not far from his home, in order to contemplate God in greater tranquillity. When he had been there scarcely a full week, it happened that one day while he was gazing intently heavenward the Lord suddenly illuminated his mind giving him the form and method for writing the aforementioned book against the errors of the unbelievers.[31]

From the 1270s to his death in about 1316 he tried hard to interest the kings of Majorca, France, Naples, Cyprus and the papacy in his schemes to combat Islam by persuasion rather than by war. He himself went to preach the faith in Africa. He had a good understanding of Arabic and probably of Hebrew as well, and aimed to meet his opponents on their own ground: he was well read in Islamic and Jewish theology. Although much of his work was conducted outside the Balearics, he did attempt to make Mallorca into a base for the training of missionaries, by founding the convent at Miramar which lasted for a few years under royal patronage. In his novel *Blanquerna* he described Miramar this way:

That king [James II of Majorca] is a man of noble customs, and has much devotion as to the manner wherein Jesus Christ may be honoured by preaching among the unbelievers; and to this end he has ordained that thirteen friars minor shall study Arabic in a monastery called Miramar, established and set apart in a fitting place, and he himself has provided for their needs; and when they have learned the Arabic tongue they will be able

[31] Life of Ramón Llull, iii. section 14, from the translation by A. Bonner, *Selected Works of Ramon Llull (1232–1316)*, 2 vols. (Princeton, NJ, 1985), the introduction to which constitutes a very good survey of Llull's life. See also J. Hillgarth, *Ramon Lull and Lullism in fourteenth-century France* (Oxford, 1971).

to go, by leave of their General, to honour the Fruit of Our Lady, and in his honour suffer hunger and thirst, heat and cold, fears and torture and death.[32]

It is, however, debatable whether Llull was a real pioneer in these attempts to convert non-Christians. In some respects he lagged behind the ideas of the Catalan friars at the court of James I in Barcelona, and his algebraic method, or 'Art', owed much to early medieval writers.[33] Llull's career, already much-studied, is not a theme of this book, but his early career in Mallorca and his obsession with the souls of Jews and Muslims are important reminders that the newly created kingdom was a gateway not merely for merchants but for missionaries entering Africa.

III

The Llulls were prominent merchants, and in the early fourteenth century Ciutat de Mallorca continued to grow in importance as a safe haven from which western merchants could venture into the less safe ports of north Africa. Soon after the Catalan conquest of Mallorca, Popes Gregory IX and Innocent IV stated that it was permissible for the Christian merchants of Mallorca to trade with the infidel in north Africa, in order to provide a livelihood for the island's inhabitants and to encourage settlement there.[34] The island could not survive without trade; by the start of the fourteenth century perhaps half the population lived in the capital, and agricultural resources were insufficient to feed everyone.[35] Imports of Sicilian grain and other basic produce became more and more vital. Not surprisingly, Mallorca benefited from its position as a major Christian possession facing the Muslim world by becoming an important centre of the international slave trade. There were many Muslim domestic slaves on the island, in Christian or Jewish households, but most of the slaves who passed through Mallorca were in transit to mainland Spain, Italy or north Africa. Both Christians and Jews were active in

---

[32] Ramón Llull, *Blanquerna*, transl. E. A. Peers and ed. R. Irwin (London, 1987), cap. 65, 256–7.

[33] On the 'art' see F. Yates, 'Ramon Lull and John Scotus Erigena', *Journal of the Warburg and Courtauld Institutes*, 17 (1954), 1–44. On the friars, see J. Cohen, *The friars and the Jews* (Ithaca, NY, 1982) and R. Chazan, *Daggers of faith. Thirteenth-century Christian missionizing and Jewish response* (Berkeley/Los Angeles, 1989).

[34] See chapter 6 for a fuller discussion of the papal privileges.

[35] See Alomar, *Urbanismo*, for population estimates.

handling this traffic.[36] Regional sources of supply varied from the mountains of Cyrenaica in modern Libya to Black Africa, but the Balearics were well placed to act as a clearing house for this trade and for the accompanying and lucrative business of ransoming captives.

Mallorca also increased in importance as a way-station along a fragile and extenuated sea-route from Italy through the Straits of Gibraltar to Seville, northern Spain, Gascony, England and Flanders. Since about 1280 Mallorcan ships had been sailing alongside those of Genoa as far as London, thus making possible the transfer of high or medium quality English wool to the Florentines and other Mediterranean cloth producers.[37] A Mallorcan woollen cloth industry began to develop in the early fourteenth century, really taking off around 1350, and remaining quite successful until the fifteenth century, by when exports of Mallorcan and Menorcan raw wool had also become a major feature of the islands' economy. In addition, the Mallorcans built up a lucrative trade in Moorish Granada and Atlantic Morocco.[38] Mallorcan Jews were able to exploit family ties with north African Jews, and were heavily engaged in commerce. At this period, too, the monarchy appears to have begun to draw a handsome income from trade taxes, after a slow start, and lavish building programmes, including the magnificent round Bellver Castle on the western edge of Ciutat de Mallorca and the refurbished Almudaina Palace in the old city, testify to the monarchy's prosperity.[39]

IV

At the same time, the capacity of the Majorcan rulers to resist Aragonese pretensions was constantly being weakened. The Majorcans made a substantial contribution, as vassals of Aragon–Catalonia, to the fleet that invaded Sardinia in 1323–4, and Mallorcan merchants were rewarded with trade privileges in Sardinia as a result.[40] Technically, under the terms of King James I's will, the kingdom of Majorca should have reverted to the Aragonese when King Sanç died without an heir in 1324. But the Aragonese

---

[36] Larry Simon is proposing to publish further studies of the Mallorcan slave trade in the thirteenth century, originally prepared under the direction of Fr R. I. Burns.
[37] See chapter 10.
[38] On the Mallorcan presence in Almeria, Granada's outport, see chapter 9.
[39] M. Durliat, *L'art dans le royaume de Majorque* (Toulouse, 1962). See chapter 8 for further details concerning royal revenues from trade in the early fourteenth century.
[40] See appendix 1.

were still facing tough resistance in Sardinia; they grudgingly accepted that the crown could pass to Sanç's nephew James. James III's policies were built on an unequivocal assumption that as king of Majorca he could be subject to no other secular power. Characteristic was his decision to issue a set of 'laws,' the so-called *Leges Palatinae*, which in fact consist almost entirely of descriptions of the ceremonial duties of the king's principal courtiers: the butler, the marshal, the constable and so on. He was irked by King Peter IV's insistence that he should kneel on a cushion no higher than that of ordinary barons when he came to perform homage to the king of Aragon. Arguments broke out between James III and Peter during a visit to the pope at Avignon; James was reluctant to ride behind Peter as his underling.[41] The problem was that Peter too was a stickler for correct form; he has acquired the sobriquet 'the Ceremonious' as a result. Indeed, James III's 'laws' were later reissued by his rival Peter IV of Aragon; nor were these kings alone in their obsession with etiquette and ceremonial, as a brief glance at the reign of Peter's contemporary the Emperor Charles IV would reveal.

Peter IV's view is recorded in his own memoirs, which insist that the original grant of a kingdom to James II of Majorca 'was not valid in law, for the gift was an immense one and took away the greater or a great part of the patrimony of the house of Aragon'.[42] James appears to have taken the advice of Roman lawyers, notably those of the University of Montpellier (a city which was largely under his lordship), who insisted that monarchs enjoyed full authority in their own kingdoms; their rights could not be compromised by subjection to another. Either James was a king or he was not. In a sense, similar arguments were being propounded by each side to prove that the authority of the king of Aragon, or that of Majorca, was undermined by the present arrangement.

As tension grew in the years around 1340, accusations and counter-accusations flew back and forth from Barcelona to Mallorca. The king of Majorca was said to have tried to kidnap the king of Aragon on a visit to Barcelona during which a half-hearted attempt was made to settle the differences between the two kings; his galley was moored next to a seaside palace, and a closed wooden bridge was constructed from the ship to the palace. James would spirit Peter

---

[41] There is a detailed account of their differences in Book III of Peter IV's chronicle: see Peter the Ceremonious in *Les quatre grans cròniques*, ed. F. Soldevila (Barcelona, 1971).
[42] Chronicle of Peter the Ceremonious, III.3.

away without anyone noticing. More serious, perhaps, was the infringement of the agreement that the king of Majorca should not mint his own coins in Roussillon, where Catalan money circulated. In addition, James was known to be making polite noises to the king of England, with a view to a marriage alliance. This was more troubling than it sounds, since the English possessions in the foothills of the northern Pyrenees lay no great distance from the Majorcan ones in the southern Pyrenees.[43] James also dreamt up grand schemes for expansion into the Atlantic; expeditions were sent to the Canary islands in 1342, to claim them for Majorca and to create bases there for a two-pronged assault on Muslim Africa.[44] There was perhaps a *folie de grandeur* in all this.

In 1343 Peter IV invaded Mallorca. As in 1285, there was no sudden upsurge of enthusiasm for the Majorcan monarchy. The mainland territories too were overwhelmed in 1344, though there Peter encountered more resistance. Only Montpellier and nearby lands were left in the hands of James III; and, desperate to raise money with which to pay an army, James sold Montpellier to the king of France in 1349. He attacked Mallorca with his followers, but was almost immediately killed in battle. This marked the effective end of the kingdom of Majorca. There are doubts about the sanity of his son James IV, who tried to reactivate his claims in the late fourteenth century; but neither he nor other claimants to the throne such as Duke Louis I of Anjou–Provence, a member of the French Valois dynasty, could dislodge the Aragonese. A kingdom of Majorca persisted, shorn of its mainland territories, which were henceforth simply appendages of Catalonia; but Mallorca did not enjoy the same status as the core states of Aragon, Catalonia and Valencia and was much less often visited by the kings of Aragon, except en route to their troublesome Sardinian lands. A governor exercised authority on behalf of the king.

V

The Balearics experienced the same economic uncertainties as the other lands of the Crown of Aragon in the late fourteenth and fifteenth centuries. The cloth industry retained some importance, though there were severe banking crises, as at Barcelona. Foreign merchants continued to frequent the islands around 1400, notably

---

[43] For the negotiations with England, see chapter 10.   [44] See chapter 10.

the prominent Tuscan merchant Francesco Datini, the 'Merchant of Prato,' who had very extensive business interests in Mallorca and Menorca. Ibiza appears to have increased in importance as a source of good quality salt, though it was increasingly the Genoese who handled this trade. Although by then trade through Mallorca had passed its medieval peak, the business community of Ciutat de Mallorca saw fit in the late fifteenth century to erect a stunningly beautiful *Lonja* or *Llotja*, which functioned as an exchange and as the seat of the Sea Consuls, who were responsible for the administration of merchant law.[45] Designed by Guillem Sagrera, it consists of a large Gothic hall whose roof is supported by a soaring forest of slender columns. Its beauty lies to a large extent in its austerity. It is arguably one of the most spectacular secular Gothic buildings to have survived; it is hardly testimony to an economy in severe recession.[46]

Nevertheless, depopulation, after the Black Death, changes in the international trade routes and war taxes combined to induce an economic crisis, marked by faction struggles in the capital. Trade on Mallorcan ships to Flanders and England faltered and died by the mid-fifteenth century. A particularly ugly manifestation of unrest was the attack on the Jewish community in 1391, which started as a rural protest aimed at the lieutenant governor, and which ended in the sack of the *Call* or Jewish quarter in Ciutat de Mallorca. Despite royal attempts to protect the Jews, whose economic contribution was much valued by the monarchy, there was a noticeable increase in anti-Jewish agitation, culminating in a mass conversion, effectively under duress, in 1435. Thereafter the converted Jews, or *Xuetes*, remained a distinct group on the island, subject to investigation by Inquisitors and subject also to discrimination by the old Christian population.[47] Mallorca was thus the first region of Spain in which the open practice of Judaism disappeared. Islam had already vanished, except among the imported slave population of the islands.

The history of the Balearic islands in the Middle Ages appears at one level as a success story: newly arrived merchants, settling in this frontier territory early in the thirteenth century, made Ciutat de Mallorca into one of the major centres of international trade, serving not merely the Mediterranean but the Atlantic. The fifteenth century

---

[45] For this institution, see R. S. Smith, *The Spanish gild merchant. A history of the consulado, 1250–1700* (Durham, NC, 1940); *The consulate of the sea and related documents*, transl. S. S. Jados (Alabama, 1975). On the state of the economy after 1343, see chapter 11.

[46] For a good description of this building, see *The Balearic islands*, ed. Jacques Heers (Nagel's Encyclopedia Guide, 2nd edn, Geneva, 1969), 43–5.   [47] See chapter 5.

did, it is true, see a check placed on Mallorcan economic expansion, but there was still some optimism, as the building of the *Lonja* suggests. Against this, there is the paradox of the failure of the Majorcan monarchy. Its political weakness contrasts strikingly with Mallorca's economic strength. Attempts to secure real independence from Aragonese overlordship culminated in the suppression of the separate Majorcan crown, first briefly in 1285, and then permanently in 1343. The loss of the Balearics by Islam detached the islands from Africa; the disappearance of the Majorcan kingdom detached them from what is now southern France; the final Aragonese conquest in 1343 brought them decisively into Spain.

CHAPTER 2

The kingdom and its historians

I

There are reasons why the Catalan kingdom of Majorca has received less attention than other Spanish kingdoms: the brief existence of a Majorcan dynasty, before its reincorporation into the Crown of Aragon in 1343; its limited territorial extent; the emphasis in Spanish historiography on Castile, are all factors that have diverted attention away from a kingdom that sat astride some of the key trade routes of the late medieval Mediterranean, that had a significant role in the dramatic events of the War of the Sicilian Vespers, and that poses important questions about the nature of royal autonomy in late medieval Europe. Above all, the fact that its territories are now divided between France and Spain has resulted in a general failure to look at the mainland territories of Roussillon, Cerdagne and Montpellier together with the Balearics. The sheer diversity of its archives, now spread between Paris, Perpignan, Montpellier and Palma, has combined with a natural reluctance among historians trained in the history of their nation and its regions to speak in one breath about what are now the French Pyrenees and the Balearic Autonomous Region. Even with the resurgence of Catalan national consciousness, there has been a tendency to articulate research around the regions established by the democratic government of modern Spain, with the result that the wider setting of the Balearics (and even on occasion the question of their links to their Catalonian motherland) has taken second place to their internal history.

One of the principal vehicles for the study of Catalan–Aragonese history is the periodic Congress of the History of the Crown of Aragon, held in one or another of the key cities of the Catalan–Aragonese commonwealth. Two congresses in succession were held on what was once Majorcan territory. However, looking at the acts of the congress held in Montpellier (1985)[1] and of that held in Palma (1987)[2], it appears that the study of the rôle of the Crown of Aragon, and in particular the kingdom of Majorca, in southern France and the study of the late medieval Balearics have rather little in common. Other physically divided kingdoms in the Middle Ages have fared better: English historians have insisted on the need to understand Norman and Angevin policy in France (though French historians have become curiously neglectful of England), and the history of the kingdom of Sicily has generally, though not always, been written as that of both the mainland and the island territories, until their separation in 1282. Indeed, the study of 'multiple kingdoms and federal states' has attracted increasing interest in an age of speculation about European federation, and of the creation, or recreation, of regional governments in such areas of the former Catalan commonwealth as Catalonia, Valencia, Sicily, Sardinia and the Balearics themselves. At the same time, broader based descriptions of Mediterranean politics at the time of the Sicilian Vespers have often had much less to say about Majorca than the island and the kingdom deserve. Neither Sir Steven Runciman's *Sicilian Vespers* nor Peter Herde's *Karl I. von Anjou* makes more than passing reference to the involvement of the Majorcan king in the complex diplomacy of the years around 1282, even though the sub-plot of the French invasion of Catalonia in 1285, in which the Majorcans appear to have been implicated, looms large in Runciman's overall approach.[3] Coverage of Majorca in works devoted to the lands of the Crown of Aragon has also been patchy, though Hillgarth's studies are a notable exception here.[4]

Those works that do pay close attention to the Majorcan kingdom

---

[1] *Montpellier, la Couronne d'Aragon et les pays de Langue d'Oc* (1204–1349). *Actes du XIIe Congrès d'Histoire de la Couronne d'Aragon, Montpellier, 26–29 septembre* 1985 = *Mémoires de la Société archéologique de Montpellier*, 15–16 (1987–8), in three separate parts. (Hereafter CHCA xii.)

[2] *XIIIe Congrés d'Història de la Corona d'Aragó, Palma de Mallorca, septembre 1987*, 4 vols., (Institut d'Estudis Baleàrics, Palma de Mallorca, 1989–90). The first volume consists of the longer lectures (*Ponències*), the next three of shorter *Comunicacions*, so that *Comunicacions* i, of 1989, is vol. ii of the overall set. (Hereafter referred to as CHCA xiii, followed by volume number.)

[3] Steven Runciman, *The Sicilian Vespers. A history of the Mediterranean world in the later thirteenth century* (Cambridge, 1958); cf. Peter Herde, *Karl I. von Anjou* (Stuttgart, 1979), 102.

[4] Hillgarth, *Problem*; J. N. Hillgarth, *The Spanish kingdoms, 1250–1500*, 2 vols. (Oxford, 1975–8). Jocelyn Hillgarth's interest in Mallorca reflects both his expertise in Ramón Llull and his residence on the island. See now J. N. Hillgarth, *Readers and books in Majorca, 1229–1550*, 2 vols. (Paris, 1992).

often emphasise the first phase, the period of the conquest and settlement under James I of Aragon; an engaging and widely ranging study of conquest and colonisation in the Mediterranean and the Atlantic by Felipe Fernández-Armesto treats the colonisation of Mallorca as the essential prelude to the creation not merely of a Catalan–Aragonese 'space' in the western Mediterranean, but also as the beginning of a more or less continuous (though also in some respects haphazard) period of expansion culminating in the arrival of Castilian *conquistadores* in the Canaries and the Caribbean. Moreover, Mallorca has special importance as a major centre of geographical knowledge in the early fourteenth century, and as an early leader in what the author calls the late medieval 'space-race': it was the Majorcans who first tried to lay claim to the Canaries around 1340.[5] Even so, Fernández-Armesto concentrates his comments on the Balearic islands within the decades before the creation of the autonomous kingdom of Majorca. When looking briefly at the fourteenth century, he rightly insists that Mallorca had become 'a land of medieval *Wirtschaftswunder*, comparable with Madeira in the next century with its new products and "nodal" trade'.[6] For Fernández-Armesto, the autonomous kingdom created the conditions for an economic boom, offering, as Muntaner himself realised, low taxation and limited government intervention as incentives to enterprise.[7] At the same time, 'Majorca was never genuinely viable as a wholly independent state', for its inhabitants were mainly Catalans and trade with the Spanish mainland was crucial to its survival; the inhabitants of Mallorca welcomed rather than resisted Peter IV of Aragon's invasion in 1343.[8] There is an apparent contradiction here, and it is one of the purposes of this book to resolve the problem of the viability of the Majorcan entity, both within the political arena of Aragon–Catalonia and within the trading circuits of the western Mediterranean. Clearly, a coherent answer must pay some attention to the connections between the mainland territories of Roussillon, Cerdagne and Montpellier as well as the Balearic islands.

Among modern Spanish historians of the Majorcan kingdom, only Antoni Riera i Melis has attempted a global view that encompasses

[5] Fernández-Armesto, *Before Columbus*, 11–36, 156–9, 245–7.
[6] Fernández-Armesto, *Before Columbus*, 26.
[7] Fernández-Armesto, *Before Columbus*, 27; Muntaner, *Crònica*, cap. 29.
[8] Fernández-Armesto, *Before Columbus*, 30–1.

the mainland and island regions.[9] Further attention to his analysis of Majorcan-Aragonese relations at the start of the fourteenth century will be provided in a later chapter.[10] Yet a nineteenth-century pioneer in the study of the kingdom, Lecoy de la Marche, was well aware of the need to examine closely the links between the Balearics and France.[11] His research on Majorca was the product of serendipity: stuck in Paris, in the Archives Nationales, during the Prussian siege of 1871, he diverted his attention from current horrors by delving into the history of the second dynasty of Anjou–Provence, established in the late fourteenth century by Louis I, unsuccessful claimant to any number of thrones: Sicily and Naples, Jerusalem, Sardinia and Majorca itself. In the vast mass of Angevin documentation he found what appeared to be the royal archive of Majorca, carried away to Montpellier and later to northern France after the loss of the Balearics and the Pyrenean counties in 1343–4. In fact, this consisted of a large number of transcriptions, and some originals (which lie mostly in the Bibliothèque Nationale), which had as their purpose the demonstration that Majorca was a separate kingdom from Aragon-Catalonia; the aim was to provide a secure legal basis for the revival by Louis I of the now vanished Majorcan state. Lecoy's substantial history of the Majorcan kingdom thus devotes a disproportionate amount of space to the period after its dissolution by the Aragonese, and to the survival of the title with virtually no lands attached to it; the Angevin claimants are of greater importance for their role in the history of France and Provence, even of southern Italy, than they are in the history of the Balearics and Roussillon, where they never succeeded in establishing themselves. All this gives his book a slightly crooked configuration, for the opening chapters concern the Catalan conquest of Muslim Mayurqa and the French emphasis comes into focus quite gradually. In a sense, Lecoy's study of Majorca must be read as a companion to his well-regarded life of the last major Angevin pretender, the fifteenth-

---

[9] A. Riera Melis, *La Corona de Aragón y el reino de Mallorca en el primer cuarto del siglo XIV*, vol. I, *Las repercussiones arancelarias de la autonomía balear (1298–1311)* (Madrid/Barcelona, 1986); see also A. Riera Melis, 'El regne de Mallorca en el context internacional de la primera meitat del segle XIV', *Homenatge a la memória del Prof. Dr Emilio Sáez* (Barcelona, 1989), 45–68; A. Riera Melis, 'Mallorca 1298–1311, un ejemplo de "planificación económica" en la época de plena expansión', *Miscellanea en honor de Josep Maria Madurell i Marimon*, in *Estudios Históricos y Documentos de los Archivos de Protocolos*, 5 (1977), 199–243.

[10] See chapter 8.

[11] A. Lecoy de la Marche, *Les relations politiques de la France avec le royaume de Majorque* (2 vols., Paris, 1892).

century ruler of Anjou, Lorraine and Provence, René of Anjou, would-be king of Sicily, Jerusalem and even of Aragon, a book which he actually published first.[12] Lecoy also shows a clear contempt for Saracen savages and for Jewish usurers that reflects the cultural patterns of late nineteenth-century France; he explicitly compares the colonisation of Mallorca with the conquest of Algeria in his own time. The Catalans were engaged in a civilising mission. However, the supposedly objectionable character of King Peter the Great of Aragon, evinced in his bitter opposition to France, disqualified the Catalans from the highest praise. Here the close links between the court of Majorca and the court of France were taken to be a sign that the Majorcans recognised the essentially French destiny of their mainland territories such as Roussillon and Montpellier. What Catalonia had achieved, it had partly achieved through its French connections. France, not Spain, possessed a Mediterranean imperial destiny. Lecoy's work thus fits neatly alongside those French histories of the crusader East which sought to portray the lands *outremer* as France's first colony in the Islamic world.[13]

More disinterested treatment was offered in Germany. Briefly, the kingdom of Majorca attracted the attention of pupils of the distinguished German scholar Heinrich Finke, collector of the *Acta Aragonensia* of James II of Aragon. Carl Willemsen examined the political history of Majorca in the early fourteenth century, and adopted a global view encompassing islands and mainland, before developing an obsession with the art and culture of Frederick II's time.[14] Another exception to the general rule, this time in France, is Marcel Durliat, whose work on the art of the kingdom looks at islands and mainland, linking artistic styles at Perpignan to those at Ciutat de Mallorca, and who has provided a masterly introduction to the history and economic structure of the kingdom; he has in addition worked closely on its excellent commercial records.[15]

Modern Mallorcan historiography has tended to utilise the phrase *reino privado*, *regne privatiu* to describe the new entity created by James

[12] A. Lecoy de la Marche, *Le roi René*, 2 vols. (Paris, 1875).

[13] E. G. Rey, *Les colonies franques de Syrie aux XII* et XIII* siècles* (Paris, 1883).

[14] C. A. Willemsen, 'Der Untergang des Königreiches Mallorka und das Ende des Mallorkinischen Dynastie', *Gesammelte Aufsätze zur Kulturgeschichte Spaniens*, 5 (Munster in Westfalen, 1935), 240–96; C. A. Willemsen, 'Jakob II. von Mallorka und Peter IV. von Aragon (1336–1349)', *Gesammelte Aufsätze zur Kulturgeschichte Spaniens*, 8 (1940), 88–118; an older study is Auguste Störmann, *Studien zur Geschichte des Königreichs Mallorka* (Abhandlungen zur mittleren und neueren Geschichte, 66, Berlin/Leipzig, 1918).

[15] M. Durliat, *L'art dans le royaume de Majorque* (Toulouse, 1962).

I's will. This term has overtones of 'autonomous kingdom', and is used to express the paradox of its separateness from Aragon–Catalonia but also its formal dependence on the king of Aragon. Alvaro Santamaría Arández, the most prolific modern historian of medieval Mallorca, devotes his recent *Ejecutoria del reino de Mallorca* to the islands, and mainly to Mallorca proper at that; in addition, he concentrates most heavily on the reign of James I of Aragon, thereby offering a very different perspective to this book.[16] Santamaría addresses the social structure of what he sees as a 'predominantly bourgeois society' and looks at the exploitation of the soil and at the fiscal machinery available to the Majorcan kings. The emphasis is therefore much more on the internal history of Mallorca than on the 'international' position of the Balearics, stressed in this book. The collaborative history of Mallorca, to which Santamaría has contributed important chapters, has something to say about the mainland territories, but understandably its main concern is the continuities in the history of the island.[17] A study of town foundations in Mallorca by Gabriel Alomar makes extensive reference to the mainland cities, but is securely rooted in research on Mallorca and (briefly) Menorca.[18] The lesser islands have not lacked energetic historians. Generally, however, studies of Menorca (and *pari passu* Ibiza) have been more inward-looking than those of Mallorca, and have largely consisted of brave attempts by local historians to pull together large amounts of documentation with little overall analysis. What is needed is a discussion of the relations between Menorca and the outside world in the three distinctive periods of its late medieval history: Muslim Menorca between 1231 and 1287, when it was subject to the higher authority of the Aragonese ruler of Mallorca, but retained its autonomy under a surrender treaty; Menorca as part of the Balearic realm of James II of Majorca, Sanç and James III; and Menorca under Peter IV and the other kings of Aragon, a period which has received some attention.[19] Here, attention concentrates on

---

[16] Alvaro Santamaría, *Ejecutoria del Reino de Mallorca* (Palma de Mallorca, 1990).

[17] *História de Mallorca*, ed. J. Mascaró Pasarius, vol. III (Palma de Mallorca, 1978).

[18] Alomar, *Urbanismo regional*. The publisher's decision to print Alomar's book in brown ink on orange paper has a curious effect on the illustrations, particularly the photographs of the rural habitat.

[19] All credit is due to the Consell Insular de Menorca, Ciutadella, which has published a series of books and pamphlets on medieval Menorca, including several by Ramón Rosselló Vaquer, who has offered handlists of documents in the Mallorcan archives relevant to the history of the lesser isle: *Aportació a la història medieval de Menorca. El segle XIII* (a mere 27 pp., 1980); *Aportació a la història medieval de Menorca. Segle XIV (Reis de Mallorques i Pere el*

two issues: the fate of the Muslims of Menorca; and the evidence for trade between Menorca and the rest of the Catalan world, both in the period of Muslim autonomy before 1287, and after the island was resettled by Christian Catalans.

The valuable studies of the history of the mainland territories have generally retained their local character, be they studies of Montpellier, Roussillon or the Pyrenean territories of the kingdom. There is little to indicate in Rogozinski's excellent analysis of the political tensions in early-fourteenth-century Montpellier that the city stood in an awkward relationship with the king of France's officials.[20] Few historians are as emphatic about the Majorcan connection of Montpellier as Michael McVaugh, whose examination of the medical history of Aragon necessarily alludes to the special role of the Medical Faculty of Montpellier, long the only *studium generale* in the Catalan–Aragonese lands.[21] Occasional conferences have laid stress on the links between Languedoc, Roussillon and the Balearics, but apart from some fine miniature studies by Guy Romestan there have been few attempts to look at the trade and other links in precisely this period.[22]

Cerimoniós) (a much fuller 355 pp., but a real rag-bag of summaries of documents, with gems buried in the mass of material; 1985); *Aportació documental a la història medieval de Menorca. El segle XV* (112 pp., 1982), as well as his *La revolta menorquina contra Joan II (1463–1472). Aportació documental a la història medieval de Menorca* (1981); and his *Llibre del notari de Ciutadella Jaume Riudavets 1450–1453* (1982). To the same batch belongs A. Murillo i Tudurí, *Documentació medieval menorquina. El llibre de la Cort Reial de Ciutadella. Index de cartes registrades de 1350 a 1403*, *segons còpia conservada a l'arxiu del regne de Mallorca* (1981). A more cohesive study by Maria Perelló i Mas, *Menorca a l'epoca de Pere el Cerimoniós*, looks at the government of the island in the late fourteenth century, and again makes available substantial amounts of new documentation; this was published by the Consell in 1986. Similar initiatives appear to have stimulated publications on medieval Ibiza, with an emphasis, however, on the Islamic period. There is further material on Menorca and Ibiza in the acts of the thirteenth Congress of the History of the Crown of Aragon, cited earlier, one theme of which was the lesser islands.

[20] J. Rogozinski, *Power, caste and law. Social conflict in fourteenth-century Montpellier* (Cambridge, MA, 1982). But see now K. Reyerson, 'Flight from prosecution: the search for religious asylum in medieval Montpellier', *French Historical Studies*, 17 (1992), 603–26.

[21] M. McVaugh, *Medicine before the plague. Practitioners and their patients in the Crown of Aragon, 1285–1345* (Cambridge, 1993).

[22] See for instance G. Romestan, 'Draperie roussillonnaise et draperie languedocien dans la première moitié du XIVe siècle', *52° Congrès de la Fédération historique du Languedoc méditerranéen et du Roussillon*, (Montpellier, 1970), 31–59; G. Romestan, 'Les marchands de Montpellier et la leude de Majorque pendant la première moitié du XIVe siècle', *Majorque, Languedoc et Roussillon de l'Antiquité à nos jours. 53° Congrès de la Fédération historique du Languedoc méditerranéen et du Roussillon* (Montpellier, 1982), 53–60. The work of Kathryn Reyerson also bears on Montpellier's links to Mallorca, e.g. her *Business, banking and finance in medieval Montpellier* (Toronto, 1985). An older study of great value is L. J. Thomas, 'Montpellier entre la France et l'Aragon pendant la première moitié du XIVe siècle', *Monspeliensia. Mémoires et documents*

A particular problem has been the lack of native chronicle sources from the Majorcan kingdom. It is possible that a description, partly in rhyming prose, of the conquest of Mallorca forms the core of the chronicle usually regarded as the autobiography of King James I; valuable clues are provided concerning royal policy towards the Balearics before their detachment from Catalonia–Aragon at James I's death. The statement that there are no native chroniclers should also be qualified in the sense that the Catalan chronicler Bernat Desclot's family may well have hailed from Roussillon, eventually part of the Majorcan lands, and in the sense that Ramón Muntaner had close links with the Majorcan royal family. But Desclot was very definitely not on the side of the Majorcans when conflict broke out after 1282 between Peter the Great of Aragon and James II of Majorca. Muntaner attempted, at times at great risk to veracity, to argue that the Majorcan dynasty was always really on good terms with the Aragonese; but he observed the Majorcan monarchy mainly from outside its territory. The royal chronicles of James I and Peter IV are illuminating on the question what the Aragonese kings thought the status of the Majorcan kingdom to be; but Peter was deeply hostile to its existence, and seems to have conceived its suppression as a marvellous way to unite the Aragonese baronage behind himself. This is abundantly clear from the chronicle of his own life, which devotes a disproportionate amount of space to relations with James III of Majorca, amounting to almost exactly one-third of the entire surviving work.[23] It is plain too from the accompanying short history of his predecessors Peter commissioned, which is known as the *Chronicle of San Juan de la Peña*, and which belongs alongside the four Catalan 'pearls', and which seems to have had the status of an official history of the Crown of Aragon.[24] Here the first ruler of an independent Majorcan state, James II of Majorca, is portrayed in exceptionally unflattering terms, except, for some reason, when the chronicle writes a brief obituary of him. It is stated that the creation of the Majorcan state under the will of James I 'displeased his subjects immensely'. James of Majorca, 'unmindful of his father's advice, was extremely disobedient to his brother Pedro' (Peter III of

relatifs à Montpellier et à la région montpelliéraine publiés par la Société archéologique de Montpellier,
1 (1928/9), 2–56.

[23] As well as Soldevila's Catalan edition, see Pere III of Catalonia (Pedro IV of Aragon), *Chronicle*, transl. Mary Hillgarth, ed. J. Hillgarth, 2 vols. (Toronto, 1980).

[24] *The Chronicle of San Juan de la Peña. A fourteenth-century official history of the Crown of Aragon*, transl. Lynn H. Nelson (Philadephia, 1991).

Aragon). James of Majorca was guilty of nothing less than 'treachery'.[25] Only the compliant King Sanç of Mallorca, 'a straightforward man', who performed his act of homage to the king of Aragon in the full public view of the assembled *Corts*, wins real approval from the chronicle.[26]

II

Despite the unevenness of treatment of this kingdom, its documentary sources are of unsuspected richness, and on occasion they appear to surpass even the excellent records of Barcelona in quality and quantity. Fuller discussion of the key primary sources is deferred until they are brought under close examination, but some general points need to be stressed here. As early as 1240 a series of registers, analogous in many ways to the notarial cartularies of Genoa, begins to provide a marvellously detailed picture of a colonial society in the making. This material is preserved in the Arxiu del Regne de Mallorca in Palma, but deterioration has meant that it may only be consulted on microfilm.[27] Merchants can be seen making business deals for trade to Muslim Spain, Africa, Barcelona, Sicily and elsewhere a mere dozen years after the Catalan conquest; traders set out for Menorca, still ruled by Muslims under the loose suzerainty of the Aragonese king, and for Ibiza, captured only in 1235. All this is happening at a time when land deals and house purchases are defining the human geography of Catalan Mallorca for the first time, and when the Muslim population is experiencing rapid erosion. Similar documentation, only briefly utilised by Durliat, exists in the archive of Palma Cathedral, and sheds particularly strong light on the trade of Mallorca around 1340.[28] Alongside this promising material can be placed similar documents from the archives of Montpellier and Perpignan: the notarial registers of Perpignan have mainly been exploited for a noteworthy study of the city's Jews in the late thirteenth century, while those of Montpellier have been scoured thoroughly for commercial contracts by Kathryn Reyerson.[29] On

[25] *Chronicle of San Juan de la Peña*, 70–1, 77, 79, 85–6, 98, 101–2.
[26] *Chronicle of San Juan de la Peña*, 98–101.
[27] See chapter 6 for an analysis of this material, of which a little was used by F. Sevillano Colom and J. Pou Muntaner, *História del puerto de Palma de Mallorca* (Palma de Mallorca, 1974).
[28] See chapter 9.
[29] R. W. Emery, *The Jews of Perpignan in the thirteenth century* (New York, 1959); Reyerson, *Business, banking and finance* and her Yale thesis 'Commerce and Society in Montpellier, 1250–1350' (2 vols., University Microfilms, 1974), especially vol. II, 115–278 (tables). Some early notarial acts from Montpellier have been published in summary: *Archives de la ville*

this basis, as will be seen, it is possible to reconstruct some episodes in the history of trade between the constituent parts of the Majorcan kingdom, as part of an attempt to see how far the kingdom functioned as a coherent unit.

Looking beyond the period of conquest, the Mallorcan documentation also provides a good opportunity to compute the profits a monarchy could hope to make out of the economic activities of its subjects. The possibilities were first revealed in the fine study by Durliat and Pons of the revenues received from the *ancoratge* tax, levied on ships coming into port in the early fourteenth century.[30] Other sources are even more eloquent about royal revenues: the *Reebudes* and *Dades*, the records of the receipts and outgoings of the Majorcan crown, were analysed to potent effect by Jaime Sastre Moll in a study which provides the basis for further discussion in Santamaría's monograph.[31] The picture that emerges from the statistical tables and pie-charts of Sastre and Santamaría is of a monarchy quite well endowed with resources; possession of those resources may arguably have been as important a motive in the final Aragonese conquest of 1343 as the issues of principle concerning the respective rights of the kings of Aragon and of Majorca.

The kingdom of Majorca may have been one of the shortest-lived and smallest of the medieval Spanish kingdoms, but the central position of its territories on the Mediterranean trade routes, and eventually on the routes running out of the Mediterranean to the Atlantic, has meant that historians of other western Mediterranean kingdoms have been drawn into its history. This process is clearly visible in the acts of the thirteenth Congress of the History of the Crown of Aragon, with their emphasis on the theme of the *regne privatiu*. These conferences have played a major role in stimulating research into the relations between the far-flung territories of the Crown of Aragon; for, even when the theme has been a particular Aragonese territory – Sicily in 1982, Montpellier and southern France in 1985, Mallorca and Menorca in 1987, Sardinia in 1990 – there has often been a strong emphasis on ties to the other territories,

de Montpellier, vol. XIII, *Inventaire analytique série BB* (*Notaires et greffiers du consolat 1293–1387*), ed. M. de Dainville et al. (Montpellier, 1984).

[30] M. Durliat and J. Pons i Marquès, 'Recerques sobre el moviment del port de Mallorca en la primera meitat del segle XIV', *VI Congreso de Historia de la Corona de Aragón, Cerdeña 8–14 diciembre 1957* (Madrid, 1959), 345–63.

[31] Jaime Sastre Moll, *Economia y sociedad del reino de Mallorca. Primer tercio del siglo XIV* (Trabajos del Museo de Mallorca, Palma de Mallorca, 1986).

whose historians are well represented at the congresses. Even if, as has been suggested, the conference held in Mallorca rather turned its face away from the mainland possessions of the Majorcan crown, it also provided a chance to weigh up the current state of research on the Balearics and their international connections. Manuel Riu demonstrated in his conference address on the current state of research, delivered at Palma in 1987, how many gaps are being filled in the social, economic and religious history of the medieval Balearics, quite apart from the continuing publication of sources.[32] A major paper given at Palma by Professor Santamaría on 'El contexto historico del reino de Mallorca' casts doubt on some of the gloom-laden approaches to the Majorcan kingdom. The crown of Majorca was not doomed to auto-destruction; indeed, it showed remarkable resilience during two political crises: the succession of King Sanç in 1311 and the long minority of his successor James III, whose royal title was perhaps even more in doubt.[33]

Another feature of the Palma conference was the understandable stress laid by scholars from outside the Balearics on links with other parts of the Mediterranean and even the Atlantic. Some of these links are ecclesiastical, such as those between the church of Tarragona and Ibiza–Formentera, islands originally captured by licensed *conquistadores* under the authority of the archbishop of Tarragona; the existence of a Tarragonese enclave in the Balearics placed obstacles in the way of attempts to consolidate royal authority.[34] Several international orders had important branches on the Balearics, notably the Templars, the Friars of the Sack and the Trinitarians.[35] Another important problem arises from the settlement of large numbers of Catalans and southern French in Mallorca, and from the granting to them of generous privileges after the conquest.[36] Indeed, the contacts between Genoa and Mallorca are of crucial importance in understanding the commercial expansion of Ciutat de Mallorca

[32] Riu's lecture is, in effect, a guided tour through the recent bibliography of the *regne privatiu*: CHCA XIII, vol. I, 119–36. [33] CHCA XIII, vol. I, 25–61.
[34] R. Urgell Hernández, 'Proceso entre Sancho de Mallorca y la Iglesia de Tarragona por derechos de jurisdicción en Ibiza y Formentera', CHCA XIII, vol. 2, 15–31.
[35] J. García de la Torre, 'La Orden del Temple como ejemplo de atipismo social de la Edad Media en Mallorca medieval', CHCA XIII, vol. II, 199–204; G. Cipollone, 'L'ordo Trinitatis et Captivorum. Il suo insediamento nelle Baleari', CHCA XIII, vol. II, 169–78 and vol. III, 37–45 (why there are two versions of the same paper is not explained by the publisher). For the Friars of the Sack see the article by Larry Simon, 'The Friars of the Sack in Majorca', *Journal of Medieval History*, 18 (1992).
[36] J. Massip, 'Les franqueres dels ciutadans de Tortosa al regne de Mallorca', CHCA XIII, vol. II, 125–35.

after the Catalan conquest; for Georges Jehel, Mallorca was the 'véritable pivot de l'espace méditerranéenne'.[37] If anything, Pisa had an even longer history of links to the Balearics, indicated as early as 1113–15 by the briefly victorious Pisan and Catalan invasion of Mallorca and Ibiza. But by the late thirteenth century Genoa had apparently stolen a lead.[38] Since the importance of Mallorca to international merchants lay not in what the Balearic islands produced (at least at this stage) so much as in the easy access they gave to north Africa, the role of Catalan merchants trading through Mallorca towards the Maghrib is a subject of special significance; moreover, the whole question of the relative importance of Catalans, Proven-çaux and Italians in the creation of the Mallorcan trade network is one that needs thought.[39] Links with foreign merchants extended through Seville and the Basque ports as far as Flanders and England, which in the late thirteenth and early fourteenth centuries were the targets of Mallorcan ships; whether or not Roberto Lopez was right to argue that it was the Mallorcans who first forged maritime links between the Mediterranean and the North Sea, it is now clear that he exaggerated the rapidity of the decline of Mallorca's English and Flemish trade.[40]

What can be seen in medieval Mallorca is the creation almost *ex nihilo* of a settler society: not a colonial society, in the sense of Valencia, for Muslim Valencia was conquered soon after Mallorca and ruled by a minority of Christians; the Valencians long remained predominantly Muslims, whereas what is visible in Mallorca is the steady evaporation of its Islamic community, whose members left the island, were sold into slavery, converted to Christianity, bred themselves out of existence. The result of these processes was that Mallorca in the early fourteenth century had become a Christian society, with a sizeable Jewish population but a negligible Muslim one. As its Christian identity became more clearly defined, the rulers of Mallorca drew limits, physical, legal, economic, even moral, around the Jewish community, which was confined to its special

---

[37] G. Jehel, 'La place de Majorque dans la stratégie économique de Gênes aux xiiᵉ et xiiiᵉ siècles', CHCA xiii, vol. ii, 99–110.

[38] S. Petrucci, 'Tra Pisa e Maiorca: avvenimenti politici e rapporti commerciali nella prima metà del XIV secolo', CHCA xiii, vol. ii, 137–46.

[39] C. Batlle, J. Busqueta and C. Cuadrada, 'Notes sobre l'eix comercial Barcelona-Mallorca-Barbaria, a la meitat del s.XIII', CHCA xiii, vol. ii, 33–47.

[40] D. Abulafia, 'Les relacions comercials i polítiques entre el regne de Mallorca i l'Anglaterra, segons fonts documentals angleses', CHCA xiii, vol. iv, 69–79. Unfortunately all the title after the word 'Mallorca' has been omitted by the printer. See chapter 10.

quarter in the capital at the end of the thirteenth century, and which was increasingly discouraged from close daily contact with the Christian community, for apparent fear of 'contamination'.[41] The most noticeable similarity is not between Mallorca and Valencia, even though both formed part of the lands of the Crown of Aragon, but between thirteenth-century Mallorca and twelfth to early thirteenth-century Sicily, in the period when the Muslim population was rapidly declining to its final point of singularity, the far-off, exiled community of Saracens in the Apulian town of Lucera.[42] Another similarity to Sicily, this time of the early fourteenth century, is that the Aragonese rulers of both Sicily and Mallorca transferred the Jews of the capital into a reserved area surrounded by walls. In view of the intensity of interest in the Jews and Muslims of Mallorca, it may seem surprising that the history of Christianity in the Balearics has attracted rather less attention. The origins of Christianity in Mallorca and Menorca, including the early conflicts between Jews and Christians in Menorca, have at last been revealed in a new Catalan study.[43] Religious learning has also been examined in a major new work by Jocelyn Hillgarth.[44] Further work, concentrating on the period just after the conquest, is being prepared by Larry Simon in the United States.[45] But there are still major gaps. Less attention than the subject deserves is, accordingly, paid to the ecclesiastical history of Mallorca in this book; the subject is one of the missing colours in the medieval Mallorcan mosaic.

III

The conquest of the Balearics by Peter IV, in 1343, was, as Pau Cateura Bennàsser points out, seen as an act of reunion, restoring the natural ties between the Catalans of the islands and those of the mainland.[46] A major question raised in the works of Pau Cateura

---

[41] See chapter 4, and, for an earlier discussion, D. Abulafia, 'From privilege to persecution: crown, church and synagogue in the city of Majorca, 1229–1343', in: *Church and city, 1000–1500. Essays in honour of Christopher Brooke*, ed. D. Abulafia, M. Franklin and M. Rubin (Cambridge, 1992), 111–26.

[42] David Abulafia, 'Monarchs and minorities in the Mediterranean around 1300: Lucera and its analogues', *Christendom and its discontents*, ed. Scott L. Waugh (Berkeley/Los Angeles, 1994).   [43] Amengual i Batle, *Els orígens del Cristianisme*.

[44] Hillgarth, *Readers and books in Majorca*.

[45] Larry Simon, 'Society and religion in the Kingdom of Majorca, 1229–c.1300' (Ph.D. thesis, University of California, Los Angeles), sections of which are in course of publication.

[46] Pablo Cateura Bennàsser, *Política y finanzas del reino de Mallorca bajo Pedro IV de Aragón* (Palma de Mallorca, 1982). A broader picture of the social structure of the islands is provided in the

Bennàsser is how far the islands shared the fate of the mainland territories under Peter IV. The whole question how far the dissolution of the autonomous Majorcan kingdom affected the economic vitality of the Balearics is especially tricky, since the arrival of the Black Death severely jolted all the lands of the Crown of Aragon only a few years after the fall of James III of Majorca. Increasing tax demands, accompanying the ravages of plague throughout the late fourteenth and the whole of the fifteenth centuries, arguably induced as severe a social and economic crisis as historians have identified in Catalonia itself. Yet this was also a period of active trade, of the expansion of the textile industry, of the development of a lively export trade out of Mallorca and Menorca in raw wool: around 1400, a major customer for Balearic wool was the famous Merchant of Prato, Francesco di Marco Datini. It is not intended here to offer anything more than a brief survey of events and developments after 1343; however, the history of the autonomous kingdom will make more sense if it is understood in the wider context of antecedents and consequences. Fortunately, it is a period whose trade has been studied closely by Pierre Macaire, in the published version of a French thesis.[47]

The history of Mallorca thus provides a focus for the study of the trade and politics of the western Mediterranean in the later Middle Ages. The Balearics, and the mainland territories of the independent kingdom, formed a crossroads between Spain, southern France, Italy and Africa, and the political life of the Balearics was largely determined by wider events in that space, such as the Sicilian Vespers. The economy was heavily dependent on international trade, with the capital city functioning as a point of transit and, eventually, as a source for local goods, notably wool and cloth. This interdependence between the lands of the crown of Majorca and the surrounding coasts of the Mediterranean was not greatly altered by first the creation and then by the extinction of the independent kingdom of Majorca; in commercial terms, medieval Mallorca never could be truly independent.

same author's *Sociedad, jerarquia y poder en la Mallorca medieval* (Fontes rerum Balearium, Estudios y textos, vol. VII, Palma de Mallorca, 1984).
[47] P. Macaire, *Majorque et le commerce international (1400–1450 environ)* (doctoral thesis, Université Paris IV, Sorbonne, 1983, Atelier réproduction des thèses, Université de Lille III, Lille, 1986).

CHAPTER 3

The constitutional problem

I

The Catalan kingdom of Majorca had a 'split personality'. Not merely did its lands lie both in the Balearics and in scattered parts of modern France, but its reputation is variously that of a feeble state ruled by meddlesome kings and of a major commercial centre whose three main cities, Ciutat de Mallorca, Perpignan and Montpellier, were focal points of trans-Mediterranean and trans-continental trade. This chapter aims to examine the paradox of apparent political weakness set alongside formidable economic strength. Emphasis is placed on the definition of its political identity, and especially on the reasons for its creation in the will of James I of Aragon. Was it merely a shapeless mélange of territories from the Auvergne to Ibiza or was it a carefully devised frontier state, poised between France, Aragon and the infidel foe? In later chapters attempts by the Majorcan monarchs at the economic integration of these territories will be examined, and trade between the constituent parts of the kingdom will come under special scrutiny; in addition, the main trade routes beyond the kingdom are analysed in order to see how far the three principal trading cities pursued complementary, competing or disinterested commercial objectives. Throughout, attention is paid to arguments for and against the concept of a Catalan–Aragonese 'Empire' embracing Majorca, Valencia, Sicily, Sardinia and elsewhere, whether this 'Empire' is understood to have existed in a political, cultural or economic sense.

As has been seen, the kingdom of Majorca left no native chronicles to express its rulers' rights; what is known of its political history is largely derived from the chronicles of the rulers of the house of Barcelona and those of its courtiers, men who sought to justify the incorporation of the kingdom of Majorca into the realms of

Aragon–Catalonia, beginning from the time before the independent kingdom was even born. The kingdom of Majorca has tended therefore to share in studies of medieval Spain the fate of the kingdom of Navarre, and to be dismissed in footnotes as a political football tossed between Spanish and French kings, little more, in fact, than a specially honoured fief of Aragon, a *feudum honoratum sine omni seruicio*. Indeed, it was in such words that the rulers of Aragon tried to describe the relationship of the kings of Majorca to their Aragonese overlords in those periods when such overlordship was claimed or acknowledged.[1]

An attempt to write a constitutional history of Majorca was, however, made in the 1370s, more than thirty years after Peter IV of Aragon reincorporated Majorca into the dominions of the house of Barcelona.[2] At this time Louis, duke of Anjou, was seeking to extend his influence via Languedoc and Provence into the Mediterranean. Majorca, and later Sardinia, Naples, Sicily and Jerusalem, were seen as sources of a royal crown; moreover, in the case of Majorca Louis was able to purchase the rights to its vanished crown from Ysabella, marchioness of Montferrat. Her own rights had been inherited from the son of King James III of Majorca, who wished to be known as James IV and whose grasp of reality, not least when he was third husband of the much-married Queen Joanna I of Naples, was apparently slight.[3] Louis assiduously gathered together an archive detailing the relations between the kings of Majorca and their neighbours in France, Aragon and elsewhere, and he commissioned practised lawyers to present a defence of his pretensions. The dossiers he created are now preserved in the Archives Nationales in Paris, alongside similar dossiers documenting his and earlier claims to royal authority in the other kingdoms he craved.[4] Few dynasties have been less successful than the second house of Anjou in their attempts to turn mere titles into practical reality. What is striking in Duke Louis'

---

[1] Paris, Archives Nationales (hereafter Paris, AN), KK 1413, f.77r. The parallel with Navarre can be followed in B. Leroy, *La Navarre au Moyen Age* (Paris, 1984); J. Lacarra, *História del reino de Navarra en la edad media* (Pamplona, 1976), 275–422.

[2] Paris, AN, KK 1413, ff.1r–7v.

[3] For Louis, see A. Coville, *La vie intellectuelle dans les domaines d'Anjou–Provence de 1380 à 1435* (Paris, 1941); F. Piponnier, *Costume et vie sociale. La cour d'Anjou, xive-xve siècle* (Paris, 1970). The major account of his political career is to be found in the collected articles of E. R. Labande, *Histoire de l'Europe occidentale, xie-xive siècle* (London, 1973). On James IV, see for instance the colourful account in V. and E. Gleijeses, *La regina Giovanna I di Napoli* (Naples, 1990).

[4] See the documentary appendices of Lecoy de la Marche, *Relations politiques*.

archive is the attention paid to the claims and counter-claims of the Majorcan and Aragonese kings. The Majorcan, and Angevin, position can be reduced to a simple formula: one king cannot be subject to another; whatever agreements had been entered into to bind Majorca to Aragon were nul and void. Peter IV's assumption of the title king of Majorca, to be added to his Aragonese, Valencian and other titles, was illegitimate. The operative principle was that a king is emperor in his own kingdom.[5] Such arguments certainly were circulating at the court of Majorca in the years around 1340, under the stimulus, most likely, of lawyers from Montpellier (part of the Majorcan dominion); and of course other rulers, including close blood relations in Naples, were adept at this argument in the face of imperial or papal pretensions to overlordship.[6] The problem was that the king of Aragon, Peter IV, was himself no less insistent on the fullness of his royal authority, and was driven by an urgent need to demonstrate that neither the *Corts* of Catalonia nor, later on, the rebellious Unions of Aragon and Valencia possessed ultimate sovereign power in his realms. His bullying of James III of Majorca was in significant measure a public manifestation of the reality of Aragonese royal power, all the more important to a king who was small, feeble-looking and no physical match for his ancestor James I, Mallorca's first conqueror.

Duke Louis' advisers began their account with the creation of the kingdom by the will of Majorca's Catalan conqueror James I.[7] But in many ways the crux of the problem lay three years after James I's death, when the first independent king of Majorca (generally known as James II) had been recognised as sole ruler by his subjects in the Balearics and in what is now south-western France.[8] In 1279 King Peter III of Aragon bullied his younger brother the king of Majorca into accepting Aragonese overlordship over the Majorcan territories; in 1285 Peter sent his elder son Alfonso to Mallorca in order to

---

[5] Paris, AN, кк 1413, f.8r: 'Aduertendum est consistens in facto quod reges omnes Maioricarum sic in omnibus et per omnia fuerunt visi tamquam reges non habentes superiorem'.

[6] W. Ullmann, 'The development of the medieval idea of sovereignty', *English Historical Review*, 64 (1949), 1–33, reporting the views of Marinus de Caramanico and Andreas of Isernia on the Angevin monarchy in southern Italy. Ullmann notes that these ideas developed in Naples independently of similar ideas in France. There it was once again Montpelliérain lawyers who had at least some influence on ideas of royal authority, notably Guillaume de Nogaret. An instructive contemporary parallel also exists from Scotland, where the English kings claimed overlordship over another king.

[7] Paris, AN, кк 1413, ff.2r–3r.   [8] Paris, AN, кк 1413, f.3v.

suppress entirely the fledgling Majorcan kingdom.[9] Peter was acting directly contrary to the wishes of his father James I, who had envisaged the kingdom of Majorca as a completely independent monarchy.[10] Contrast the position a few years later. In 1285 Peter III left the Spanish lands of the Crown of Aragon (including now the Balearic islands) to Alfonso, but separated the crown of Sicily, acquired only three years earlier, from the other Aragonese territories, to form an independent kingdom ruled by his younger son James. The contrast between the attempts to incorporate Majorca and its dependencies in the Crown of Aragon and the attempts (of which this was only the first) to maintain the separation of the Sicilian crown from that of Aragon have to be understood in the context of the violent confrontation between the house of Aragon and its arch-rivals in the Mediterranean, the Angevins of Provence and Naples. The growing tension between Anjou and Aragon was of major importance in determining not merely the future of Sicily, but also the viability of the kingdom of Majorca that lay suspended between Sicily, Provence and Aragon. Sicily, in any case, was too far from Aragon–Catalonia to be governed directly from Saragossa and Barcelona; even when, during a brief period, King James I of Sicily was also King James II of Aragon, Sicily required the presence of a royal Lieutenant, James' brother Frederick, who before long seized the island crown for himself anyhow.

This chapter aims, then, to contribute to the wider discussion of the intentions (if any) behind the expansion of the Crown of Aragon in the late thirteenth century by looking at the kingdom of Majorca and its relationship with the kingdom of Aragon. Any discussion of the expansion of Aragonese influence in the Mediterranean must take as its starting-point the eminently reasonable arguments of Jocelyn Hillgarth.[11] Here we are presented with rulers who are not, or not mainly, led by the commercial interests of the merchants of Barcelona; rulers who had a surprisingly narrow financial base and rather small fleets; who seized a number of diplomatic and military initiatives in the western Mediterranean as they arose, and met with

---

[9] Duke Louis' advisers noted the opposition of Peter III, 'qui erat homo terribilis et austerus', to the creation of the Majorcan kingdom: AN, κκ 1413, f.3v.

[10] Paris, AN, κκ 1413, f.3v: he sought to 'infrangere paternam voluntatem et dispositiones'.

[11] Hillgarth, *Problem*; these arguments involve a well-sustained and vigorous rebuttal of the views of J. Lee Shneidman, *The rise of the Aragonese–Catalan Empire, 1200–1350*, 2 vols. (New York, 1970).

much sheer luck (especially during the War of the Vespers); but who had no coherent concept of an Aragonese empire, and generally made few attempts to impose direct rule from Aragon over the other lands ruled by kings of Aragonese descent. For before the invasion of Sardinia in 1323 the only major new territory to be permanently incorporated in the lands of the king of Aragon was the kingdom of Valencia. This study proposes to take the arguments of Hillgarth a stage further. A close study of the structure of the kingdom of Majorca concentrates attention on the nature of the issues dividing the French and Angevin rulers of Languedoc and Provence from the Aragonese, and specifically Majorcan, rulers of Roussillon and Montpellier. The tensions that were to erupt in the War of the Vespers are seen to be expressed over thirty years earlier in the struggle for control of most of what are now the coasts of southern France.

Most authorities see a clear distinction between the policies and interests of the Crown of Aragon before and after 1258, the date of the Treaty of Corbeil between Louis IX of France and James I of Aragon.[12] The French monarchy renounced all its rights of overlordship in Catalonia and Roussillon, rights dating back to the time of Charlemagne. But in return Aragon promised not to press its claims in southern France: in the county of Toulouse, in the viscounty of Milhau, at Nîmes and elsewhere. A firm boundary was thus drawn between Aragon and France, such as had not existed before. But there were also things left unsaid. Montpellier was not mentioned in the treaty. This was the city of James I's birth; but French suzerainty was neither stated nor denied at this point, though endlessly debated thereafter. So too the lordships of Aumelas (*Homelades*), on the outskirts of Montpellier, and of the Carlat, some way to the north, were not mentioned and remained in Aragonese hands.

A second issue that arose in this period was the relationship between the Aragonese and the Angevins. Louis IX's brother Charles of Anjou had acquired the county of Provence in 1246 by marriage to the heiress; so ended over a century of Aragonese rule in Provence, generally by way of a cadet dynasty.[13] It can be argued that Provence had provided the Aragonese with essential means to secure their

---

[12] Published in *Layettes du Trésor des Chartes*, ed. J. Teulet (Paris, 1863–75), vol. III, 405–8.

[13] For Charles' career, consult Herde, *Karl I. von Anjou*, also available in Italian in *Dizionario biografico italiano*, vol. XX, s.v.; É. Léonard, *Les Angevins de Naples* (Paris, 1954); G. Galasso, *Il regno di Napoli Angioino e Aragonese 1266–1494* (Storia d'Italia UTET, Turin, 1992).

interests in the south of France, and further afield: the large Provençal contingent in the conquest of Mallorca suggests as much; moreover, any attempt to create a band of Aragonese vassals between Roussillon, Montpellier and the Rhône would also perhaps depend on the assistance of cousins and allies in Provence itself. It was papal refusal to countenance a marriage within the prohibited degrees between the heiress to Provence and the royal house of Aragon that allowed the Capetians to instal their most ambitious cadet prince in the territory; more than that, the French monarchy was able to reverse the process of Aragonese encroachment in Languedoc by installing Alfonse of Poitiers in the county of Toulouse and by building the first French port on the Mediterranean at Aigues-Mortes.[14]

Thus the Treaty of Corbeil appeared to ensure the immunity of Languedoc, other than the enclave of Montpellier, from Aragonese intervention. But in a sense all that had happened was that Aragonese interests remained unchallenged in the largest, most prosperous city between Barcelona and Genoa, Montpellier; while the Aragonese and Majorcan kings plied likely sympathisers, such as the abbots of Valmagne near Montpellier, with privileges and sought on occasion to nullify the treaty entirely.[15] In 1280 Peter III of Aragon came to Toulouse to demand from Philip III of France the return of Milhau, Carcassonne and Rodez.[16] An inveterate opponent of French and Angevin interests, Peter aimed not merely to claim his wife's rights in Sicily but unashamedly to combat Angevin and French influence in an area traditionally regarded as part of the Aragonese sphere. The *Chronicle of San Juan de la Peña* makes it plain that the issue of control of Majorcan Roussillon and of Montpellier weighed on Peter's mind when he met Philip III:

King Peter, thereby being at peace and harmony with all those of Catalonia, wished to have a meeting with the king of France. Gathering a large and distinguished army of his subjects, he met with his brother-in-law, Philip, king of France. After they had had a long discussion, King Peter most urgently asked Philip for the viscounty of Fenollades, the counties of Carcassonne, Gévaudan, Milhau, and Béziers, and certain other lands. He also asked the king for all the rights due from his brother, King James of

[14] G. Jehel, *Aigues-Mortes. Un port pour un roi. Les Capétiens et la Méditerranée* (Roanne, 1985).
[15] J. Baumel, *Histoire d'une seigneurie du Midi de la France*, vol. II, *Montpellier jusqu'au rattachement à la France (1213–1349)*, (Montpellier, 1971), 275.
[16] Lecoy de la Marche, *Relations*, vol. I, 162–3: 'ce n'était rien moins que l'annulation du traité de Corbeil'.

Majorca, by reason of the lordship of Montpellier and other lands he possessed appurtenant to the county of Barcelona. But the king of France was not willing to grant him any of these requests.[17]

All this is not to suggest that the wilful Charles of Anjou was the agent of Capetian any more than of papal interests. There was hardly a corner of the Mediterranean where Aragonese and Angevin interests failed to clash. His Tunis crusade of 1270 interfered with the attempts of the Catalan merchants and of the Aragonese monarchy to create a loose series of protectorates in key commercial centres in the Maghrib.[18] The request of Charles of Anjou to the papacy for recognition of his son Philip as king of Sardinia collided with Aragonese aspirations to gain lordship over Sardinia: in 1267 James I provisionally attached a proposed Sardinian kingdom to the kingdom of Majorca, which was to be inherited by his second surviving son, declaring himself confident that the pope would cede him the island; in 1269 Philip of Anjou was elected king of Sardinia by Guelf partisans in Sassari, who hoped for papal approval (an election of no practical effect).[19] These events are discussed further in appendix I. What is clear is that yet again the Aragonese dynasty had been cheated of its hopes by the Angevins. The marriage of the future Peter III to Constance of Hohenstaufen, daughter of Manfred king of Sicily, enlarged the conflict further, since a couple of years after the wedding Charles of Anjou was nominated by the pope as rightful king of Sicily. Manfred died in battle in 1266 fighting him, and Constance surrounded herself with refugee courtiers from Sicily, a visible reminder of the vendetta between Anjou and Aragon.[20]

The intention so far has been to suggest that there was no dramatic shift in Aragon from a continental to a Mediterranean policy: there was no real sense of a separation between important aspects of what we might too easily describe as separate policies.[21] In the entire western Mediterranean, Christian and Muslim, Aragonese and Angevin interests were in violent opposition long before the War of

[17] *Chronicle of San Juan de la Peña*, 71. The spelling of proper names has been standardised here.
[18] C. E. Dufourcq, *L'Espagne catalane et le Maghrib au XIIIe et XIVe siècles. De la bataille de Las Navas de Tolosa (1212) à l'avènement du sultan mérinide Aboul-Hasan (1331)* (Bibliothèque de l'École des Hautes Études Hispaniques, 37, Paris, 1966).
[19] Paris, AN, p1354¹, 800, f.1r. This is printed as document 1 attached to Appendix 1.
[20] Hillgarth, *Problem*, 23, points out that the famous Giovanni di Procida did not actually become Chancellor of Aragon till after the Vespers, whatever his role in planning Aragonese policy towards Sicily.
[21] An intelligent restatement of the traditional view appears in F. Fernández-Armesto, *Before Columbus*, 70.

the Vespers. Aragon's 'continental' and 'Mediterranean' interests overlapped, and were challenged by Capetian and Angevin. Archibald Lewis has emphasised the existence of a large Provençal and Montpelliérain contingent during the conquest of Majorca, and has stressed the Occitan character of the settlement of the Balearic islands.[22] (Others have even spoken, somewhat wildly, of the large settlement of refugee Cathar noblemen in Mallorca.)[23] It seems, in corroboration of Lewis' views, that the dialect of Catalan spoken today in Mallorca and Menorca shows significant grammatical similarities to the Catalan of Roussillon and even to Provençal; Mallorquin, Menorquin and Eivissenc are dialects of eastern Catalan despite the fact that the Balearics lie on the same latitude as the western Catalan-speaking region of Valencia.[24] The intense links between the Balearic islands and both Languedoc and Provence were a reminder of the past history of Aragonese–Catalan interests to the east of the Pyrenees; conquered Mallorca might almost be described as an extension out of the Aragonese lands in Languedoc and Provence, as well as out of Catalonia itself. The kingdom of Majorca, when it came into independent existence in 1276, included all the lands of the Crown of Aragon that are now part of France. Was it then a kingdom with a special political and cultural identity, no less Occitan than Catalan, and not simply an inelegantly constructed series of slices cut out of the Crown of Aragon? In order to answer this question it is necessary to examine the constitutional status of the constituent parts of the kingdom, Iberian and Occitan.

II

From the moment of the conquest of Mallorca in 1229, James I of Aragon called himself king of Majorca. An act of 22 September 1230, in which King James rewards the men of Lleida (Lerida) for their aid, is issued in the name of 'James by the grace of God king of

[22] A. R. Lewis, 'James the Conqueror, Montpellier and southern France', in A. R. Lewis, *Medieval society in southern France and Catalonia* (London, 1984), essay no. XVI; and in R. I. Burns (ed.), *The worlds of Alfonso the Learned and James the Conqueror* (Princeton, NJ, 1985), 130–49; cf. A. Santamaría, 'Comunidades occitanes en la conquista y repoblación de Mallorca,' in *El regne de Mallorca i el Sud Francès. IV Jornades d'Estudis històrics locals* (Palma de Mallorca, 1986), 9–19.

[23] G. Alomar Esteve, *Cataros y occitanos en el reino de Mallorca* (Palma de Mallorca, 1978) documents amply the southern French, though not strictly speaking the Cathar, settlers in Mallorca.

[24] F. de B. Moll, *Gramática catalana, referida especialment a les Illes Balears* (Palma de Mallorca, 1968).

Aragon and of the kingdom of Majorca [*regni Majoricarum*], count of
Barcelona and lord of Montpellier'.[25] Thus there was notionally a
separate Majorcan kingdom. At first the government of Mallorca fell
into the hands of a freewheeling Iberian prince, Pedro of Portugal.
Pedro had already performed signal service to James by marrying the
royal mistress Aurembiaix, countess of Urgell, after James had tired
of her (but not of the wish to gain influence in the County of Urgell).
In return for respecting James' claims over Urgell, Pedro acquired
the tempting bait of the Mallorcan lordship. He toyed with his rights
in Mallorca during a long and eventful life in Aragonese royal
service, spent more in Valencia than in the Balearics; by the time he
died in 1256 he had once again asserted his rights in Mallorca.[26]
However, he never seems to have been closely involved in the day-to-
day government of the island, and was absent for many years at a
time, during which James I began to develop schemes to hand
Mallorca over to one of his own sons. In a sense, Pedro can be seen as
a stop-gap lord of Mallorca who was keeping the island warm for one
of James' future heirs. It was only when James I became aware of the
need to cater for the interests of all his sons that the idea of
establishing rule over the island under an Aragonese prince began to
take definitive shape, and his son the Infant James was granted rights
over the island preparatory to the creation of a separate Majorcan
kingdom for him. Until then, Mallorca had the character of many a
frontier territory in medieval Europe, entrusted to the control of
semi-autononomous lords who were permitted to enjoy extensive
rights in return for a promise of loyalty and a commitment to defend
the land against resurgent infidels. As in other frontier lands, and as
in the Latin East, the Knights of the Temple secured extensive lands
in Mallorca; they made efforts to improve exploitation of the soil,
and do not seem to have been a disruptive presence, as they were in
the kingdom of Jerusalem.

King James granted Pedro rights as *dominus regni Majoricarum*, 'lord
of the kingdom of Majorca', over conquered Mallorca, dependent
Menorca and unconquered Ibiza. It seems clear, then, that the
kingdom of Majorca was originally, and quite logically, thought to
consist of all of the Balearic islands. According to the autobiography

---

[25] *Documenta regni Majoricarum* (*Miscelanea*), ed. J. Vich y Salom and J. Muntaner y Bujosa
(Palma de Mallorca, 1945), no. 1, 9.
[26] Fernández-Armesto, *Before Columbus*, 29–30, describes him as 'that extraordinary condot-
tiere-cum-gigolo'.

of James I, *Mallorca era cap de les altres illes*, '[the island of] Mallorca was head of the other islands', all three together originally forming a single Muslim 'kingdom';[27] but, even after the Aragonese conquest of Mallorca, Menorca was left for several decades under the charge of a Muslim governor who acknowledged the suzerainty of the ruler of Mallorca whose flag had been ceremonially raised over the main castle in 1231, so that Menorca too must be regarded as part of the Majorcan kingdom.[28] As for Ibiza and Formentera, they were conquered by an army and fleet organised by the archbishop of Tarragona, the then count of Roussillon, Nunyo Sanç, and Pedro of Portugal, lord of Mallorca, in 1235: an expedition that has been described as the last private act of reconquista in Spain.[29] However, the licence to invade Ibiza did emanate from the king of Aragon. In 1235 the king was still happy with control solely of the islands' strongholds. He also insisted that no other overlord should be acknowledged by those who held the island, other than the cathedral church of Tarragona, which was directly involved in the planning of the expedition. In fact, the leader of the expedition, Guillem de Montgrí, shared control of Ibiza with Pedro of Portugal and Nunyo Sanç, while taking care to reserve for himself a lion's share of the land and of revenues from salt, the island's most precious 'crop'. Since this was all there was on Ibiza to attract Christian settlers, the island's rulers soon had to concede shares in the salt harvest to newcomers.[30] By the mid-fourteenth century there was an exceptionally vigorous trade in salt and in Mallorcan goods tying Ibiza to Ciutat de Mallorca. On Formentera the local lord, Berenguer Renart, a vassal of Guillem de Montgrí, concentrated on drawing revenue from fisheries, and left salt to any settlers who might be prepared to settle the furthest outpost of the Balearics.[31] When Pedro of Portugal's rights in Mallorca reverted to the crown (in the person of Prince James of Majorca), his lands in Ibiza also fell under royal control.[32]

Early in his reign, even before the conquest of Mallorca, James seems to have been thinking of the eventual separation of Catalonia plus the lordship of Montpellier from Aragon, with his elder son inheriting the highland kingdom.[33] This aroused violent protest, but

---

[27] James I, *Crònica*, cap. 47.   [28] Fernández-Armesto, *Before Columbus*, 35–6.
[29] Fernández-Armesto, *Before Columbus*, 31–3.
[30] Fernández-Armesto, *Before Columbus*, 31–3; for the status of the Muslims, see chapter 4.
[31] Fernández-Armesto, *Before Columbus*, 32.
[32] Fernández-Armesto, *Before Columbus*, 32.
[33] Lecoy de la Marche, *Relations*, vol. I, 102.

such a measure would have been very much of a part with established practice in Spain. By the early thirteenth century the idea of transmitting a compact inheritance appears to be gaining ground; but, equally, James believed in the principle of catering for all his sons. By 1242 James had decided to leave his second son Mallorca, Valencia, Roussillon (newly inherited from Nunyo Sanç) and Milhau, the last of which was ceded to France in 1258. In 1248 Valencia was to be hived off as an independent kingdom. Catalonia and Mallorca were to be united in the hands of the future King Peter. The southern French lands, with Roussillon, were to go to James' fourth son, Ferdinand. Poor Sanç, number five, was to have a career in the Church and 3,000 marks.[34] It was only in 1262 that the Aragonese king 'designed' the future kingdom of Majorca, whose territory included both the Balearics and the lands in what is now southern France, and, it was anticipated, Sardinia as well.[35] Two important factors must be considered here. The first is, quite simply, that many of James' sons predeceased him. By 1262 the task of catering for his legitimate heirs was more straightforward: a kingdom for Peter, the eldest, and one for his sibling James. A second point is that the Treaty of Corbeil had made it possible to guarantee most of the rights claimed by James I on behalf of the future James II of Majorca. There was little danger that the French kings would try to overwhelm Roussillon.

A fundamental feature of the Majorcan kingdom was to be its complete independence of Catalonia–Aragon. There is no reason to doubt that James hoped his sons would work together; however many separate kingdoms he created in his will, he saw them as a loose commonwealth bound together by the ties of blood and affection. Assuming that neither dynasty, that of Aragon proper and that of Majorca, died out, the two kingdoms would have complete parity and would not trade territories or divide themselves further.[36] This is important: the mainland territories were seen not as a make-weight that would extend the resources and influence of the fledgling Majorcan kingdom but as an integral part of it. They were not to be a mere fief of Aragon–Catalonia. Yet in fact the will of James I did bind James II of Majorca to make use of the *Usatges* of Barcelona in Roussillon, and the only money that was to circulate freely in

[34] Lecoy de la Marche, *Relations*, vol. 1, 102–8.
[35] Lecoy de la Marche, *Relations*, vol. 1, 109–19.
[36] Paris, AN, KK 1413, ff.2v-3r; doc. 4, f.52r-v (= Lecoy de la Marche, *Relations*, 1, doc. 15).

Roussillon was to be that of Barcelona (this issue was in fact to help spell the downfall of the kings of Majorca).[37] Moreover, James' autobiography speaks of the king's wish that the younger brother should show due respect to the elder; respect is not the same as subjection, but it seems that James was optimistic that a sense of family duty would cement together Aragon and Majorca, despite the vocal doubts of the Infant Peter:

Then I commanded and prayed Peter to love and honour my son, the Prince Lord James, who was his brother both on his father's and on his mother's side, to whom I had given already a certain heritage, in such wise that they might have no contention with each other. And since I gave him, the oldest, a greater heritage and more honourable, he should hold himself content with it; this would be the easier for him to do, as the Prince Lord James, I was sure, loved him and would obey him in all he should command as his elder brother.[38]

The kingdom of Majorca combined the old Catalan lands of Roussillon, Cerdagne, Conflent and Vallespir with the new Catalan lands of Mallorca proper and of Ibiza, as well as sovereign rights over Menorca. This combination of old and new is strikingly similar to the inheritance of the elder Aragonese line: the old territories of Catalonia and Aragon plus the new and restive kingdom of Valencia. It can be argued that James saw by 1262 the need to provide a solid basis of resources in old Christian territories while also enabling his sons to continue from Valencia and the Balearics in the struggle against Islam. Thus there was a greater degree of logic to the creation of the Majorcan kingdom than is easily supposed. It is now necessary

---

[37] Paris, AN κκ 1413, ff.59v-60r refers to the practice of using Valencian money in Mallorca under James I, though a Mallorcan currency was also envisaged. See Lecoy de la Marche, *Relations*, vol. I, doc. 17, 431–2. The Mallorcan coinage only began to be minted in 1300: see chapter 8.

[38] James I, *Crònica*, cap. 563: 'E puís faem manament a ell e el pregam que degués amar e honrar l'infant En Jacme, fill nostre, qui era frare seu de part de pare e de mare, e al qual nos havíem dada ja certa heretat, en guisa que ab ell no havia en res a contendre. E que, pus a ell donàvem l'heretat major e de tot l'honrament, que s'en tengués per pagat. E així que li era pus lleu de fer. E, encara, que l'infant En Jacme, fill nostre, l'amaria e l'obeïra en ço que fer degués, així com a frase major.' Soldevila, *Les quatre grans cròniques*, 399–400, cites the codicil of James I's will which expresses the hope 'quod ipsi se invicem diligant et honorent'. Soldevila remarks that if James I had wanted James II of Majorca to become the feudatory of Peter III of Aragon he would hardly have used such language. In fact, the balance of the passage in his autobiography suggests strongly that the old king was (not without good reason) worried at Peter's known hostility to the division of the Aragonese lands; the passage shows James I casting Peter in the role of Esau to his brother Jacob(us). Attempts in 1266 and on other occasions to secure Peter's agreement to the division only confirm the view that it was not what he sought: Lecoy de la Marche, *Relations*, vol. I, doc. 16, 429–30.

to look in detail at the rights and lordships that made up the mainland territories: Montpellier, Aumelas, Roussillon with Cerdagne, and Carlat.

Even in recent studies the rôle of Montpellier in the crown of Majorca has often been left vague.[39] The king of Majorca (and, between 1204 and 1276, the king of Aragon) was styled *dominus* of Montpellier. But the city did not constitute a single jurisdiction. The bishop of Maguelonne, whose see lay a little to the south-west of Montpellier, was recognised as overlord over all Montpellier; however, the bishop retained under his direct control only a small suburb, known as Montpelliéret. In 1255 the bishop was quite definite that the city of Montpellier was held by the king of Aragon not as king but as seigneur–*non ut rex, sed ut dominus Montispessulani.*[40] But equally the king of Aragon was quite definite that the French were not his overlords in Montpellier. Thus when in 1264 citizens of Montpellier brought an appeal before the seneschal of Beaucaire, James I of Aragon denied the seneschal's authority and almost unleashed a war.[41] The city itself was not free from civil strife; further conflict erupted in 1280, after the assassination of Pere de Claramunt, the lieutenant of the king of Majorca in Montpellier.[42] The French argued that this crime should be tried by the seneschal of Beaucaire; irritated at the conduct of the case, they further argued that the whole city should be returned to the hands of the French king, 'because of the failings of the officials of the lord king of Majorca, lord of Montpellier'.[43] Finally it was left to the French king to make a decisive move: in 1293 Philip IV of France bought out the bishop's interests in the city, and thus became immediate lord of the king of Majorca in the greater part of Montpellier.[44] The French had always argued that they were the ultimate suzerains of the city anyway, but the acquisition of the bishop's rights had some down-to-earth consequences. The seneschals of Beaucaire began to interfere in the administration of justice in Montpellier, offering the services of a

[39] See chapter 2 for examples.   [40] Lecoy de la Marche, *Relations*, vol. I, 143.
[41] Lecoy de la Marche, *Relations*, vol. I, 142–3.
[42] Lecoy de la Marche, *Relations*, vol. I, 170–2.
[43] Lecoy de la Marche, *Relations*, vol. I, 179.
[44] J. Strayer, *The reign of Philip the Fair* (Princeton, NJ, 1980), 53, 106–7, 408; W. C. Jordan, *The French monarchy and the Jews. From Philip Augustus to the last of the Capetians* (Philadelphia, 1989), 196. Jordan remarks that Philip IV had already in 1284 allowed Montpellier to import French grain so long as it was not re-exported to Aragonese territory – another sign of the process whereby Philip exploited the War of the Vespers to tighten his hold on Montpellier and the kingdom of Majorca.

court of appeal and gradually beginning also to demand taxes of the citizens. This led in the early fourteenth century to a double burden of taxation, French and Majorcan, on the inhabitants of Mont-pellier.[45] The intrusion of the French crown and of French officials could not easily be resisted after 1293.[46] In essence the choice lay between co-operation with the French and the danger of a blockade of the city's trade, dependent as it was on access to the sea via the indubitably French port at Aigues-Mortes. As Riera Melis has now shown in a close analysis of the period from 1298 to 1311, such blockades occurred even when the kings of France and of Majorca were otherwise on good terms; they were facts of life for the citizens of Montpellier.[47] Philip IV had no qualms about forcing ships bound for the small outports of Montpellier to call in first at Aigues-Mortes, and he tried to force Lombards resident in Montpellier to live in the completely French-controlled suburb of Montpelliéret.[48] So it is no surprise, after years of strong pressure, that in 1311 the compliant King Sanç of Majorca, under pressure from Philip the Fair, offered the French king homage and fealty for Montpellier.[49] At the same time we find James II of Aragon, Sanç's cousin, making requests that Sanç recognise Aragonese suzerainty over the so-called barony of Montpellier or Aumelas.[50] This was a separate entity to the town, consisting of a ring of lands around the city, and containing important castles such as Frontignan. What James II sought to achieve was recognition that even in Montpellier the king of Majorca owed him obligations: not, perhaps, in the city itself, but certainly in the outskirts. But this territory had lost much of its importance by 1300; its tiny ports could not compete with aggressive Aigues-Mortes, and were very nearly suffocated by the canal building which not merely

---

[45] Rogozinski, *Power, caste and law*, 142–5, a table of taxes raised in Montpellier from 1315 to 1340, including (for instance) taxes both to the French and to the Majorcan king in 1317 and in 1335.

[46] This process is well documented in Thomas, 'Montpellier entre la France et l'Aragon'.

[47] Riera Melis, *Corona de Aragón*.

[48] Lecoy de la Marche, *Relations*, vol. I, 327; Reyerson, *Business, banking and finance*, 12. The general tendency of French policy was to push the Italians towards Nîmes, and to deprive Montpellier of Italian capital.   [49] Lecoy de la Marche, *Relations*, vol. I, 368.

[50] Paris, AN, KK 1413, ff.5r, and f.82v–86v, docs. 28–9. The French king secured recognition from Sanç of his authority in Lattes and its dependencies, because this part of the outskirts of Montpellier was originally part of the territory of the bishop of Maguelonne; but Sanç reserved his rights over the remaining segments of Aumelas and also over the Carladès. See further Lecoy de la Marche, *Relations*, vol. I, 368, 386; and vol. I, 140, where it is pointed out that much of the barony was at first held not from the bishop of Maguelonne but from the count of Mauguio; also Thomas, 'Montpellier entre la France et l'Aragon'.

improved access to the French port but made the seaside lagoons of Aumelas inaccessible.[51]

It is not surprising that the complex interweaving of jurisdictions in Montpellier gave rise to bitter argument at the courts of France, Aragon and Majorca. The most remote of the Majorcan possessions on the soil of modern France raises difficulties of a different order. The Carladès or Carlat lay on high ground on the boundaries of Auvergne and Rouergue, and consisted of ten castles, none of them of great moment. Yet these lands, already under Aragonese over-lordship in the twelfth century, were attached to the new kingdom of Majorca under the will of James I.[52] They were not mentioned in the Treaty of Corbeil; maybe there is truth in the idea that they were so unimportant that nobody cared about their fate. Lecoy de la Marche suggested that they were granted to James of Majorca simply because they were nearer Montpellier than they were to Catalonia–Aragon.[53] Yet the Carlat emerged as an issue of moment in 1322, when James II of Aragon tried to score points off both the king of France and the king of Majorca. James gave the following instructions to the ambassadors he was sending to Charles IV of France: 'tell him that the baronies of Aumelas and Carlat are held in fee of the king of Aragon, whose allods they are, which lands the king of Majorca holds on his behalf. And it is certain that in the past the officials of the previous kings of France (of good memory) have made many errors and injustices, above all in the time of King Philip his father.'[54]

The kings of Aragon were, in any case, far more interested in realising their rights of lordship in Roussillon and Cerdagne, on the Pyrenean borders of Aragon–Catalonia, than they were in pressing a claim to Montpellier and the Carlat which the French would see as an irritating intrusion. For there was no doubt that Roussillon was not part of France; even when Louis XI conquered Roussillon in the fifteenth century he found it hard to deny that he held it from the

---

[51] Riera Melis, *Corona de Aragón*, 102–3; see chapter 8.

[52] Lecoy de la Marche, *Relations*, vol. I, 146–7: in 1167 Alfonso II of Aragon reserved rights of homage and fealty while permitting the descendants of the region's former viscounts to administer the territory; the ten castles were those of Carlat, Vic, Boisset, Cromières, Calvinet, Vigouroux, Turlande in Auvergne, and of le Mur de Barrès, Vinzelles and Barre in Rouergue.   [53] Lecoy de la Marche, *Relations*, vol. I, 147.

[54] Lecoy de la Marche, *Relations*, vol. I, doc. 48, 495, March 1322: 'Item, li diguen com les baronies de Omelades et de Carlades son tengudes en feu per lo rey d'Arago, de qui son alou, lesquals te per ell lo rey de Mallorcha. E es cert que en los temps passats y son estats fets molts torts et molts greuges per los officials dels reys de França, de bona memoria, passats, e specialment del temps del rey Phelip, pare seu, a en ça.'

Aragonese.[55] And the kingdom of Majorca could not have acquired its rights in Roussillon without the agreement at Corbeil. The only area of the French border with the Aragonese kings to remain a serious matter of dispute was the Val d'Aran, north-west of Andorra; as a matter of fact, the kings of Majorca administered this area between 1298 and 1313, during the long years of intricate negotiation between France, Aragon and the papacy concerning its ownership.[56] But clearly this was no more than a neutral temporary administration more or less agreeable to the competing parties, and there was no serious attempt to grant the Majorcan king actual possession. James II of Majorca would have been glad to hold on to the territory, but he was aware that he could not risk further upsetting the already delicate relations between Aragon and France.[57] Moreover, the Val d'Aran was physically detached from the main Majorcan territories in the Pyrenees.[58]

Roussillon and Cerdagne, the lands between Andorra and the Mediterranean, experienced an economic upsurge at the end of the thirteenth century. Perpignan, the largest city in this part of the kingdom of Majorca, was already a significant trading and industrial centre in the mid-thirteenth century; but it became a boom town with a lively textile industry.[59] Puigcerdà, the main town in the Cerdagne, lying just south of Andorra, also became a textile centre; Villefranche de Conflent bloomed as a result of its fairs.[60] Perpignan drew inhabitants, Jewish and Christian, from Languedoc, acting as a bridge between such southern French cities as Narbonne and Toulouse and the major Aragonese trading centres of Barcelona and Montpellier.[61] Collioure, its flourishing outport, was a valuable stopping-point for shipping bound between the far-flung territories of

[55] J. Calmette, *La question des Pyrénées et la marche d'Espagne au Moyen Age* (9th edn, Paris, 1947) indicates, however, that what Louis XI really wanted was ruthlessly to incorporate Roussillon into France.
[56] J. Reglà Campistol, *Francia, la Corona de Aragón y la frontera pirenaica. La lucha por el Valle de Arán, siglos XIII-XIV*, 2 vols. (Madrid/Barcelona, 1951), vol. I, 206–17. Reglà points out, p.207, that the Val d'Aran was integrated into the lieutenancy of Roussillon, Vallespir, Conflent and Cerdagne, functioning as an autonomous territory under a governor.
[57] Reglà, *Francia*, 210.
[58] The Pyrenees provide an ideal environment for mixed jurisdictions (such as Andorra), or for enclaves (as the modern case of Llivià, physically separate from Spain, demonstrates). See P. Sahlins, *Boundaries. The making of France and Spain in the Pyrenees* (Berkeley/Los Angeles, 1989). [59] See chapter 9. [60] Durliat, *Art*, 55–6.
[61] Emery, *Jews of Perpignan*, 12–13, points out how few names of Perpignan Jews appear to originate south of the Pyrenees, while a good number can be traced to Lunel, Montpellier, Béziers, Narbonne and other southern French centres. See chapter 5.

the crown of Majorca. Perpignan was the administrative, Mallorca the ceremonial capital, of the kingdom; the two royal palaces of the Almudaina in Palma and of the kings of Majorca in Perpignan mirror one another down to the architectural details of the chapel doorways. Now, by the late twelfth century the authority of the counts of Barcelona had been recognised by the counts of Roussillon, who had played a substantial rôle in the conquest of the Balearics; it is hardly surprising that Peter III of Aragon saw the loss of Roussillon and Cerdagne to his younger brother the king of Majorca as a blow to his interests.[62] If a completely independent king controlled the frontier lands between France and Aragon, Peter's own ability to conduct a decisive anti-French policy would be hampered. Cerdagne or Cerdanya actually straddled the watershed of the Pyrenees, and so the Majorcan kingdom also included some lands in what is now mainland Spain, though they were far from extensive, and were intimately linked to the economy of Old Catalonia. From a military perspective, Majorcan involvement in Cerdagne was potentially dangerous to Aragon–Catalonia. Proof of Peter's doubts is provided by the War of the Vespers, when James II of Majorca allowed the French 'crusaders' to march through Roussillon on their way (they hoped) to the destruction of Peter III, but in fact to ignominious failure.

It is thus no surprise that Peter attempted to anticipate this difficulty by presenting himself in 1279 at Perpignan and securing by threats a recognition of his suzerainty over the kingdom of Majorca from his brother James.[63] If, as is likely, Peter already had in prospect ambitious campaigns in north Africa and ultimately Sicily, it was essential to guarantee the security of the French frontier, for the usurper of Sicily's throne, Charles of Anjou, was uncle to the king of France. By 1279, Peter had a different view of the status of the Balearics to his view of Roussillon and Cerdagne. The latter were treated as counties held from him as count of Barcelona.[64] The point

---

[62] Lecoy de la Marche, *Relations*, vol. I, 128 dates the first close ties of Roussillon to Barcelona to 1172, but regards the Aragonese succession in 1258 as the real moment of union.

[63] Lecoy de la Marche, *Relations*, vol. I, 156.

[64] Yet earlier he had acknowledged that at least one of his most powerful vassals in Cerdagne and Conflent, Roger, count of Foix, would have to transfer allegiance to James of Majorca: Lecoy de la Marche, *Relations*, I, doc. 15, 428–9 (of 1263). Not surprisingly this document features in the dossiers of Louis of Anjou: Paris, AN, KK 1413, f.52r-v. More generally, see the agreeable narrative of J. E. Martinez Ferrando, *La tràgica història dels reis de Mallorca* (Barcelona, 1960), 51–4; A. Pons, 'El reino privativo de Mallorca. Jaume II', in *Història de Mallorca*, ed. J. Mascaró Pasarius, vol. III (Palma de Mallorca, 1978), 59.

seemed proved by the practice in Roussillon of following the *Usatges* of Barcelona, enjoined on James II in his father's will.[65] The Balearics, on the other hand, were a kingdom in their own right, even though their ruler was a vassal of the king of Aragon. In a sense (as Riera Melis has said), Roussillon and the Balearics had become a special apanage, whose prince simply possessed an unusually grand title, that of king.[66] Peter's view thus contradicts the clear statement in James I's will that Roussillon and Cerdagne were indissolubly bound to the Balearics. Between 1276 and 1279 Roussillon was not just an additional dependency of the kings of Majorca on another king's soil; it was an integral part of the kingdom of Majorca. James II of Majorca, once restored to the Balearic islands in 1298, seems to have soft-pedalled on the issue of the status of Roussillon and Cerdagne. His correspondence with the king of Aragon appears to define the *regnum Maioricarum* as the Balearics, while the mainland territories were often described as *alie terre*, 'other lands', of the king.[67]

Later, King Peter IV of Aragon tried to explain how the arrangement between Peter the Great and James II of Majorca, as also their descendants, was supposed to work:

The king of Majorca should remain king and count of Roussillon and of Cerdagne and lord of Montpellier and hold and possess his realm, counties and lands with entire jurisdiction, but, for the said realm, counties and lands, the king and his successors should be vassals and liegemen of the king of Aragon and his successors. He should hold the kingdom, counties and lands in fief for the king of Aragon, and should do all those things that a vassal was bound to do for his lord and, especially, he should be present at and come to the Corts of Catalonia, every time that the king of Aragon summoned them.[68]

The *Chronicle of Peter the Ceremonious*, reflecting closely the views of Peter IV of Aragon, insists that under the second and third kings of Majorca, Sanç (1311–24) and James III (1324–43), the dangerous view was spreading that the Majorcan king could deny Aragonese overlordship 'for the land had been given in old times in free allod'.[69] Peter attributes these wrong-headed notions to the bad influence of southern French nobles, but there is no reason to doubt the help and advice of Montpellier's able law professors. The chronicler contrasts the readiness of Sanç for most of his reign to follow the Catalan

[65] Peter IV, *Chronicle*, ed. Hillgarth, vol. I, 229.
[66] Riera Melis, *Corona de Aragón*, 32, 258: the king of Majorca was a 'feudatario honrado del rey'. [67] See chapter 8; Riera, *Corona de Aragón*, doc. 63, 319–20.
[68] Peter IV, *Chronicle*, III.3. [69] Peter IV, *Chronicle*, III.6.

Usatges, and even to attend the *Corts* of Catalonia when summoned, with the growing, and in Peter IV's view treacherous, pretensions of James III of Majorca around 1340. But even Sanç, according to the chronicle, began to waver towards the end of his life.

The French 'crusade' against Aragon, and other events of 1285, make it clear that the attempts of Peter of Aragon to impose his suzerainty over the kingdom of Majorca, in 1279, had backfired. The Majorcans took advantage of the rivalry of the houses of France, Anjou and Aragon to favour France and the Angevins against Peter and his successors. In 1283 Peter laid siege to Perpignan and tried to trap James of Majorca in his palace, but James escaped down the sewers, leaving his wife at Peter's mercy.[70] In fact, between 1285 and 1298 all the Majorcan kings had was Roussillon and Montpellier, since Peter sent his heir Alfonso to recover the Balearics for the king of Aragon. There was no problem in justifying this, for to Peter James II of Majorca was clearly a contumacious vassal who had rebelled against his rightful lord. Thus between 1285 and 1298 there were two 'kings of Majorca': the king of Aragon himself, who resumed using the title, and the king of Majorca, count of Roussillon and lord of Montpellier, James II. A similar situation of course prevailed in southern Italy and Sicily, where Charles II, king of Sicily was confronted by the Aragonese kings of Sicily, James and Frederick. In both the Majorcan and the Sicilian cases the displaced ruler had lost control of the core territory from which his royal title in the first instance derived, but had retained control of most of the mainland territories. The Majorcan king was reinstated in the Balearics in 1298, under pressure from France and the papacy for an end to the War of the Vespers; but he could not be reinstated as a completely autonomous king free of Aragonese overlordship.[71] The kingdom had the added bonus of including Menorca, newly conquered in 1287 by Alfonso III, but still largely uninhabited after the evacuation of its Muslim population.[72] Yet even after 1298 plentiful symbols of the anomalous status of the kings of Majorca remained. The complex monetary history of the dispersed kingdom reveals the continuing difficulties. In Mallorca, they were free to mint their own silver coins,

[70] Bernat Desclot, *Crònica*, caps. 134–6.
[71] Martinez Ferrando, *Tràgica història*, 96–107.
[72] E. Lourie, 'La colonización cristiana de Menorca durante el reinado de Alfonso III "el Liberal", rey de Aragón', *Analecta sacra Tarraconensia*, 53/4 (1983), 135–86, repr. in E. Lourie, *Crusade and colonisation. Muslims, Christians and Jews in medieval Aragon* (Aldershot, 1990).

as they did from 1300 in an attempt to assert their independence. Until then they made use of the Valencian coinage in the islands, thus using a total of three coinages at any one time: Valencian or Balearic in the islands, Barcelonan in Roussillon, and the famous money of Melgueil in Montpellier, itself challenged after 1293 by a French royal mint in the city.[73]

At least one of the kings of Majorca had plans to extend his dominion far southwards. Arguably the idea behind the foundation of the kingdom had been precisely that of the creation of a new frontier crusading state. In the early fourteenth century considerable influence was acquired over the Abdalwahidid state of Tlemcen, and it may be justified to describe the coastal towns of Algeria as a Majorcan protectorate; there was a long tradition of attempts by Christian rulers, Castilian, Catalan, Sicilian, to create zones of influence on the shores of Africa opposite their own lands.[74] Independent Majorcan efforts to establish control of new lands (other than the privately advocated schemes of Ramón Llull) point away from the coast of Africa towards the Canary islands. The Majorcan Jewish cartographers were well informed about the Canaries by 1340; the many Majorcan traders who followed the coast of Atlantic Morocco southwards may have brought news of the islands. In 1342 and 1343 several expeditions were sent to the Canaries, with little apparent success, to spread the faith and to provide a base from which the gold resources of west Africa could (supposedly) be exploited. If the conquest succeeded, its leaders were enjoined to acknowledge the king of Majorca as their suzerain and to refer appeals to his court. The conquest of the Canaries was thus seen to have useful implications for the authority of the kings of Majorca; indeed, there may have been some idea of establishing there the first Majorcan lordship that would be free of either Aragonese or French claims to suzerainty. After 1343 the Aragonese themselves began to patronise expeditions, initially by Mallorcan ships, to the Canaries. It is likely the Majorcans aimed to stimulate interest in a great pincer-shaped crusade which would assault north-west Africa simultaneously from west and north.[75]

---

[73] Reyerson, *Business, banking and finance*, 139–46.

[74] David Abulafia, 'The Norman kingdom of Africa', discusses a twelfth-century example of this process. For the Majorcan 'protectorate' in the fourteenth century, see Dufourcq, *Espagne catalane*.

[75] See chapter 10 for details of the large literature on this, and for further discussion of the political implications.

III

The intention of this discussion has been to examine some of the ways in which the kings of Aragon and their Majorcan kinsmen interacted, in the period of violent conflict before and after the Sicilian Vespers. It has been seen that the assertion of the authority of the king of Aragon over the king of Majorca must be understood in the context of the tension between the house of Aragon and the houses of France and Anjou, and that this tension itself hardened the resolve of Peter III to redeem his wife's Sicilian inheritance. The fundamental principle that was at work here was the defence of the honour of the house of Aragon. Peter sought to claim the rights of his and his wife's bloodline. He did not even intend to unite the crown of Sicily permanently to that of Aragon: his will stipulated that Aragonese Sicily was to be fully independent of Aragon, under the rule of his second son James. Yet his wish to make the kingdom of Majorca a *reino mediatizado* (to cite Riera Melis[76]), by insisting that his brother recognise his suzerainty, might appear to speak for higher, 'imperial', objectives. James I had sought to create an association of crowns that would be bound together by the bond of fraternal affection.[77] Peter saw that if he did not assert his authority in the kingdom of Majorca others, particularly the French kings, would do so. In fact the whole history of the kingdom of Majorca is a history of attempts to fight loose of the suzerainty of Aragon. Sheer proximity made this a hazardous business. Moreover, the inhabitants of Mallorca made very little resistance to the conquest by Alfonso III in 1285 or to that of Peter IV in 1343. The Majorcan monarchy excited surprisingly muted enthusiasm, at least in the Balearic islands.

The vulnerability of the kingdom of Majorca is thus very striking. James I had not in fact created a kingdom that was too disparate to be viable; as will be seen, James II of Majorca, the author of vigorous economic policies, did attempt to knit together the territories into a well-integrated economic unit.[78] But he could not resist the pressure of Aragon, and to some degree of France, which saw Roussillon, Montpellier and even the Balearics as a highly accessible strategic zone between their kingdoms. The kingdom of Majorca thus never really fulfilled its function as a frontier territory looking south to

[76] Riera Melis, *Corona de Aragón*, 253.   [77] James I, *Crònica*, cap. 563.
[78] See chapter 8.

Africa, and was condemned to a fragile existence as a permeable frontier looking north, stuck between France and Aragon.

All this should be taken to confirm the arguments of Hillgarth that the whole concept of a Catalan 'empire' is a mirage. The pursuit of the hereditary interests of the royal family of Aragon, and the desire to cater for the needs of the princes of the dynasty, resulted in haphazard, inconsistent policies. For even the ideal of fraternal co-operation between kings of one blood proved hard to turn into reality. Conciliatory marriage alliances between Aragonese and Angevin princes (such as Sancia of Majorca's marriage to Robert the Wise of Naples) brought new family obligations.[79] Far from helping to create the so-called Aragonese empire, the War of the Sicilian Vespers tore the Aragonese dynasty apart, setting both Sicily and Majorca against Aragon. It was, in fact, the disunity of the apparent parts, not their unity, that dominated the diplomacy and commerce of the Mediterranean around 1300.

[79] R. G. Musto, 'Queen Sancia of Naples (1286–1345) and the Spiritual Franciscans', in *Women of the medieval world. Essays in honor of John H. Mundy*, ed. J. Kirshner and S. F. Wemple (Oxford, 1985), 179–214.

CHAPTER 4

One kingdom, three religions: the Muslims

I

The kingdom of Mallorca provides a useful laboratory in which to examine the breakdown of the *convivencia* of Jews, Christians and Muslims in the late Middle Ages. However, the focus of such a study has to be the island parts of the kingdom, particularly Mallorca, where the Jewish community is especially well documented, and Menorca, where the destruction of the Muslim community is the dominating theme. Although even Montpellier may have possessed a small Muslim population at some time, the Muslim inhabitants of this kingdom were concentrated in the Balearics;[1] Jews lived in all parts of the kingdom, though they suffered expulsion from Montpellier when the French king cleared his lands of Jews in 1306. The Jewish population of Mallorca has attracted considerable attention from historians interested in its survival as a coherent *converso* community, the *Chuetas* or *Xuetes*, subject to discrimination more or less until the twentieth century; some interest has also been expressed in its achievements in cartography and astronomy, notably under King Peter IV of Aragon, who acquired Mallorca in 1343. Perpignan was also a centre of Jewish astronomy and science; the Jews of Roussillon have been the subject of a now classic study of their moneylending activities by R. W. Emery.[2] However, the earlier history of the Jews and the Muslims in the Majorcan lands is still the subject of much controversy. The aim here is as much to make clear some areas of disagreement as to resolve them. In particular, the aim is to indicate where the treatment of the two groups coincided and where it differed. Why did the Jews of Mallorca possess an *aljama*

---

[1] At Notre-Dame-des-Tables in Montpellier, casts of Muslim tombstones of perhaps the twelfth century are displayed. But their origins and significance remain mysterious.
[2] Emery, *Jews of Perpignan.*

56

when the Muslims of the island did not? Were the Mallorcan Muslims predominantly free or unfree? Why were the Muslims of Menorca sold *en masse* into slavery? Why did the kings of Majorca resist the temptation to follow the lead of the French and English kings in expelling the Jews? Each of these questions deserves extended treatment on its own; but equally it is only by linking these questions that they can be understood at all.

II

The question whether a significant Muslim population survived in Mallorca and Ibiza after the Catalan conquest has now been answered in the affirmative.[3] In a sense, this only compounds the problem of what happened to the Mallorcan Muslims. The Muslim population appears to have withered away during the period of the autonomous Majorcan kingdom. On the other hand, James I's own memories were of Muslims who remained on the island, cultivating the soil in some instances as serfs or slaves: *els poblassen per la terra en manera de catius*, at least if they had earlier resisted the conquest; there was some last ditch opposition as late as June 1232 in the mountains.[4] The leader of the resistance was Xuaip (Shuayb) but he had already given way to James by May 1231, though James' autobiography

[3] E. Lourie, 'Free Moslems in the Balearics under Christian rule in the thirteenth century', *Speculum*, 45 (1970), 624–49; repr. in Lourie, *Crusade and colonisation*, essay VI. Much of what follows in this section is a friendly critique of Elena Lourie's important article. My own views coincide at some points with those of Alvaro Santamaría, in his *Ejecutoria del Reino de Mallorca* (Palma de Mallorca, 1990), 51–265, and of Larry Simon, in his unpublished papers and thesis; both approaches are based on the notarial protocols preserved in Palma. The latest discussion (in large part methodological) of the Muslims appears in R. Soto Company, *L'ordenació de l'espai i les relacions socials a Mallorca en el segle XIII (1229–1301)* (doctoral thesis, Autonomous University of Barcelona, published in microfiche, Bellaterra, 1992), 174–202; here Soto asks whether Mallorca was a society based on slavery, or merely one in which slaves were to be found, an important question from the Marxist perspective; in addition, he reviews progress on the problem of the Muslims in post-conquest Mallorca since the publication of Lourie's pioneering article and his own earlier studies: R. Soto Company, 'La población musulmana de Mallorca bajo el dominio cristiano (1240–1276)', *Fontes Rerum Balearium* (Palma de Mallorca, 1978–80), vol. II, 65–80, vol. III, 549–64, and the same author's study 'Sobre mudèixars a Mallorca fins a finals del segle XIII,' *Estudis d'història de Mayurqa i d'història de Mallorca dedicats a Guillem Rosselló i Bordoy* (Palma de Mallorca, 1982), 195–221. For the framework, see Robert I. Burns, 'Muslims in the thirteenth-century realms of Aragon: interaction and reaction', in *Muslims under Latin rule, 1100–1300*, ed. J. M. Powell (Princeton, NJ, 1990) 57–102.
[4] James I, *Crònica*, cap. 124; Santamaría, *Ejecutoria*, 60–71, for the guerrilla war in the cordillera and the capitulation of Xuaip, and 71–84 for the single documentary reference to *casatos*, Muslims in what can be described as an intermediate state between *catius* and *libres*.

dates the capitulation to the next year.[5] Whether Xuaip remained permanently on the island is unclear, but he seems to have entered into a surrender treaty with the king of Aragon; another Saracen of high standing, the thirteen-year old son of the last Muslim king of Mallorca, was captured, baptised and granted lands near Calatayud in Catalonia with extensive rights of jurisdiction over both Christians and Muslims.[6] Something like 15,000 to 16,000 Muslims are believed to have accepted the new reality of Catalan rule on the island, and their status was probably rather better than those who fought to the end.[7] Large areas of Mallorca are not covered by the *Repartiment* documents, and it is sometimes assumed that here there might have been a substantial Saracen population tilling the king's lands. It seems that the Saracens of the region around Pollença in the north-east of Mallorca were tenant farmers, but the freedom of such cultivators was often limited in a significant way by the obligation to pay tithes.[8] The question whether non-Christians were liable for tithes was an important one in *reconquista* Spain. In this case, the obligation may indicate some unease at the reliance of the Catalan conquerors on a continuing agricultural population of Saracens. It is also likely that areas where Muslim farmers were liable for tithes were areas where the self-same Muslims had not farmed the land continuously since the days of Islamic rule. If lands had been in Christian ownership they remained subject to the tithe even when the cultivators were no longer Christian.[9]

Elena Lourie has moved beyond supposition to argue that a sizeable free Muslim population existed in the Balearics after 1229.[10] Her definition of 'free' is all who were not actually enslaved, including manumitted slaves, former debt slaves and serfs of very debased condition, who nonetheless cannot be described as slaves. On the other hand, some of her evidence confirms, rather, that there

[5] Santamaría, *Ejecutoria*, 66.   [6] Santamaría, *Ejecutoria*, 67–9.
[7] James I, *Crònica*, cap. 113; Soto, *L'ordenació*, 193. But cf. Desclot's figures, in Soldevila, *Les quatre grans cròniques*, 439–40, criticised by Santamaría, *Ejecutoria*, 52–7: the idea that 30,000 Saracens were captured when Ciutat de Mallorca fell is described as 'una magnificación jactanciosa'.   [8] Lourie, 'Free Moslems', 627, 629.
[9] Lourie, 'Free Moslems', 627–8; Lourie's clever and complex argument at this point seems to benefit from the application of Occam's razor, with the result that a diametrically opposite conclusion is reached: the Saracens she analyses from 1241 are more likely than not resettled ones, whether or not born in Mallorca. For further doubts, see Soto, *L'ordenació*, 196–7.
[10] See also Santamaría, *Ejecutoria*, 84–108, for a different approach to Lourie, well documented from the notarial protocols. An authority who agrees strongly with Lourie is Fernández-Armesto, *Before Columbus*, 21.

was a sizeable unfree Muslim population; and some evidence goes further to show that Mallorca's Muslims, free or unfree, in the mid-to late thirteenth century were not necessarily of Balearic origin. This should occasion little surprise; in Castile and Andalucia new Moorish quarters or *morerías* grew up in cities recently cleared of Muslims, and only some of the new settlers can be assumed to be of local descent.[11] What rulers wanted was to break the continuity of Muslim settlement; they might still require Muslim technological skills and value the taxes they could draw from Muslims. But they preferred to ensure that the old communities were shattered in pieces first.

It is true that in 1231 James I issued a charter agreeing to let the Order of the Temple settle thirty Saracen families at Inca in the Mallorcan interior.[12] The king was prepared to guarantee to protect these Muslims. But it is quite likely that these Saracens were not from Mallorca, or at least from Inca itself; some Muslim settlers were of north African origin.[13] The papacy was keen to ensure that the Templars and the Hospitallers should not celebrate their success in being granted generous estates on Mallorca by bringing in Saracens from outside the island.[14] Native Muslims in rural areas may well have started as unfree serfs but have been allowed to purchase their freedom, so that the proportion (but not necessarily the overall number) of free Saracens in what was probably a sharply declining Muslim population gradually increased. In 1247 the free Muslim Alí was granted a lease for an *alquería* which he was to cultivate with the help of two captive Muslims.[15]

In Ibiza there were certainly local Muslims who were apportioned farms, and who were treated as unfree serfs; in the words of the new lord of the island, Pedro of Portugal:

predictas alquerias et predictum rafal, cum domibus ejusdem et cum omnibus pertinentiis sius, cum terminis, terris, pratis, paschuis, herbis, aquis, lignis, vineis, arboribus diversorum generum, et cum omnibus ibi pertinentibus et pertinere debentibus ad predicta omnia de abisso usque ad celum, habeatis vos et vestri, teneatis, possideatis et expetetis in proprium; tali conditione quod non elegatis vel proclametis ibi alium dominum nisi nos et successores nostros.[16]

[11] Fernández-Armesto, *Before Columbus*, 43–67.
[12] Lourie, 'Free Moslems', 625.
[13] Lourie, 'Free Moslems', 626, 636.
[14] Lourie, 'Free Moslems', 628.
[15] Santamaría, *Ejecutoria*, 95, citing Prot. 343, f.232.
[16] Paris, Bibliothèque Nationale (hereafter BN), MS latin 9261, no. 2; L. de Mas Latrie, *Traités de paix et de commerce et documents divers concernant les relations des Chrétiens avec les Arabes de l'Afrique septentrionale au Moyen Age* (Paris, 1868), part II, 185–6; Fernández-Armesto, *Before Columbus*, 31–3; Lourie, 'Free Moslems', 631.

On the other hand, the Muslim population was treated harshly after the conquest in 1235: captured Moors were obliged to redeem themselves for a not inconsiderable sum of money, and many were sold into slavery. The Christian conquerors, notably Pedro of Portugal, soon found themselves forced to bring in Muslim settlers to occupy the empty land; this annoyed the pope, who insisted that they should be 'placed beneath the yoke of slavery'.[17] Fernández-Armesto may be right to claim that many Saracen cultivators were Ibizans who had returned from slavery abroad or who had been excused the ransom, but this is supposition; moreover, the picture remains of a Muslim society that had been shattered to pieces. If Ibizan Muslims worked the soil, it was not necessarily the soil they had habitually worked in the past, and they worked alongside Valencian Moors and other new settlers of low status.[18]

That there were free Muslims in Ciutat de Mallorca is clear, though some became unfree as a result of debt slavery. Although it is impossible to be sure that most were of Balearic origin, their role as dyers, blacksmiths, swordsmiths, bakers, shoemakers suggests the survival in the city of an established Muslim artisan population.[19] In 1302, the plasterer Alí acquired by emphyteusis some houses in the portion of Mallorca City originally granted to Nunyo Sanç.[20] Some were certainly foreign Muslims: Mahomat was a free Saracen of Bougie, who received a loan from a Christian, Andrés Safer, in July 1279, so that he could set up an ironsmithery in Mallorca; but he was also liable for a payment to the crown *per stando in terra Maiorice*.[21] Relations with the Christians were good enough to enable Muslims and Christians to operate joint workshops.[22] Free Muslims occasionally took loans from Jews: in April 1279 the Muslim woman Ocsona borrowed fifty *solidi* from the Jew Yucef Alvarandi; the deal was witnessed by a Saracen silversmith, Abdalla.[23] The free Muslim Mahomet Cauzoni engaged in the cloth trade on behalf of the Jew Maimon Aben Nono in 1280.[24] There is some evidence that the Muslims had a mosque.[25] But they were not permitted to organise themselves into an *aljama*. In 1286, the monarchy wrote to the Jewish

---

[17] Fernández-Armesto, *Before Columbus*, 32–3.
[18] For Formentera, the fourth of the Balearic islands, see Fernández-Armesto, *Before Columbus*, 32.   [19] Lourie, 'Free Moslems', 633–4.   [20] Santamaría, *Ejecutoria*, 95.
[21] Santamaría, *Ejecutoria*, 95, citing Prot. 351, f.104.   [22] Lourie, 'Free Moslems', 638.
[23] Santamaría, *Ejecutoria*, 94, citing Prot. 351, f.197.
[24] Santamaría, *Ejecutoria*, 96, citing Prot. 350, f.19.
[25] Lourie, 'Free Moslems', 646, citing evidence of 1327.

aljamas of Catalonia, Valencia, Mallorca and Aragon, but to the Saracen *aljamas* only of Catalonia, Valencia and Aragon.[26] The monarchy did find ways of taxing them, but as individuals rather than as a community. It has been seen that a Saracen from Bougie found himself liable to a tax licensing his right to stay on the island; this was in fact payable by native Mallorcan Muslims too, at least from the middle of the thirteenth century. The *dret de estada dels sarrayns franchs* was first set at eight *solidi* of Valencia, or one *morabetin*, but by the early years of James II of Majorca it had been doubled for adult women, and quadrupled for adult men.[27] In May 1283 Abdala Abnelferiq, a Saracen, borrowed 160 *solidi* of Valencia, *salvis morabatinis quatuor quos dare teneor quolibet ano* [sic] *ratione standi in Maiorice*; in other words, the Saracen remained liable to pay this tax and it did not form part of the loan, nor was any obligation to pay it transferred to the lender.[28] If the annual income of a free servant in Ciutat de Mallorca was around three to four *morabetins* in the mid-thirteenth century, it can be seen that the tax imposed by the crown was fairly onerous: a quarter or more of the income of a domestic servant.[29] It is possible that this tough policy stimulated the migration of Muslims away from Mallorca, or the baptism of those less solid in their faith. The only Muslim beneficiaries were the merchants, who were exempt from the *leuda* or *lezda* imposed on foreign traders, so long as they paid the residence tax and the *dret de exida* on leaving the island.[30] Lourie herself argues that 'the right to reside was essentially an individual favour'; this can be compared to the position of the Jews, who compounded their taxes as a community, and were dealt with by the crown as a homogeneous unit. All the signs are, then, that the Christianisation of the island was a priority from the earliest days of the conquest; but it was a priority that was easily compromised when landlords had urgent need of cultivators and when Catalan or other Christian settlers were not available in sufficient numbers.

The free Muslims were, then, free in two senses. They were no one's slave or serf, but they also were unattached to a community. It is not surprising that Muslims should have sought to escape from so unpromising an environment. The *dret de exida* records not merely

[26] Lourie, 'Free Moslems', 645–6.   [27] Santamaría, *Ejecutoria*, 97–8.
[28] Santamaría, *Ejecutoria*, 99, from Prot. 350, f.178; there are plenty more examples of loans containing this or similar expressions: Santamaría, *Ejecutoria*, 98–9.
[29] Santamaría, *Ejecutoria*, 101–2.
[30] Sastre Moll, *Economía y Sociedad*, 48–56; Santamaría, *Ejecutoria*, 104–5.

those who left on trading expeditions, and subsequently returned, but those who emigrated to Africa, Granada, Valencia. Nine Muslims travelled to Anfa (modern Casablanca) in Atlantic Morocco in 1311, 24 in 1314, ten in 1316; a total of 55 journeys is on record for the four years between 1311 and 1320 for which records survive. Ceuta attracted 38 visitors or émigrés, Algiers 24, Mostaganem 55, Bougie 47, Tunis 99, Valencia 25, Almería 94 and Sicily 28. In the three years 1325, 1328 and 1329, Anfa, Ceuta, Oran, Tunis, Valencia and Almería were especially popular. To some extent the patterns in these figures reflect patterns of trade, but they also suggest where the Muslims of Mallorca retained close contacts, and where some at least found solace after abandoning the land of their birth.[31] More specific data bring detail to this picture. In 1257, two Saracens agreed to redeem themselves over an eight-year period, serving a master called Bolfaray (Abulfaraj) de Messina on a farm on the island. They would then be free to go on *transitum in terra Sarracenorum*. In 1273 a certain Fatima sold herself to a Catalan for over eight pounds of money of Valencia, with which she proposed to redeem her daughter Nussa, a slave, and send Nussa *in terram Sarracenorum*.[32] Meanwhile Muslims were converting to Christianity, like the new Christian Laurence who shared a workshop with the Muslim Alí in 1286.[33] The number of Muslim domestic slaves can be assumed to have been substantial: the early career of the mystic Ramón Llull serves as a reminder that Muslim household slaves were far from out of the ordinary; and this group would have included concubines as well.[34] Finally, it is clear that several Muslims who were identifiably free were visitors to Mallorca: merchants subject to special taxes on Saracen merchants; Menorcans too, who, as will be seen, were explicitly guaranteed their freedom in an Aragonese royal charter of 1231.

A number of issues of wider significance in the history of Mediterranean slavery have been raised by Alvaro Santamaría in his studies based on the notarial protocols in Palma. What was the status of enslaved captives who accepted baptism? Apparently it differed little, if at all, from that of Muslim slaves. The main area where baptised slaves could hope to benefit was in the rules concerning

---

[31] Sastre Moll, *Economía y Sociedad*, 53–6; the evidence suggests a considerable shrinkage in the Muslim population of Mallorca by the mid-fourteenth century.

[32] Lourie, 'Free Moslems', 637, n.55, citing documents from Prot. 344 and Prot. 348, without folio number.　　　[33] Lourie, 'Free Moslems', 638.

[34] Ramón Llull, 'Vita coetanea', in *Selected Works of Ramon Llull*, ed. and transl. Bonner, introduction, 18, 21.

manumission, which were more generous (especially for those who found themselves the slaves of Jews); after release, baptised slaves joined the free Christian community of Mallorca. But they did not automatically become free, unless their master or mistress was a Jew.[35] It is clear that quite a number of Saracen slaves, some of whom must have been non-Mallorcan, went to the font in the thirteenth century. In April 1242 a Catalan of Mallorca accepted 400 *solidi*, over four times the average cost of a slave on the markets of the island, as the redemption price of the baptised Berenguer.[36] In 1243 P. de Torre released his Saracen Abrahim along with the baptised Bertomeu for 100 *besants*, or 350 *solidi*, payable over seven years, and granted them lands near Sineu, with two pairs of oxen and a plough.[37] The baptised Jacob or Jaume sold a white Saracen slave of his own, named Asmet, to R. Costa of Valencia in 1256, a sign, perhaps, of the integration of the new Christians into the social and economic life of the settler population.[38]

It is certainly striking how few Muslim names appear in the documentation concerning Mallorcan trade during the thirteenth century.[39] This confirms the suspicion that many of the Muslims who paid the *dret de exida* were leaving Mallorca for good or were short-term visitors. Even if there was some Muslim-controlled trade out of Mallorca, it is apparent that it was not intimately tied to the trade networks of the Christian and Jewish Catalans of Barcelona and Mallorca, nor to those of the Italians. It most likely consisted of small-scale trade in low-value goods. The earliest notarial acts from Mallorca, from the early 1240s, concern Christian merchants; even the case of Jacobus de Abennacer (Yaqub ibn Nasser), who was involved in trade towards Valencia, probably in Menorcan butter, seems not to disprove this rule, for he was most likely a member of a Christian Mozarab family that had subsisted under Muslim rule.[40] The same acts reveal that local merchants brought back from Valencia Saracen slaves, male and female.[41] In any case, Mallorca was a major slave market in the Mediterranean, ideally placed

[35] Santamaría, *Ejecutoria*, 229–51.
[36] Santamaría, *Ejecutoria*, 237, no. 2; Prot. 342, f. 92.
[37] Santamaría, *Ejecutoria*, 238, no. 7.   [38] Santamaría, *Ejecutoria*, 243, n.231.
[39] See e.g. the register of licences for ships and sailors leaving Mallorca in 1284, though it could perhaps be argued that only Christians were subject to the requirement to pay for a licence to leave Mallorca in 1284: chapter 7.
[40] Sevillano Colom, *História del puerto*, 454, no. 298; but for this family, see Santamaría, *Ejecutoria*, 195–220, and comments later in this chapter.
[41] Sevillano Colom, *História del puerto*, 254–5, no. 299.

between Africa and Europe; some free Muslims on the island were undoubtedly emancipated non-Mallorcan Muslims who had first arrived as slaves. The Jews were involved, like the Christians, in this slave trade, and they had particular need for Muslim slaves, since the law of both king and church forbade Jews to own Christian slaves.[42] In 1240 and 1248 the papacy gave its approval to Mallorcan appeals for trade with the Muslim world to be permitted, acknowledging that without some such means of financial support, Christian settlers would be even more reluctant to come to the Balearics.[43]

The intention here has been to suggest that the case for a substantial free Muslim population on Mallorca and Ibiza after the conquest is not proven. The Muslims were disadvantaged by not possessing a communal organisation of their own, and (even if for a time they were a majority) they were still treated as a marginal element in the population. Clearly, such a policy could not be followed in the more open *reconquista* territories of Valencia and Murcia which were invaded by the same Aragonese conqueror. In the Balearics, the programme was to create a new society of Catalans, Provençaux and indeed some Jews. The open welcome to Jews but not to Muslims may reflect security fears, just as other rulers, such as Frederick II in Sicily, adopted a not dissimilar policy of allowing Jews to settle while even expelling Muslims.[44] The silence of the sources leaves the historian speculating otherwise about the fate of Mallorca's Muslims: enslavement and sale on the open market for those who most persistently resisted the conquerors; abasement and a life of toil on the soil for others; a greater variety of responses, including conversion to Christianity, in the capital city, where no doubt a large artisan population survived for some time. And yet contact through trade with the *dar al-Islam* served to remind the city's Muslims that it was their duty to seek refuge in the Islamic principalities of al-Andalus and the Maghrib. There was no clearly enunciated royal policy against the Muslims, but an atmosphere had been created in which the former rulers of the island were made aware that they had become outsiders.

---

[42] Larry Simon presented a paper on the Mallorcan slave trade at the conference 'Medieval Spain and the Mediterranean' held in honour of Fr Robert I. Burns at the University of California, Los Angeles, in October 1991.

[43] L. Perez, 'Documentos conservados en los archivos vaticanos relativos al primer episcopado de Mallorca', *Bolletí de la Societat Arqueològica lulliana*, 32 (1961/2), 61–2, 64; Santamaría, *Ejecutoria*, 35, nos. 4 and 6.

[44] David Abulafia, *Frederick II. A medieval emperor* (London, 1988), 335–6.

III

On two occasions in this period entire Muslim populations of a small territory were arrested and deported into slavery. The first case is that of Menorca in 1287, the second that of Lucera in Apulia in 1300.[45] Both events raise fundamental questions about the attitude of Christian rulers to their Muslim subjects. There is a notable contrast with the practice followed even by the aggressive Castilian conquerors of Andalucia, who in the 1240s expelled the Muslims from the major towns, such as Córdoba and Seville, but did not round them up almost to a man, woman and child in order to sell them into slavery. As Lourie has said, the Menorcans were denied the chance to become *mudéjares*.[46] There are some important analogies between Menorca and Lucera: like Lucera, Menorca was a tolerated notch of Muslim-inhabited land within a Christian kingdom. It had submitted to James the Conqueror in 1231, in the wake of his conquest of Mallorca, and was in Catalan eyes a fief held by its headman or *almoxerif* from the king of Aragon and/or Majorca.[47] The Menorcans were frightened into submission when the Aragonese–Catalan army massed at night on the eastern tip of Mallorca, apparently ready to invade Menorca. The Menorcans were convinced that the lights they saw on the horizon at night heralded the arrival of a far larger army than was in fact the case.[48] But they must also have realised that the Aragonese were not now likely to be dislodged from Mallorca; the amount of succour received by the Mallorcan Muslims from north Africa had been small, and the Mallorcan countryside was being resettled with Christian colonists. The only safe option was to preserve the Menorcan polity by coming to terms with the Aragonese. Indeed, this may have seemed an opportunity to secure a greater degree of autonomy than the Menorcans had ever really possessed.

The text of a treaty between James I and the Muslims of Menorca survives; here Abu Abdallah Muhammad, described as the son of the

---

[45] For Lucera see P. Egidi, *La colonia saracena di Lucera e la sua distruzione* (Naples, 1915); this originally appeared in the *Archivio storico per le provincie napoletane* between 1911 and 1914: 36 (1911), 597–694; 37 (1912), 71–89, 664–96; 38 (1913) 115–44, 681–707; 39 (1914), 132–71, 697–766; for a different approach, see Abulafia, 'Monarchs and minorities'.

[46] E. Lourie, 'Anatomy of ambivalence: Muslims under the Crown of Aragon in the late thirteenth century', in Lourie, *Crusade and colonisation*, essay VII, 2–6. This volume is mainly a collection of reprinted articles; the article cited here is published for the first time.

[47] Strictly, from James I of Aragon and Majorca till 1276; from James II of Majorca from 1276 to 1285; from Peter III of Aragon and his heir Alfonso III for the remaining couple of years.

[48] James I, *Crònica*, caps. 117–23.

alfaqui, alcady and *alcaid* of Menorca, with a large band of companions, accepts James I as *dominum naturalem et proprium* of the island.[49] Homage and fealty is offered; all other oaths and obligations are renounced. The main castle in Menorca is ceded to the king of Aragon, who will fly the flag of Aragon there and will then allow the Menorcans use of the castle.[50] The provision of a tribute payment, in wheat, barley, goats, sheep, cattle and butter is agreed upon; this reflects the pastoral nature of the island's economy. The Menorcans were to aid the king in war, if required to do so; they were not to allow enemies of Aragon, including pirates, to make use of the island; they were to conserve the goods of shipwrecked Christian boats and they were not to provide asylum for escaped Mallorcan slaves. James for his part promised the Menorcans extensive guarantees: he would, of course, protect the Menorcans and their goods on land or at sea, but he would also permit them to deny rights of residence to any Christian or Jew whom they did not wish to have on the island. The king confirmed the right of the present chief *alfaqui* to rule the island, and of the islanders freely to elect their own *alfaqui* thereafter. The king would only intervene significantly were there to be a contested election. But even then he would choose a headman from among the Muslims of Menorca. Menorcan merchants were stated to be free of all trade taxes when they entered the other lands of the Crown of Aragon. Muslim ships arriving in Menorca would be safe from attack by the Catalan navy, though only so long as they remained in port; on leaving the island the king refused to take responsibility. Menorcans were welcome to go and live wherever they liked, whether in Muslim or Christian lands, and if they came to Mallorca they would be subject to the same law as the Muslims of the part of Mallorca where they settled. Moreover, if a subject of King James were to seize a Menorcan Saracen, the captive could go free with all his goods.

There is thus no doubt that the inhabitants of Menorca were originally permitted the free practice of Islam, and were even encouraged to come to Mallorca, in the hope, it has been suggested, that contact with Christians would be to their spiritual benefit; a letter of Gregory IX urges James I to ensure that the ruler of Menorca give free passage to *neophitos* and others interested in the

---

[49] BN, ms latin 9261, no. 1; Mas Latrie, vol. ii, 182–5; James I, *Crònica*, 61, cap. 121.
[50] Soldevila, *Les quatre grans cròniques*, 253, suggests that this must be the *muntanya del Toro*, though maybe it represents a post near Ciutadella.

Christian faith who seek to leave for Mallorca.[51] On the other hand, Menorca was not an artificial settlement like Lucera, but the rump of a disappeared Muslim state in the Balearics; the aim of the treaty was to emasculate the Balearic Muslims by denying them any chance of entering into dangerously close relations with the Muslims of north Africa. The general tone of the treaty is very similar to that of other surrender arrangements made in Spain at this period.[52] The status of Menorca was such that the king of Aragon could claim the satisfaction of an easily won victory, and of valuable tribute in grain and pastoral products; the Menorcans had retained freedom to conduct their internal affairs as they wished in a way that was to become typical of the Muslim communities of Valencia too.

A close relationship persisted between Mallorca and Menorca after 1231.[53] The tribute payments agreed upon that year arrived with regularity, at least between 1266 and 1273, in 1278 and in 1280.[54] Particularly interesting is the frequent sale by the king's officers in Mallorca to fellow Catalans of the right to claim the annual tribute in animals from the island; what appears to be in operation here is an auction system, with the income to the crown varying from £180 in 1277 to £193 in 1276, £210 in 1278, and as much as £250 in 1285.[55] This tax farm therefore bears comparison with the sale to bidders of the Catalan consulates in north Africa at the same period, which was, however, incomparably more lucrative. However, Menorcan goods reached Mallorca and elsewhere not simply as tribute. Commercial ties existed between Menorca and both Mallorca and Ibiza before 1287.[56] Further afield, there were visits to Ceuta in north-west Africa around 1240.[57] Interestingly, there were Christian Catalan and southern French investors in trade with

---

[51] Cited by Lourie, 'Free Moslems', 637, n.53.

[52] For a comparison with Lerida (Lleida), see Burns, 'Muslims in the thirteenth-century realms of Aragon', 61–2 and 67. For examples in Valencia, see the important study of surrender constitutions of R. I. Burns, *Muslims, Christians and Jews in the crusader kingdom of Valencia* (Cambridge, 1984), 52–79.

[53] See R. Rosselló Vaquer's pamphlet, *Aportació a la història medieval de Menorca. El segle XIII*, where details are given of links with Mallorca before 1287, with the help of the notarial protocols in the Arxiu del Regne de Mallorca in Palma. Florenci Sastre Portella, 'La conquista de Menorca en 1287: estado de la cuestion y perspectivas de futuro', CHCA XIII, vol. I, 137–61, is especially valuable on the vexed question of the Christian population between 1231 and 1287, and contains a valuable bibliography of recent works.

[54] Rosselló Vaquer, *Segle XIII*, 8.

[55] Rosselló Vaquer, *Segle XIII*, 8–9. The figures represent money of Valencia.

[56] Rosselló Vaquer, *Segle XIII*, 9.

[57] Rosselló Vaquer, *Segle XIII*, 9–10; Sastre Portella, 'La conquista', 155.

Menorca, such as Ramonet de Montpellier in 1243 and Berenguer Solset of Narbonne in 1247.[58] Moreover, there was a local slave trade, once again involving both Christians of Mallorca and Muslims of Menorca, such as the sale of the slave Xep by the wife of En Saltell to Mahumet Abdelgani of Menorca in 1248.[59] In view of Mallorca's important role as a centre of the slave trade this is hardly a surprise, but the tone of the treaty of 1231 and the events following the final Aragonese conquest mask the fact that there were Menorcan Muslim slaves before 1287.

The dispersal of the Menorca Muslims forms part of the side-history of the War of the Sicilian Vespers. The Muslims of Menorca were suspected of plotting with the north African emirs against the Aragonese, notably during Peter's assault on Collo in north Africa which preceded his successful invasion of Sicily in 1282. It appears that advance notice of Peter's arrival was sent to Africa by the Menorcans when the large Catalan fleet stopped at Maó on its way to Collo. The Menorcans were thus held to have broken the terms of the agreement of 1231 by entering into relations with the enemies of the king of Aragon. It is certainly not impossible that the Menorcans set out to damage Peter's campaign, though events in Sicily quickly came to dominate his plans and any serious ambitions he may have had in Africa were rapidly forgotten. With the struggle for Sicily on his hands and with the prospect of a French invasion of Aragon, Peter had little time to spend on punishing the Menorcans; when the Aragonese did so, it was not simply in recompense for the betrayal of 1282, but as part of a wider policy of building their naval power in the western Mediterranean.

It has been seen that the Aragonese had fought back against the French invasion of 1285 by attempting to dispossess James II of Majorca, brother of Peter of Aragon but apparent ally of Philip III and IV of France. Mallorca and Ibiza were occupied in 1285 by the Infant Alfonso and there was fighting in the Majorcan-held lands in the Pyrenean foothills that separated Catalonia from Languedoc. Besides, there was a danger that the French or Angevins might try to use the island, with its superbly endowed port at Maó, as a base from which to attack Aragonese positions.[60] In 1287 Alfonso, now king of

[58] Rosselló Vaquer, *Segle XIII*, 9, citing Prot. 343 of the Palma archive; Sastre Portella, 'La conquista', 155–6.   [59] Rosselló Vaquer, *Segle XIII*, 10, also citing Prot. 343.
[60] Ramón Muntaner, *Crònica*, cap. 170.

Aragon, invaded Menorca by way of Maó.[61] A substantial fleet and army were used to overwhelm the island; the sources are unclear how much fighting was involved. But clearly Alfonso had no qualms about attacking his nominal subjects. They had broken faith with their lord.

The broad facts about the fate of the Menorcans are related in the chronicle of Ramón Muntaner, who was generally more interested in heroic deeds than in the niceties of Muslim–Christian relations. His insistence that Alfonso 'thought that it was a great scandal for the house of Aragon that the isle of Menorca was occupied by Saracens, and thus that it would be good to throw them out, and conquer it', must be understood as part of his wider attempt to project a view of his masters as paragons of chivalry.[62] He even papers over the deep gulf between Alfonso III and his uncle the king of Majorca by pretending that a victory in Menorca would serve James II of Majorca's interests; the opposite was the case, but Muntaner constantly insisted that the deep rift between the Majorcan and the Aragonese kings was simply a diplomatic ploy to entrap the king of France.[63]

More revealing of Alfonso's outlook is what he did on his arrival in the island. Once he had reached the capital, Ciutadella, he 'took all the women and children throughout the island, and the men who remained alive, who were few, because in the battle the men had all been killed'.[64] Muntaner estimates the number of captives at forty thousand, which may be a considerable exaggeration, as, clearly, are his assumptions about the extirpation of the male population. The entire population was to be sold into slavery in Mallorca, Sicily and Catalonia.[65] Exceptions were made for those who could pay a ransom

[61] Ramón Muntaner, cap. 172; Mata, *Conquests and reconquests of Menorca*, 9–62, especially 30–1 where stress is laid on the betrayal by the Muslim ruler of Menorca of Peter the Great's plan to attack Collo in 1282, and the conquest is explained as punishment for this betrayal, and as an attempt to gain papal approval for a war against Islam; see also Sastre Portella, 'La conquista', 143–5. The useful older work of C. Parpal, *La conquista de Menorca en 1287 por Alfonso III de Aragón* (Barcelona, 1901) has been reissued in Mahón in 1987. E. Lourie's studies in *Crusade and Colonisation* add much new documentation from the Arxiu de la Corona d'Aragó in Barcelona.

[62] Muntaner, *Crònica*, cap. 170: 'se pensà que gran vergonya era de la casa d'Aragon que l'illa de Menorca tenguessen sarraïns, e aixi que era bo que els ne gitàs, e que la conqueris'.

[63] See the commentary by Soldevila, *Les quatre grans cròniques*, 975, on Muntaner, *Crònica*, cap. 170.

[64] Muntaner, *Crònica*, cap. 172: 'féu pendre totes les fembres e els infants de tota la illa, els hòmens qui romases eren vius, qui eren assats pocs, que en la batalla foren tots morts.'

[65] Muntaner, *Crònica*, cap. 172.

for themselves, who were nonetheless generally obliged to leave the island, which was to be repopulated 'by good Catalan stock': 'de bona gent de catalans'.[66] The headman and his (very large) family were allowed to depart by ship without interference; he had been expected to help pay a ransom for many of the Menorcan Muslims, but did less for his former subjects than King Alfonso had expected; and some families were split apart when enslaved.[67] In fact, as Elena Lourie has discovered, some Muslims were retained on the island as agricultural labourers, but they were few – a little over one hundred – and they were needed because of the great difficulty the kings of Aragon (and, after 1298, the restored kings of Majorca) had in attracting settlers to their wind-blown conquest.[68] These labourers were 'neither slave nor free', 'ni esclaves ni libres', in Lourie's view.[69] An ambiguous description of their status is offered by the terms of the charter permitting them to settle: 'they are miserable and poor; we sent them into the island of Menorca *causa populandi*, that is, they shall pay nothing for their redemption'.[70] Some Christian proprietors ransomed enslaved Menorcans in order to acquire a cheap labour force, since the price paid for a Menorcan slave appears to have exceeded the ransom.[71] It does not appear that they simply were permitted to remain in place where they had always worked. Once again, the Muslim community had been shattered and resettlement by a few Saracens did not threaten the Christian ascendancy on the island.

Recently, the mass enslavement of the Menorcan Muslims has been singled out by Henri Bresc as an important moment in the development of western attitudes to slavery. This was not just an expulsion, but an appropriation of human bodies and of their possessions, notably their lands, their cattle and sheep.[72] According to this view, even if earlier isolated examples of similar conduct can be found, the clearance of a whole territory in this manner cannot be paralleled, whether or not Muntaner greatly exaggerated his figure of forty thousand captives. For Bresc, the assertion of royal rights over

---

[66] For evidence that a few freed Muslims stayed on Menorca, see Lourie, 'Anatomy of ambivalence,' 5.   [67] Lourie, 'Anatomy of ambivalence', 4–5.
[68] Lourie, 'Free Moslems', 632–3; Lourie, 'La colonización cristiana de Menorca', 135–86; Jaime Sastre Moll, 'La salida de los Musulmanes menorquines tras la conquista de la isla por Alfonso III (1287)', CHCA xiii, vol. iii, 373–82, and other studies in the same volume.
[69] Lourie, 'Colonización cristiana de Menorca', 135.   [70] Lourie, 'Free Moslems', 632.
[71] Lourie, 'Anatomy of ambivalence', 6.
[72] H. Bresc, 'L'esclavage dans le monde méditerranéen des xive et xve siècles: problèmes politiques, réligieux et morales', CHCA xiii, vol. i, 89–102.

the Menorcans is an expression of the growing power of the state. The reappearance of slavery in the Christian Mediterranean world is thus seen as a symptom of the centralisation of government during the late thirteenth and fourteenth centuries. Untidy exceptions such as enclaves of Muslims within Christian territories lay under threat from powerful unitary governments. There is an interesting parallel in the sale of the Luceran Saracens, together with their cattle and other goods, into slavery thirteen years later; the Lucerans were quite simply the property of the king of Naples, *servi camere regie*, whose status was in effect that of slaves even before they were arrested and deported.[73] Bresc's assessment makes good sense, but there is a danger of exaggerating the novelty of what had occurred in Menorca. The evidence already cited from Mallorca and Ibiza leads to the supposition that the enslavement of a considerable part of the Muslim population of those islands followed on from their conquest by the Catalans in 1229–35. What was new was the systematic and all-embracing nature of the decision to enslave the entire Moorish community of Menorca, a decision which was itself rapidly compromised by the agreement to let a handful of Muslim families remain on the island as cultivators. There is also a noticeable contrast with the practice followed during the Aragonese conquest of Valencia; but the analogy in that case is with the original surrender by Menorca in 1231, rather than the violent invasion of 1287.

The occupation of Menorca was undoubtedly prompted by immediate political considerations. Alfonso III had financial motives, and hoped to raise large sums from the sale of so many slaves.[74] Similar explanations have been adopted of the mass sale of the Luceran slaves in 1300, on behalf of an impecunious King Charles II of Naples.[75] It has been seen that Mallorca was itself a leading centre of the international slave trade, and there were very close trading links to the slave markets of north Africa at this period. However, the scale of the Menorcan sale may have depressed the price of slaves, though Lourie denies this. The king seems to have been of the opinion that he was free to dispose of the persons of the Menorcan Muslims since they were faithless on two counts: as Muslims, certainly, but also as people who had placed his father in

[73] For this interpretation, see David Abulafia, 'Monarchs and minorities'.
[74] Lourie, 'Anatomy of ambivalence,' 2–6.
[75] Egidi, *Colonia saracena*, laid an extreme emphasis on this aspect, almost forgetting that the victims were Muslims: cf. Abulafia, 'Monarchs and minorities'.

jeopardy by alerting the north Africans to Peter's plans five years before. In a sense, then, they were war captives; captivity in war was an established justification for enslavement in Spain. In another sense, Aragonese policy had perhaps only moved a few stages beyond what had been effected when Mallorca was captured. There the erosion of the Muslim community was much slower, but the basic aim of creating a Christian advance post in the Mediterranean, looking towards Africa (with which, indeed, it conducted much of its trade) was not dissimilar.

IV

An area of great interest that has been explored by Santamaría is the existence of a Mozarab community, the *Arrom*, that is, the *ar-Rumi*. This group is very poorly documented in the pre-conquest period, and its traceable history really begins with references to *alquerías* possessed by *Arrom* soon after the conquest.[76] The *Ripartiment* document of 1 July 1232 speaks of the *alqueria Cudia Arrom* and of the *alqueria Dar-Arrom*, while a beneficiary of the shareout of lands is *J. Tome arrom*. From 1240 onwards there are references to *Arrom* in the notarised acts already mentioned. In one, of 23 August 1241, Dominicus Abenmor sells a white Saracen slave named Abraym and a black one named Sayt to his wife María Abenjohan, for the sum of fifty *besants*.[77] In another, of 21 December 1242, Dominico *arrom* buys the white Saracen slave Hazmet for 80 *solidi* from the Catalan Pere de Sabadell. One of the witnesses to this act is Bernardus Abennacer.[78] This witness appears to be a member of a prominent Mozarab family, perhaps the ancestors of the later Bennàssers of Mallorca, among whose members can be counted the merchants Johannes and Jacobus Abennasser, the latter of whom is known to have traded towards Valencia in dairy products or animal fats produced on the still Muslim-inhabited island of Menorca.[79] There were lands that bore the name of *rahal* or *alquería* of the Abennazar (spelt in various ways) at the time of the *Repartiment*; Johannes Abinnascer had life-time use of a house in the Almudaina district of Mallorca City, in the area ceded at the conquest to Nunyo Sanç.

This figure, or his namesake, appears again and again in Protocol 342 of 1241–3 preserved in the archives of Palma. In 1240 he sent

[76] Santamaría, *Ejecutoria*, 201.   [77] Santamaría, *Ejecutoria*, 205, from Prot. 342, f.35.
[78] Santamaría, *Ejecutoria*, 202, citing Prot. 342, f.20r.
[79] Sevillano Colom, *Historia del puerto*, 454, no. 298; Santamaría, *Ejecutoria*, 195–220.

goods worth 255 *solidi* of Melgueil to Ceuta on the vessel of Oberto da Trapani.[80] He can be observed witnessing a deal between the Jew Salomón Bendarech and the Menorcan Muslim Halef Ybenadarahamen (ibn Abd-ar-Rahman), entering into a *commenda* contract with the baptised Jaume Ferrer, with the merchants Ramón de Berga (a frequent partner) and Ramón de Montpellier, purchasing slaves and livestock, and trading in oil and wine. He handled these commodities on a grand scale, with one deal, of 1249, involving over 20,000 litres of oil; the contract was witnessed by three Abennassers, creating the image of a family of wealthy merchants and landowners similar in character to the patrician élites of Catalonia and Italy.[81] Johannes Abennasser represents an elusive group of people, probably in fact a very small group which he himself dominated: businessmen who dedicated their commercial interests to the transport of foodstuffs and other basic goods out of, and perhaps back into, the Balearic islands. Whereas most of the merchants who appear in the Mallorcan documentation, Catalan, Occitan or Italian, were engaged in the first instance in transit trade through Mallorca, Johannes was one of those who managed the supply system carrying Mallorcan and Menorcan agricultural and pastoral products. It is arguable that the conquest made his fortune, opening up new markets on the one hand, destroying more powerful Muslim competitors on the other. The sale of slaves captured during the Aragonese conquest may well have been the foundation of his initial fortune. But the secret of his success can only be guessed at, and it is unlikely that his family's wealth could compare with that of the great Italian and Catalan traders who passed through the island.[82] The links of Johannes and his relatives to the merchant communities of mainland Catalonia and of Languedoc suggest that they, unlike the Muslim merchants, were rapidly integrated into the expanding commercial economy of Catalan Mallorca. What is known about their links to Italy is, however, less certain evidence of regular ties. The Abennassers appear to have suffered seizure of their goods by the Genoese off the small island of Cabrera near Mallorca; the value of the goods was estimated at £100 of Valencia, or 2,000 *solidi*; this outrage occurred, however, in the midst of the War of the Vespers, some time before 8 August 1285,

[80] Santamaría, *Ejecutoria*, 217.
[81] Santamaría, *Ejecutoria*, 207–10, provides abridged texts of nineteen documents, plus three further ones in a footnote to 210, all concerning the Abennàssers. A further discussion of Johannes Abennàsser is then offered from 217 to 220.
[82] Cf. the speculations of Santamaría, *Ejecutoria*, 217–20.

when the seas were hardly safe. Representations were to be made to
the consul of the Genoese in Mallorca, with the support of the royal
baile or *batlle*.[83]

It is less clear whether those with the appellative *Christianus,
xrispianus*, are also of Mozarab origin, as Santamaría believes.[84] The
Christian population of Muslim Mayurqa is generally believed to
have been very small. Santamaría believes about five distinct *arrom*
lineages can be identified in Catalan Mallorca, which is really rather
few; and allowance must be made for the possibility that some were
mainland Mozarabs who followed the Conqueror into the Balearic
markets. However, one religious minority that certainly did persist
under Muslim rule, even under the hostile gaze of the early
Almohads, was the Jewish community. It is here that evidence can be
found for continuity in settlement beyond the conquest, though even
so there was substantial growth through immigration after it. Thus
the history of Mallorca's Jews in some respects is an inversion of that
of its Muslims.

---

[83] Santamaría, *Ejecutoria*, 210.   [84] Santamaría, *Ejecutoria*, 200–1.

CHAPTER 5

One kingdom, three religions: the Jews

I

This book is concerned with the 'international' standing of the Majorcan kingdom, its outside relations, both commercial and political. In such a study, the Jews must have a special place. Family and business links with mainland Spain, southern France and the Maghrib, close supervision of their affairs by the monarchy, a shared destiny with the Jewries elsewhere in the lands of the Crown of Aragon – in Barcelona, Sicily, eventually Sardinia – all make the history of the Jews in the kingdom of Majorca highly relevant to the wider argument of this book. It is not, then, surprising that the Jews of Mallorca have attracted widespread attention from historians both of the island itself and of the Spanish Jews, while those of the mainland territories, especially Perpignan, have been examined in the wider context of southern French Jewry in the late thirteenth century, a time of growing menace from the French if not to the same degree the Majorcan crown.[1] Interest in the Jews of Mallorca has been further stimulated by the distinct survival of their descendants as a shunned caste for centuries after their mass conversion in 1435. Claims have, indeed, been made for the survival of shadowy Jewish beliefs among the inhabitants of Ibiza and Formentera until the twentieth century.

The emphasis here is on two themes that stand out in the source material: the increasing seclusion of the Jews of Ciutat de Mallorca, as royal policy gradually shifted from one of privilege to one of persecution; and the role of the Jews, more particularly of Perpignan and Puigcerdà, in the provision of credit. It should not, of course, be

---

[1] On the question of royal involvement in the persecution of the Jews of thirteenth-century France, see W. C. Jordan, *The French monarchy and the Jews. From Philip Augustus to the last of the Capetians* (Philadelphia, 1989).

75

assumed that the trends visible on the mainland automatically apply
to the islands as well; what is striking, in fact, is the diversity of
function and experience between the Balearics and Roussillon–
Cerdagne; and as for the Jews of Montpellier, their fate was
determined by the actions of the French king as supreme overlord in
the city.

II

In the cities of Spain, southern France and most of the Mediterranean
islands that fell under Latin rule by about 1350, churches were not
the only place of worship, and sizeable communities of Jews and on
occasion Muslims required and obtained the right to conduct their
own religious services in their own buildings. Toledo was perhaps
exceptional in possessing at least ten synagogues by the middle of the
fourteenth century, one of which, that built by the royal treasurer
Don Samuel Abulafia, was brand new; there were also several
smaller study centres that were used for prayer.[2] A walled *judería*
developed by the same period, but (as in other parts of the
Mediterranean) the Jewish quarter had earlier been defined by the
preference of the Jews to reside fairly close together, rather than by
compulsion. In Erice (Monte San Giuliano) in Sicily the Jews lived
intermingled with the Christians at the start of the fourteenth
century, and a *Giudecca* probably came into existence only in the late
fourteenth century.[3] In Palermo a predominantly Jewish quarter can
be traced back to Norman times; but around 1311, under the
Aragonese king Frederick III, the Jews were regrouped in a new zone
under much tighter restrictions.[4] In northern Europe, Jewish
quarters were already being contained within walls by 1084, to judge
from the example of Speyer. Here the Jews were being offered special
protection by the bishop, who apparently shared their fears for safety
at a time of growing hostility to the Jews of *Ashkenaz* (Germany). The

---

[2] F. Cantera Burgos, *Sinagogas de Toledo, Segovia y Córdoba* (Madrid, 1973), 17–32; B. de
Breffny, *The synagogue* (London, 1978), 75–6; G. Wigoder, *The story of the synagogue*
(London/Tel Aviv, 1986), 63–8.

[3] David Abulafia, 'Una comunità ebraica della Sicilia occidentale: Erice 1298–1304',
Archivio storico per la Sicilia orientale, 80 (1984), 7–39, repr. in David Abulafia, *Commerce and
conquest in the Mediterranean, 1100–1500* (Aldershot, 1993), essay VIII; also published in Hebrew
as 'Yehudei Erice (Monte San Giuliano) sheb^eSitsiliah, 1298–1304', *Zion: a quarterly for
research in Jewish history*, 51 (1986), 295–317.

[4] David Abulafia, 'Le attività economiche degli Ebrei siciliani attorno al 1300', *Convegno
internazionale di Studi Italia Judaica*, 5, Palermo, *June 1992* (1995).

precocity of this development reflects the more embattled position of the north European Jews from a much earlier time.

There was, nonetheless, a broad trend. Jews were gathered into defined areas of the city partly to protect them from Christian hostility, and partly because of fears that they would 'contaminate' the Christian population with their unbelief. The appearance of Jewish quarters in which only Jews may live (i.e. ghettos) is thus an interesting barometer of changing attitudes to the Jews among those possessing power over them, and also among the local Christian population. Needing security, the Jews did not necessarily resent the command to gather together, so long as they were provided with suitable facilities; what was worst about the ghettos of sixteenth-century Venice and Rome was the appalling overcrowding, but this had not always been the case in earlier times. In the newly conquered territories like medieval Mallorca, the Jews may well have received an especially spacious and fairly empty area of the capital city.

What is offered here is an examination of one case where Jews were guaranteed their rights of freedom to practise their religion, but at the same time were constrained within a prescribed inner-city territory: Ciutat de Mallorca from the Catalan conquest of 1229 to 1435, when the Jews converted *en masse* to Catholicism, with an emphasis on the period of the autonomous Majorcan kingdom. There are a number of instructive features of the Mallorcan evidence. In the first place, this was a frontier territory, an area of new settlement by the Catalans, seized from Islam, to which the Christian conquerors welcomed Jewish settlers too (but not Muslims). The conquerors valued the Jewish presence, more, it seems clear, for financial reasons than out of a spirit of *convivencia*. In the second place, the privileged position of the Jews shows striking analogies to that of other communities in Mallorca and elsewhere, notably the Genoese and the Pisans.

Another good reason for singling out this community is the coherent nature of the surviving evidence. One hundred and thirteen documents containing privileges for the Mallorcan Jews have been preserved in a single manuscript, the 'Codice Pueyo', and have been edited by Spanish scholars.[5] This manuscript was compiled between 1328 and 1387 by notaries of the kingdom of Majorca, but the earliest

---

[5] F. Fita, 'Privilegios de los Hebreos mallorquines en el Códice Pueyo', scattered throughout *Boletín de la Real Academia de la Historia*, 36 (1900) (hereafter Privilegios).

document it contains dates back much further, to 1247. Additional privileges, court decisions and royal mandates have also been brought to light by Yitzhak Baer, the great historian of Spanish Jewry,[6] and by Jean Régné.[7] The work of Régné focussed on the Jews of Catalonia–Aragon, but he discovered a mass of material in the Barcelona archives referring to Mallorca during the period from 1285 to 1298 when it was ruled by the kings of Aragon. Finally, Antonio Pons Pastor published a large selection of documents from the Majorcan archives in an eclectic series of studies of the medieval Mallorcan Jews.[8] And yet, despite the good quantity and quality of the evidence, Mallorca's medieval Jews have not received as much attention as their modern Christian descendants, whose separate identity even after conversion has justifiably excited much interest.[9] The Jews of medieval Mallorca are mainly remembered for their important contribution to medieval cartography.[10]

The existence in the Balearics not merely of an old Jewish community but of new settlement after 1229 is striking. In fact, the Jews had welcomed James I to the City of Mallorca, probably out of impatience at the ungenerous attitude of the Almohads to non-Muslims. Catalan Jewish financiers had apparently given some help to the conquering army, and it is not surprising that privileges to the Jews rapidly followed the conquest; these privileges were extended to north African Jews as well, such as Salomon ben Ammar of Sijilmasa, the important staging post on the gold routes to Black Africa.[11] Salomon ben Ammar and his family make very regular appearances in the notarial protocols from Palma, as financiers, traders and

[6] F. (later known as Y.) Baer, *Die Juden im Christlichen Spanien. Erster Teil: Urkunden und Regesten*, vol. 1 *Aragonien und Navarra* (Berlin, 1929; repr. with additional material by H. Beinart, Farnborough, 1970).

[7] J. Régné, *History of the Jews of Aragon. Regesta and Documents*, ed. Y. T. Assis from the original publication in separate parts of the *Revue des Études juives* (Hispania Judaica, 1, Jerusalem, 1986),

[8] A. Pons, *Los Judíos de Mallorca durante los siglos XIII y XIV*,. 2 vols. (Palma de Mallorca, 1957–60); the older work of A. L. Isaacs, *The Jews of Mallorca* (London, 1936; Catalan translation as *Els jueus de Mallorca*, Palma de Mallorca, 1986) has a useful register of documents, though the text is very dated. References here are to the page number of the English edition of Isaacs and to the document number shared by the English and the Catalan editions.

[9] There is a large literature on the *Xuetes*, notably K. Moore, *Those of the street. The Catholic Jews of Mallorca* (Notre Dame, IN, 1976); Angela S. Selke, *The Conversos of Majorca. Life and death in a crypto-Jewish community in seventeenth-century Spain* (Hispania Judaica, 5, Jerusalem, 1986); B. Porcel, *Los Chuetas mallorquines. Quince siglos de racismo* (6th edn, Palma de Mallorca, 1986).   [10] See chapter 10.

[11] Pons, *Judíos*, II, 203, doc. 2; *Privilegios*, 482–3, no. 110; Isaacs, *Jews of Majorca*, 225, doc. 2.

property owners;[12] it might be right to see in the ben Ammars the Jewish equivalents of the Mozarab Abennassers, with the striking distinction that the latter were probably natives of Mallorca, whereas the ben Ammars were immigrants. And while the Abennassers were interested in the trade in basic foodstuffs, the ben Ammars were more attracted to luxury goods, including precious metals, and the financing of operations by other parties.[13]

In fact, Mallorca became something of a haven for foreign Jews, and on one occasion the Jews asked the king to expel some new arrivals who were deemed to be of bad character.[14] Jews in Mallorca were certainly closely involved in trade with north Africa, and as at Palermo and elsewhere they played a major part in the slave trade too during the middle and late thirteenth century.[15] Jews might even sell slaves to the king, as a case from 1289 reveals.[16] In July of the same year a Jew petitioned the *baile* of Mallorca concerning the seizure of his goods aboard a Christian-operated Mallorcan ship *in parte de Tenez*, that is, near Ténès in modern Algeria.[17] Later, in 1326, Jews were to be accused of complicity in the contraband trade to Tlemcen and Mostaganem in the same region, at a time when commercial relations with parts of north Africa were officially frozen.[18] Cultural links to the Maghrib appear to have remained strong, while the flight of refugee scholars such as Shimeon ben Zemah Duran to Africa in the late fourteenth century suggests that, under threat of persecution, the African links provided an important lifeline.[19] Many of the leading Jews of Mallorca had Arabic surnames; this was not, of course, unusual among Spanish Jews, but it is likely that the Mallorcan Jews retained their use of Arabic alongside Catalan and of course Hebrew.

What distinguished the Jews from the Muslims was the existence of a Jewish *aljama*. The Jews were not seen as a Fifth Column, tied by

[12] Palma de Mallorca, Arxiu de Regne de Mallorca (hereafter ARM), Prot. 341, 342.
[13] For the commercial setting in which Solomon ben Ammar operated, see chapter 6.
[14] Isaacs, *Jews of Majorca*, 240, doc. 82.
[15] Evidence for this can be found in ARM, Prot. 341 and subsequent notarial registers, and has been examined by Larry Simon, in studies that are being prepared for publication.
[16] Régné, *History of the Jews of Aragon*, 354–5, no. 1996; Isaacs, *Jews of Majorca*, 235, doc. 55.
[17] Baer, *Die Juden*, 146–7, no. 130; Isaacs, *Jews of Majorca*, 235, doc. 54. The document does not concern Tunis, as Baer and Isaacs assumed. Mallorcan trade with Ténès was already established at this date, as is revealed by a register of licences for ships and sailors leaving Mallorca in 1284: chapter 7.
[18] Privilegios, 187–91, nos. 39–40; Isaacs, *Jews of Majorca*, 246, docs. 114–15.
[19] See chapter 11 for a discussion of evidence for trade found in Rabbi Shimeon's *responsa*.

emotional or more practical secret links to foreign and hostile governments such as the Hafsids of Tunis. Jewish government had no expression anywhere in the world above the level of autonomous communities, self-governing within a Christian or Muslim state; indeed, for medieval Christians the lack of Jewish statehood was seen as proof of the loss of divine favour by the Jews and their state of *servitudo*. The Jews collected their own taxes, which, as elsewhere, were compounded by the whole community; as at Barcelona, they were administered by a board of four elected Jewish secretaries; they maintained their own archives, and marriage contracts and wills were to be valid even when drawn up in Hebrew and Aramaic, as a privilege of 1252 made clear. The dowry contracts of the Jews were in fact to have identical force to notarised Christian acts.[20] In 1278 James II of Majorca reiterated the statement that contracts *in littera hebraica* were to be valid when drawn up before Jewish witnesses; that is, Jewish marriage law was to be binding in the instance of Jewish marriages.[21] Not surprisingly there were Jewish cemeteries, though one was lost in the early fourteenth century when King Sanç, who had grand schemes to build a powerful navy, turned it into a shipyard.[22]

The right to live under Jewish law was an early, and fundamental, concession, matching contemporary practice in areas of the Mediterranean where there existed substantial Jewish or Muslim communities. In 1250 James I confirmed that Jews could settle their own differences among themselves, but insisted that especially grave crimes must be brought to the royal courts; this accords with a wider tendency at this period (for instance, in the Sicily of Frederick II) to insist on the authority of royal courts in such cases as capital crimes.[23] The decree is also reminiscent of the privileges accorded to Italian and Catalan merchants in the Mediterranean, guaranteeing their

---

[20] J. L. Villanueva, *Viage literario a las Iglesias de España*, vols. XXI–XXII, *Viage a Mallorca* (Madrid, 1851–2), vol. XXII, 331; summary only in Privilegios, 20, no. 3; Isaacs, *Jews of Majorca*, 226–7, 229, docs. 7, 21; the reference by Isaacs to contracts in Hebrew is the result of confusion (apparently as far back as 1252) at the use of Hebrew script for Aramaic *ketubot* or marriage contracts, and the text mentions *carta ebraica* and *instrumenta vestra judaica*. Cf. Pons, *Los Judíos*, vol. II, 207–8, doc. 8, of 1278, confirming this right.

[21] Privilegios, 27–8, no. 11; Isaacs, *Jews of Majorca*, 229, doc. 21.

[22] Villanueva, *Viage*, vol. XXII, 330–1; Privilegios, 20, no. 3 (summary); Isaacs, *Jews of Majorca*, 226–7, doc. 7; Fernández-Armesto, *Before Columbus*, 26.

[23] Villanueva, *Viage*, vol. XXII, 328–30 (not 301 as Isaacs indicates); Isaacs, *Jews of Majorca*, 226, doc. 5; a case of adultery was brought to the attention of the baile in 1314: Pons, *Los Judíos*, vol. II, 237, doc. 49.

rights of separate jurisdiction in such places as Acre, Tunis and indeed the City of Mallorca itself, where the Genoese had a loggia that was frequented by Italians and by Jews in search of business and of banter about the relative merits of Judaism and Christianity.[24] When Christians brought cases against Jews, there must be Jewish as well as Christian witnesses.[25] This provision was made in 1250 but confirmed after only two years, with particular reference to cases concerning debts to Jews; this suggests that there was some tension between Jews and Christians over this problem.[26] By special royal grace, Muslim slaves were forbidden in 1269 from giving evidence against Jews.[27] Some would have been slaves of the Jews, and the Jews were apparently worried at the danger of vexatious attacks from people who were looking for a chance to cast off their shackles.[28] In fact, the slave trade was protected by special tax exemptions for Jewish slave dealers.[29]

Another similarity with the privileges obtained by communities of foreign merchants in Mediterranean ports was that weights and measures were controlled by the *aljama*, as a result of a privilege of Alfonso III of Aragon issued soon after the reoccupation of Mallorca by the Aragonese in 1285.[30] In effect this meant that the *aljama* could levy its own taxes on merchandise brought in and out of the Jewish quarter and on sales of goods within the quarter. King Alfonso extended this right to include exemption from trade taxes on Jews of Mallorca who traded anywhere in the Aragonese realms.[31] It was an opportunity to celebrate the reincorporation of Mallorca into the Aragonese realm and the suppression of the all-too independent

[24] Fernández-Armesto, *Before Columbus*, 22–3, for the rights of the Genoese; O. Limor, *Vikuah Mayurqa*, published in offset by the Hebrew University of Jerusalem (2 vols., Jerusalem, 1985).

[25] Villanueva, *Viage*, vol. XXII, 328–30 (not 301, as Isaacs indicates); Isaacs, *Jews of Majorca*, 226, doc. 5.

[26] Privilegios, 20–1, no. 4; Isaacs, *Jews of Majorca*, 227, doc. 8. But in 1269 the king confirmed that the provision applied to all types of civil and criminal charges, not specifically debts: Privilegios, 24, no. 8.

[27] Privilegios, 24, no. 8; Isaacs, *Jews of Majorca*, 227, doc. 12. See also Pons, *Los Judíos*, vol. II, 204–6, docs. 4–5.

[28] Privilegios, 24, no. 8 appears to Isaacs, *Jews of Majorca*, 227, doc. 12, to speak of slaves owned communally by the *aljama*; but the wording is at best ambiguous: *captivus vel captiva alicujus judei vel judee aljame predicte*. Most likely this means 'male or female slave of any Jew or Jewess of the said *aljama*'. [29] Isaacs, *Jews of Majorca*, 226–7, 230, docs. 4, 12, 27.

[30] Régné, *History of the Jews of Aragon*, no. 1479 (summary) and 438–9, doc. 20 (full text); Isaacs, *Jews of Majorca*, 230–1, doc. 27.

[31] Régné, *History of the Jews of Aragon*, 438–9, doc. 20, and Régné, *History of the Jews of Aragon*, no. 1481; Isaacs, *Jews of Majorca*, 230–1, docs. 27, 29.

Catalan kingdom of Majorca, by bonding the inhabitants of the Balearics to the mainland Aragonese territories from which they had been isolated for several years.[32] Alfonso's warm-hearted approach to the Jews of Mallorca was no doubt prompted in part by the awareness that they might help him out of growing financial difficulties.[33] In 1286, he tried to squeeze 10,000 *solidi* (£500 of Valencia) from the *aljama* of Mallorca, but 100,000 from the entire city of Mallorca. The money was needed for supplies of wheat and barley.[34] Yet it was the same king who created the reserved area, the *Call*, in which the Jews of Mallorca City were required to live.

The transfer of the Jews from the shadow of the Almudaina Palace, where most had lived since the conquest, to the south-east of the old city may simply reflect the need for more space; it also in a sense reflects the increase in privileges for the Mallorcan Jews, some of which, such as the right to use their own weights and measures, might be said to be conditional on the existence of a coherent territory in which they could be applied. The exercise of justice by Jewish officials was easier to achieve if there were no non-Jewish neighbours with whom to enter into property or other disputes. James I had already forbidden Jews and Christians to live in the same houses or share the same front door, though he permitted Jews to buy houses from Christians in Mallorca City.[35] It was common, too, for Italians and other merchant communities in the Mediterranean to be assigned prescribed areas under their jurisdiction, as at Acre; though the requirement actually to reside in their quarter was not necessarily made explicit.[36]

Early in 1286 Alfonso III issued a privilege to the city of Mallorca (and not, in fact, to the Jews) indicating that he wished the Jews to foregather on a specially assigned site in the city, within the next five years. He promised that the Jews would be allowed their own kosher butcher's shop.[37] This part of the privilege can be read as an

---

[32] The licences of 1284 (see chapter 7) indicate that there was very little direct commercial contact between Mallorca and Catalonia in early 1284, when Peter of Aragon and James II of Majorca were taking opposite sides in the Vespers conflict.

[33] See Isaacs, *Jews of Majorca*, 230–7, docs. 24–68, for a handlist of acts of Alfonso concerning the Jews of the City of Mallorca.

[34] Régné, *History of the Jews of Aragon*, nos. 1595, 1611, 1624; Isaacs, *Jews of Majorca*, 232, docs. 35–7.

[35] Régné, *History of the Jews of Aragon*, no. 562; Isaacs, *Jews of Majorca*, 229, doc. 18.

[36] But the case of Palermo reveals that confinement in a Jewish ghetto was the policy of one Aragonese prince: see note 3.

[37] Régné, *History of the Jews of Aragon*, no. 1483; Isaacs, *Jews of Majorca*, 231, doc. 31.

improvement on the position established by James I in 1273, which was that the Jews were to follow their own rituals in slaughtering animals, but were to arrange for the sale of the meat in Christian butcher's shops.[38] In fact, James I's privilege may have been more generous, since it enabled Jews to dispose directly to Christians of certain parts of the carcass which Jewish law did not permit to be eaten, or of carcasses that were found to contain certain lesions that prohibited their consumption by Jews. In Spain, Jewish butcher's shops were generally separate, but this was less often the case in Germany. Thus German Jews often found it easier to pass the carcasses of animals which had not been approved for consumption directly to the Christian butchers alongside whom they worked. This became more difficult when the kosher slaughterhouse was within the Jewish quarter, where, moreover, the noise and smell would have to be tolerated by residents. Some differences between the legal rulings of Sephardi (Spanish) and Ashkenazi (German) rabbis on the fitness for consumption of slaughtered animals may be attributable to this difference, the principle being that excessively severe controls would force up the price of meat to intolerable levels. Once again, the Sephardim were less strict here than the generally rigorous Ashkenazim.[39] Thus the appearance of a special kosher meat shop was a further stage in the disentanglement of Jews and Christians in Mallorca City. It was not a sign of greater 'tolerance' at all.

What is visible, then, is a steady process of dissociation of the Jews from the Christian community in Mallorca City. Thus the king issued orders in 1288 that Jews should not be obliged by the city administration to contribute to taxes and other royal or municipal levies; the Jewish *aljama* would always be assessed separately. It was the Mallorcan Jews who brought this to the king's attention, for fear that they would find themselves liable to double taxation.[40] In 1289 Alfonso ordered the Jews of Mallorca to pay taxes to the royal treasurer, Dalmau Suyner or Sunyer.[41] The crown was seeking to

[38] Régné, *History of the Jews of Aragon*, nos. 561–2; Privilegios, 26–7, no. 10; Isaacs, *Jews of Majorca*, 228–9, doc. 17–18.

[39] On the general question, see H. J. Zimmels, *Ashkenazim and Sephardim: their relations, differences and problems as reflected in the rabbinical responsa* (London, 1958), 200–1. The Sephardim took the view that their leniency reflected an emphasis on the quality of mercy, while Ashkenazi rigour reflected an emphasis on strength of character. But, as Zimmels shows, even principles could give way to economic determinants.

[40] Régné, *History of the Jews of Aragon*, no. 1915; Isaacs, *Jews of Majorca*, 234–5, doc. 52; cf. the earlier privilege of 1254: Pons, *Los Judíos*, II, 204, doc. 3.

[41] Régné, *History of the Jews of Aragon*, no. 2044; Isaacs, *Jews of Majorca*, 235, doc. 56.

exploit Jewish resources, in the awareness that the Jews were themselves a royal possession. Competition from (say) the city government in Mallorca in taxation of the Jews was not tolerable.

The aim of transferring the Jews to a defined zone was not forgotten. In late 1290, there were consultations between the king's representative in Mallorca, the *baile* Pere de Libian, and prominent Jews.[42] Both the city administration and the Jews of Mallorca sent agents to Barcelona to petition the king about the proposed transfer, but the king was too busy to give much thought to the affair.[43] In early December the king confirmed the decision of his *baile* that the Temple and Calatrava areas of the city, in the south-east of the town, were to be enclosed as a Jewish quarter. It is noticeable that Pere de Libian is said to have consulted the consuls and leading men of the city about the choice of a site, which was made 'by the advice and wish not merely of the said consuls and worthy men, but indeed of the whole city government of Mallorca' (*concilio et voluntate non solum dictorum consulum et proborum hominum, immo tocius universitatis Maiorice*).[44]

The king did, nevertheless, show understanding of the special needs of the Mallorcan Jews. He stated that the community could build a synagogue, at a time when church policy greatly discouraged new synagogues; the point was, quite simply, that they needed one: 'they must have one', *eam habere debent*.[45] A bakehouse was also permitted the Jews; this was a right often granted to Italian merchants in their trading colonies, but it had special significance for the Jews, above all at Passover. The rationale cited by the king was not Jewish ritual requirements but the lack of need for them to send for bread outside their quarter. Alfonso may have seen this as another way to reduce undesirable association between Jews and non-Jews in the city. However, he still insisted that the bread tax (*panegia*) should be levied as elsewhere in the city.[46] Later, in 1294, James II of Aragon gave special permission to Juceff ben Salamon Coffe to build a bakery in the Jewish quarter, against a weighty annual rent of ten gold *morabetini*; this was to be the sole bakery in the area.[47]

---

[42] Régné, *History of the Jews of Aragon*, no. 2252; Isaacs, *Jews of Majorca*, 236, doc. 61.
[43] Régné, *History of the Jews of Aragon*, no. 2254; Isaacs, *Jews of Majorca*, 236, doc. 62.
[44] Régné, *History of the Jews of Aragon*, nos. 2267–8 (summaries) and 440–1, doc. 22 (full text of no. 2267); Isaacs, *Jews of Majorca*, 236–7, docs. 63–4.
[45] Régné, *History of the Jews of Aragon*, no. 2267; Isaacs, *Jews of Majorca*, 237, doc. 63.
[46] Régné, *History of the Jews of Aragon*, 441, doc. 22; cf. Régné, *History of the Jews of Aragon*, no. 2271 and Isaacs, *Jews of Majorca*, 237, doc. 67.
[47] Isaacs, *Jews of Majorca*, 238, doc. 72.

The whole quarter was to be enclosed by a wall, with gates and doors. The intention was to create what Alfonso called a *callem unicum*. This term was translated by Régné to mean 'une rue unique';[48] but the charter of 1290 is clearly speaking of something more substantial, incorporating a substantial network of streets either side of the modern Calle de Montesion; so too in Barcelona and other contemporary Catalan towns the term evidently means more than one street.[49] As a matter of fact, the term *rua* or *ruga* was used in merchant settlements such as Acre and Messina to mean not just a street but a whole quarter.[50] There are several possible explanations of the origin of the term *Call*, notably the reading of *Call* as *Calle*, 'Street'. But *Calle* is not a Catalan term; it arrived in the Catalan-speaking lands from Castile after the medieval period, and is unlikely to have given rise to the usage *Call*. Even so, a particular *Calle* in modern Palma deserves attention in this context. The Calle de la Platería in Palma de Mallorca was in modern times the street par excellence of the gold and silversmiths of Jewish descent, the so-called *Xuetes* or *Chuetas*; it lies on the north side of the church of Santa Eulalia, where a mass conversion of Jews took place in 1435. The *Platería* is divided from the area of the original *Call* by the church and its plaza, from which access can be gained to the western end of the old *Call*, and thence to a modern street called '*Call*'; but the *Platería* was never part of the Jewish settlement.[51] The *Xuetes* were talked of until recent times as 'Those of the Street', but what was intended by this term was not the *Call* but the Calle de la Platería. Almost certainly, the term 'Those of the Street' has no connection with the term *Call*. *Call* is most likely derived from the Hebrew *qahal*, 'community', and thus means not a single street but the area in which the Jewish community of Mallorca City, or, *pari passu*, Barcelona, lived. What is interesting is that the use of *callis* seems to

---

[48] Régné, *History of the Jews of Aragon*, no. 2268; cf. Isaacs, *Jews of Majorca*, 237, doc. 67, with 'single street', where Régné, no. 2271, has '*call unique.*'

[49] E. Lourie, 'A plot which failed? The case of the corpse found in the Jewish *Call* of Barcelona (1301)', *Mediterranean Historical Review*, 1 (1986), 209, repr. in Lourie, *Crusade and Colonisation*, essay X.

[50] D. Jacoby, 'Crusader Acre in the thirteenth century: urban layout and topography', *Studi medievali*, ser. 3, 20 (1979), 14–16, repr. in D. Jacoby, *Studies on the crusader states and on Venetian expansion* (Northampton, 1989), essay X, makes this point emphatically, as against, e.g., P. Aebischer, 'Ruga "rue" dans les langues romanes', *Revista portuguesa de filologia*, 6 (1951), 170–85.

[51] However, the parish of Santa Eulalia technically included part of the *Call*: Pons, *Los Judíos*, vol. II, 214, doc. 16.

be confined to the physical area of the Jewish quarter; the word used for community in the sense of an organised body of people was still *aljama*. The *aljama* was the commune or *universitas* of the Jews of Mallorca; the *Call* was their place of habitation.

King Alfonso wished all Jews to gather there: 'all Jews of Mallorca City are to live at the same time in a certain part of the said city, where they may create one *Call*' (*quod omnes Judei Majorice habitarent simul in aliqua partita dicta civitatis, ubi facerent callem vestram*).[52] For the privilege of being grouped together, the Jews of Mallorca were to pay 12,000 *solidi* (£600), and those who refused to pay were to be coerced.[53] While the Almudaina district had merely been the focus of Jewish settlement, the *Call* was to be the home of all the Jews of Ciutat de Mallorca;[54] James II of Majorca was irritated that as late as May 1303 there were still Jews living outside the *Call*, and issued orders to his lieutenant in Mallorca that 'you do not permit nor allow that any Jews stay, remain or delay outside the said *Call*' (*non permitatis nec sustineatis, quod aliqui judei stent extra dictum callem, maneant nec morentur*).[55] Pleas of poverty on the part of Jews who could not afford to move to the *Call* were ignored, but Jews not yet living in the *Call* were permitted to maintain workshops and to put goods on sale outside the *Call*.[56] Eventually, in 1320, the bishop complained against this and it seems the permission was revoked.[57] Later, the Jews of the small town of Inca were to experience the same process of separation from the surrounding Christians, as part of a slow but steady tendency to force Jews to live apart.[58]

Having arrived in the *Call*, the Jews not surprisingly decided that it would be an even worse imposition were they to be forced to move yet again. Soon after the return of James II of Majorca to the Balearics, the restored king promised the Jews that they could remain in perpetuity in the *Call*. The Jews had already begun to build houses in the area, and they seem to have been worried that space for further building would soon run out. They were therefore to be permitted to encroach on adjoining land, close to the Templar buildings in the far

---

[52] Régné, *History of the Jews of Aragon*, 440, doc. 22.
[53] Régné, *History of the Jews of Aragon*, nos. 2269–70; Isaacs, *Jews of Majorca*, 237, docs. 65–6.
[54] Isaacs, *Jews of Majorca*, 231, doc. 31; Régné, *History of the Jews of Aragon*, no. 1483; cf. Isaacs, *Jews of Majorca*, 236–7, no. 63 and Régné, *History of the Jews of Aragon*, no. 2267. Cf. the case of Palermo, again involving a transfer from one area (the *Cassaro*) to a new quarter.
[55] Pons, *Los Judíos*, vol. II, 215, doc. 17.   [56] Pons, *Los Judíos*, vol. II, 216–17, doc. 19.
[57] Pons, *Los Judíos*, vol. II, 248, doc. 60.
[58] Isaacs, *Jews of Majorca*, 252, doc. 147; Pons, *Los Judíos*, vol. I, 33–42.

corner of the city: *in locis dicto callo contiguis, et versus dictam domum Templi.*[59] The Jews had begun to build a synagogue, and this had been done with the approval of the bishop of Mallorca; this too could be finished.[60] Worries at a possible move persisted, and King Sanç again confirmed that the *Call* would not be disbanded, either by expelling the Jews *à la française* or by requiring the Jews to transfer elsewhere within the city. In the wake of Philip the Fair's expulsion of the Jews in 1306, the Mallorcan Jews, and still more their brethren in Roussillon, subjects of the Majorcan monarchy, *valde erant timidi et stupefacti.*[61] In fact, the Jews of Montpellier, most of which was held by the king of Majorca from the king of France, were forced to leave in 1306, and many from there and elsewhere came as refugees to Majorcan Roussillon, so the realm of Majorca was not untouched by the French persecutions.

Yet the *Call* both protected and restricted the Jews. Christian women were to be chaperoned if they entered the area; but such rules were perhaps as pleasing to the rabbis as to the churchmen, who would share a fear that immoral associations might be formed.[62] In 1296 James II of Aragon decreed that the lieutenant of the king in Mallorca would have to give special permission before preachers could enter the *Call*. Even those who were allowed to preach could only be accompanied by ten people; there were to be no large crowds baying at the Jews and demanding their conversion.[63] When James II of Majorca reissued these provisions, he also put to an end the practice whereby priests entered the *Call* on Easter Saturday and sprinkled Jewish houses with holy water, in return for which they expected gifts of eggs. As the king pointed out, this meant nothing to the Jews.[64] The Jews were not to be forced to go out of the *Call* to hear sermons. There were even important limitations on conversions:

[59] Villanueva, *Viage*, vol. XXII, 332–3; Privilegios, 31, no. 14 (summary); Isaacs, *Jews of Majorca*, 240, no. 78.

[60] Pons, *Los Judíos*, vol. II, 231–14, doc. 15; Villanueva, *Viage*, XXII, 332; Isaacs, *Jews of Majorca*, 240, doc. 78, has 'synagogues', but the privilege appears only to refer to a single 'sinagoga in dicto callo.'

[61] Villanueva, *Viage*, XXII, 333–4; Privilegios, 123, no. 17 (summary); Isaacs, *Jews of Majorca*, 242, doc. 90, (of 1311) for the fears arising from the French expulsion; Privilegios, 131–2, no. 23; Isaacs, *Jews of Majorca*, 243, doc. 96, for the promise to let the Jews stay put (1318).

[62] Cf. the prohibition in Barcelona in 1319: Lourie, 'A plot which failed?', 209.

[63] Isaacs, *Jews of Majorca*, 239, doc. 75.

[64] F. Fita, 'Los Judíos mallorquines y el Concilio de Viena', *Boletín de la Real Academia de la Historia*, 36 (1900), 241–2, no. 3; Pons, *Los Judíos*, vol. II, 227, doc. 35; Isaacs, *Jews of Majorca*, 241, doc. 87.

minors were not to be baptised, and teenagers were given several days to think over what they were planning to do before going to the font.[65]

Guarantees for the Jews were dependent on royal goodwill, of course. The relationship between Jews and Christians declined sharply early in the fourteenth century. The Jews of Roussillon and Mallorca may have escaped from the fate of the French Jews, but it was clear that anti-Jewish factions were emerging and that they were beginning to influence the Majorcan monarchy. It will be seen shortly that conditions in Perpignan were turning sour under King Sanç. In 1309 a priest named Galceron began to spread rumours in Mallorca that the Jews had put to death a Christian child, and these rumours were firmly suppressed by the crown and indeed the bishop, who was requested to deal toughly with Galceron.[66] He was to be punished in such a way that anyone who thought of repeating such accusations would be struck with terror.[67] More problematic was the case a couple of years later of two German Christians who came to the island and converted to Judaism. In 1315, King Sanç turned on the Jews in fury, fining them £95,000 and confiscating all Jewish property, including the synagogue.[68] Even the Torah bells and crowns, made of silver, were taken into custody.[69] The *aljama* continued to be managed by Jewish officials, or secretaries, but Sanç deprived the *Call* of all 'privileges, liberties and immunities' granted by himself or former kings.[70] He did permit a replacement synagogue to be built, but it is clear that the Jews had virtually no resources with which to do this, and nothing seems to have been done.[71] The main synagogue was turned into the church of Santa Fé, but it remained difficult of access, isolated within the *Call*. Once Sanç had secured the major part of the fine he was claiming from the Jews, he could look

---

[65] Isaacs, *Jews of Majorca*, 241, docs. 85–6.   [66] Isaacs, *Jews of Majorca*, 241, doc. 87.

[67] Fita, 'Los Judíos mallorquines y el Concilio de Viena', 240–1, no. 2; Isaacs, *Jews of Majorca*, 241, doc. 87; cf. Lourie, 'A plot which failed?', 187–220, and especially 202–3, where she observes that the ritual murder charge had now arrived in the Mediterranean. Its origins lay in Norwich in 1144; neither the closely argued denunciation by Frederick II nor papal condemnation under Innocent IV checked its progress and elaboration into the 'blood libel'.   [68] Pons, *Los Judíos*, vol. II, 32–41.

[69] Pons, *Los Judíos*, vol. II, 252, doc. 64, recording their return by the Regent Philip in 1326. The *rimonim* (Torah bells) in the Cathedral Treasury are apparently of fifteenth-century Sicilian workmanship and probably never belonged to the Mallorcan community; they were made into staffs for the bishop. For illustrations, see Pons, *Los Judíos*, vol. I, plates 3–5.

[70] Privilegios, 132–3, no. 24; Isaacs, *Jews of Majorca*, 243, doc. 97.

[71] Fita, 'Los Judíos mallorquines y el Concilio de Viena', 249, no. 6; Isaacs, *Jews of Majorca*, 242–3, doc. 93.

more kindly on their grievances. In 1323 he decided to reward the Jews for the help they had given the royal treasury (£2,000) and for their contribution to the cathedral building fund (£300) by transferring the chapel of Santa Fé to the garden of En Cassa close to the Temple Gate, on the outer edge of the *Call*. The king claimed the support of the bishop of Mallorca in making this move. Sanç also conceded the Jews the right to open a new gate into the *Call* at the bottom of the road leading past the disused synagogue and chapel. The old synagogue was not to be restored to Christian use.[72] There was, not surprisingly, a backlash. The bishop apparently assented to the move of Santa Fé, but assumed that the chapel within the *Call* would still remain Christian property. He was worried that it was about to be turned back into a synagogue, and opposed any transfer of disused churches to Jewish or Muslim hands. No doubt the bishop had received complaints from other churchmen in Mallorca City that the king was in breach of canon law.[73]

The Jewish community of Mallorca City thus experienced great practical difficulties under King Sanç. There was no central synagogue. At least one of the secretaries of the community was nominated by the crown from the Jewish community of the city.[74] Technically, since part of the massive £95,000 fine was still outstanding, the privileges of the *aljama* were still in a state of abeyance. On the other hand, Jews from Mallorca frequented south Italian business centres, whether as migrants leaving behind the dismally impoverished *Call* or as visitors in search of profit; King Robert of Naples, married to a Majorcan princess, urged them to come to his kingdom in 1329, four years after he had sealed a general (and generous) trade pact with the Majorcan court granting access to Majorcan merchants.[75] The climate improved markedly after Sanç's death in 1325. The Regent Philip in 1328 acknowledged that the fine

[72] Pons, *Los Judíos*, vol. II, 249–50, doc. 61; Villanueva, *Viage*, XXI, 300–2; Privilegios, 139–42, no. 31 (correcting errors in Villanueva); Isaacs, *Jews of Majorca*, 244–5, doc. 105.

[73] Fita, 'Los Judíos mallorquines y el Concilio de Viena', 257–8, no. 7; Villanueva, *Viage*, XXI, 302–3; Isaacs, *Jews of Majorca*, 245, doc. 107.

[74] Privilegios, 197, no. 45; Isaacs, *Jews of Majorca*, 248, doc. 124. Isaacs, 60, wrongly implies that the king appointed Christian secretaries, but the document says explicitly *judeus secretarius*. In the late fourteenth century, though, Christians were being appointed to the headship of Muslim *aljamas* in the Aragonese mainland territories.

[75] N. Ferorelli, *Gli Ebrei nell'Italia meridionale dall'età romana al secolo XVII*, ed. F. Patroni Griffi (Naples, 1990; original edition Turin, 1915), 73, based on the lost Angevin Register 1329B, f.180v, in the Archivio di Stato, Naples. For Robert's policy towards trade with Majorca, see below, p. 186. Alfonso IV of Aragon brought forty Mallorcan Jewish families to Sardinia: C. Pillai, CHCA XI, vol. IV, 94.

had now been paid and reconstituted the *aljama*, against an annual tribute of £165. The *aljama* secretaries were to be elected by the Jews as in the days of Sanç's predecessors, without intervention by the king or any royal officials.[76]

In 1331 James III finally permitted the Jews to re-establish a synagogue; moreover, the building used was not to be decorated in the sumptuous fashion of the previous Great Synagogue, which had been *curiosam et valde formosam*.[77] James was careful to pay lip service to the requirements of canon law, which had already been cited to deny the Jews the return of Santa Fé. The law as he understood it prohibited the erection of new synagogues in new places, but not by any means the rebuilding of synagogues where they had earlier existed. The new synagogue was not to be thought of as a new building, in fact, so much as the *reparatio et refectio* of what had been in the *Call* in former times (though he was most certainly not offering them back Santa Fé). In fact, it was not to be a synagogue at all, but a 'school' or 'house of prayer'; this was a code word for a synagogue, but understandably the king preferred to avoid using the word that would bring ecclesiastical censure upon him. From the point of view of the Jews this all made little enough difference: synagogues functioned as house of prayer and of study, as well as assembly halls.[78] He thus advanced a whole range of arguments, some of which almost contradicted one another, in order to justify his policy. At one moment he talked of the building as a synagogue, at the next it was a 'house suitable for praying according to their rites and customs' (*domum aliquam decentem ad orandum juxta ritus et consuetudines eorum*). Maybe too he was influenced by the aid he received from able Jewish cartographers; a ruler of impossibly ambitious schemes, James contemplated the conquest of the Canary islands, and Jewish maps were an important key to the Atlantic. The contribution of the Jews to Mallorca's economy was recognised in a privilege of 1329 when King James III pointed out that the Jews of Mallorca were primarily

---

[76] Isaacs, *Jews of Majorca*, 247, doc. 122; cf. Privilegios, 191–4, no. 41 and Isaacs, *Jews of Majorca*, 246, doc. 117; Privilegios, 197–8, no. 45; Isaacs, *Jews of Majorca*, 248, doc. 124.

[77] Pons, *Los Judíos*, vol. II, 271–2, doc. 88; Isaacs, *Jews of Majorca*, 48–9, doc. 127. One of the candelabra hanging from the ceiling of Palma Cathedral is said to have been brought there from the Great Synagogue. Some idea of how sumptuous a new fourteenth-century Spanish synagogue could be can be obtained from the so-called Tránsito Synagogue in Toledo, built c. 1360 in *mudéjar* style for Samuel Abulafia and designed by Meir Abdeli: see note 1.

[78] Hence the use of the term *Scuola* for synagogues in sixteenth-century Venice and Rome, not to mention the continuing use of the term *Shul* among Ashkenazi Jews.

engaged in commerce: *judei dicte aljame mercantiliter vivant pro majore parte.*[79]

The fall of the kingdom of Majorca to Peter IV of Aragon in 1343 did not result in a significant change of status for the Jews of the *Call*. The monarchy continued to give vocal support to the *aljama*, for example against those found guilty of misconduct.[80] Protection was given to African Jews who wished to settle in Mallorca.[81] The right of the Jews to operate their own weights and measures was confirmed.[82] A Mallorcan Jew was compensated by the king when a cargo of grain was appropriated for the army in Sardinia.[83] Following complaints from the *aljama*, even the bishop of Mallorca concurred with the requirement that Jews had been rushed to the baptismal font faster than canon law permitted.[84] The Jews of Mallorca City were commended by the crown for helping efforts to alleviate famine, and the city government was praised for protecting the Jews from angry mobs that were threatening their safety: *molts christians de aqueixa ciutat han comensat e quaix continuen vituperar envilogar e, so que es pijor, avolotar los juheus de la dita ciutat.*[85] It was the Christian population who made scapegoats of the Jews now, in 1374, and then on a much more severe scale in 1391, when a violent wave of anti-Jewish hatred swept through Spain and coincided with social unrest in the Mallorcan countryside, and with economic convulsions throughout the lands of the Crown of Aragon.

The slaughter and forced conversions of 1391 and the mass conversion of 1435 stand in direct contrast to the benign outlook of Peter IV of Aragon. Nor, indeed, were the *conversos* of Mallorca allowed to forget their origins. They were a caste apart, pursuing in many cases the sort of artisan crafts in gold and silver in which the Jews of medieval Mallorca had also been involved; until the twentieth century even wealthy *Xuetes* could only escape from discrimination by travelling to mainland Spain, where their status in Mallorca was held of no account. Many were devout Catholics, and the churches of Santa Eulalia and of Montesion became their special places of prayer: the one the place of their ancestors' conversion, the other the

[79] Privilegios, 199, no. 46; Isaacs, *Jews of Majorca*, 248, doc. 126.
[80] Privilegios, 281–2, no. 61; Isaacs, *Jews of Majorca*, 252, doc. 149.
[81] Isaacs, *Jews of Majorca*, 255, doc. 166.
[82] Privilegios, 377–9, no. 81; Isaacs, *Jews of Majorca*, 257, doc. 179.
[83] Baer, *Die Juden*, 435–6, no. 301; Isaacs, *Jews of Majorca*, 258, doc. 185.
[84] Villanueva, *Viage*, xxii, 253; Isaacs, *Jews of Majorca*, 259, doc. 190.
[85] Privilegios, 393–4; Isaacs, *Jews of Majorca*, 260, doc. 195.

site of the Great Synagogue which had been seized from the Jews by King Sanç. They did not retain their religion, but their sense of identity was forced on them, and they maintained a territory which was contiguous with that of the medieval *Call*.[86]

III

The picture changes somewhat when the Jews of Roussillon and Cerdagne are brought under examination. It is a moot point how far the Jews contributed to the economic expansion of Perpignan and Puigcerdà. Many were themselves recent migrants into Roussillon and Cerdagne, whose origins must be sought among the Jewries of Languedoc and Provence, for about half the Jews who can be identified bore surnames indicating their origin, and of these more than 80 per cent have southern French names;[87] they retained family ties to Lunel, Carcassonne, Narbonne and elsewhere until Philip IV's expulsion of the French Jews, when many of their relatives joined them. Not surprisingly, they were greatly alarmed at the expulsions from France in 1306, and in fact received in their midst settlers from the Majorcan fief of Montpellier, which was not exempt from the persecutions because it lay under French suzerainty.

The initial arrival of the Jews in Perpignan, and the expansion of the *aljama*, are both, as Emery pointed out, aspects of the city's own rapid growth in the thirteenth century. There is, indeed, a chicken-and-egg problem here: it is unclear whether the Jews came because they saw a city in full process of expansion, or whether they themselves fuelled that expansion. Predictably, the answer is something of each. The surviving records present a picture of them as largely involved in moneylending, with clients at all levels of society.[88] It can be argued that there was a shortage of capital in the boom town of Perpignan, which lacked a large, established Christian élite, such as one finds in contemporary Narbonne; this, and the good rates of interest chargeable under James I's edicts, may have attracted moneylenders from southern France, and (Emery believed) might also explain the strange lack of Jewish artisans in the town.[89] Yet there were very few

---

[86] A few *Xuetes* have emigrated to Israel, but the new synagogue in Palma serves the need of a very different community: English and other modern settlers on the island.

[87] Emery, *Jews of Perpignan*, 13. Emery further states that 'only nine names imply origin south of the Pyrenees'.

[88] P. Wolff, 'Un grand centre économique et social', in *Histoire de Perpignan*, ed. P. Wolff (Pays et villes de France, Toulouse, 1985), 55–60.   [89] Thus Emery, *Jews of Perpignan*, 99.

Italians in the town, and this probably reflects the royal hostility to small-scale Italian banking operations, generated in part by the rivalry of the Catalans, in part, perhaps, by ethical principles: this attitude is discussed further in a later chapter.[90] Although there are parallels in nearby Catalonia, notably at the small town of Santa Coloma de Queralt, the emphasis on lending at interest seems to differentiate the Perpignan and Puigcerdà communities from the Jews of the Catalan–Aragonese world as a whole, where a great variety of economic activities is documented.[91] The extensive participation of Jews of Perpignan in long-distance or local trade is particularly hard to prove. Only Salomon Sullam de Porta and Samuel Secal of Narbonne were active in trade, according to surviving records. Salomon Sullam is found entering into a *commenda* contract with Vives Septim, Jew of Barcelona, in August 1273; the commodity to be traded was cloth of Narbonne.[92] He had some links with Jews of Toledo and Seville, and he had contacts in northern Catalonia, which may suggest that he hailed from that area and that he was only in Perpignan to represent the mercantile interests of his wider family.[93] Samuel Secal appears slightly later, during the War of the Vespers. In November 1283 he came before a notary to declare that he owed £115, payable within fifteen days, to A. de Castilione, a Christian merchant from Mallorca, who had sold him a quantity of saffron.[94] In April 1284 he was owed money by a merchant of Perpignan, having sold him a quantity of lac and of *porcelanes*, cowrie-shells, a commodity that on occasion passed through southern France to Mallorca and the Maghrib.[95] He had some dealings with Mosse Davini (Moshe ben David), Jew of Collioure, who had travelled with cloth on his behalf, but whose work had not satisfied Secal.[96]

One problem that has to be faced is how representative of their wider economic activities the major records of Jewish moneylending are. The Perpignan records consist of notarial registers of the late thirteenth century (the fourteenth-century records have not yet been studied adequately) and it is possible that so many Jewish loans were

[90] See chapter 6.
[91] Cf. Yom-Tov Assis, *The Jews of Santa Coloma de Queralt* (Jerusalem, 1988); also I. Ollich i Castanyer and M. Casas i Nadal, *Miscellània de Textos Medievals*, vol. III, *Els 'Libri Iudeorum' de Vic i de Cardona* (Barcelona, 1985).   [92] Emery, *Jews of Perpignan*, 17.
[93] Emery, *Jews of Perpignan*, 18.   [94] Emery, *Jews of Perpignan*, 168, doc. 104.
[95] Emery, *Jews of Perpignan*, 182, doc. 122. On cowrie-shells, see chapter 6.
[96] Emery, *Jews of Perpignan*, 18–19.

recorded because lenders and clients insisted that a careful public record be made of each transaction; many other types of business, less likely to give rise to controversy, would never be brought before the notary. The presence in the registers of signatures and annotations in Hebrew makes it plain that the Jews themselves valued recourse to a notary, which removed all doubt about the date and value of the transaction, crucial information in the moneylending business. It is thus not surprising that the notarial registers have nothing to say about Jewish artisans and shopkeepers, though kosher butchers must certainly be postulated; precisely because common sense demands that such Jews existed, the value of these documents as a record of all Jewish economic activity must be seriously doubted. In fact, a large number of Jews are only mentioned once or twice in the surviving records, and it would be hazardous to assume that they lived off these periodic loans.[97] Occupational surnames are not found among the Jews of Perpignan, though the significance of this must not be exaggerated.[98] The evidence for Jewish economic activity in Puigcerdà in fact consists of a register exclusively dedicated to Jewish loans.[99] It simply does not speak about other activities; nor can it be expected to do so. Moreover, the impression that remains is of a community that could not compare in wealth and status with that of Narbonne, the great centre of southern French Jewry, nor with that of Barcelona. Jacob of Montpellier died in Perpignan worth a highly respectable £2,000 of Barcelona; there were one or two competitors in wealth, but the overall wealth of the *aljama* has been assessed at £30,000 of Barcelona, some way behind the £95,000 King Sanç assumed he could find in the *Call* of Mallorca City. Assuming there were about a hundred families, this works out at an average of £300 per family, but there must have been enormous variations either side of this figure.

It does, all the same, appear to be the case that the Jews of Mallorca (and also Barcelona) were more heavily involved in commerce and in artisan work than the Roussillon community. Emery even insisted, with excessive confidence, that 'most Jews of Perpignan seem to have engaged in moneylending', though in

[97] Emery, *Jews of Perpignan*, 31, should have seen the implications here. He, however, preferred to take this as evidence for large numbers of small loans which were not entered into notarial registers.

[98] Emery, *Jews of Perpignan*, 21–4, appears to make concessions to this view, but concludes that 'only a negligible proportion' of the Jews of the city could have been artisans.

[99] M. Delcor, 'Les Juifs de Puigcerdà au xiiie siècle', *Sefarad*, 26 (1966).

different degrees.[100] He also extended the image of the Jew as in first place a moneylender to Montpellier, which was better established as a commercial and industrial centre.[101] The Jewish lenders of both Montpellier and Perpignan were very active in providing small-scale loans in the countryside to peasants, mainly in early autumn, when improvement projects could be set in motion;[102] this is a picture not greatly dissimilar from that in, say, Cambridge during the thirteenth century, where the Jews concentrated on rural loans and were not greatly involved with the townspeople. Loans to villagers account for about 60 per cent of the known new loans to Christians made by Perpignan Jews in the late thirteenth century.[103] Emery saw in the evidence signs of considerable rural prosperity, for guarantees are rarely offered in the documents, and the peasants who took loans were presumably seen as viable risks.[104] In Perpignan, however, the Jews also lent to royal officials, to the local monasteries such as Saint-Michel de Cuxa, to merchants; and around one-third of known loans were directed to artisans and retailers of modest means within the city or from neighbouring towns such as Elne, the former regional capital, Villefranche, the major centre in Conflent, or Collioure, the main port.[105]

Several local merchants, all Christian, obtained advances from the Jews of Perpignan, and this is especially revealing: the Jews may not have been directly involved in regional trade, but they had a key role in the financing of the operations of others. Too sharp a distinction should not be drawn between the finance they offered and other types of commercial financing such as the *commenda* contracts and *cambium* loans amply recorded in contemporary Genoa, Barcelona and Mallorca. The difference is that the Jews did not take a direct interest in the purpose for which capital was being made available; but a sleeping partner who offered funds to support a commercial venture away from home carried the risks of the venture on his shoulders in a way that the disinterested moneylender did not. Christian businessmen such as Arnau de Codaleto of Rivesaltes (born soon after 1220)

---

[100] Emery, *Jews of Perpignan*, 29.
[101] Emery, *Jews of Perpignan*, 131–3. He bases himself on the Montpellier notarial register BB I in the Archives Municipales, aspects of which are discussed in chapter 9.
[102] This is the implication of Emery, *Jews of Perpignan*, 65.
[103] Emery, *Jews of Perpignan*, 61. In Erice (Sicily), the practice appears to have been direct investment by Jews in agricultural improvement schemes, especially vineyards, rather than loans: Abulafia, 'Una comunità ebraica della Sicilia occidentale'.
[104] Emery, *Jews of Perpignan*, 63.
[105] Emery, *Jews of Perpignan*, 44, for Saint-Michel de Cuxa.

were also active in Perpignan;[106] indeed, not very far away was the notorious centre of moneylending, Cahors. Emery saw the money-lending of the Christians as more episodic, but this is to ignore the fact that so many Jews appear only once or twice in the notarial registers; the lack of reference to interest in the loans made by Christians is very often an attempt to cover up activities which, though extremely regular, were still labelled immoral by the Church.[107] Arnau himself raised money from the Jews of Perpignan, and is an outstanding example of a Christian merchant who made good in the age of expansion. Links to local monasteries, notably Lagrasse (which raised funds from the Jews)[108] carried him up the social scale, and two of his sons became royal officials in the region. He was unusual in his knowledge of the Flemish cloth trade through Champagne: most Perpignan cloth dealers preferred to wait in their home city for goods to arrive on the mules and wagons of the merchants of Saint-Antonin near Quercy, further to the north, but Arnau invested with travelling merchants, mainly along the cloth routes and only to a minimal extent, and very locally, in maritime traffic.[109] The truth is that in the western Mediterranean those with spare cash kept it on the move, and were often accepted not as a necessary evil but as a general good.[110]

The dangers of an *argumentum ex silentio* have been indicated; nonetheless, the lack of references to Jews involved in the textile industry of Perpignan may be significant. The better-off Christian textile manufacturers appear to have turned mainly to fellow-Christians for loans, and the divorce of the Jews from Perpignan's own major industry is striking. It surely reflects the fact that Perpignan had begun to expand as an industrial centre before the Jews arrived in large numbers; the textile industry was the creation of Catalan and Occitan Christians, and similarly the trade in Roussillonnais textiles was primarily a Christian business. As in northern Europe, the Jews found that the moneylending business was the economic sector where they were most needed and where they possessed the appropriate skills.

As in the rest of the Catalan and Occitan world, these activities cannot be shown to have aroused deep resentment. In the long term,

[106] Emery, *Jews of Perpignan*, Appendix 1, 109–27.
[107] Emery, *Jews of Perpignan*, 100, seems to miss the point here.
[108] Emery, *Jews of Perpignan*, 44.
[109] Emery, *Jews of Perpignan*, 109–27. For the links to Saint-Antonin, see chapter 9.
[110] J. Shatzmiller, *Shylock reconsidered* (Berkeley/Los Angeles, 1990).

the Jews of Roussillon experienced the same process of gradual marginalisation and exclusion as in the other lands of the Crown of Aragon, protected and exploited by kings of Majorca and of Aragon who saw in them an economic asset. The parallels between the treatment of the Jews of Mallorca and those of Roussillon are as exact as could be. In 1275 King James I declared his support of the city's Jews, particularly against Christians who had presumed to cite Jewish moneylenders before Church courts; this was not permissible.[111] In 1317 the king of Majorca confiscated many Jewish loan contracts, as part of his efforts to fine the Jewish communities of the kingdom.[112] The passage of the Pastoureaux, or Shepherds' Crusade, through Roussillon in 1320 created a climate of fear; there were Talmud burnings at this time, too. But the difficult atmosphere under King Sanç gave way by the time of Peter IV to improvement: in 1372 and 1377 the king assured Jewish traders travelling into or out of Roussillon of his protection, and in 1383 Jewish apostates were forbidden to enter the *Call* and make trouble.[113] The Jewish community of Perpignan received royal protection during the pogroms of 1391; the Jews were brought into the castle, though this did not save their property in the *Call* of Perpignan. The autonomy of the *aljama* was guaranteed in 1408, but seven years later King Ferdinand I forbade the construction of a new synagogue or the repair of the old one. Tension was further aroused by the pressure to convert that followed the great public disputation at Tortosa in 1410. But a few years later, in 1413–14, evidence from the levy of a tax on the Jews suggests that the community had retained its moderate prosperity, as well as its appeal to rulers ever in search of funds: the *aljama* contained about 150 families, but its wealth hovered around £60,000, making a fourfold increase since the late thirteenth century (but without allowing for the considerable variations over time in the value of the Catalan coinage).[114] Even so, seclusion in the *Call* was increasingly rigorous, and life became disrupted by the contest between the kings of Aragon and Louis XI of France for control of Roussillon: Perpignan itself fell to the French in 1475, and was still in French hands when the Jews were expelled from Castile and Aragon

---

[111] Emery, *Jews of Perpignan*, 88–91; H. Beinart, 'Perpignan', in *Encyclopaedia Judaica*, s.v.
[112] Emery, *Jews of Perpignan*, 83.　　　　[113] Beinart, 'Perpignan'.
[114] R. W. Emery, 'The wealth of the Perpignan Jewry in the early fifteenth century', *Les Juifs dans l'histoire de la France* (Haifa, 1980); I. Loeb, 'Histoire d'une taille levée sur les Juifs de Perpignan en 1413–1414', *Révue des Études juives* (1887); Wolff, 'Un grand centre', 59; for the coinage, see Wolff, 'Un grand centre', 60.

in 1492. Sephardi refugees headed for Perpignan, but were expelled again in September 1493, setting out thereafter, like so many of the exiles, for Naples and Constantinople.[115] Indeed, the *Call* became a model for the seclusion of another group of late-medieval outcasts, the prostitutes of Perpignan, whose red-light district was also surrounded by walls and placed under guard; a blue-print for such a scheme can be found in a diploma of Peter IV, of 1380; but by 1500 Perpignan, and other cities of the Crown of Aragon such as Valencia, certainly possessed special enclaves for their prostitutes.[116]

IV

The Jews, like the Muslims, were at the mercy of the monarchy. What protected the Jews was also in a sense what made them most vulnerable: their relative wealth, or at least their assumed wealth; their lack of political and religious ties to the rulers of the Maghrib; their special status as a religion and people whose right to exist under Christian rule was circumscribed but also traditionally guaranteed. These guarantees were increasingly ignored in the late thirteenth century, in Gascony, Anjou, the French crown lands, southern Italy and elsewhere. The thin cover of protection had worn away. For the Muslims, the cover was even thinner. What rights they had were guaranteed by treaty arrangements that could be ignored by an exercise of *force majeure*; John Boswell has shown how Muslim rights were eroded in fourteenth-century Aragon, as the Muslims became more and more isolated.[117]

In dealing with their Jewish subjects, the Aragonese kings in mainland Spain, Majorca and Sicily avoided the maximum punishment of exclusion by expulsion, but opted for a lesser punishment of exclusion by seclusion. It was internal, rather than external exile. The *Call* became an obligatory place of residence in the great cities; in small towns, such as Inca in Mallorca or Erice in Sicily, the process of segregation was long delayed. The end of the thirteenth century

---

[115] Beinart, 'Perpignan'; for the routes taken by the exiles see David Abulafia, *Spain and 1492. Unity and uniformity under Ferdinand and Isabella* (Bangor, 1992), 44–7.

[116] L. L. Otis, 'Prostitution and repentance in late medieval Perpignan', *Women of the medieval world*, ed. J. Kirshner and S. F. Wemple (Oxford, 1985), 141–3; see more generally L. L. Otis, *Prostitution in medieval society. The history of an urban institution in Languedoc* (Chicago, 1985).

[117] J. Boswell, *The royal treasure. Muslim communities under the Crown of Aragon in the fourteenth century* (New Haven, 1977); but there was some recovery in the fifteenth century: M. Meyerson, *The Muslims of Valencia in the age of Fernando and Isabel* (Berkeley/Los Angeles, 1991).

and beginning of the fourteenth was a time when the Christian kings of Europe appeared to have lost patience with the irrational obstinacy of the Jews in their refusal to accept the Christian faith. Even the gentle persistence of Ramón Llull was punctuated by expressions of deep sorrow and impatience at the 'blindness' of the Jews and Muslims.[118] He, after all, was convinced that Jews, Christians and Muslims shared a belief in the same God, but that Judaism and Islam were incomplete, and incapable of providing a vehicle for worshipping God in the best and truest way. Less spiritual perspectives on the presence of Jews and Muslims in the lands of the Crown of Aragon also existed. What were they worth? Jews seemed often to be involved in trade and credit. The Muslims of Valencia were an essential agricultural work force, and were valued as artisans. But the problem for the Muslims of the Majorcan kingdom was that they had no place in the polity that was being devised. They were not particularly wealthy, as far as is known; they had no powerful leaders, for the élite had had the sense to leave; there was no political organisation outside Menorca. Their value consisted in their bodies, as labourers in the fields, as skilled artisans, and finally as expendable objects of commerce, sold into abject slavery. No clearer statement could be made of the lack of interest of the kings of Majorca in the *convivencia* of the three religions within the Balearic islands.

[118] This is evinced, for instance, in Llull's semi-autobiographical novel *Blanquerna*.

PART II

The crossroads of the Mediterranean

CHAPTER 6

The rise of the trade of Mallorca City

I

The chapters that follow look at the ways in which the major trade routes of the late medieval western Mediterranean were transformed by a series of related developments in the Catalan political world: the conquest and settlement of the Balearic islands from 1229 onwards; the creation by the will of James I of Aragon of the notionally independent kingdom of Majorca; and then the reincorporation of this kingdom into the lands ruled by the king of Aragon and count of Barcelona after 1343. The subject is thus not simply the commerce of the island of Mallorca and the kingdom of Majorca, but the relationship between the changing views of the function of the Majorcan kingdom in the Aragonese commonwealth and the expansion or contraction of its trade that accompanied its changing status. An attempt is made to place the kingdom's trade in a wider context by looking at Latin trade with the Balearics before the Catalan invasion of 1229, and at the trade of Mallorca after the fall of the autonomous kingdom in 1343. Above all, this study seeks to examine the trade of Mallorca mainly by way of the documents left by the merchants themselves, such as the commercial contracts for trade to and from Mallorca.

It will be seen that the Aragonese kings acquired a clearer view not merely of the commercial potential of Mallorca after 1229, but also of the interrelationship between the economy of Mallorca and that of their other Mediterranean territories; having been acquired by means of a crusade in which mercantile considerations took second place, Mallorca eventually became a fundamental prop of an integrated trade network and of a system of political alliances. In addition, it will be seen that the economic role of Mallorca changed significantly in the course of the fourteenth century, as a result of wider regional economic changes, the most important of which was the greatly altered structure of demand that was created by the Black Death. Expressed differently, it is clear that Peter the Ceremonious' vision of the links between Catalonia and Mallorca or Sicily was novel, in the sense that he sought to incorporate both kingdoms into an enlarged association of realms that would stretch from Syracuse to Saragossa; but it is also clear that his approach did not mark a radical break with an emerging set of principles concerning the relationship between Catalonia–Aragon and the island conquests of the Crown of Aragon. The famous comment made in 1380 by Peter IV in a letter to his heir is worth citing again: *perduda Sardenya, pot fer compte que axi mateix li tolra Mallorques, car les vitualles que Mallorques sol haver de Sicilia e de Serdenya cesseran e per conseguent la terra se haura a desebitar e perdre.*[1] It is not just the inclusion of all the Mediterranean islands that is striking here, but the insistence that the economies of the islands are by now closely interrelated. The function of the trade between Mallorca and Sicily or Sardinia is not simply to enrich Catalan merchants, but to sustain the population of Mallorca, and, by extension, to make possible the continued political stability of the west Mediterranean islands.

The integration of the Mallorcan economy into the commercial networks of the Catalan–Aragonese world was paralleled by the integration of the Majorcan state into the Catalan–Aragonese polity. It is argued that this process was delayed, at times quite deliberately, by the creation of a separate Majorcan kingdom: for two-thirds of a century the kings of Majorca pursued a policy of drawing together the mainland and island sectors of the kingdom into a coherent realm. The Majorcan monarchs saw their economic programme as a means towards the assertion of their independence from Aragon: the establishment of tariff barriers between Majorcan and Catalan territories; the creation of Majorcan consulates overseas; the inception of an independent foreign policy in the Maghrib; the establishment of a Mallorcan coinage in the Balearic islands, and later, with a disastrous political outcome, in Roussillon too.[2]

---

[1] V. Salavert y Roca, *Cerdeña y la expansión mediterránea de la Corona de Aragón 1297–1314*, vol. I (Madrid 1956), 213–14, n.37, translated on p. 248 infra.

[2] Antoni Riera Melis, *La Corona de Aragón y el reino de Mallorca en el primer cuarto del siglo XIV*, vol I, *Las repercusiones arancelarias de la autonomía balear (1298–1311)* (Madrid/Barcelona, 1986); see also his article 'El regne de Mallorca en el context internacional de la primera meitat del segle XIV', *Homenatge a la memòria del Prof. Dr Emilio Sáez* (Barcelona, 1989), 45–68,

While stressing the importance of control of Mallorca in the political programme of the late-fourteenth-century Aragonese kings, sight must not be lost of its importance as a centre for maritime trade far beyond the areas of Catalan–Aragonese influence.[3] Sea links were forged with England by 1281, with Atlantic Morocco around the same time, and with the ports of the Levant. It is argued here that it was no more than the strategic position of the Balearics that first drew western merchants to Mallorca, and the development of the islands as a source of locally produced commodities, notably salt and wool, was the result, rather than the cause, of its initial commercial success. After the Catalan conquest an attempt seems to have been made to stimulate grain production; a similar phenomenon is visible in another Mediterranean island conquered by Christians some time earlier, Sicily; but the disparity between the size of Mallorca City relative to its island and the fertility and extent of Sicily meant that such initiatives could ease but not solve the problem of feeding the Mallorcans. The Balearics themselves could not meet their own food needs, though there were exports of oil and figs in the thirteenth and fourteenth centuries; by the fifteenth century olive oil was a massive export.[4] The prime exportable resource of the Balearics lay on the third island, and was the famous salt of Ibiza, which probably grew in importance between the thirteenth and the fifteenth centuries.[5] Mallorca's textile industry came into its own more slowly than that of Barcelona; there are references to an incipient cloth industry around 1304 and in 1321, but the island was not a particularly important supplier of finished cloths before the middle of the fourteenth century;[6] thus it did not possess the importance of Sicily

which takes a more pessimistic view than I do of the kingdom's coherence: see chapter 3; A. Riera, 'Mallorca 1298–1311, un ejemplo de "planificación económica" en la época de plena expansión', *Miscelánea en honor de Josep Maria Madurell i Marimon*, in *Estudios Históricos y Documentos de los Archivos de Protocolos*, 5 (1977), 199–243.

[3] From a Spanish perspective see in the first instance F. Sevillano Colom, 'Mercaderes y navegantes mallorquines. Siglos XIII-XV', in the collaborative *História de Mallorca*, J. Mascaró Pasarius (ed.), Vol. VIII (Palma de Mallorca, 1978), 1–90; Sevillano Colom, *História del puerto de Palma de Mallorca*; to which should now be added Santamaría, *Ejecutoria*.

[4] A. Santamaría, *El reino de Mallorca en la primera mitad del siglo XV* (monograph of IV Congreso de História de la Corona d'Aragón, Palma de Mallorca, 1955), 25–6. See also the Pisan evidence cited below. For a statistical survey of Mallorca's economic resources, see Sastre Moll, *Economia y sociedad*. For the argument that grain production increased after the conquest of Mallorca, see Soto, *Ordinació de l'espai*.

[5] J. C. Hocquet, 'Ibiza, carrefour du commerce maritime et témoin d'une conjoncture méditerranéenne (1250–1650 env.)', *Studi in memoria di Federigo Melis*, vol. I (Naples, 1978), 493–526; Riera, *Corona de Aragón*, 36.

[6] Durliat, *L'Art*, 38; Santamaría, *Reino de Mallorca*, 29; Riera, *Corona de Aragón*, 36.

and Sardinia as an exporter of agricultural products, nor had it yet acquired the importance of Florence and Barcelona as an exporter of industrial goods. What we are looking at is the transformation during the fourteenth century of a commercial entrepôt into a centre of production. Interestingly, this resulted around 1400 in the reaffirmation, and not the loss, of the island's role as entrepôt, just at a time when another major centre of Catalan trade, Barcelona, was finding it increasingly difficult to maintain its own position.

It is fortunate that a series of snapshots of the state of Mallorcan trade can be provided from a wide variety of sources, public and private. The notarial registers of late-twelfth-century Genoa give the first clues to Mallorca's value in international trade; similar material, this time preserved in Mallorca, illuminates the trade networks out of Mallorca in the 1240s; the trade contracts of Marseilles provide unusually detailed information on the commodities carried to and from Mallorca in the thirteenth century; a remarkable set of licences for merchants and seamen wishing to leave the island in 1284 conveys important information about links to the Maghrib; in the 1320s, 30s and 40s the government records of Mallorca include the tax lists of incoming ships, foreign and Mallorcan, and from the same period there survive in Mallorca records of Pisan trade, of licences to export monitored goods, and a rich set of commercial contracts preserved in a notarial register of 1340. At the end of the fourteenth century the massive archive of Francesco Datini of Prato provides well over ten thousand letters concerning Mallorca (apart from other documentation); and for the early fifteenth century we have the registers of the notary Anthoni Costanti, analysed by Pierre Macaire.

II

Early Catalan trade, of the late twelfth and early thirteenth centuries, has been taken out of the realm of conjecture as more documents have been subjected to close scrutiny, notably those from the cathedral archive in Barcelona. The tendency has been for them to be studied first for their legal form, with the result that they have been classified by three main types (*commenda* contracts, exchange documents, simple partnerships).[7] Among these documents, there are sufficient

[7] J. M. Madurell Marimón and A. García Sanz, *Comandas comerciales barcelonesas de la baja edad media* (Barcelona, 1973) (hereafter *Comandas*); A. García Sanz and M. T. Ferrer i Mallol, *Assegurances i Canvis marítims medievals a Barcelona*, 2 vols. (Barcelona, 1983) (hereafter

references to Mallorca, before and after its conquest by James I, to make plain the existence of regular, if not necessarily intense, commercial links between Barcelona and Mallorca at this period; Mallorca seems still to have been valued as a bridgehead between Christian Europe and Africa. A famous story recounted in the autobiography of James I suggests that Mallorca was an occasional destination of major Catalan shippers before 1229: Pere Martell, the Barcelona merchant based in Tarragona, answers King James' question 'what sort of island is Mallorca?' It turns out that Pere Martell has been there a few times, though the impression is that, while he has an idea of their broad configuration, he does not know the Balearics very well. Alongside the evidence from the mainland it is, however, possible to place commercial contracts from Mallorca itself, beginning in 1240. This is especially precious material because it reveals a commercial élite in the process of formation, a combination of Catalans, Italians, Provençaux, of Jews and Christians, even the occasional Mozarab and Muslim; wealthy merchant families of the Catalan mainland, notably the Llulls, acquire power in Mallorca both as landholders and as merchants. It is difficult to think of other frontier societies in the medieval Mediterranean where on-the-spot commercial documentation is to be found so soon after the Christian takeover.[8]

The question being posed here is to what extent Ciutat de Mallorca was a clone of Barcelona and the southern French or Catalan ports from which it drew much of its population; or to what extent it developed a distinctive character as a centre of trade that was able to meet new commercial needs of the mid-thirteenth century. In certain respects its character clearly does resemble Barcelona: as it grew, it became increasingly dependent, like the mother city, on imported grain; its merchant community, though predominantly Christian, had, like that of Barcelona, a significant Jewish element and a small Muslim component. There is even a

Assegurances); A. García Sanz and J. M. Madurell i Marimón, *Societats mercantils medievals a Barcelona*, 2 vols. (Barcelona, 1986).
[8] The evidence for Sicily, for example, begins a century after the Norman invasion began and derives from north Italian archives; that from Crete postdates the Venetian conquest by several decades, though it originates on the island. The nearest analogy might be the Cypriot notarial acts preserved in Genoa, which date from a decade after the fall of Acre, and which document the rapid emergence of Famagusta as a major centre of trade; but the Christian conquest had actually taken place over a century earlier. Studies based on some of these materials can be found in Abulafia, *Italy, Sicily and the Mediterranean*, and Abulafia, *Commerce and conquest*.

rough physical comparison, with both cities possessing a centre of gravity to the east of a water course, and both combining a sea-front with parishes set back from the harbour. Yet the obvious contrast lies in the simple fact that Ciutat de Mallorca had no real hinterland, for the city accounted for perhaps 50 per cent of the population of an island that was not especially fertile, and that included steep mountain ranges. Mallorca's 'countryside' was the sea that surrounded it, and that joined it to two dependent islands, Menorca and Ibiza (plus Ibiza's own dependency of Formentera). It was as navigators, map-makers, merchants that the Mallorcans made an impact on the world around them; they were a maritime people, specialists in sea trade and shipping services, to an greater degree than the Catalans of the mainland.[9] Mallorca's role was that of an entrepôt, poised on the outermost edge of the Christian world, or, equally, just above the Mediterranean boundaries of Islam. Here was a Christian territory, a land of *conquistadores* (notably, King James I *el Conqueridor*), which actually depended for its survival on its links to the Muslim enemy. In some respects, as will be seen, the conquest, even though it repopulated the island, could not shatter the identity of Mallorca's trade; it would take events on the scale of the Black Death to do that. Christian conquest did not and could not turn the face of the island towards Europe, as happened, arguably, to Palermo after its absorption into the Christian world (and Palermo at least faces north, unlike Palma).[10]

The first theme that needs to be examined is the rôle of non-Mallorcans in the island's trade: the involvement of Latin merchants in the Balearics even before the Catalan conquest; the effect of a Catalan–Aragonese victory on the trading interests of the north Italian and Provençal merchants; the gradual emergence of the Catalans of Barcelona and Mallorca as the leading operators out of the port of Mallorca.

The first clear indication of active trade between Mallorca and Latin Europe comes in the register of Oberto de Mercato, notary of Genoa, dealing with autumn 1182. This is a period of special interest, just following a failed Sicilian invasion of Mallorca, and a decision by

---

[9] C. Batlle, J. Busqueta and C. Cuadrada, 'Notes sobre l'eix comercial Barcelona–Mallorca–Barbaria, a la meitat del s.xiii', CHCA xiii, vol. ii, 33–47.

[10] This concept of Sicily turning to the north is developed in Abulafia, *Two Italies*; see especially the new introduction to the Italian edition, *Le Due Italie: relazioni economiche fra il Regno normanno di Sicilia e i comuni settentrionali* (Naples, 1991), 7–38.

the Genoese not to participate in the campaign but to confirm past truces with the Muslim ruler of Mallorca; in 1181 the ruler of Mallorca solemnly promised not to permit interference with Genoese shipping, and the Genoese stated that they would not indulge in hostile acts against Mallorca.[11] The Genoese had in the past been involved in attacks on the Balearic islands, notably a raid on Menorca in 1146, which was itself a prelude to the siege of Almería and of Tortosa in 1147–8 (the Pisans had, of course, actually conquered Mallorca and Ibiza briefly in 1113–15). There is also occasional evidence of trade with the Balearics, including Ibiza, in the oldest notarial register, that of Giovanni Scriba (1154–64).[12] The Genoese had evidently settled into a co-operative relationship with Mallorca by the 1180s, and the reason was almost certainly the value the island possessed in gaining access to the ports of the Maghrib 150 miles to the south: hence, indeed, the emphasis in their agreement of 1181 on the safe passage of Genoese and Mallorcan ships in the western Mediterranean. But it is surely no coincidence that the acts of Oberto de Mercato contain ten contracts for Mallorcan trade in 1182, alongside half a dozen for Bougie, to which access would be gained via the Balearics.[13] In fact, the prominent Genoese merchant Enrico Trencherio was investing money both in Mallorca and in Bougie that year.[14] There are also twenty-three contracts in 1182 for Ceuta, on the route to which Mallorca would have been a half-way stop: the merchant Anselmo Rivario invested £28 13s 4d of Genoese money in Mallorcan trade and a further £20 in Ceuta, making plain the links between business in the Balearics and business in the Maghrib;[15] no other Spanish port is mentioned in these contracts, so a route Genoa–Mallorca–Morocco seems very likely to have been standard. There was certainly active business along the route Mallorca–Ceuta around 1240. What is especially striking about the contracts of 1182 is the high standing of the investors; in part this reflects the distinguished clientele of the notary Oberto de Mercato,

[11] For the text of the treaty of 1181, see L. de Mas Latrie, *Traités de paix et de commerce et documents divers concernant les relations des Chrétiens avec les Arabes de l'Afrique septentrionale au Moyen Age* (Paris, 1866), part 2, 109–13, and P. Guichard, *L'Espagne et la Sicile musulmanes aux XIe et XIIe siècles* (Lyons, 1990), 181–3, with further valuable comments; also Doxey, 'Christian attempts to reconquer the Balearic islands'.   [12] Abulafia, *Two Italies*, 104–5, 111.

[13] For what follows see Archivio di Stato, Genoa (herafter ASG), Cartolare notarile 2, ff.1r–34v (Oberto Scriba de Mercato 1182, unpublished), nos. 64, 127–8, 178, 181–4, 189–90; also Abulafia, *Two Italies*, 158; Erik Bach, *La Cité de Gênes au XIIe siècle* (Copenhagen, 1955), end tables (without pagination).   [14] ASG, Cart. 2, nos. 153, 184.

[15] ASG, Cart. 2, nos. 51, 127.

but to the modern observer it is a valuable indication that Mallorca was on the map as far as leading merchants were concerned: the wife of Fulco de Castello and Ansaldo de Mari were both members of top families, while Oglerio Vento was several times consul and had a stake in the lucrative grain trade out of Sicily.[16]

The upsurge in contracts in 1182 was a temporary response to the treaty of 1181, which was renewed in 1188;[17] this happened so soon, in fact, that there may well have been some difficulties in implementing it which were felt to necessitate its reiteration and extension. The Almoravid régime in Mallorca had been under heavy pressure between 1184 and 1187; there were domestic revolts, there were rumours of a new Sicilian invasion, there was conflict with the Almohad rulers of north Africa. The Sicilian fleet that was to capture Thessalonika in 1185 was being prepared amid conjecture about its destination, a closely guarded secret: the secretary to the governor of Granada, Muhammad ibn Jubayr, reports that 'some men say its destination is Alexandria – may Allah guard and defend it – and others Mallorca – Allah defend it – while yet others say Africa', but this was thought unlikely in view of King William's treaty obligations towards Tunis.[18] The Genoese must therefore have thought it in their best interests to reaffirm their support for what was now a tiny rump state, the last remnant, in fact, of the Almoravid Empire, but also a mighty mouse: in AH 580 (1184/5) 'there came from the west the sad news that the Lord of Mallorca had seized Bajayah [Bougie]', to cite the words of ibn Jubayr who, while no friend of the Almoravids, was also fearful of Sicilian threats to Mallorca.[19] The new treaty provided the Genoese with a warehouse in Mallorca, and it is arguable that this reveals that their trade had now become fairly substantial.

There is a solitary Genoese contract for trade in Mallorca in late summer 1184, when business recorded by Oberto de Mercato was dominated by trade to Syria and Alexandria; but the merchants involved were from prominent trading families (the Trencherio and Lecanoce families) so it is likely that their investments formed part of

---

[16] ASG, Cart. 2, nos. 64, 181–2; for Oglerio Vento, see Bach, *Cité de Gênes*, 152–3.

[17] Mas Latrie, *Traités de paix*, part 2, 113–15.

[18] *The Travels of ibn Jubayr*, ed. and transl. R. J. C. Broadhurst (London, 1952), 354.

[19] *Travels of ibn Jubayr*, 353; the translator, Broadhurst, comments (387, n.170): 'ibn Jubayr's allegiance to the Almohades did not cause him to wish success to a Christian assault on the rival but nevertheless Muslim Almoravids of Majorca'. For the Sicilian treaty with Tunis (1180), see David Abulafia, 'The reputation of a Norman king in Angevin Naples', *Journal of Medieval History* 5 (1979), 135–47.

a larger consignment of goods and money of which other records are lost.[20] In addition, that year saw a trade treaty between Pisa and the ruler of Mallorca.[21] But there are no contracts for Genoese trade in Mallorca from 1186, otherwise quite a well-documented year. The reaffirmation of ties in an enhanced set of privileges two years later is reflected in the records from 1190. Some evidence exists for trade there in early 1190, when investors included the wealthy Levant trader Baiamonte Barlaira, described by Erik Bach as 'un très grand capitaliste', though he was apparently not of patrician origins.[22] The notary Guglielmo Cassinese records a trip to Mallorca in late 1191, in which five investors, including one or two women, placed funds. What is perhaps more important is that 1191 saw intense trade between Genoa and the whole Maghrib, notably Bougie, much of which must have passed through Mallorca.[23]

By this period Genoese ships were freely penetrating the waters off Muslim Spain; in 1184 ibn Jubayr, heading for Mecca, took ship in Ceuta; the vessel was Genoese, and bound for Alexandria; the description of the route that he provides serves as a reminder that by the late twelfth century the Italians had gained control of the trade routes even between Morocco and Egypt, and also of the importance of the Balearics in east–west as well as north–south traffic:

Our course lay along the Andalucian coast, but this we left on Thursday the sixth of Dhu'l Qa'dah [3 March] when we were opposite Daniyah [Denia]. The morning of Friday the seventh of the month we were off the island of Yabisah [Ibiza], on Saturday the island of Mayurqa, and on Sunday we were off Menorca. From Ceuta to Menorca is eight *majari*, a *majra* being one hundred miles. We left the coast of this island, and early on the night of Tuesday the eleventh of the month, being 8 March, the coast of the island of Sardinia all at once appeared before us about a mile or less away. Between the islands of Sardinia and Menorca lie about four hundred miles. It had been a crossing remarkable for its speed.[24]

This passage confirms neatly the evidence of the notarial acts, suggesting as they do that Mallorca and Ceuta lay on the same Genoese trade routes.

The open question is where the Catalans fit in. Of some importance is a solitary published commercial document from Tarragona

[20] ASG, Cart. 2, f.84r, no. 2; Abulafia, *Two Italies*, 161.
[21] Mas Latrie, *Traités de paix*, 55; part 2, 367–73.
[22] Bach, *Cité de Gênes*, 70 and 119–22.
[23] For an overview, see Bach, *Cité de Gênes*, end tables, and Abulafia, *Two Italies*, 174, 182.
[24] *Travels of ibn Jubayr*, 26.

indicating trade with Mallorca in 1187. Bertran Català is found declaring that he owes a certain Bernat a hundred golden *massamutini* and ten golden *morabetini*, which he will repay as soon as possible after his arrival in Mallorca; this forms part of a larger consignment of 400 *massamutini*.[25] Too much need not be made of the use of Muslim monies here, since there is no certainty that the original investment consisted of gold coins; it could very likely have been a cargo of unnamed goods, or a quantity of silver, which were to be sold or exchanged for gold coins. This partial silence is typical of *cambium* contracts of the period, and often reflects the wish to avoid accusations of usury. Nevertheless, the charter does suggest quite an active trade from Tarragona to Mallorca at this point. The obvious parallel is with the Barcelona merchant En Pere Martell, who also operated out of Tarragona, and who told the king of Aragon, on the eve of the invasion of Mallorca, that he had traded there in the past, though not, apparently, with very great frequency. The impression remains that the Catalans were not a very powerful force in Mallorcan trade even in 1229.

In the twelfth century it seemed that, if any Christian power were to seize Mallorca, it would be with the help of Italian fleets, whether Pisan, Genoese or Sicilian. But in 1229 it was a Catalan fleet, strongly backed by allied fleets from southern France and Provence, where Aragonese influence and even lordship was extensive, that led the successful invasion.[26] To some extent the event symbolised the emergence of Barcelona as a viable competitor against better established Italian rivals. And yet, according to the late-thirteenth-century chronicler Bernat Desclot, the Pisans and Genoese opposed the Aragonese invasion plans and offered counsel to Abu Yahya, ruler of Mayurqa, with the specific aim of guaranteeing their own privileged access to the Balearics and of excluding Catalan rivals.[27] Even after the conquest, the Aragonese king was afraid that the Italians would ally with the irredentists if he did not treat them well. The Genoese and Pisans were awarded some lands, plus generous commercial privileges.[28] In 1230 Andrea Caffaro of Genoa was in

[25] *Assegurances*, vol. II, 306, no. 2.   [26] See chapter 1.
[27] Bernat Desclot, *Crònica*, cap. 14.
[28] See *Liber iurium reipublicae Genuensis*, in Historiae Monumenta Patria (Turin, 1854), col. 923, no. 707; col. 924, no. 708; col. 928, no. 710; col. 938, no. 716; also B. Pitzorno, 'Il consolato veneziano di Maiorca', *Studi nelle scienze giuridiche e sociali della Facoltà di Giurisprudenza della R. Università di Pavia*, 22 (1938), 15–17 of the *estratto*. Sevillano, 'Mercaderes', 62–4;

Mallorca, explicitly aiming to recover old rights attributed to Ramón Berenguer IV in 1146 and 1153; the Pisans too expected, and gained, confirmation of the commercial privileges they had possessed under Muslim rule. Some evidence exists for Pisan trade in Mallorca around 1247; characteristically, Pisa provided access to the island for other Tuscans too, such as Ser Doto of Florence, who owned a ship.[29]

For their part, the Genoese obtained property in Ciutat de Mallorca, including a church and enough land to support five priests, and in 1233 they were granted the long-lasting *lonja dels genovesos*, by which time they had become a self-governing community with their own consuls.[30] The Italians were thus, in a sense, rewarded for being on the wrong side. However, the new relationship did not prove easy at first, and in 1246–7 there is evidence of royal reprisals against the Genoese in Mallorca.[31] The Genoese in particular were to maintain a presence in the island's trade irrespective of the constant worsening of political relations between the Catalans and the Genoese. In part this was because Genoa was so faction ridden that you could always find some Genoese who sympathised with Aragon; but mainly this was the result of the increasing importance of the Balearics as a point of transit to Africa and the Atlantic, and, eventually, as a source of salt and other goods. Even in the fifteenth century the Genoese were able to ignore their violent differences with Alfonso the Magnanimous and to trade in Mallorca and Ibiza, where, apparently, they were tolerated.

A more subtle hint of the existence of an active trade from Mallorca in other directions than Catalonia is provided by the evidence for large numbers of Italian, Provençal and Jewish settlers in Mallorca immediately after the Catalan conquest. Quite apart from the evidence of the Genoese and Pisan negotiations for privileged status, there is the substantial grant of property to the men of Marseilles in Ciutat de Mallorca. The part of the capital city that was reserved to Nunyo Sanç, count of Roussillon, was granted out to immigrants from 1234 onwards; they included both foreign Jews (often from Nunyo's mainland possessions, such as Collioure) and Genoese, and it seems unlikely that these groups had been attracted

A. Santamaría, 'La reconquista de las vías marítimas', *Actas del Iº Congreso internacional de História mediterranea*, in the *Anuario de Estudios medievales*, 10 (1980), 55–7; C.E. Dufourcq, 'Aspects internationaux de Majorque durant les derniers siècles du Moyen Age', *Mayurqa*, 11 (1974), 6–7, 13–17. [29] Santamaría, *Ejecutoria*, 620–1, no. 36.
[30] Santamaría, 'Reconquista', 56.
[31] Santamaría, *Ejecutoria*, 610–11, 614–15, nos. 25, 29.

to Mallorca simply to exploit its relatively limited natural resources.[32] Tommaso di Donato of Genoa received a house next to the orchard of a certain Master John;[33] Benmont Zacolad of Marseilles, apparently a Jew, received property near the arsenal, and Jucef of Marseilles was granted houses in the Jewish street;[34] Barobe of Alexandria, son of the Jew Aaron, received 'quasdam domos in carrario Judeorum';[35] Boneto of Collioure and Astruc de Quillano, Jews, were granted an *operatorium* or workshop in the city, as well as other properties;[36] some Jewish beneficiaries such as Ceyt Abenceyt may have arrived from the Islamic world;[37] a large patch of territory was conceded to Ogerio di Mazanello, 'consuli statuto in terra et civitate ab universitate januense', so that the Genoese could build houses and shops there, subject to the provision that the land could not be alienated by the Commune of Genoa.[38] This picture of the creation of a lively business community is confirmed by the grant of King James I to Salomon ben Ammar of Sijilmasa, in north Africa, and his family of the right to settle in Mallorca and the other lands he ruled. It has been seen that the plentiful references to Salomon and his kinsmen in the Mallorca notarial acts make it plain that he was a major financial presence in Mallorca during the 1240s.[39]

The men of Provence, who at the time of the invasion of Mallorca were subjects of an Aragonese count of Provence, played a large enough role in the conquest to lead Archibald Lewis to the view that

---

[32] ARM, Prot. 341; printed by E. K. Aguiló, 'Capbreu ordenat l'any 1304 dels establiments y donacions fets per Don Nunyo Sanç, de la seu porció', *Bolletí de la Societat arqueológica Luliana*, 14 (1913), 209–24, 241–56, 273–85.   [33] Aguiló, 'Capbreu', no. 4, 209c2.

[34] Aguiló, 'Capbreu', no. 5, 209c2–210c1; no. 228, 250c1; this is perhaps the same person as Jucep de Marsilia Judeus who appears 'in carrerio Judeorum ... in via dicti calli' in Prot. 342, f.16v1.

[35] Aguiló, 'Capbreu', no. 195, 246c2; the use of the term *carrario* for the street (*Carrer*) of the Jews should be contrasted with the use of the term *Callis* (*Call*) for the Jewish quarter, especially after the reign of Alfonso III: see chapter 5.

[36] Aguiló, 'Capbreu', no. 83, 218c2; no. 213, 248c1; no. 214, 248c2.

[37] Aguiló, 'Capbreu', no. 181, 245c1.

[38] Aguiló, 'Capbreu', no. 219, 249c1. Interestingly, similar provisions about alienation applied to the Jews too; see the grant to Pietro di Pavia of houses in 'callo nostro judayco', i.e. the Jewish quarter as a whole, which must be occupied by Jews (Aguiló, 'Capbreu', no. 370, 282c1); also there is no. 214, 248c2, which is a grant to the Jew Astruc de Quillano of houses in the Jewish *Carrer* which 'non possitis uendere nisi judeis nostris'. The similarities between treatment of Jews and that of Italians have been mentioned in chapter 5.

[39] ARM, Prot. 342, f.15r2, f.19r4, f.73v2, etc., for Solomon; the second document is a loan he makes to a Provençal and a Catalan or Provençal of £6 2s 0d of Melgueil, guaranteed by textiles edged with fur. The borrowers were themselves planning a trading expedition to *Yspania*, that is, Muslim Spain: Prot. 342, f.16v2. A compatriot and probably a close kinsman of Solomon was Ammar Abenyacop de Sigilmaza Judeus: f.20v4, f.42r1–2, f.47r1, etc.

Mallorca was as much a New Occitania as it was a New Catalonia.[40] Marseilles received 297 houses in the capital, as well as lands
outside; and the success of its trade in Mallorca is explicitly revealed
in the commercial documents from thirteenth-century Marseilles.
The Manduels, merchant princes of Marseilles, acquired one of the
houses in Ciutat de Mallorca; in 1244 they renewed for a further six
years a lease held since 1240 by another Provençal merchant on this
logerio seu pensione illius honoris Mayoricharum.[41] In fact they allowed the
rent to fall from £25 of Marseilles to £15. Maybe this implies that
business was not as good as had at first been hoped, but the
Provençaux responded rapidly to the opportunities presented by the
need to provision the newly conquered territory. In Narbonne on 4
September 1233 Pere de Puig or Delpech of Marseilles bound himself
by contract to carry grain worth £60 of Melgueil from Narbonne to
Mallorca (*Malorgas*) on behalf of a leading Provençal merchant,
Bernard de Manduel; he was to buy goods in Mallorca and bring
them to Marseilles.[42] The same Pere de Puig carried cloth valued at
£100 of Marseilles money from Marseilles to Mallorca in 1235.[43]
Around the same time Bernard was claiming the return of some cloth
and of £38 of money of Marseilles, the latter of which at least had
recently been sent in trade to Mallorca.[44] After Bernard's death,
Petrus de Podio de Blancquaria (to give his full Latin name) still had
outstanding debts arising from his cloth-bearing expeditions to
Mallorca on Bernard's behalf, as a document of March 1239 makes
plain.[45] The impression is that Pere was a draper specialising in the
cloth trade to Mallorca, but he was not averse to taking other goods
there too.[46]

The plentiful acts of the Marseilles notary Amalric, of 1248,
concentrate heavily on business linked to St Louis' crusade, but here
too Mallorca is represented in interesting ways. Not unusually in
Marseilles, we see Jews and Christians working together in trade. A
certain Bonisaac Ferrusol, a member of a prominent Jewish trading
family, acted as agent for several Christian and Jewish investors

[40] See chapter 3.
[41] L. Blancard (ed.), *Documents inédits sur le commerce de Marseille au Moyen Age*, 2 vols.
(Marseilles, 1884–5), vol. I, 249–51, Manduel doc. 146.
[42] Blancard, vol. I, 56, Manduel doc. 41.   [43] Blancard, vol. I, 92–3, Manduel doc. 63.
[44] Blancard, vol. I, 83–4, Manduel doc. 58.
[45] Blancard, vol. I, 128–9, Manduel doc. 85.
[46] Blancard, vol. I, 227, 231, 380–4; vol. II, 259–60, Manduel docs. 138, 139, Amalric docs. 284,
927, and also 348, 351, 365, for other references to this figure.

trading to or through Mallorca around the end of May, 1248.[47] Brazilwood, cloves and muscat were sent with him from Marseilles to Mallorca and the Maghrib on the ship of Domènec Esfonts;[48] he also carried linen cloth worth £28 10s od and a sum of money southwards either to Mallorca or to Algiers or to Ténès.[49] In fact, the Ferrusol family had a record of wider contact with the Maghrib, and their Mallorcan trade fits neatly into the argument that those who traded intensively with the island also had major commitments in north Africa. Nor was Domènec Esfonts the only ship's master bound for Mallorca. In early June, the Lucchese merchant Rolando Vendemmia entered into a *societas* contract with another Lucchese and promised to take £32 to Mallorca on the ship of Guglielmetto de Nervi, whose name indicates a Genoese origin; the same merchant was also trading towards Montpellier at this time.[50]

At this point, it is worth making a quick jump across time, for of particular importance is a document of 1296 concerning a galley master, Guillem Franc, against whom a law suit had arisen. The master insisted on requiring a written copy of his bill of lading for two journeys made in 1289 from Marseilles and Aigues-Mortes to Mallorca, and conducted, apparently to their displeasure, on behalf of a group of merchants of Piacenza, Genoa and Marseilles. The Piacenzans loaded pepper, lac and *porcellanas* (of which more shortly). On the first journey, Provençal merchants placed wine, lac, incense, cinnamon and *porcellanas* on board; a Pisan added some more wine, lac, cloves, aspic and similar luxuries. On the second voyage the cargo was rather more varied, since a moderate amount of cloth, some ginger and some coral were also included. These commodities are what one would expect to find on a galley: smallish consignments of high value goods. Interestingly, they are being shipped out from a European entrepôt back towards the outer edge of the Latin world. The spices would have arrived in Marseilles direct from the Levant for redistribution.

Special interest attaches to the commodity labelled *porcellanas*: these were cowrie shells. These small shells apparently derived their

[47] For this family, see J. Pryor, *Business contracts of medieval Provence. Selected notulae from the cartulary of Giraud Amalric of Marseilles, 1248* (Toronto 1981), 86–7.

[48] Blancard, vol. II, 204, 206–7, Amalric docs. 807, 815.

[49] Blancard, vol. II, 205–6, Amalric docs. 810, 814.

[50] Blancard, vol. II, 231–2, Amalric docs. 870–1. On the other hand, the factors of another Marseilles merchant cancelled their plans to travel to Mallorca and Barbary in late July, 1248: Blancard, vol. II, 306, Amalric doc. 1023.

name from their broad similarity to the shape of a piglet's back; their sheen and partial transparency eventually resulted in the conferment of the name on Chinese pottery, but this occurred well after the thirteenth century. Such cowrie shells were seen by Marco Polo in China (*porcellani*), and they were still known as 'porcelains' in eighteenth-century Marseilles. The *porcellane* were packed in tubes similar to those used for pepper. Cowrie shells from the Maldive islands were certainly carried by Venetian shippers in the late Middle Ages, who transported them most probably from Alexandria westwards, for despatch to Africa, where they resumed their Indian Ocean use as a means of exchange.[51] For the Latin merchants, the sale for specie of humble cowrie shells in north Africa was literally a golden opportunity.[52]

The same document carries information about what was loaded in Mallorca for both return journeys; most of the items are luxury or semi-luxury goods typical of Spain and the Maghrib: the red dyestuff known as *grana*, indigo, paper, fine leather, cow-hides, cheeses, dates, figs, cumin, wax. A significant amount of alum and more cloves also figure. On each return trip, the owners of the cargoes were all or mainly from Piacenza and Genoa, and there were some distinguished merchants involved: Antonio Brancaleone of Genoa, on the first trip; Percivallo di Mari on the second.[53]

The Piacenzans were clearly well organised in trading companies, to judge from the bill of lading just examined. However, the Majorcan kings were also capable of turning on them and other wealthy foreigners. They joined with the business community of Barcelona in trying to impede the installation of medium-sized Italian banks of Florence, Siena, Lucca and Piacenza, while at the same time welcoming the great Florentine firms, the Bardi, Peruzzi and Acciaiuoli, whose credit was too valuable to ignore. What has been called a *batalla del proteccionisme* was waged, but the Majorcan effort

---

[51] J. Hogendorn and M. Johnson, *The shell money of the slave trade* (Cambridge, 1986), 15–16.

[52] Mallorca exported pottery to the Latin west, at least in the eleventh century: David Abulafia, 'The Pisan *bacini* and the medieval Mediterranean economy: a historian's viewpoint', *Papers in Italian Archaeology 4: The Cambridge Conference*, vol. IV, *Classical and medieval archaeology*, ed. C. Malone and S. Stoddart (Oxford, 1985), 291, repr. in David Abulafia, *Italy, Sicily and the Mediterranean, 1100–1400* (London, 1987). However, the reason why maiolica was named after the island when it was actually produced in Valencia and Andalucia remains a puzzle; it is generally assumed to be further testimony of the ready availability of a wide variety of western Mediterranean goods in late medieval Mallorca.

[53] Other evidence shows a trade in incense and *porcellanas* from Marseilles to Mallorca (also in 1289, but on another ship): Blancard, vol. II, 443, Pièces commerciales diverses, doc. 70.

cannot have been very successful: decrees expelling the Italians were reiterated often enough to leave the impression that they were barely heeded. The first decree, of 1269, followed closely on one issued four years earlier in Barcelona, but even when Majorca was under the rule of its own dynasty the Italian bankers remained under suspicion, at least until 1327.[54] To some extent, this series of edicts may reflect a dislike for usury, but the main motive was clearly the desire to ensure that local, or at least Catalan, merchants retained their primacy in the financing of commercial enterprises.

The argument here that Mallorca was valued as a transit point rather than for its own commodities is confirmed by the readiness, observed already, of Popes Gregory IX and Innocent IV to permit the Catalan settlers in Mallorca to trade with the Maghrib, on the grounds that otherwise they would lack a livelihood. We thus have the paradox that a crusader conquest depended for its continued existence on the infidel.

III

The role of the foreigners is, then, accessible to observation through archival materials in Genoa, Marseilles and elsewhere. It is now necessary to turn to the documentation from Mallorca itself, which is especially revealing for the Catalan business community settled on the island after 1229. Even without the help of the Mallorcan documents, those from Barcelona make a case for a rapid response by the Catalans to the acquisition of the island: an early text now preserved in the cathedral archive at Barcelona states that on 26 June 1231, in Mallorca, Arnau Guillem, who worked in the cotton industry, received nine *solidi* to be carried to Barcelona on the galley of Berenguer de Poses.[55] Less than a year later Arnau Eimeric and Ramón Agramunt entered into a business partnership for trade from Catalonia to Mallorca; the former was patron of a small ship, a *barcha*.[56]

The fortunate survival of notarial registers from the Mallorca of the 1240s, which contain significant numbers of trade contracts, means that it is possible to look closely at the direction of Mallorcan commerce in the very years when the popes were ceding the right to

---

[54] Sevillano, 'Mercaderes', 66; Santamaría, 'Reconquista', 58; M. T. Ferrer i Mallol, 'Els italians a terres catalanes (segles xiii–xv)', *Actas del I° Congreso internacional de História mediterranea*, in the *Anuario de Estudios medievales*, 10 (1980), 396; Dufourcq, 'Aspects internationaux', 16–18.   [55] *Assegurances*, vol. ii, 311–12, no. 8.

[56] *Assegurances*, vol. ii, 312–13, no. 9.

trade with the Muslim world. It is possible, too, to move beyond the bare recital of trading destinations, commodities and sums of money to observe the merchants themselves, confidently preparing business ventures in a highly commercialised corner of the Catalan trading world that had come into existence almost overnight. The commercial documents reveal that north Africa, newly conquered Valencia City and al-Andalus were the preferred destination of the earliest Catalan merchants in Mallorca.[57] In August 1241 two brothers arranged a trading voyage to *Yspaniam* (probably Muslim Spain) or to *Sabut*, that is, Ceuta: Pere de Bages and Guillem de Puiglliure, brothers, declared and acknowledged to Guillem son of the late Ver, to Jaume de Clareto de Forns and to their associates, that they had received in *commenda* 50s. of Melgueil, which they would carry to Spain in the ship of the Stornelli, or to Ceuta.[58] A considerable number of ships are identifiable bound for *Yspania*, or Muslim Spain, at this juncture; what is especially striking is the lack of repetition of the names of ships bound for this region in the commercial contracts of 1240 to 1243. The evidence does not consist of two dozen deceptively impressive contracts for trade in what turn out to be only one or two ships, as occasionally is the case in series of Genoese commercial contracts; rather, it is spread over time, involves a good many investors, and the shipowners, whether mainland Catalans or Mallorcans, are very varied: Jaume de Negero, Pere Arnau, Ser Lancelini, Berenguer Roig (*Rubi*), and many others who were clearly ready to set out at much the same time. The ship of the first captain was to carry cloth belonging to Ramón de Clergue valued at £114 of Melgueil as well as 350 silver *besants*, property of the same investor.[59]

[57] The major source is ARM, Escribanía de Cartas Reales, Serie Civitatis et Partis Foraneae, Prots. 342 and 343. A number of the commercial documents have now been published; some are scattered in the notes to Sevillano, *História del puerto*, and are mainly transcribed from ARM, Prot. 342. More recently, Alvaro Santamaría has published several dozen more of these texts, including groups from Prot. 343, in the appendices to his *Ejecutoria*.

[58] Sevillano, *História del puerto*, 449, n.238; cf. 449, n.237 for a contract for trade in *Yspaniam* and Valencia on the same ship.

[59] For trade to *Yspania* in the period 1240–3, see Prot. 342, f.83v5 (Santamaría, *Ejecutoria*, no. 10); f.87v2; f.91v2; f.105v4; f.109r1; f.115r3–4,6, f.118r3; f.119r2; f.129r1; f.132v1; f.133v3; f.136r2; f.138r5; f.140r3; f.192v1; f.194v5; f.196r3; f.196v2; f.209r1 (Santamaría, *Ejecutoria*, no. 20); f.209r2 (Santamaría, *Ejecutoria*, no. 21); f.210v3; f.211v1. Some documents specify a route via *Yspania* to Ceuta, making plain the fact that the term *Yspania* refers to the southern part of Mediterranean Spain, i.e. effectively the kingdom of Granada. Prot. 342, f.194r1, mentioned in Sevillano, *História del puerto*, 455, n.305, offers a choice between a voyage to Valencia and one to Ceuta.

In some other cases the purpose of a visit to the waters of Muslim Spain was to prey on enemy shipping, *ad lucrandum contra Sarracenos*, which is of little surprise at a time when the war for Valencia was still incomplete; Bernat de Roig (*Rubi*) and Ser Boni were evidently pirate captains with an eye on human booty (captives for sale on the slave market) as well as humbler goods.[60] However, the investment required before a pirate raid could be launched was far from negligible: Jaume and Joan de Alba received nearly £100 from Arnau de Font in September 1242, for a voyage *contra sarracenos* with the ship *Sanctus Dominicus*, and they pledged the ship and its rigging as guarantee for the investment.[61] It would be interesting to know if this is the same Arnau de Font who was royal *baiulus* in Mallorca, and who is found ceding mining rights for precious metals in a document of November 1247.[62] Elsewhere we see a merchant who originated in Marseilles, Porcellus de Marcilia, taking six pounds of money of Melgueil to Valencia to be invested *in sarracenis et sarracenabus*, Muslim slaves, a very important commodity throughout the trading history of Catalan Mallorca.[63] Porcellus' backer was one Stefan Sastre (*Sartor*), who reappears elsewhere as a slave dealer with links to a Valencian shipper; this time it is Sastre who is taking a baptised slave to Sicily.[64] There was some demand in *Yspania* for figs exported from Mallorca, to judge from a contract of April 1243.[65]

A consistent feature of Mallorcan trade, whether in the mid-thirteenth, mid-fourteenth or mid-fifteenth century, is the primacy of the Maghrib as a commercial destination. North Africa also dominates the series of licences, dating from 1284, permitting sailors to leave the island in time of danger; at that moment, when trade to Catalonia was severed by the quarrel between the kings of Aragon and Majorca, the primacy of the Maghrib comes as little surprise. But in the 1240s too it had a place of fundamental importance in Mallorcan trade. The region was even supplied with Mallorca's own foodstuffs: in January 1241 Jaume Correger and Arnau de Vallespir were already capitalising on the dairy produce of Menorca, since 1231 a tributary of James I; Jaume Correger planned to take a quintal of Menorcan butter to Ceuta aboard the ship of Ser Gilineo.[66] Other merchants were about to depart for Ceuta, which had already

[60] Prot. 342, f.98r2, f.102v1.   [61] Prot. 343, f.218r; Santamaría, *Ejecutoria*, no. 12.
[62] Prot. 343, f.236v; Santamaría, *Ejecutoria*, no. 48.
[63] Prot. 342, f.134r2; Sevillano, *História del puerto*, 454–5, n.299.
[64] Prot. 343, f.144r; Santamaría, *Ejecutoria*, no. 14.   [65] Prot. 342, f.196r3.
[66] Prot. 342, f.11v4; Sevillano, *História del puerto*, 454, n.298.

emerged as a major centre of Genoese trade:[67] in October 1241 Pere Genever intended to travel there via Muslim Spain, as a whole series of contracts reveals;[68] Berenguer de Tarragona was also bound for either al-Andalus or *Sabut* in November 1241;[69] as was Berenguer Burgeti.[70] Grain bound for Ceuta and Bougie passed through Mallorca in the 1240s. On 15 October 1246 Arnau de Font received from Jaume de Marí over 2,000 Moroccan silver *besants* which were to pay for the export of 800 measures (*mudini*) of barley and 100 of wheat to Ceuta; of this, the greater part was to be loaded on the ship of Bernat de Molí or Molendino, the remainder in the galley of Pere de Tortosa.[71] Whether Pere was based in Tortosa or was a settler in Mallorca, other shipping moved from Tortosa to Mallorca and then via Ibiza to Algiers or Bougie.[72] Arnau de Font reappears in a document of 7 November 1247, when he sends 140 quarters of wheat to Bougie with his agent Jaume, on what is described as the *navi de Palma*.[73]

Ceuta was understandably tied more closely to the trade of al-Andalus than were Bône, Bougie and other points in modern Algeria; indeed, it was in this zone that the Catalans as a whole were most successful in extending their political and economic influence, as the work of Charles-Emmanuel Dufourcq reveals, even though he seems to have been unaware of the existence of Mallorcan protocols from the 1240s.[74] Links to north Africa were further consolidated by the treaties arranged by James I with several Maghribi rulers; even where the aims were the assertion of Aragonese political influence in Tlemcen and its neighbours, there were major benefits for Majorcan, as for other Catalan, merchants.[75] What is striking is the large

---

[67] Sevillano, *História del puerto*, 449–50, nn.239–41; cf. Santamaría, *Ejecutoria*, 423, 425 for the arming of pirate ships on this route at the same period; also Santamaría, *Ejecutoria*, 597–8, no. 13, for the ransoming of Christian and Muslim captives in Ceuta.
[68] Prot. 342, f.115r4–5, f.116r2–3, f.116v2. [69] Prot. 342, f.118v2.
[70] Prot. 342, f.119r2.
[71] Prot. 343, f.104v1; Santamaría, *Ejecutoria*, 609–10, 632, no. 24, suggesting location is f.104r.
[72] Santamaría, *Ejecutoria*, 619–20, no. 35: it is not certain the ship arrived directly from Tortosa, but the captain and his business partner came from there.
[73] Prot. 343, f.228r; Santamaría, *Ejecutoria*, 609–10, 632, no. 45.
[74] C.E. Dufourcq, *L'Espagne Catalane et le Maghrib aux XIIIᵉ et XIVᵉ siècles. De la bataille de Las Navas de Tolosa (1212) à l'avènement du sultan mérinide Aboul-Hasan (1331)* (Paris, 1966), with a note on the Mallorcan sources he employed, 7–9.
[75] BN, MS latin 9261, no. 8; Mas Latrie, *Traités de paix*, part 2, 280–4 (a treaty of 1271 between James I and the ruler of Tunis) and 187–8, which is a confirmation by James II of Majorca of 1278; other treaties binding the kings of Majorca to north African rulers are known from 1313 (Tunis) and 1339 (Tlemcen): BN, MS latin 9261 nos. 29, 37; Mas Latrie, *Traités de paix*, 188–95.

number of destinations at which Mallorcan vessels were being pointed in the 1240s: the Hafsid capital at Tunis,[76] Marinid Ceuta,[77] and, along the coast of the Abdalwahidid state of Tlemcen, Algiers,[78] Ténès,[79] Bougie,[80] Brechk[81], not to mention Oran[82] and Bône.[83] In one case, there are instructions to travel either to Algiers or to Ténès 'vel usque ad quemcunque locum de Alguer ad Tenes'.[84] In May 1241 Guillem Mir and Pere de Lleida entered into a contract for the carriage of nine jars of oil and certain other goods to Bône on the barque of Arnau Galart.[85] This shipowner appears also to have acquired a share in the use of his brother's *sagetia*, which was to travel to Denia or Alicante or to the Maghrib (*Barberiam*) or simply to Menorca, at differential rates of 18, 22 and 44 *besants* for the first three destinations, and a mere fifty *solidi* of Melgueil if only bound for Menorca.[86]

As elsewhere in the Catalan trading world, the handling of cloths was a major source of profit; significant quantities of cloth from a wide range of sources, Catalan, Valencian, Provençal and Flemish, were forwarded through Mallorca to north Africa. The island evidently functioned as a clearing house for European and Andalusi cloths destined for markets in the Islamic world. Evidence is provided very early in the Mallorcan protocols of a cloth trade towards Algiers: on 19 April 1240 Pere de Palau received from Berenguer Salicrup linen cloth worth £14 6s 0d of Barcelona for carriage *apud Alguer*, or to whichever other port Pere might go for trade.[87] In November 1242 twenty linen cloths of Xàtiva (Játiva) and four other 'Saracen linen cloths' are sent in *commenda* to Ceuta; in January 1246 more Xàtiva cloth is sent on a ship of Marseilles to Ceuta, Málaga or Morocco.[88] The famous white cloths or 'blankets' of Narbonne feature in April 1240, when debts are stated for two and four pieces;[89] in August 1241 the Jew Salomon of Sijilmasa sells a

---

[76] E.g. Prot. 342, f.134v1, involving Bonafos Jafie Judeo.   [77] E.g. Prot. 343, f.104v1.
[78] E.g. Prot. 342, f.120r1.   [79] E.g. Prot. 342, f.120r1.   [80] E.g. Prot. 342, f.149v2.
[81] E.g. Prot. 342, f.204r3; Santamaría, *Ejecutoria*, no. 17.
[82] Prot. 342, f.139r; Santamaría, *Ejecutoria*, 402.   [83] Prot. 342 f.73v4.
[84] Prot. 342, f.120r1.   [85] Prot. 342 f.73v4.
[86] Prot. 342, f.84; Santamaría, *Ejecutoria*, 595–6, no. 11. Other documents concerning the sale of *sagetie* include Santamaría, *Ejecutoria*, 595–6, nos. 26–7, printed from Prot. 343, f.136r, f.139v.
[87] Prot. 342, f.9v1; Sevillano, *História del puerto*, 449, n.236; Santamaría, *Ejecutoria*, 583, no. 1 (giving f.9r instead of 9v).   [88] Santamaría, *Ejecutoria*, 401.
[89] Prot. 342, f.10r1: 'cxci sol. melg. racione duarum panarum albi de narbona'; Prot. 342, f.10r2: 'ix lib. melg. racione quatuor peciarum pannis albi de narbona'. The purchaser in the latter contract is Guillem de Banyeres, very probably a member of the prominent

similar amount of the same cloth at a higher price.[90] Among the prestigious cloths of Flanders and northern France, 'stamfort' cloth of Arras and St Omer is sent in January 1243 from Mallorca to Oran; in September 1242 cloth valued at 480 *solidi* arrives from Ghent and is reclaimed.[91] Such items were collected together by merchants in Mallorca for redistribution to Tunis and elsewhere: in April 1247 Joan de Bas arranged to take a mixture of north French and Flemish cloths from Mallorca to Tunis: *vij blaus de Proins et in uno camalino de Provins et in ii reyets de Ipres et in v barrecanis de Locri*.[92] Among Catalan cloths, it is woollen cloths of Lleida that appear most often in the contracts.[93] At this period, Mallorca had still not developed an important cloth industry of its own.

The Mallorcan protocols provide evidence that not just settler Catalans, Provençaux and Italians, but Muslims, Mozarabs and Jews were involved in trade out of the island in the 1240s. Muslims of the mainland territories of the Crown of Aragon, as well as of al-Andalus, utilised Catalan ships to gain access to north Africa: Acmet Abenyequir hired half a ship; he came from Alicante, as yet unconquered by the Christians, and the ship he was interested in was owned by a mainland Catalan, Bernat de Quart, of Sant Feliu; it was to sail from Alicante to Algiers or Bougie. It is uncertain from the text whether the ship was to begin its voyage from Mallorca or from Alicante; most likely the captain was to sail from Mallorca to Alicante, there to load Acmet's cargo.[94] What appears to be a partnership between Muslims of the Aragonese mainland and Christian businessmen was formalised in February 1242, when Amicus de Caldis, Farraj of Saragossa and Abdella Alferichy of Lleida, the last two Saracens, invested money with Berenguer de Briansono on the eve of their own departure for Bougie or, if not, Ceuta, *in ligno Arrelli*.[95] In June 1243 Abdella and Farraj were once again in Mallorca, planning an expedition to Tunis with a relative of Amicus de Caldis, whose original investment was reinvested in the new project; the Muslims had apparently recently returned from a

Barcelona trading family of Banyeres, on whom see Abulafia, 'Catalan merchants and the western Mediterranean', 217.　　　　[90] Santamaría, *Ejecutoria*, 401.
[91] Santamaría, *Ejecutoria*, 402.
[92] Prot. 343, f.155v3; Santamaría, *Ejecutoria*, 617–18, no. 32.
[93] Santamaría, *Ejecutoria*, 401: Berenguer Ferrer de Milán sells a piece of green cloth of Lleida in February 1242; in November of the same year P. de Santa Coloma promises another person a Leridan tunic in the style of Arras (both from ARM, Prot. 342).
[94] Prot. 343, f.243v–244r; Santamaría, *Ejecutoria*, 639–40, no. 51 (29 December 1247).
[95] Prot. 342, f.160r4.

side trip to Tortosa.[96] Jews, too, took an interest in the Africa trade, which is hardly surprising when one of the most prominent of the Mallorcan Jews was himself the north African settler Salomon of Sijilmasa. In January 1242 Bernat Marellus agreed to travel to Bougie with some money of Samuel filius Jafie, that is, Abinafia or ibn Yahya; as guarantee of his debt the Christian shipper offered ten jars of oil aboard his ship.[97] Later sources suggest that links between the Jewish communities of Barcelona and Mallorca were expressed through commercial as well as religious channels.[98]

As well as oil, animal fats, notably butter, featured in trade from Mallorca to Spain and the Maghrib; the butter may often have been Menorcan, as will be clear shortly.[99] In this trade, Catalan merchants can be seen working very closely in conjunction with Mallorcans of pre-conquest times: Jacobus de Abennacer gives a substantial quantity of *mantega*, butter or another animal fat, in *commenda* to Bernat de Dana, who will sell it on his behalf in Valencia.[100] It has been seen that this Abennasser was very probably a member of a family of native Mallorcan Mozarabs of the same surname. There are many references in the Mallorcan protocols to Johannes Abennasser *Arrom*, that is, *ar-Rumi*, or 'the Christian', who had especially strong interest in the oil and wine trade, and who seems to have specialised in the handling of foodstuffs passing out of Mallorca itself.[101]

As well as Mallorca, Menorca and Ibiza were exploited from the start by Catalan businessmen, a mere decade after the submission of the Menorcan Muslims to James I and less than a decade after the conquest of Ibiza. Not surprisingly, the dairy produce of Menorca, already cited in the surrender treaty of 1231, appears in the trade of the Balearics ten years later. In January 1241, there were exports towards Ceuta of butter from Menorca (*unum quintalium butiri de Minorica*), to be carried on the ship of Ser Gilineo, already mentioned.[102] In one contract of the 1240s, already discussed,

[96] Prot. 342, f.210v1. [97] Prot. 342, f.149v2.

[98] García and Marimon, *Societats mercantils*, vol. II, no. 21, Barcelona, 16 August 1314, reveals business links between Isaac Benhaembran Tahvellí of Mallorca and Samuel Faquim and Abraham Bisbe of Barcelona, all Jews; cf. *Comandas*, no. 67.

[99] Sevillano, *História del puerto*, 454, nn.295, 298; in modern Spanish a distinction is generally made between *manteca*, indicating lard, and *mantequilla*, indicating butter. See also for Valencia Santamaría, *Ejecutoria*, 589–90, no. 7.

[100] See Santamaría, *Ejecutoria*, 217–20, for the career of the Muslim businessman Johannes Abennàsser. See Santamaría, *Ejecutoria*, 630–1, no. 44, for a safe-conduct issued in Mallorca for two Saracens (one from Murcia) and their goods (10 October 1247).

[101] See chapter 4 for a further discussion of this figure and his family.

[102] Prot. 342, f.11v4; Sevillano, *História del puerto*, 454, n.298.

Menorca is cited as one of several viable destinations alongside Denia, Alicante and the Maghrib.[103] In April 1243 Ramón of Montpellier was one of two merchants who invested a sum of 'twelve silver besants [of the sort] circulating in Menorca' in trade with that island, to be repaid either in Menorca or back home in Mallorca; in other words, the travelling partner, Guillem de Tholosa, did not propose to move beyond Menorca, but only to make a quick round trip.[104] The presence in this deal of a Montpelliérain (assuming he is not simply one of many settlers from the city in Mallorca) provides an interesting comparison with evidence from a century later, in the notarial archives of Montpellier, for close business links between Menorca and Montpellier.[105] A ship bound for Ibiza is recorded in late April, 1243, though it appears from the contract that the captain has the option to sail as far as Ceuta.[106] Similarly, in April 1247 Guillem de Segas of Tortosa rented out an eighth part of his *leny* to Berenguer Miquel of the same town; the ship was travelling from Mallorca (*de terra*) to Ibiza, and then to Algiers, Bougie or such other place as God should decide.[107] Ibiza thus already possessed the role it held during the time of Francesco Datini, around 1400, as a jumping-off point from the Balearics towards Africa or Spain. Menorca, by contrast, seems to have fed its supplies into the trade network of Mallorca, though the surrender treaty of 1231 did envisage some navigation between Menorca and the Muslim world, which would not be entirely immune from Catalan interference.[108]

In fact, there is hardly a corner of the western Mediterranean that is ignored in the commercial contracts of the 1240s. By comparison with similar material of the 1340s, the absence of Sardinia is striking, and contact with Genoa was clearly limited as a result of letters of marque issued in favour of the Mallorcans against Genoese ships; a merchant of Tortosa, Jaume Roig, conceded his share of the royal *sisa* of Genoese property to the Jew Bonissach Dax in February 1247.[109] A document of April 1247, concerning a legal claim by Ser Doto the Florentine, and the appointment of two Pisans as procurators, suggests that links between Mallorca and Tuscany were much alive, for the law suit concerned ownership of a boat, and Ser Doto was

[103] Santamaría, *Ejecutoria*, 595–6, no. 11, citing Prot. 342 f.84r.
[104] Prot. 342, f.197v3.   [105] See chapter 9.   [106] Prot. 342, f.198v2.
[107] Prot. 343, f.16or; Santamaría, *Ejecutoria*, no. 35.
[108] See chapter 4 for the failure of King James I to guarantee the security of Menorcan shipping outside local waters.
[109] Prot. 343, f.142v6; Santamaría, *Ejecutoria*, no. 29.

evidently a bird of passage.[110] Sicily was already enjoying close links to Mallorca, and arguably it is already possible to see evidence here for the creation of a primitive *ruta de las illas* across the western Mediterranean: in January 1242 Pere de Valencia and Pere de Ripullo were organising the despatch of a ship bound for Sicily;[111] some thought was given to the need to ensure it was properly armed.[112] A few days later, Stefan Sastre sent on board two ounces of gold, for repayment a fortnight after the vessel reached Palermo or wherever it should arrive.[113] The same Stefan Sastre agreed in March 1243 to take a baptised slave named Bernat to Sicily on the ship of Pere de Valencia.[114] Fragmentary though the evidence is, the recurrence of names suggests that Valencian shippers used Mallorca as a stopping-off point on the route to Palermo. Pere de Valencia was not the only shipper looking in that direction: a contract for a hundred *solidi* of Melgueil was drawn up in April 1247, for trade *apud Seciliam*.[115] Ramón Penitensi was to carry a female black slave named Maymona to Sicily in April 1247, and she was to be sold there on behalf of Arnau de Font, who has already been encountered trading in wheat to north Africa, whence, perhaps, the Saracen slave had been obtained; the travelling partner, Bernat Tolsá, hailed from Tortosa.[116] Southern Italy too was on the map, as a recipient of Provençal iron forwarded through Mallorca in April 1247 by Bernat Ferrer, described as a lawyer, and Bernat Boxan.[117]

Well before Roussillon and Mallorca were united under the single Majorcan crown, commercial links between the Balearics and Collioure had been forged; these links speak for wider links, via Perpignan, to the trade routes running across France. On 7 May 1243 Bartomeu de Sipiá and Gerbert Pellicer declared that they had received £33 of Melgueil from Pere de Vallespir, a merchant of Perpignan; this sum was to be invested in goods and sent to Collioure on the ship of a certain Ribe.[118] Ships also arrived in Mallorca from Collioure bound for north Africa, such as a vessel on which a merchant of Tarragona was due to take two barracan cloths to Ceuta on behalf of a certain Guillem de Guarda in October 1241.[119] Merchants of Collioure appeared in Mallorca, for instance Berenguer

[110] Prot. 343, f.165v; Santamaría, *Ejecutoria*, no. 36.
[111] Prot. 342, f.149v1.
[112] Prot. 342, f.138r4.
[113] Prot. 342, f.151r1.
[114] Prot. 343, f.144r; Santamaría, *Ejecutoria*, no. 14.
[115] Prot. 343, f.159v5.
[116] Prot. 343, f.159r; Santamaría, *Ejecutoria*, no. 33.
[117] Prot. 343, f.159v6; Santamaría, *Ejecutoria*, no. 34.
[118] Prot. 342, f.202v3; Santamaría, *Ejecutoria*, no. 16.
[119] Prot. 342, f.123v3.

of Collioure, who was bound for *Yspania* aboard the *Sanctus Johannes* in January 1242, and who seems to have had an interest in the cloths of Lleida.[120] Links with Montpellier have already been mentioned; here too was a way into continental European markets, and there was an export trade in what may well be Mallorcan luxury foodstuffs towards this Aragonese base in Languedoc. On 18 August 1240 Arnau de Fluxà sent two hundred quintals of figs on the barque of the Catalan Jazbert de San Feliu; the document implies a series of such journeys may be about to be undertaken.[121]

Paradoxically, the relative lack of evidence in the commercial contracts for trade between Mallorca and Barcelona is perhaps the best sign such trade existed on a very intensive scale. Arguably, it was the riskier, less frequent voyages to Muslim territory that needed the extra security of a permanent written record, by contrast with regular cabotage in small barques of which a few reflections exist in the charters of Barcelona cathedral. Similarly, in the Genoese collections of commercial acts, material on local trade along the coast of Liguria, and even to Provence, is rather sparse; yet the number of boats passing along these routes certainly far surpassed the number of ships bound for Alexandria or Acre. Even so, there are references to voyages to Barcelona in the Mallorcan acts: having returned from a trip to Bône the year before, Guillem Mir was on his way there in late March, 1242;[122] and Guillem de Puig was involved in a business deal worth £23 10s od of Melgueil with a partner who was setting out for Barcelona around the start of June 1242.[123] A trip 'in Cataloniam' and back to Mallorca is mentioned in March 1247.[124] In September 1242 Berenguer de Maressa received two Saracen male slaves and one female slave from Barcelona.[125]

One problem that cries out for attention is how far the merchant community of Ciutat de Mallorca was dominated by a patriciate of Catalan or Occitan merchants who carried with them to the island their wealth and status; and how far, by contrast, Mallorca proved the making of merchants of middling condition, who in the new, opportunistic environment of a settler society were able to create a fortune and gain power and influence in the community. The documentation examined here, and later in this book, suggests that

---

[120] Prot. 342, f.140r3.
[121] Santamaría, *Ejecutoria*, 588–9, no. 6: 200 quintals of figs bound for Montpellier.
[122] Prot. 342, f.93r3; cf. his earlier trip mentioned in Prot. 342, f.73v4.
[123] Prot. 342, f.78r1. [124] Prot. 343, f.151r2. [125] Prot. 342, f.102r2.

few tremendously powerful merchant families emerged, and that those who appear in the notarial acts and in the government records are run-of-the-mill businessmen who do not compare in influence to the Banyeres and other merchant élites of Barcelona. This is, admittedly, an argument from silence; or rather, it is an argument from names such as Roig, de Rosis and Renart which at best suggest an ancestry on the Catalan mainland (as in the second case), and at worst are vague epithets that make the individual hard to place socially. It really does seem that Mallorca was a land of opportunity for merchants; equally, those of grander station who settled on the island, such as the Llulls, patrician merchants of Barcelona, actually became landed gentry and courtiers, working alongside the Roussil-lonnais nobility and Occitan lawyers who frequented the royal court at Perpignan. It seems therefore that for some success was marked by the abandonment of trade for more gentlemanly pursuits. To say that powerful merchant élites are hard to identify is not, however, to say that Mallorca City was an irredeemably 'bourgeois' place. The special character of the city as a large centre of trade in a smallish island, about half of whose population lived in the capital, created social relationships quite different to those of, say, Perpignan and Montpellier, not to mention Barcelona.

The commercial documentation from Mallorca thus makes abundantly plain the effective, enthusiastic response of the Catalans, notably the new settlers, to the invasion of the island. It has been seen that the monarchy drew little direct income from the Balearics, entrusting their care to Pedro of Portugal, and exempting large groups of merchants from the main burden of commercial taxation. Perhaps, indeed, this *laissez-faire* attitude stimulated trade more than a policy of protectionism might have done. It was in the era of the autonomous rulers that government intervention in trade became more significant; and this is not surprising, given the need of the Majorcan kings to find an adequate income for themselves out of the resources of their motley lands.

CHAPTER 7

Commerce in the age of the Vespers

I

The creation of the autonomous kingdom of Majorca strengthened several of the links so far examined; but it weakened others. In the early days of the independent kingdom, trade with Barcelona continued unimpeded. Thus in 1280 Maria, widow of the successful Barcelonese entrepreneur Pere de Malla, sent from Barcelona to Mallorca ten jars of oil, as well as fustians of various colours and silk, on the ship of Pons Calafat of Mallorca, expecting wax, a major African export, to be sent from the island in return.[1] A century or so later, Mallorca functioned as a clearing-house for African wax. However, the War of the Vespers resulted in a distortion of the Balearic trade routes, since the alignment of the king of Majorca with France and the papacy made direct contact with Catalonia and Valencia dangerous; James II of Majorca was, indeed, to lose the Balearics as a result of his links to France, between 1285 and 1298. The effects of the crisis are visible already in a series of licences to leave the port of Ciutat de Mallorca dating from the winter of 1284.[2] The Majorcan government insisted that each native merchant and sailor departing from the island should register his movements and promise to return by early summer; the growing conflict between France and Aragon brought the threat of an Aragonese invasion of the Balearics, as in fact occurred in 1285. According to Charles-

---

[1] *Comandas*, no. 43; Abulafia, 'Catalan merchants', 220–1.
[2] These licences have been published by A. Riera, 'La Llicència per a barques de 1284. Una font important per a l'estudi del commerç exterior mallorquí del darrer quart del segle XIII', *Faventia*, 2 (1980), 53–73; published also in *Fontes Rerum Balearium*, 3 (1979–80) 121–40. Original text: ARM, RP 1105/1, Libro de licencias para barcas. In these notes, the first page number indicates the introduction to the edition in *Faventia*, the second that in the *Fontes*. References to individual licences are expressed by simply using the number of the licence in the Riera edition.

Emmanuel Dufourcq, such documentation as the 1284 licences makes it possible to establish the general characteristics of movement through the port of Mallorca City. He said of these licences:

On peut donc affirmer que même en plein hiver il y a en moyenne un départ tous les deux jours, et parfois un départ quotidien, de Majorque vers la Berbérie; et ce trafic avec les ports maghribins représente les deux tiers du trafic majorquin total. Rien permet de penser que l'année 1284 est exceptionnelle.[3]

Elsewhere he repeated and amplified this observation:

On est ainsi en présence d'une réalité essentielle de la vie méditerranéenne d'alors: même en plein hiver, il arrivait que deux ou trois petits navires majorquins partissent en une semaine vers les rivages abdalouadides; malgré les tempêtes, la course, la Guerre Sainte, les conflits, les Catalans avaient toujours l'ardent désir d'aller en Afrique: ils s'y enrichissaient.[4]

However, what makes this analysis more questionable is the difficulty in knowing whether the years around 1284 were indeed typical ones for trade through Mallorca. In fact, as has been seen, they were a troubled period for the Majorcan kingdom. The policies of James II of Majorca, so intimately tied to French interests, or rather to the doubtful possibility that the French might give their support to a Majorcan state independent of Aragonese interference, led the Majorcan government to control the movements of the kingdom's premier port; there were two good reasons for this. First of all, Mallorca needed to be defended by a home fleet against the real menace of a Catalan invasion led by King Peter, who was furious at the 'treason' of his younger brother; and the validity of such fears was amply demonstrated by the Catalan takeover of Mallorca in 1285. In the second place, the break with Catalonia meant that the provision of foodstuffs to Mallorca was at risk, for Peter's newly acquired Sicilian kingdom was an important supplier of grain to Mallorca.

Marcel Durliat and Antoni Riera have emphasised the special conditions under which Mallorcan trade had to be conducted during the Vespers crisis.[5] According to Riera, 'la redacció de la *Llicència* té lloc, efectivament, durant un hivern bastant especial', 'the issue of the licences occurred, to all intents, in a special winter'. The

---

[3] Dufourcq, *Espagne Catalane*, 68.   [4] Dufourcq, *Espagne Catalane*, 320.
[5] Durliat, *Art*, 29–30; Riera, 'Llicència', 58–9/125.

fundamental problem was that of the lack of cereals in the western Mediterranean; but the presence of warring Genoese and Pisan fleets in the same waters added to the chaos of the War of the Vespers; international trade was made difficult until Genoa settled its claim to primacy at the battle of Meloria. Merchant fleets, caught between two major conflicts, risked either the closure of traditional trade routes or the seizure of their vessels. Important too was the seizure of Jerba and Kerkennah by Roger de Lauria the same year, for the African islands provided good lookout posts on the edge of the Sicilian Channel. In Genoa, 1282 saw a ban on the departure of home vessels, according to the *Annales Ianuenses*; the Catalans of Barcelona were placed under comparable restrictions that year and the next.[6]

It is striking that only a single manual of *Llicències per a barques* exists in the *Arxiu del Regne de Mallorca* at Palma. Given the well-preserved nature of this archive, the explanation of the uniqueness of the licences may not lie with the accidental survival of one out of many now lost manuals of the same sort. More likely, as Riera points out, is the explanation that there never did exist other such collections of licences; these are special documents which were drawn up to meet the critical situation of 1284. Thus the preponderance of voyages towards the Maghrib would reflect the danger of landing in the territories controlled by King Peter, not merely in Catalonia and Valencia but in Sicily. In addition, the lack of involvement in trade beyond Seville would reflect the terms of Majorcan ordinances requiring Mallorcan sailors not to absent themselves from the island for more than a few weeks at a time.[7] On the other hand, trade with Flanders, England, Egypt, the Holy Land was not normally conducted during the winter anyway, and it is only for the winter months that the record survives.[8] Thus it is quite possible that in this respect the licences give a reliable picture, typical of the late thirteenth-century Mediterranean, and that at this season the Mallorcans simply would not have tried to navigate to the eastern Mediterranean or the North Sea (the latter route was in any case very new, and almost certainly involved only a small number of ships a year). It is true that the Mallorcans were adept at navigation during the winter months, as has been made plain from the analysis

---

[6] *Annales Ianuenses* of Jacopo Doria in *Annali Genovesi di Caffaro e de'suoi Continuatori*, ed. L. T. Belgrano and C. Imperiale di Sant'Angelo (Fonti per la Storia d'Italia, Roma, 1890–1929), vol. v, 25.   [7] Riera, 'Llicència', 59–60/126.   [8] See chapter 10.

of the contracts of the 1240s;[9] but the prime task in winter was to be able to sail out of sight of land in the western Mediterranean, so as to link the Balearic islands with Catalonia and north Africa; the opportunity to breach the Straits of Gibraltar was, as will be seen, a bonus provided by technological improvements.

The issue of how representative the licences are thus needs careful consideration; but there are in fact two issues: whether the document was unique even in late-thirteenth-century Mallorca, and whether the information it conveys about Mallorcan trade routes is typical of the period. The licences of 1284 date from the period 23 January to 18 March. The manual contains a brief introduction in which the royal lieutenant on Mallorca, Pons de Guardia, advises the Mallorcans that he has received royal letters forbidding the island's sailors to absent themselves without obtaining a special licence, and without providing a guarantee *per idoneas cauciones* that they will return to Mallorca before the end of April. This in itself makes plain the unique character of the document, reflecting the political conditions of 1284.

It is important, however, to realise that the title the document carries in the Palma archive, 'licences for boats', is inexact. In fact, what the document contains is licences for merchants, sailors, shipowners who wished to leave the island, apparently for trade overseas. These are licences for people, not for ships. An example will prove the point:

Item Pascalinus de Nervis, civis Maioricarum, habuit licenciam eundi apud Eivissam cum barca sua; et promisit redivisse ad terram Maioricarum per totum mensem aprilis proxime venturum. Et dedit fideiussorem Oberto Pelos, qui obligavit et cetera (xvi kal. mar.)[10]

Obviously, too, the time span of the licences does not permit an all-year analysis of Mallorcan trade. Only the month of February is represented in its entirety. On the other hand, the question of winter navigation is one of special interest, since the traditional consensus has been guided by Braudel's assumption that the winter saw little maritime movement even in the sixteenth century. The *ancoratge* documents of the fourteenth century indicate that winter traffic through Mallorca was always intense. Durliat and Pons remark in their study of the *ancoratge* records that 'el màxim d'activitat tant pot coincidir amb l'estiu, per exemple en 1324, com amb el desembre i gener, com és el cas per a 1332 i 1340'. (It should be noted that these

---

[9] See chapter 6; also Dufourcq, *Espagne catalane*, 45–6.   [10] Licence no. 38.

authors follow the practice of the registers, and include the period from 1 January to 24 March as part of the old year; thus for 1332 and 1340 one should read 1333 and 1341.) It seems, however, that February was generally a quieter time of the year; they counted 17 movements towards Mallorca in February 1321/2, 24 in February 1324/5, 20 in February 1331/2, 26 in February 1332/3, 27 in February 1340/1. By contrast, the maximum and minimum arrivals, by month, in the *ancoratge* lists are: for 1321/2, 34 arrivals in September 1321 and 9 in March 1322; in 1324/5, 49 arrivals in August 1324 and 20 in November 1324; in 1331/2, 42 arrivals in May 1331 and 20 in February 1332; in 1332/3, 48 arrivals in December 1332 and only three in September 1332 (this year was evidently atypical); in 1340/1, 48 arrivals in January 1341 and 25 in April 1340.

At first sight, the licences of 1284 indicate that departures from Mallorca were much more spasmodic than the arrivals known from the *ancoratge* registers. However, the licences only concern the departure of Mallorcans, or at any rate of Genoese domiciled in the Balearics; the only references to Catalan or Italian ships arise when they are to carry Mallorcan sailors or merchants on board. A reflection of this reality can be seen in the mention among the licences of a ship's patron called En Renart de Barchinona, who is bound for Bougie and Djidjelli in January 1284;[11] it is possible too that En Bargayó or Guillielmus Bargayoni, who is travelling in February to Ibiza and Tortosa is a Catalan of Barcelona.[12] The presence of Genoese patrons and vessels is analysed shortly.

Since the exact date of departure of vessels is not mentioned in the licences, it is necessary to use the last reference to a specific boat to establish an approximate departure, which is no more than a *terminus post quem*. This is not unduly risky, since in several cases it is evident that a boat left soon after the last licence; some sailors reappear after their return from what are obviously brief hops across to Africa or Europe.[13] In this way it is possible to chart the chronological sequence of departures from Mallorca between 23 January and 18 March (or a few days thereafter): see Table 7.1.

During February it is possible to observe twenty-five departures, which is a striking figure, given that the arrivals mentioned in the *ancoratge* registers surpass this only in February 1341. Four ships that

[11] Licence no. 9.   [12] Licence nos. 22, 26.   [13] Licence nos. 11–14, 28, 33–5.

Table 7.1 *Departures from Mallorca, winter 1284*

Week 1 (23–29 Jan.)	13 ships
Week 2 (30 Jan.–5 Feb.)	2 ships
Week 3 (6–12 Feb.)	4 ships
Week 4 (13–19 Feb.)	5 ships
Week 5 (20–26 Feb.)	14 ships
Week 6 (27 Feb.–4 March)	0 ships
Week 7 (5–11 March)	1 ship
Week 8 (12–18 March)	3 ships
Total	42 ships

apparently left in February 1284 possessed a shipowner or captain from Genoa, and one barque was the property of En Bargayó; the others were the property of citizens of Mallorca. To these figures must be added the invisible Genoese, Pisan, Provençal and indeed Venetian ships that did not carry Mallorcans out of the island, or carried Mallorcans who wished to avoid the trouble of obtaining a licence (which no doubt cost money); even on the eve of Meloria the Genoese at least were evidently not averse to voyages to the Balearics and Seville.

It is likely, in fact, that it was precisely because the prospects for trade in 1284 looked rather grim that activity was relatively intense during the winter, before the great fleets could manoeuvre into their war positions. There has, however, been a tendency to argue that the ships used in winter 1284 were all quite small. It is possible to identify twenty-four *ligna*, or *lenys*, and only six *barce*, that is, barques specialising in trade in the waters around the Balearics (despite the fact that the document bears the title 'Llicències per a barques'). The idea that the Mallorcan vessels tended to be quite small is based on references to very small crews aboard these boats.[14] The first licence is a good example. Guillem Godafre, *civis Maioricarum*, wants to go to Ténès with four men of Mallorca, Pere Bostans, Berenguer Seva, Romeu de Saragossa and Guillem Seguini, *marinarii dicti ligni*; the licence is granted on 23 January.[15] Pere Reya, who is himself bound for Djidjelli, presents himself as *fideiussor*.[16] Dufourcq concludes from this that 'on appelle *leny* même de très petits bateaux, qui n'ont que

---

[14] Dufourcq, *Espagne catalane*, 38, 320; Batlle, Busqueta and Cuadrada, 'Notes sobre l'eix comercial Barcelona–Mallorca–Barbaria, a la segona meitat del s. XIII', 37–8.
[15] Licence no. 1.   [16] Licence no. 2 for the voyage to *Giger*.

quatre ou cinq matelots, tandis qu'on donne le nom de *barca* à des embarcations plus importantes, dont l'équipage est formé par une dizaine ou une quinzaine d'hommes, voire plus encore'.[17] This is an unsafe assumption; the number of Mallorcan sailors given in the licences is in no way an indication of the total number of sailors aboard. Crews aboard *ligna* were certainly larger than many licences suggest; a look at the *ancoratge* records reveals that a good many vessels arriving in port had mixed crews.[18] On these boats particularly evasion of the requirement to obtain licences may have been rife.

Besides, the *ancoratge* registers are dominated by *lenys* to such a degree that it has to be concluded that the word *leny* was employed in a very general sense, meaning no more than 'a small or medium sized boat'. On this question it is necessary to agree with Jal that a *leny* is 'un navire, en général';[19] the point is confirmed in the analysis by Dufourcq of a treaty between the king of Majorca and a north African ruler in which there are to be found references to a *lignum magnum vel parvum*.[20] There is no reason to doubt that the *leny*, like the barque, was never very large, and that its main use for the Catalans was on the short trajectory from Mallorca to Spain or the Maghrib; but it would be unsafe to conclude that *lenys* were necessarily small, or that they were all the same type of ship.

Nearly all the departures of *barce* are for Spanish ports, and the *barca* was certainly the regular medium for establishing close links with the lands of the Crown of Aragon nearest to Mallorca.[21] The only barque bound for north Africa is that of Bernardus de Rosis, heading for Alcol (Collo) and Djidjelli.[22] Another licence mentions a voyage aboard a barque as far as Valencia;[23] a *barca armata* leaves in February 1284, but she has returned before 13 March, after a trip to

[17] Dufourcq, *Espagne catalane*, 38.
[18] E.g. ARM, RP 1102, *ancoratge* of 1330, f.11v: *Bn. de Tores de Cocliure entra xviij yorns dagost. Galea. Ay v setzenes domens de mayorca*. The next entry concerns a *barca* containing five-eighths *omens de mayorca*. ARM, RP 1097 (*ancoratge* of 1321/2), f.29v (September 1321), no. 4: Mateu Alseyo *ay la meytat domens de Maylorca* in his *coca*; f.30r (September 1321), no 1: En Bernat Sifre pays 2s *per la parte qu'an omens de Barzelona el seu ley*.
[19] A. Jal, *Glossaire nautique* (Paris, 1848), s.v.
[20] Dufourcq, *Espagne catalone*, 38–9; Paris, Bibliothèque Nationale, MS latin 9261, no. 8; Mas Latrie, *Traités de paix*, part 2, 187.
[21] For the terminology used to describe Spanish ships, see R. Eberenz, *Schiffe an den Küsten der Pyrenäenhalbinsel. Ein kulturgeschichtliche Untersuchung zur Schiffstypologie und terminologie der iberoromanischen Sprachen bis 1600* (Europäische Hochschulschriften, Iberoromanische Sprachen und Literaturen, series 24, no. 6, Bern/Frankfurt-am-Main, 1975). There are references to *barce* in the important *lezda* documents of Collioure (1249?), Tortosa (1251), etc.: Eberenz, 36; M. Gual Camarena, *Vocabulario del comercio medieval* (Tarragona, 1968/Barcelona, 1976), 73, 80, 97.   [22] Licence no. 55.   [23] Licence no. 24.

Almería.[24] Three cases are recorded of barques bound for Ibiza, in one case without mention of any other destination,[25] but in the other instances with a further port of call on the Catalonian coast, at Tortosa[26] and Tarragona.[27] In addition, there is the twenty-oared barque (*barca viginti remorum*) of Ramón de Rosis, which leaves for Collioure in March,[28] thus linking the Balearics to the mainland territories of the crown of Majorca, especially with the administrative capital at Perpignan, and to the trans-continental land trade. An inhabitant of Collioure owned the *lignum* in which Guillem Pol and Bernat Sant Joan (Bernardus San Iohan) were leaving for Collo and Bône in late February,[29] and a certain Berengarius Cotliure, described, despite his name, as a Mallorcan, was travelling on the *lignum* of Berenguer Lobet bound at the same time for Brechk.[30]

Larger ships, *naus* or *naves*, of something like 200 tons, were employed for longer voyages, to Italy or out into the Atlantic.[31] It has been argued that many *lenys* and *barques* could not carry a cargo weighing more than ten tons, while the *naus* might displace several times that weight.[32] Two of the three voyages to Seville were made on board *naves*;[33] and one of the shipowners, Berenguarius Mattelli, was a Genoese from Noli (it should also be mentioned that the third voyage to Seville, even though aboard a *leny*, was also the work of a Genoese vessel, with a ship's master from Chiavari).[34] Such visits to Seville are especially interesting because the first indications that the Catalans and the Italians were regularly penetrating beyond the Straits of Gibraltar are traditionally said to date from only a short time before (1277–81).[35] It is likely that historians have failed to distinguish between the grand navigation by galley, or later by cog, that linked Flanders and England to the Mediterranean, and the more modest Atlantic voyages towards south-eastern Spain and Portugal, or to Atlantic Morocco, where Genoese merchants are visible well before 1277.[36] What is certain is that the presence of

[24] Licence nos. 33–5.   [25] Licence no. 38.
[26] Nos. 22, 26; Durliat, *Art*, 30, is wrong when he denies the existence of licences for trade to Catalonia, but what is striking is the total absence of references to Barcelona.
[27] Licence no. 71.   [28] Licence no. 72.   [29] Licence no. 68.
[30] Licence no. 69.
[31] Riera, 'Llicència', 60/127; Eberenz, *Schiffe an den Küsten der Pyrenäenhalbinsel* 223; Gual, *Vocabulario*, 66 (*lezda* of Tamarit, 1243) and 80 (*lezda* of Collioure, 1249?).
[32] Riera, 'Llicència', 60/127.   [33] Licence nos. 43, 57.   [34] Licence no. 32.
[35] See chapter 10.
[36] Batlle, Busqueta and Cuadrada, 'Sobre l'eix', 39, reveal the interest of the Catalans in Safi (Atlantic Morocco) in 1278 and 1282.

Mallorcans at Seville was of fundamental importance in the creation of a series of maritime links tying Italy to the Balearics, the Balearics to Seville, Seville to Bayonne, Bayonne to the English Channel.

It would be unwise to jump to a conclusion about the lack of participation by larger ships in the trade of Mallorca at this period. Riera observes that 'large vessels did not adapt themselves so well to the chronological limits imposed by the licences, since there normally passed a considerable number of days, even weeks, between the announcement of a voyage and the renting out of enough space on board to assure the shippers of the profitability of the venture'.[37] He remarks too on the absence of galleys and *taride* in the licences; as a matter of fact, this is the very decade in which evidence survives for the presence of Mallorcan galleys in London. The registers of *ancoratge* say little about tarides (there are five examples in 1331/2, four in 1332/3).[38] Besides, it is probable that in 1284 the king of Majorca banned the use of home-based galleys in overseas trade; the international crisis demanded the presence of Mallorca's potential war-fleet either off Mallorca or at Collioure.

Naves departed in addition for the classic destinations of Catalan trade in the Maghrib: for Bougie,[39] or for Tunis with the requirement to stop off also at Bougie.[40] A Genoese *navis* was bound for Alcudia at the end of January, and a Mallorcan *navis* was destined for the same place at the end of February.[41] It was for Genoa itself that the *navis* of Guillem Salembe left soon after 26 February.[42] *Lenys* or *ligna* were more worthwhile in trade with middling ports such as Oran,[43] Alcol,[44] even Bône,[45] Honein and 'Togo',[46] Mazagran[47] or Ténès.[48] A voyage to Valencia was made by *leny*, too.[49] All this reflects the wish to obtain large quantities of goods in major ports such as Tunis and Bougie, as against the more modest opportunities offered in towns of secondary importance. Thus the fact that a single vessel was bound for Tunis does not demonstrate the feebleness of ties between

[37] Riera, 'Llicència', 60/127; Batlle, Busqueta and Cuadrada, 37.
[38] Durliat et Pons, 'Recerques sobre et moviment', 355; for tarides, see Eberenz, *Schiffe*, 271 and Gual, *Vocabulario*, 73 (*lezda* of Valencia, 1243). For *lenys*, Eberenz, 213; Gual, 65–6 (*lezda* of Tamarit, 1243) and 73 (*lezda* of Valencia (1243).
[39] Licence nos. 27, 37, 48, 58–60.   [40] Nos. 36, 39–42, 45–6, 49–53, 56, 63.
[41] Licence nos. 3, 5, 67.   [42] Licence nos. 54, 61, 64–5.   [43] Licence nos. 4, 62, 70.
[44] Licence nos. 7, 8, 66, 68.   [45] Licence nos. 7, 8, 11–14.
[46] Licence nos. 10, 15. The identity of *Togo* is problematic. Dufourcq, *Espagne catalane*, 24, 134, 369, believed it was Taount, near Honein and Tlemcen. But Batlle, Busqueta and Cuadrada, 'Sobre l'eix', 39–40, are less certain and speak of Tegon and also (without conviction) of Tetuan.   [47] Licence nos. 18, 74.   [48] Licence no. 1.   [49] Licence no. 47.

Mallorca and Tunis at this time; as has been seen, the cargo of a *nau* could be large enough to surpass that of a flotilla of barques.

Thirty-one out of a total of forty-two voyages were directed towards the Maghrib: in the far west, to Badis, Motzema and Alcudia in Mediterranean Morocco, towns lying west of Melilla; looking the other way, as far as Bône and Tunis. But it was the ports closest to Mallorca that not unnaturally were most favoured by Mallorcan merchants, notably Algiers, Brechk, Tédèllis and Bougie.[50] Among the habitués of African trade there was Guillem Renart, patron of a *leny*, who visited Brechk in late January and Oran at the end of February.[51] One shipowner, Jaume Mercader, set out in his *leny* twice for the same destination (Mazagran) within the period of the surviving licences, first towards the end of January, and then in the second half of March.[52] No doubt Jaume Mercader made the Mallorca–Maghrib crossing several times a year. Between the two voyages there are some revealing variations. The number and identity of the sailors changes somewhat: there were two sailors who participated in both voyages, named Pere Guasc and Pere Oliver, but Domingo Ninet was replaced by Enrico Ninet (possibly his brother) and the *magister axie* Michel was replaced by the carpenter Bernat, with the same duties. The licences record seven names the first time but only five the second, suggesting that some significance has to be attached to the words *qui sunt de Mayoricis* in licence no. 18, and to the words *vadunt cum eo isti homines Mayoricarum* in licence no. 74. An additional non-Mallorcan element in the crew, about which the documents remain silent, can thus be postulated; this might just as well include Muslims as Christians. As has been seen, the *ancoratge* records attest to the existence of mixed crews, for example half Barcelonese and half Mallorcan.

Noteworthy too is the lack of absolution from their obligations following the return of Jaume Mercader, Pere Guasc and Pere Oliver. Sometimes the shipowners or sailors obtained such an absolution, presumably because their guarantor or *fideiussor* wished to be quit of further liability. Thus Beneto de Levanco returned to Mallorca before 13 March, having left for Algiers on 11 February or a little after;[53] Michel de Castelnou returned from Almería aboard his *barca armata* before 5 March, having left Mallorca not earlier than

---

[50] Dufourcq, *Espagne catalane*, 320, speaks of 45 departures; but it is necessary sometimes to consolidate groups of licences which appear to refer to the same departure.
[51] Licence nos. 21, 70.   [52] Licence nos. 18, 74.   [53] Licence no. 28.

13 February;[54] Bernat Bertrandi travelled to Bône and Honein at the end of January, but he was again in Mallorca on 2 March.[55] Ramón Vay left not before 28 January for Bougie and Collo or Alcol, returning to Mallorca during February;[56] he left again, this time for Collioure, in the second half of March, and there is no sign of his absolution after his visit to Collioure.[57]

Once again, it is a daunting task to place the shipowners mentioned in the documentation in the social fabric of thirteenth-century Mallorca. The impression remains of a large number of small enterprises; the predominance, too, of relatively small boats (even allowing for flexibility in the meaning of the term *leny*) suggests that the licences are not evidence for the existence of a medieval Mallorcan version of Onassis or Ellerman. This argument is further underlined by the evidence from the *ancoratge* records of the early fourteenth century, where a multiplicity of small shipowners appears. The Mediterranean did see, in this period, Catalan shipping entrepreneurs of some distinction, such as Mateu Oliverdar, well known from the Sicilian sources; but generally even the names that appear in the records as shipowners hide a multiplicity of shareholders whose names it is often impossible to recover.

A notable aspect of the licences is the presence of several Genoese, shipowners and sailors, to the exclusion of other Italians.[58] In one licence, Joan Darassa announces that he is leaving for Algiers; aboard his vessel is a crew that includes *Examenus ianuensis et Girorfus ianuensis*.[59] Those Genoese who were not resident on Mallorca did not have to register their absence from the island, but they do appear in the manual of licences in another guise: as shipowners who provided space on board for sailors or merchants of Mallorca. These shipowners acquired licences not for themselves, but for the use of their employees. Nicholas Matalaf of Mallorca was going to Africa, to Alcudia, in the ship of Brexo Çeba of Genoa,[60] and this was also the case for Andriol de Bolasco and Manuel de Rapallo, two sailors, one of whom has a self-evidently Ligurian name.[61] Their *fideiussor* was himself Genoese, Lanfranco Zeba or Çeba, and in fact there are quite a few Genoese *fideiussores* in the licences. Indeed, the co-operation between Catalans of Mallorca and Genoese on the sea routes out of Mallorca is an impressive feature of the licences. The origins of this

---

[54] Licence nos 33–5.   [55] Licence nos. 11–14.   [56] Licence no. 16.
[57] Licence no. 72.   [58] G. Jehel, 'La place de Majorque', 103–4.
[59] Licence no. 6.   [60] Licence no. 5.   [61] Licence no. 3.

collaboration can be traced to the relationship between the Genoese
colony and the Catalan conquerors after 1229, when the Genoese had
been obliged to accept the new political régime in order to safeguard
their basic trading interests. The confirmation of Genoese rights after
the conquest of Mallorca had two results: the creation of a strong
Genoese colony within Catalan Mallorca, and the intensive use of
Mallorca as a way-station to Africa and the Levant by Genoa-based
Genoese. The relationship was strengthened by the creation of
Genoese consuls in Mallorca, with primary interest in civil rather
than criminal cases. Interestingly, 1282 saw a further agreement
between Genoa and the ruler of Mallorca, this time for the creation
of a consulate in Ibiza. Whether it ever really began to function is
unclear.[62] There were benefits too for Mallorcans. In the licences
there appears a Mallorcan whose precise origins are unclear, but who
is bound for Genoa; he is the owner of a *navis*.[63] A parallel indication
of the presence of the Genoese on the island is furnished by the text of
the debate of 1286 between the Genoese Ingheto Gontardo or
Contardo and several Mallorcan Jews on the relative merits of
Judaism and Christianity; the first debate began in the *loggia* of the
Genoese in Ciutat de Mallorca.[64]

The central problem in analysing this material is not that of
deciding whether the licences portray a typical image of Mallorcan
trade in the era of the *regne privatiu*. That the circumstances of 1284
differed from those of 1298–9 (when there is plenty of evidence for
Mallorcan merchants in Palermo and even at Erice and Trapani) is
clear; the War of the Vespers was almost over by then, and trade with
Sicily, on which the licences are mute, could be re-established.[65] The
registers of *ancoratge* say little about the origins of the ships that
arrived in Mallorca during the first half of the fourteenth century; it
is more than likely, nevertheless, that north Africa retained its prime
position, the more so in view of the existence of a series of Mallorcan
warehouses or fonduks along the coast of the Maghrib, beginning
with that at Bougie in 1302. Moreover, Mallorcan influence in the
Abdalwahidid state of Tlemcen was at a peak in the 1330s, after

---

[62] *Liber iurium reipublicae Genuensis*, col. 938, no. 716; Pitzorno, 'Il consolato veneziano di
   Maiorca', 17n.   [63] Licence nos. 54, 61, 64–5.
[64] Ora Limor, *Vikuah Mayurqa* (2 vols., Jerusalem, 1985), vol. II, 1: 'Contigit autem quod
   quidam Iudeus qui publice vocabatur rabi, qui et ipse erat magister Iudeorum, venisset ad
   logiam Ianuensium... Cui per aliquas Ianuenses responsum fuit: "O rabi, tu venis huc et
   loqueris de lege tua, quia vides quod Ingetus non est hic".'
[65] See later in this chapter for discussion of the Sicilian evidence (pp. 144–9).

decades of frustrated diplomatic endeavours complicated by the rivalry of Aragon–Catalonia and Majorca.[66]

The foundation of consulates is, in fact, an important sign that the kings of Mallorca were seeking to establish an autonomous trading network independently of Barcelona. The framework would be provided by the political links between the Balearic islands and the continental lands of the crown of Majorca, Roussillon, Cerdagne, Conflent and Montpellier. The attempts to impose *lezde* on the Catalan merchants who were subject to the king of Aragon failed;[67] and the most durable result of this economic policy was the foundation of new towns in Mallorca, Menorca and the Pyrenees. Of this more shortly. But when Mallorca was caught up in international conflict, or when its rulers sought to erect tariff barriers, the result was much the same: Mallorca found itself forced to depend even more heavily on its African trade, which it could use to obtain wool, leather, gold and even grain. In the twelfth century Muslim Mallorca had found its wealth in African trade, and the island had functioned to all intents as an offshore extension of Africa. This rôle was not abandoned after the Catalan conquest, still less after the creation of a separate Majorcan kingdom. It was because Mallorca was on the edge of Africa, but safely Christian too, that it attracted so many Italians as settlers and by-passers. Even the passage of ships via Mallorca to the Atlantic did not lead to a shift away from African preoccupations, for much of the Mallorcan traffic aimed at the Atlantic was directed to Atlantic Morocco, not to England or Flanders. A second conclusion is that the Mallorcans were able to maintain an intense trade out of the island aboard their own ships, with back-up, certainly, from the Genoese. The impressive fact is that in 1284 the level of Mallorcan and Genoese departures compared well with that of Mallorcan, Italian and Basque ships attested in the *ancoratge* records dating from the so-called golden age of Mallorcan commerce half a century later (see Table 7.2).

II

Some trading destinations, notably Sicily, which became important at the end of the century, are not listed in the licences of 1284; Mallorcan penetration of Sicily is well documented in the surviving Sicilian trade contracts of 1298–9, and it is not hard to see why: the

---

[66] Dufourcq, *Espagne catalane*, 419–87.   [67] See chapter 8.

Table 7.2 Destinations and shipowners in the licences of 1284

Licence number	Destination	Date	Owner	Type of boat
	North Africa			
3, 5	Alcudia	23–4 Jan.	Brexo Çeba G	*navis*
67	Alcudia	26 Feb.	Petrus Andree	*navis*
17,20	Alcudia/Motzema	28 Jan., 4 Feb.	Agost Ferrarii	*lignum*
6	Algiers	24 Jan.	Ioh. Darassa	*lignum*
23, 25, 29	Algiers	8, 9, 13 Feb.	Domènec Tayada	*lignum*
28	Algiers	11 Feb.	Beneto de Levanco	*lignum*
33–5	Almería	13 Feb.	Michel de Castelnou	*barca armata*
11–14	Bône/Honein	26 Jan.	Bertrandus Bertrandi	*lignum*
21	Brechk	27 Jan.	Guill. Renart	*lignum*
69	Brechk	11 Feb.	Bereng. Lobet	*lignum*
27	Bougie	11 Feb.	Bern. Poncii	*navis*
37, 48	Bougie	25 Feb.	Nicoloz Matalaf	*navis*
58–60	Bougie	26 Feb.	Nicolosus Pontixello G	*navis*
16	Bougie/Collo	28 Jan.	Guill. Balafia/Petrus Cortey	*lignum*
9	Bougie/Djidjelli	25 Jan.	En Renart de Barchinona	*lignum*
66	Collo	26 Feb.	Petrus Isarn	*lignum*
68	Collo/Bône	26 Feb.	Ioh. Calmila de Collioure	*lignum*
7, 8	Collo/Bône/Motzema/Badis	24–5 Jan.	Guill. des Puyol	*lignum*
55	Collo/Djidjelli	26 Feb.	Bern. de Rosis	*barca*
4	Oran	24 Jan.	Lorandus Scorba G	*lignum*
62	Oran	26 Feb.	Simon Corney	*lignum*
70	Oran	26 Feb.	Guil. Renart	*lignum*

2	Djidjelli	Petrus Reya	23 Jan.	*lignum*
10	Honein/Touant or Tegon	Peironus de parrochia S. Crucis	25 Jan.	*lignum*
15	Honein/Touant or Tegon	Petrus Riboti (?)	26 Jan.	?
18	Mazagran	Iac. Mercader	28 Jan.	*lignum*
74	Mazagran	Iac. Mercader	18 March	*lignum*
19	Tédellis	Bern. de Pertogas	4 Feb.	*lignum*
73	Tédellis	Nicolosus de Rapallo G	18 March	*navis*
1	Ténès	Guill. Godafre	23 Jan.	*lignum*
36, 39–42, 45–6, 49–53, 56, 63	Tunis/Bougie	Petrus Ebri	26 Feb.	*navis*
	Crown of Majorca			
72	Collioure	Raim. de Rosis	18 March	*barca* xx *remorum*
22, 26	Ibiza/Tortosa	En Bargayó (G. Bargayoni)	8, 11 Feb.	*barca*
38	Ibiza	Pascalinus de Nervis	Feb.	*barca*
71	Ibiza/Tarragona	Guill. Peyro	11 Mar.	*barca*
	Other Destinations			
54, 61, 64–5	Genoa	Guill. Salembe	26 Feb.	*navis*
24	Valencia	Bern. Caner	9 Feb.	*barca*
47	Valencia	En Sabatero	25 Feb.	*lignum*
32	Seville	Petrus Bo de Xavari G	13 Feb.	*lignum*
43	Seville	Anticus Salavert	22 Feb.	*navis*
57	Seville	Bereng. Mattelli de Noli G	26 Feb.	*navis*
30–1	Unknown port	Guill. Bola de Noli G	13 Feb.	*lignum*

Note: G = Genoese shipowner

re-establishment of the Majorcan kingdom under papal pressure in 1298 was an important step towards the pacification of the western Mediterranean, and Mallorca's own merchants were able to respond by building up trade in the latest Aragonese acquisition.[68] Considerable interest was shown in the provision of shipping services: Bernat Miquel of Mallorca rented out his ship the *Santa Maria de Nazaret* to Tuscan merchants who wished to ferry wheat from Sciacca in southern Sicily to Pisa, Genoa or another north-west Italian port.[69] Bernat Perfect of Valencia leased his ship the *Sanctus Vincentius* to a group of Catalans from Barcelona, Mallorca and Trapani, for a voyage from Sicily to Bougie by way of Cagliari.[70] In 1298–9 the Mallorcan shippers had a special importance, for direct trade links between Sicily and Barcelona were to all intents suspended, as a result of the continuing dispute over Frederick III's royal title; this served the advantage of potential intermediaries such as the Mallorcans and the Genoese.[71] After the Treaty of Caltabellotta in 1302 Mallorcan trade in Sicily seems to have intensified, partly because the routes to Barcelona were now open as well: a contract recorded by the Sicilian notary Bartolomeo da Citella in January 1309 reveals the transport of a sizeable quantity of raw cotton, raw wool, pepper, sugar, cinnamon, cowhides, salted meat, sulphur, butter and other items from Palermo and Trapani to Mallorca and Barcelona.[72] Mallorcans were entering into contracts with Tuscans and mainland Catalans, and the wheat trade from Termini Imerese to Genoa and to Africa was partly in their hands.[73] Sicilian cheese was carried out of the island by Mallorcans.[74]

Not every Mallorcan trader found that his affairs in Sicily ran smoothly. The Sicilian notarial acts, especially the second register of the Sicilian notary Adamo de Citella of 1298–9, are rich in

[68] Abulafia, 'Catalan merchants', 229, 235, 236–41.

[69] P. Gulotta, *Le imbreviature del notaio Adamo de Citella a Palermo (2° Registro: 1298–1299)* (Fonti e studi del Corpus membranarum italicarum, ser. 3, Imbreviature matricole statuti e formulari notarili medievali 2, Rome, 1982), no. 201, R. Zeno, *Documenti per la storia del diritto marittimo nei secoli XIII e XIV* (Documenti e studi per la storia del commercio e del diritto commerciale italiana 6, Turin, 1936), no. 45.

[70] *Adamo de Citella*, no. 283; Zeno, *Documenti*, no. 72.

[71] Abulafia, 'Catalan merchants', 233, for some of the dangers.

[72] Zeno, *Documenti*, no. 152.

[73] Zeno, *Documenti*, nos. 153–4, 164; the last document in fact blocks a shipment from Girgenti (Agrigento) to Tripoli in north Africa, but also indicates that Mallorcans wished to use this route. Others, such as the Genoese, meanwhile helped supply Mallorca with Sicilian grain: Zeno, *Documenti*, no. 167.　　　　[74] Zeno, *Documenti*, no. 178.

information about a certain Pere de Gradu or de Grau, who was an associate of the Catalan businessman Francesc de Sant Feliu, from Sant Feliu de Guixols, on the coast near Girona. They did not, however, remain on good terms for very long. The first reference to both these figures appears in the records of the mountain-top city of Erice (Monte San Giuliano), in the register of the notary Giovanni Maiorana, which is now preserved in Trapani.[75] On 12 March 1298 the notary drew up what is an odd document by any standards, the more so by those of Giovanni Maiorana, who was otherwise exclusively concerned with local, land-based activities, such as the agricultural investments of the town's numerous Jews.[76] One would expect maritime business to be transacted before a notary not of Erice but of the neighbouring port of Trapani, where Pere de Grau had colleagues – and enemies too. Perhaps he chose to appear before a notary in an out-of-the-way hilltown precisely because he wanted to avoid his Trapanese contacts. For the very contents of the document Giovanni Maiorana drew up for him indicate trouble. Pere declares that he has appointed his relative Nadal de Virioles (*Natalis de Viriolis*), also of Mallorca, to act as his agent in the recovery of sums he believes are owing to him as a result of a decision to lease his ship the *Sanctus Nicolaus* to Francesc *de Sancto Felicio*. Like so many of the Catalan vessels trading through Sicily, the *Sanctus Nicolaus* was a grain ship, and it had already been agreed that it would sail from Sicily to Tunis, where it would unload its grain; there it would be offered for re-leasing, either for a journey along the coast to Tripoli, or for a journey back to Sicily and then outward for a second time to Tunis or Jerba or Gabes; the idea here was clearly to reload with grain in Sicily, and simply to repeat the ship's original venture, for there were always plenty of mouths to feed in Tunisia.[77] It seems that

[75] *Il registro del notaio ericino Giovanni Maiorana (1297–1300)*, ed. A. Sparti, 2 vols. (Palermo, 1982), 22–4, no. 9; *Il registro notarile di Giovanni Maiorana (1297–1300)*, ed. A. de Stefano (Memorie e documenti di storia siciliana, 2, Documenti 2, Palermo, 1943), 13–16, no. 9.

[76] David Abulafia, 'Una comunità ebraica della Sicilia occidentale: Erice 1298–1304', *Archivio storico per la Sicilia orientale*, 80 (1984), 7–39, repr. in David Abulafia, *Commerce and conquest in the Mediterranean, 1100–1500* (Aldershot, 1993), essay VIII; also published in Hebrew as 'Yehudei Erice (Monte San Giuliano) sheb°Sitsiliah, 1298–1304', *Zion: a quarterly for research in Jewish history*, 51 (1986), 295–317.

[77] The mention of Jerba is especially interesting, in view of the attacks launched there by the Aragonese admiral Roger de Lauria; Jerba itself was captured in 1284, and in 1295 Pope Boniface VIII announced he wished to confer the island on Roger as a papal fief; later, in 1310, Jerba was governed by Ramón Muntaner on behalf of Frederick III of Sicily. See Dufourcq, *Espagne catalane*, 428–33.

in some unspecified way the agreement had broken down: that Francesc de Sant Feliu had failed to complete the terms of the deal and had failed to provide a *finalis et debita ratio*, a settling of accounts.

A year later, in early 1299, Pere de Grau and Francesc de Sant Feliu were both in Palermo, and it is not known how or whether they resolved their difficulties. What is known is that Pere de Grau gained more enemies in Palermo. On 10 February 1299 another merchant started action for the recovery of £34 previously entrusted to Pere de Grau, and not repaid;[78] more serious was a dispute between Pere and a certain Antonio, a Genoese carpenter or shipwright from Trapani.[79] Pere de Grau must have visited Trapani on his way to or from Erice, and his ship the *Sanctus Nicolaus* seems to have been there during 1298. It appears that Antonio, while working on Pere's ship, quarrelled with Pere and later claimed that Pere had grabbed what was either a toolbox or a sea chest that belonged to Antonio. Pere counter-claimed, asserting that Antonio had stolen a *gundula* or small boat, which formed part of the equipment of the *Sanctus Nicolaus*. The case was referred to the Catalan consul in Palermo, who found against Pere de Grau, much to the Mallorcan's displeasure.[80] Pere de Grau then made what proved to be a serious mistake: he invited two prominent Catalans of Palermo, Bernat Miquel (also from Mallorca) and Barsilono Dusay, to act as arbiters in the case; but they simply declared that there were no grounds to set aside the decision of the Catalan consul in Palermo, as the established arbiter of judicial disputes among Catalans in Sicily.[81] Indeed, the consul, Ramón Bordener, was among the witnesses to their decision. But the very next day, 18 February 1299, Pere de Grau appeared once again with the consul in the presence of the notary Adamo de Citella, and stated baldly that he had no intention whatsoever of obeying the consul's sentence in the case, and he actually warned the consul to take no action in the matter; he insisted that 'this consul does not have any jurisdiction over citizens of Mallorca but only over those who are under the dominion of the king of Aragon', that is, the Catalans of

---

[78] *Adamo de Citella*, no. 236; Zeno, *Documenti*, no. 52. But another Mallorcan was not discouraged from providing Pere de Grau with a sea loan for 32 ounces: *Adamo de Citella*, no. 285 and Zeno, *Documenti*, no. 54.

[79] As is indicated by *Adamo de Citella*, no. 251; Zeno, *Documenti*, no. 59; also *Adamo de Citella*, no. 285 and Zeno, *Documenti*, no. 73.

[80] As indicated by *Adamo de Citella*, no. 251; Zeno, *Documenti*, no. 59.

[81] A. de Capmany y de Monpalau, *Memorias sobre la marina, comercio y artes de la antigua ciudad de Barcelona*, ed. with annotations by E. Giralt y Raventos and C. Batlle y Gallart (Barcelona, 1962), vol. II, 62–3, no. 40; *Adamo de Citella*, no. 251; Zeno, *Documenti*, no. 59.

Catalonia and Valencia only.[82] The consul, not surprisingly, formally registered his disagreement.[83]

Pere de Grau had put his finger on an unresolved problem, even if his motive was to ensure that judgment could not be passed against him. The privilege of the Aragonese kings of Sicily to the Catalan merchants, of 1288, had granted the citizens of Barcelona equal status with the Genoese in Sicilian trade; but the privilege said nothing about Valencians, Tortosans, Tarragonese, Mallorcans and other varieties of Catalan who were not citizens of Barcelona.[84] At the time, the wording of the privilege was probably thought to have real advantages: it was universal practice for citizens of the great Mediterranean ports to allow friendly neighbours to travel under their flag and use their rights, and a Valencian in Palermo would simply have declared himself to be a merchant of Barcelona *tout court*.[85] Ten years after the privilege, the position was less simple. The lands of the Crown of Aragon had been divided among three kings, and James I of Sicily, who had issued the grant in favour of Catalans trading in his island, was now James II of Aragon, anxious to divest himself of responsibility for Sicily (now officially exchanged by the pope for rights over Sardinia and Corsica), and anxious also to assert his suzerain authority over his namesake, the recently restored king of Majorca. So in 1299 it was not entirely unrealistic for a Mallorcan merchant, aware of James II of Majorca's wish to claim independence in political and economic affairs, to renounce the authority of the Catalan consul in Palermo. But the problem does not end there. Ramón Bordener claimed rights of jurisdiction over the entire Catalan community, as far as can be seen, except in those criminal cases that remained the preserve of the Sicilian crown. Yet the Catalan consuls were representatives of the king of Aragon; and to that extent Bordener was the agent of an enemy power, against whom the Aragonese king of Sicily, Frederick III, was fighting a war. The Aragonese king of Sicily seems to have solved this problem by ignoring it: although direct trade with Barcelona was rendered

---

[82] *Adamo de Citella*, no. 256; Zeno, *Documenti*, no. 61.
[83] In a note attached to *Adamo de Citella*, no. 256; Zeno, *Documenti*, no. 61.
[84] Capmany, *Memorias*, 65–6, no. 42.
[85] For this phenomenon, see David Abulafia, 'The Levant trade of the minor cities in the thirteenth and fourteenth centuries: strengths and weaknesses', *The medieval Levant. Studies in memory of Eliyahu Ashtor (1914–1984)*, ed. B. Z. Kedar and A. Udovitch, published in Haifa in *Asian and African Studies*, 22 (1988), 183–202, and accompanying studies by me in the second part of *Commerce and conquest*.

impossible in 1298 and 1299 (as the notarial acts from Sicily indicate),
Catalan merchants still came freely to the island, still enjoyed rights
of tax exemption, were still supervised by their own consul.[86] There
is a parallel later in the career of Frederick III, for he welcomed the
Florentine bankers, notably the Peruzzi, to Sicily even while they
gave vigorous financial support to his rival Robert the Wise of
Naples; but he had goods for sale, notably grain, and was not
prepared to turn away good customers who could, in addition, grant
him loans.[87]

Pere de Grau was persuaded in the end that he must compromise
with the shipwright Antonio about the sea chest and *gundula*; and if
the agreement Adamo de Citella records tells the real events, there
was evidently right on both sides.[88] In any case, Pere de Grau seems
to have tired of his work. On 19 February he sold his ship to a
Palermo merchant, probably of Genoese origin.[89] Later he reappears
in the register as a bad debtor, reiterating promises to repay loans by
the due date and yet failing to do so. His Mallorcan colleague Joan
de Sales, to whom he owed thirty-two ounces of gold at one point,
threatened action in the courts against him: on 10 February 1299
Pere issued a declaration that he would, as already promised in
another document drawn up the previous December by a different
notary, repay Joan de Sales thirty-two ounces of gold received by
Pere as a sea loan; the fact that Joan de Sales requested confirmation
that the money was owed is suggestive of Pere's reputation for

---

[86] Not just Mallorcans were involved in disputes about the authority of the Catalan consuls
over subjects of the lesser Aragonese kings. In the years around 1285 there was a Sicilian
warehouse in Tunis under the authority of the Aragonese king of Sicily, and quite distinct
from the Catalan warehouse, but a single consul seems to have controlled both; the origins
of the Sicilian establishment may lie far back in the early twelfth century. A separate Sicilian
consul was re-established later; this figure was to be a Messinese; see G. La Mantia, *Codice
diplomatico dei re aragonesi di Sicilia Pietro I, Giacomo, Federico II, Pietro II e Ludovico, dalla
rivoluzione siciliana del 1282 sino al 1355*, vol. I (*1282–90*) (Palermo, 1917), 168–9, 204–7,
299–306; David Abulafia, 'The merchants of Messina: Levant trade and domestic
economy', *Papers of the British School at Rome*, 54 (1986), 211; Dufourcq, *Espagne catalane*, 274.
For the important dispute over whether the Majorcan king could have his own consuls in
Africa, see the next chapter.
[87] On the Peruzzi in Sicily, see now Edwin S. Hunt, *The medieval super-companies: a study of the
Peruzzi Company of Florence* (Cambridge, 1994), which amply documents their heavy
business in Aragonese Sicily; also F. Lionti, 'Le società dei Bardi, dei Peruzzi e degli
Acciaiuoli in Sicilia', *Archivio storico siciliano*, n.s. 14 (1908); C. Trasselli, 'Nuovi documenti
sui Peruzzi, Bardi e Acciaiuoli in Sicila', *Economia e Storia*, 3 (1956).
[88] *Adamo de Citella*, no. 285; Zeno, *Documenti*, no. 73.
[89] *Adamo de Citella*, no. 259; Zeno, *Documenti*, no. 74. The name *Guercius* was common in Genoa.
Pere de Grau promised to make certain repairs to the structure of the ship: *Adamo de
Citella*, no. 260; Zeno, *Documenti*, no. 75.

unreliability.[90] Pere promised to repay the money within fifteen days, but nineteen ounces twelve *tarí* were still outstanding on 25 March, when Jaume de Odina, agent for Pere de Grau, at last delivered that sum to Joan de Sales and secured the quittance from further obligation recorded by Adamo de Citella.[91] There was also a criminal case pending against Pere, for he was accused of attacking one of his Sicilian sailors while the *Sanctus Nicolaus* was standing in port at Cagliari in Sardinia.[92] The alleged attack must have taken place in 1298, but the plaintiff withdrew his accusation in February 1299, for lack of firm proof.

Thus Pere de Grau emerges from the documents as a very contentious and unpopular figure; even if several accusations against him were mischievous, he evidently had extraordinarily bad relations with his Catalan colleagues. His rejection of Catalan consular authority was not universally shared, as is plain from the collaborative ventures involving 'Catalan Catalans' and Mallorcans, such as the hiring of the *Sanctus Vincentius*, mentioned already, or the business deals of the Catalan consul in Palermo: Ramón Bordener himself entrusted modest sums of Valencian money to two Mallorcan merchants on 4 and 7 April 1299, apparently as investments in their larger trading enterprises.[93] Indeed, the best option for a Catalan in Sicily trading towards Spain was to do a deal either with the Mallorcans or the Italians, since access to the Catalan coast was still difficult. With the re-establishment of the Majorcan kingdom in 1298 conditions began to ease; with the end of the War of the Vespers, in 1302, many of the obstacles to trade in the last twenty years vanished. But there was still a central dilemma: many Catalans of Mallorca saw themselves as part of a wider trading world with focal points in Barcelona, Valencia, Palermo and the Catalan fonduks of north Africa. It was not clear, around 1300, what benefit the restoration of Majorcan rule over the Balearics would bring the island's merchants.

---

[90] *Adamo de Citella*, no. 238; Zeno, *Documenti*, no. 54.
[91] *Adamo de Citella*, no. 305; Zeno, *Documenti*, no. 84. The appointment by Joan de Sales of Jaume de Odina (and also Barsilono Dusay) as his procurator is recorded in *Adamo de Citella*, no. 233, of 9 February, 1299.   [92] *Adamo de Citella*, no. 267.
[93] *Adamo de Citella*, nos. 330 and 342; Zeno, *Documenti*, nos 88–9.

CHAPTER 8

Towards economic integration: the early fourteenth century

The political weakness evinced by the Majorcan monarchy was not matched by economic weakness within the Majorcan territories. The monarchy, if it exploited its tax rights to the full, stood to gain great wealth. There is plentiful evidence for the success of the kings of Majorca in maximising their income; the documents recording the *Reebudes* and *Dades* (receipts and outgoings) of the royal court, have been analysed by Sastre Moll and Santamaría.[1] A cursory glance at the impressive royal building programmes, which resulted in the erection of the Palace of the Kings of Majorca in Perpignan, of a smaller palace in Montpellier, and of a much rebuilt Almudaina Palace in Ciutat de Mallorca, suggests too that money was there to be spent; the kings of Majorca lived in style, and their lack of political clout was in part compensated by an attempt to project an image of themselves as real kings on familiar terms with powerful neighbours such as the Avignon popes and the Angevins of Naples, who were counts of nearby Provence.

The tendency of recent research has been to argue that the rulers of the Majorcan kingdom did initiate imaginative economic policies. There are several areas of activity in which this policy can be identified: town foundations, not merely in the Balearics but on the mainland; the establishment of trade relations with north Africa and elsewhere, without the mediation of Barcelona or the Aragonese court; the creation of Majorcan consulates in overseas ports; the building of a Majorcan commercial fleet; the creation of new coinages; and attempts, by the use of tariff barriers, to favour merchants of the Balearics and of Roussillon, in traffic through the

---

[1] For a description of these sources, see M. Durliat, *L'art dans le royaume de Majorque* (Toulouse, 1962), 360; also Durliat, 39–40 for a preliminary discussion of their content. The tables in Sastre Moll, *Economía y Sociedad* and in Santamaría, *Ejecutoria*, are especially useful.

ports of the kingdom.[2] In this chapter, use is made of archival material from all three major towns in the kingdom of Majorca, Perpignan, Montpellier and what is now known as Palma de Mallorca; particular attention will be paid to the economic ties between the three main centres of the kingdom that these archives reveal. Aspects of the economy of the Majorcan lands that have been dealt with in existing works are discussed more rapidly. The aim here is not to start from the assumption that attempts at integration were made, but to ask the question whether evidence for such attempts can be found, and, if so, how successful they were.

II

Mallorca itself was dominated by Ciutat de Mallorca, the modern city of Palma. Around 1329 its population was at most 25,000, making it rather larger than Perpignan but smaller than Montpellier. Apparently nearly half the island's population lived in Ciutat de Mallorca, with the rest divided fairly evenly between small market towns such as Pollença, Manacor and Inca on the one hand and rural settlements on the other.[3] Mallorca's economy was thus dominated entirely by external trade: trade in order to feed the Mallorcans; trade as a source of profit and employment, all the more so as the island's textile industry expanded in the early fourteenth century. The popes had been right: you could only persuade settlers to come if they could make use of the advantageous position of Mallorca on the trade routes to Africa. As a result, the primary sector of the island's economy remained rather stagnant.[4]

By 1300, however, a master-plan for the kingdom's economy began to emerge. In 1300 James II of Majorca issued ordinances for the foundation of new towns on Mallorca itself.[5] These ordinances were themselves arguably part of a wider scheme that aimed to bond the mainland and island parts of the kingdom more closely together, by reducing dependence on the mercantile network of Barcelona. They coincide with initiatives such as the establishment of a Balearic

[2] See Riera Melis, 'El regne de Mallorca en el context internacional de la primera meitat del segle xiv,' and 'Mallorca 1298–1311, un ejemplo de "planificación económica" en la época de plena expansión'.
[3] These estimates are based on the calculations of Alomar, *Urbanismo regional*, 12.
[4] Riera, *Corona de Aragón*, 35–7.
[5] *Documenta regni Majoricarum (Miscelanea)*, ed. J. Vich y Salom and J. Muntaner y Bujosa (Palma de Mallorca, 1945), 67–74; Alomar, *Urbanismo regional*, 109–113.

coinage;[6] and Majorcan consuls were appointed in rivalry with the Catalan consuls who in earlier years had assumed a brief over all subjects of all Aragonese crowns.[7] Gabriel Alomar's monograph on the ordinances of James II, stresses two motives behind the legislation: the promotion of agriculture on the island, to consist of food, such as grain and oil, but also raw materials for the slowly expanding textile industry; and the resettlement of the plains, which had experienced large-scale desertion after the conquest of the island.[8] Behind all this was the principle that Mallorca could be made if not self-sufficient, at least less reliant on imported grain and raw materials.

Alomar exaggerated the novelty of the ordinances in one respect: many of the new towns pre-existed the ordinances, but there is no doubt that they were greatly expanded and that an optimum size was set in each case. A straightforward square plan was designed, which had to fit around the existing street pattern. In Lluchmayor and Felanitx there was an existing small settlement to be incorporated, but at Sa Pobla nearly all the town was brand new. The model town of Petra provided space for 100 houses; at Sa Pobla this was expanded to 144. Spaces were designated for a church and for a town square. At Felanitx there was provision for a slaughterhouse and for a fish market. Naturally there were promises of tax exemption to settlers.[9] The master-plan was extended also to Menorca, with the foundation of Alayor, in the island's interior.[10]

There are strong parallels between the ordinances of James II and the bastide type town foundations of southern France and the Spanish Levant in the same period. Aigues-Mortes, under vigorous extension around 1300, was also built on a square plan, as was the new part of Carcassonne created by Louis IX. Along the Valencian coast similar new towns were established by James the Conqueror according to similar principles, though of necessity they were strongly fortified. Some of the most striking parallels can be found in the western Pyrenees, where the English rulers of Gascony laid down new settlements such as Baa (named after Bath) which were, not

---

[6] Riera, 'Mallorca 1298–1311', 232–9 (for the *real d'or*) and *passim* provides rich information on this; see also for reactions in Catalonia Riera, *Corona de Aragón*, doc. 28, 293–4; doc. 30, 295.   [7] See the discussion later in this chapter (pp. 159–61).
[8] Alomar, *Urbanismo regional*, 38–44, cf. Soto, *Ordenació de l'espai*.
[9] Alomar, *Urbanismo regional*, 61–72; for Felanitx, see the privilege printed by Alomar, 111–13 and in *Documenta regni Majoricarum*, 71–4.
[10] Alomar, *Urbanismo regional*, 82–3, 86–7.

surprisingly, very similar in character and objectives to those in Roussillon, Conflent and Cerdagne, the eastern Pyrenean lands of the crown of Majorca.[11] Nevertheless, there is a significant difference between small agro-towns such as Felanitx in Mallorca and towns such as Aigues-Mortes or the Valencian settlements, which had important military or naval functions. For James II of Majorca, the central consideration was the role these towns could play in an ambitious scheme to provide his kingdom with autonomy over its economic affairs. What survived in the long term from his economic policy was a Balearic coinage, new towns and a growing textile industry. But once again all attempts to escape the supervision of the king of Aragon seemed doomed to failure.

III

The first signs of serious disagreement between the Majorcan court and that of Aragon arose over the levying of a tax on Barcelona ships passing through Collioure from Catalonia to Aigues-Mortes, Marseilles and Genoa, or vice versa. James II of Aragon wrote to his Majorcan namesake on 25 February 1300 pointing out that there was a usage from time immemorial that was under threat: the custom of exempting such ships of Barcelona from tax had been observed so long that no one could remember when it had been introduced. Similarly, the rights of Catalan merchants bringing goods overland from Montpellier to Collioure, for trans-shipment there, were under threat.[12] In fact, the past history of the *lezda* of Collioure was more complicated than James II of Aragon was suggesting; a *lezda* can be traced back to 1175, and received its more or less definitive form in 1252.[13] But the question remained whether the past exemptions from taxation within the lands of the Crown of Aragon which James I and his successors had conferred on the Barcelonese applied also to ancient *lezde* such as those of Collioure, Cadaqués, Tortosa and so on.[14] Further, there was the vexed question whether the king of Majorca could unilaterally tax the Barcelonese. In fact, the practice

[11] M. G. A. Vale, *The Angevin legacy and the Hundred Years War, 1250–1340* (Oxford, 1990), 152–60.

[12] Riera, *Corona de Aragón*, doc. 8, 277–8. The account offered here is based in the first instance on the 102 documents presented by Riera, *Corona de Aragón*, 271–348.

[13] Riera, *Corona de Aragón*, 157.

[14] Riera, *Corona de Aragón*, 163. For the texts of several *lezde* (including Collioure), see Gual, *Vocabulario*, 73, 80, 97, etc.; ADP, I B 69.

at Collioure to which the letter of James of Aragon alludes was not one sanctioned by official decrees, and perhaps for that reason it had to be described as an age-old custom. There was certainly a tradition among Catalan merchants of paying a *lezda* at Collioure in the mid-thirteenth century.[15] It seems most likely, though, that James II of Majorca resolved to reform the tax system at Collioure only after he had been restored to the full extent of his dominions in June, 1298, for the issue of the *lezda* does not appear among the matters known to have been discussed between the Aragonese and Majorcan courts in previous months.[16]

In fact, as Riera has observed, there were external factors which influenced the Catalans and the Majorcans at this stage: the French were making signal improvements to the port installations at Aigues-Mortes, one result of which was to close off to shipping the *graus* or lagoons which had been one of the regular means of access from Montpellier to the Mediterranean. In future, trade to Montpellier would effectively be channelled through Aigues-Mortes, unless the Barcelonans and the Majorcans could persuade the French king to relent and permit the re-establishment of a route through Vic and Cauquilhouse.[17] Here the Majorcan king had a double interest, since as well as trying to protect Mallorcan sea-trade he needed to defend his rights as immediate lord of most of Montpellier, in the face of the strong French assertion of ultimate suzerainty since 1293.[18] Here again there was a long history of difficulties, since the French had already been trying to impose trade taxes at Aigues-Mortes since 1265.[19] The French saw the use of the *graus* simply as a chance to smuggle goods through to Montpellier without paying the taxes due to the Capetian government, though they also insisted that theirs was by far the most practicable route for normal vessels.[20] The *lezda* at Collioure should thus be seen as an attempt to secure a similar benefit from the passage of the Catalans as was being obtained by the French further down the coast at Aigues-Mortes. Since they would have to pay the French if they traded to Aigues-Mortes, the king of Majorca seems to have believed that he could also make them pay up if they tried to gain access to Montpellier via Collioure, by land or by sea.

---

[15] Riera, *Corona de Aragón*, 163–4.   [16] Riera, *Corona de Aragón*, 165–6.
[17] A. Germain, *Histoire du commerce de Montpellier*, 2 vols. (Montpellier, 1861), vol. 1, 75; Riera, *Corona de Aragón*, 86, 91, 95, 102–16, 166.   [18] Riera, *Corona de Aragón*, 102–3.
[19] Germain, *Commerce de Montpellier*, vol. 1, 326–78, especially 342–3, doc. 64.
[20] Germain, *Commerce de Montpellier*, vol. 1, 367–8, doc. 64.

They were caught in a tax trap, in some cases a double tax trap. Moreover, there was a question of principle here. Riera Melis observes that, by levying the *lezda* at Collioure, James of Majorca was following a similar course to other European monarchs of the time, who saw the creation of well-delineated frontiers defined by customs posts as an integral part of the assertion of royal authority throughout all their lands.[21] The issue of Majorcan autonomy was, in other words, of capital importance in the formulation of this policy. It is possible that tariff barriers of this sort helped stimulate the new financial initiatives in Barcelona around this time which resulted in the creation of an autonomous textile industry and the lessening of dependence on imports of northern cloths through French and Majorcan territory.[22]

By July 1301 King James of Aragon was complaining to the Majorcan king of the confiscation of Barcelonan goods at Collioure, including interference with the grain traffic from Tortosa to Genoa.[23] By December 1301 the atmosphere had darkened considerably; the issue of the tariff at Collioure was overshadowed by far more serious developments, and to all intents disappears from view.[24] The leaders of the Barcelona city council wrote to James II of Aragon advising him that the king of Majorca now intended to impose a tax of three *denarii* in the pound on goods coming into or leaving Mallorca itself. Such a decree would be contrary to the privileges of King James I for free trade in Mallorca, Menorca and Ibiza, as well as being contrary to God and to equity.[25] The answer, in the minds of the citizens of Barcelona, was to announce a boycott of Mallorca; this James of Aragon declared himself reluctant to permit, at least before proper diplomatic initiatives had been made.[26] But the Barcelona merchant leaders were convinced that it would be for the honour and advantage of the king of Aragon if indeed they banned the city's traders from

[21] Riera, *Corona de Aragón*, 172: James 'se alinea con las principales Monarquías occidentales en favor de un poder político burocrático e intervencionista, que ampía continuamente su área de competencia y procura hacer sentir su influencia en todos los límites geográficos de los mismos en auténticas fronteras, dotadas del corrispondiente aparato aduanero'.

[22] Another issue here was the Aragonese dispute with France over the ownership of the Val d'Aran, placed under temporary Majorcan administration. For the broad issues, see Abulafia, 'Catalan merchants', 219–20.   [23] Riera, *Corona de Aragón*, doc. 12, 281.

[24] Riera, *Corona de Aragón*, 177; cf. doc. 102, of 2 November 1309, where the king of Majorca exempts from the *lezda* sums of money up to £100.

[25] Riera, *Corona de Aragón*, doc. 14, 282–3. For the exemption of Barcelona merchants from taxes in Mallorca, conferred by James I in January 1231, see most conveniently Capmany, *Memorias*, vol. II, no. 6, 14–15, and Riera, *Corona de Aragón*, doc. 1, 271–2.

[26] Riera, *Corona de Aragón*, doc. 17, 285.

travelling to or sending goods to the whole Majorcan kingdom.[27] The city government of Barcelona wrote to Barcelonese merchants in Mallorca, Menorca and Ibiza to advise them of the state of affairs and to order them to adhere to the boycott.[28] They then urged the Tortosans and Tarragonese to join the trade war.[29] More problematic was the task of winning approval from King James II of Aragon.[30] The Valencians were urged by the Barcelonese to take an interest too, for one of the Majorcan innovations had been the minting of a Mallorcan coinage for the Balearic islands, to be used in lieu of the Valencian money that had mainly circulated there in the past.[31] Even an interview between the two Jameses at Girona in October 1302 did not, as had been hoped, resolve the issue, beyond talk of eventual arbitration.[32] Indeed, the Majorcan king proved that he could play the game of diplomacy as well as anyone: his increasingly close ties with the sultan of Bougie, of which more in a moment, disconcerted the king of Aragon, who was more worried about the loss of revenues from the Catalan consulates in north Africa to newly founded Majorcan ones than he was at the tariff reforms of his Majorcan uncle. He was also sensitive to the dangers that might result from the presence of Catalan armed patrols off Mallorca, even though he declared himself favourable to the general principle of the boycott; it was another matter along the coast of Catalonia, where of course measures could be taken to prohibit sailings to Mallorca.[33] Moreover, it was essential that foreign merchants should not be dragged into the conflict: one foreign ship (whose origin is not stated) had already been impounded, and yet non-Catalans could not be expected to be interested in nor to understand the issues at stake.[34] Nor were the Catalans themselves completely solid in their support of the boycott. In August 1303 the councillors of Barcelona were examining the claims of the men of Castelló d'Empuries that there was nowhere they could conduct their trade other than the Balearics and Roussillon: 'non habent alias partes ad quas possent declinare nec mercari nisi tamen insulas Maioricarum et aliam terram domini regis Maioricarum'.[35] The merchants of Tarragona also kept the

---

[27] Riera, *Corona de Aragón*, doc. 18, 285–6.
[28] Riera, *Corona de Aragón*, doc. 20, 287.
[29] Riera, *Corona de Aragón*, docs. 21–3, 288–90.
[30] Riera, *Corona de Aragón*, docs. 24–6, 290–2.
[31] Riera, *Corona de Aragón*, doc. 30, 294–6.
[32] Riera, *Corona de Aragón*, 210–13.
[33] Riera, *Corona de Aragón*, doc. 59, 316–17.
[34] Riera, *Corona de Aragón*, doc. 60, 317–18.
[35] Riera, *Corona de Aragón*, doc. 54, 312–13.

trade routes open, much to the irritation of the Barcelona councillors; they were active in the wine trade towards Mallorca, most notably: 'alcuns mercaders de vostra ciutat e de vostra ribera porten vi e altres coses a Mallorcha e que compren e venen aquí palesament so que.s volen'.[36]

The king of Majorca also began to realise that the dispute was going out of control. In July 1304 he wrote from Perpignan to his lieutenant in Mallorca to say that the new tax could not be levied on Catalan merchants while the whole matter was awaiting arbitration. His attention was concentrating now on the negotiation of a marriage between his heir Sanç and Princess Maria of Naples, and he needed James of Aragon's approval. Thus he adopted a more measured tone than he had done in the past. He was worried at the damage that might have been suffered both by his nephew's subjects and by his own. However, he did want the visits of 'Catalan Catalans' to be recorded by his tax officials, even though no payment was made: 'faciatis scribi leudam ipsam a leudariis nostris et non recipiatur ab eis'.[37] The concern for record keeping, for monitoring the potential if not actual income, was still there. On the other hand, an unpredictable factor, poor harvests in Roussillon, led James of Majorca to ban the carriage of food to Catalonia and Valencia, especially since harvests had, by contrast, been superabundant in the Balearic islands.[38] While Mallorcans clearly continued to trade towards Catalonia in 1301 to 1304, the failure to resolve the dispute generated new thought at the Majorcan court about the appropriate answer to a Catalan boycott. In the years of the War of the Vespers the Mallorcans had already found their trade routes limited, in large measure, to the north African run; now, in February 1305, James II tried to reverse the boycott by ordering his representative in Mallorca to welcome all Catalan merchants, forbidding them only access to grain supplies, but requiring him also to stop Mallorcans from trading apparently in any goods towards Catalonia.[39] In early 1308 the king of Majorca sent officials to Barcelona not to meet the city

---

[36] Riera, *Corona de Aragón*, doc. 55, 313–14.

[37] Riera, *Corona de Aragón*, doc. 61, 318–19; also doc. 62, 319. See also doc. 71, 325–6, of 12 August 1305, also printed in Sevillano Colom, *História del puerto*, 447–8.

[38] Riera, *Corona de Aragón*, doc. 63, 319–20. This is an interesting demonstration that even the Mallorcans were able to make an occasional profit from their own grain exports, though the crucial factor may be the rise in prices in Roussillon, which made such exports profitable. The document is also interesting (though not, at this period, unique) for the way it talks about the Balearics alone as the *regnum Maioricarum*, and Roussillon and its neighbours simply as 'our lands'.   [39] Riera, *Corona de Aragón*, doc. 67, 323.

councillors, but to contact the Majorcan merchants there and to instruct them that *omnes homines terrarum et locorum ipsius regis Maioricarum qui essent in Barchinona* should leave the city with all their goods. But the document implies that this command had little effect.[40]

In summer 1306, the king of Majorca declared that he was not acting out of greed when he asked the king of Aragon to arrange a flat payment of £60,000, after which he would cancel his Mallorcan tariff. This could be reduced to £40,000 if the Aragonese king wished to limit the agreement to the most important cities trading with Mallorca, that is, Valencia, Tortosa, Tarragona, Barcelona, Girona and Lleida. These sums should be compared with the income from the *leude e dret del rey* and from the *dret dels Sarrahins e de Jueus estranys*, two profitable taxes on trade and the movement of persons: taking eleven of the years 1311 to 1330, the former tax oscillates between a low of £458 (in 1318) and a high of £2,618 (1328), while the latter rendered as much as £1,337 (in 1318) but as little as £56 (1327). Taking into account the *ancoratge* tax, income from the Balearic ports may have amounted to £3,000 to £4,000 a year, and up to a quarter of royal income from the islands.[41] James of Majorca's demands were thus outrageous. But the king of Aragon was not to be drawn away from issues of principle by such a mercenary approach. As far as he was concerned, the problem had its origin in the agreement which James II of Majorca himself had made at Perpignan with his own father, Peter the Great, in 1279, ratified again when James II was restored to rule over his entire kingdom in 1298. The councillors of Barcelona had convinced James of Aragon that innovations in the tariffs of Mallorca and the other islands were possible, but only when they did not infringe the liberties of the Catalans, and in this case the immunity from taxation had its origins way back in the concessions of their ancestor James the Conqueror.[42] The insistence on the possibility of reaching an amicable conclusion masks a steely determination to assert the ultimate rights of the king of Aragon in this case. But, as ever, they were ill defined. In what senses was the king of Majorca master of the internal affairs of his kingdom if he could not set its own taxes? In a letter of 11 January 1308 James II of Aragon tactfully pressed the matter further: the Majorcan king alone did not have rights in this affair (*non ad vos solum tantumodo*

---

[40] Riera, *Corona de Aragón*, doc. 98, 345–6.   [41] Sastre Moll, *Economía y sociedad*, 33–4.
[42] Riera, *Corona de Aragón*, doc. 95, 343–4.

pertinere); the Aragonese king was duty-bound to look after the concerns of the citizens of Barcelona and of his other *fideles*.[43] The king of Majorca would accept none of this; he wrote tartly to James of Aragon in December 1310 arguing that the matter *ad nos et non ad alium noscitur pertinere, et credimus firmiter quod per dictas conveniencias quoad dictam lezdam fortificatur ius nostrum*.[44] It was ultimately a matter of right for him, too, and so, despite the attempts since 1298 to promote peace between Majorca and Aragon, in reality the problem of the ·clash of jurisdictions had proved insoluble. This was merely the final cry of anger before he was obliged to cede victory to the superior combined power of Barcelona and Aragon. In fact, the increasing role of the king of Aragon as protector of the interests of the Catalan merchants in the Mediterranean made the position of the Majorcan king more than ever anomalous. The anomaly was underlined further by the battle for control of the consulates in north Africa, which is examined next.

IV

The years around 1300 see a second diplomatic battle between the kings of Aragon and the other kings of Aragonese origin, in Mallorca and also Sicily, this time for control of revenues not from Catalan but from African trade. The Catalan consulates in North Africa were by 1280 a valuable source of funds to the Aragonese crown. Some African rulers actually remitted to the Aragonese king the revenue their officials received from Catalan trade; indeed, in 1286 Alfonso III secured the right to claim half of the revenues received at Oran and its dependencies from all Christian traders, even if not Catalan or Majorcan.[45] The establishment of 'secondary' Aragonese monarchies threatened the profitability of the consulates. In 1285 Peter III appointed a merchant of Barcelona to the post of consul over both the Catalan and the Sicilian warehouses at Tunis. The subsequent separation of the Sicilian crown from that of Aragon resulted in a successful struggle by the Sicilian merchants for the right to operate their own independent consulate in Tunis; the merchants of Messina and the other Sicilian ports had the backing of their own king who did not wish to see revenue from the Tunis trade siphoned off towards Barcelona.[46] In 1300 James II of Aragon wrote to his namesake of

---

[43] Riera, *Corona de Aragón*, doc. 97, 345. [44] Riera, *Corona de Aragón*, doc. 96, 344–5.
[45] Dufourcq, *Espagne catalane*, 321.
[46] La Mantia, *Codice diplomatico dei re aragonesi di Sicilia*, vol. I, 167–9, 204–7, 299–306.

Majorca to warn him against appointing a Majorcan consul at Bougie, in competition with the existing Catalan consul. The point was, as in the dispute over tariffs, that the king of Majorca did not have the right to innovate:

Truly, since from times of old we and our predecessors appointed and placed in charge, and were accustomed to appoint and place in charge, and indeed must so do, all the individual Catalan consuls in the said place, we require and request you not to make any innovation concerning the establishment and appointment of a consul in the said place of Bougie from among the men of your land; you should permit our faithful subject Barthomeu Déusvol, citizen of Barcelona, to occupy and exercise the office of consul to which he has been appointed some time ago in the said place, just as it has been the practice since olden days.[47]

At this stage there was not yet a Majorcan consul in post at Bougie, and the Majorcan court was anxious not to inflame the situation; accordingly, the royal lieutenant in Mallorca decreed that Mallorcan merchants who traded in Bougie, and who made use of the Catalan consulate, must most definitely pay their dues there, since the last thing the king of Majorca wanted to hear was complaints from Barthomeu Déusvol: *faens de guisa que d'aquí anant lo damunt dit senyor rey nostre non oïa clams del damunt dit Barthomeu Déusvol.*[48]

The imposition the same year of tariff barriers in Mallorca coincided with another galling setback for the king of Aragon and the Catalans: in 1302 the king of Majorca made his own treaty with the ruler of Bougie, establishing a Majorcan consulate in Bougie and promising the Majorcan king 2,000 *dinars* as indemnification for past acts of piracy.[49] But in late October 1302 the king of Majorca went, as has been seen, to Girona to meet his namesake and to discuss the difficulties over tariff barriers; his attitude to the meeting can be judged from the fact that it was while he was there, supposedly to find common ground with the king of Aragon, that he decided he was ready to order the appointment of a consul in Bougie. He wrote to the new lieutenant on Mallorca, Dalmau Sagarriga, asking him to select a suitable person. The consul was to have a fonduk in Bougie, and there he was to 'receive' those merchants who came from 'our lands' and to levy *iura*, taxes, on their transactions.[50] The consulate was to function on behalf not simply of Balearic islanders, but of men from

---

[47] Riera, *Corona de Aragón*, doc. 9, 276.   [48] Riera, *Corona de Aragón*, doc. 11, 280.
[49] Dufourcq, *Espagne catalane*, 419–22.   [50] Riera, *Corona de Aragón*, doc. 35, 299.

the other Majorcan lands too.[51] A particularly urgent and important task was to be the collection and despatch to the king of the 2,000 dinars which he required as recompense for piracy against Majorcan subjects;[52] the mercenary motive is abundantly plain throughout the project, and James of Majorca had only to look at the success of James of Aragon in drawing revenues from the original Catalan consulates to know that the new policy made good financial sense. Dalmau Sagarriga, after consulting advisers drawn from the Mallorcan business community, appointed Benet Blancas as consul for Majorca on 12 November 1302.[53] The Aragonese response was predictable: James II of Aragon wrote to the king of Bougie to say that the Majorcan consul had been installed in error, and that he had fraudulently taken possession of one of the fonduks which were already assigned to the Catalan nation. It was the custom that the kings of Aragon appoint consuls in Bougie, *e, si el rey de Malorque li posava, sería en perjudici de nós e de los nostres gens*; continued permission for the Majorcan consul to function would be a source of scandal and ill-feeling.[54] In fact in 1273 a Mallorcan had actually been Catalan consul at Bougie, but that was before the separation of the crowns of Aragon and Majorca. The issue of a Majorcan consulate in Tunis was a live one around 1307,[55] and by 1312–13 Majorcan consulates were sprouting elsewhere along the African coast too.[56] In 1308 a Majorcan consul was nominated for Seville, an important point of interchange between the Atlantic and Mediterranean trade systems visited by Mallorcan vessels.[57] Interestingly, this consul is named as Simó Abennacer or Bennàsser, probably a member of that Mozarabic trading family that has been encountered earlier.[58] Evidence from 1334 makes it plain that in Seville there was no Genoese or Catalan, let alone Mallorcan, fonduk, and none is mentioned in the privilege.[59]

---

[51] This point is made firmly by James of Majorca in Riera, *Corona de Aragón*, doc. 38, 301.
[52] Riera, *Corona de Aragón*, doc. 38, 301–2.   [53] Riera, *Corona de Aragón*, doc. 39, 302.
[54] Riera, *Corona de Aragón*, doc. 48, 308–9.
[55] A. Masía de Ros, *La Corona de Aragón y los Estados del Norte de Africa. Política de Jaime II y Alfonso IV en Egipto, Ifriquía y Tremecén* (Barcelona, 1951), 232–4.
[56] Dufourcq, *Espagne catalane*, 508, n.3, 519: there was a consul at Bône and at Collo and a joint appointment for Djidjelli and Constantine. Tlemcen, Cherchel and Mansoura also had consuls in the early fourteenth century. In addition, *Documenta regni Majoricarum*, 113–14, consists of the nomination of the Majorcan consul in Algiers; cf. Dufourcq, *Espagne catalane*, 476.   [57] See chapter 10 for Mallorca's Atlantic trade.   [58] See chapter 4.
[59] Riera Melis, *Corona de Aragón*, doc. 99, 346–7. On the lack of fonduks, see the discussion of Jaume Manfré, chapter 9.

V

A persuasive partial explanation of the weakness of the kingdom of
Majorca in the late thirteenth century lies in the failure of the
monarchy to draw substantial income from economic activities
conducted by its subjects; but there are signs of a more income-
oriented policy in the early fourteenth century, visible, for instance,
in the heavy increase of the residence taxes imposed on Muslims and
in the punitive levies on the Jewish community.[60] Obviously, too,
there were fiscal motives behind the initiatives in Bougie and the rest
of the Maghrib, and behind the tariff policy of 1299 to 1308. Yet, as
has been seen, James the Conqueror had granted the Catalan and
Provençal participants in the conquest of Mallorca and Ibiza
extensive rights of tax exemption.[61] Although the crown retained
lands for itself, the privileges of those who were granted estates and
property were very generous: it has been seen that the men of
Marseilles received 297 houses in the capital, as well as lands outside,
and that the Genoese and Pisans were also awarded some lands, plus
generous commercial privileges.[62] On the mainland, too, the income
of the kings of Majorca was severely curtailed by long-standing
grants to potentially profitable communities. In Montpellier, it was
the city government rather than the crown that secured the lion's
share of trade taxes. As has been seen, lucrative schemes to tax
merchants of Barcelona had to be abandoned under pressure from
the king of Aragon.

Looking later into the fourteenth century, the Mallorcan documentation provides a good opportunity to compute the profits a
monarchy could hope to make out of the economic activities of its
subjects. Here it is important to bear in mind that this is a period in
which the monarchy was trying to maximise its income, whereas
under James I the monarchy controlled the Catalan, Aragonese and
above all Valencian revenues and took less interest in the potential,
considerable though it was, of the Balearics. The possibilities for

[60] See chapters 4 and 5.
[61] *Documenta regni Majoricarum*, 9–16, 22–25, etc.; 22 is a privilege for the men of Montpellier.
For the privilege to the merchants of Barcelona of 1231, see Riera Melis, *Corona de Aragón*,
doc. 1, 271–2.
[62] Sevillano, 'Mercaderes', 62–4; A. Santamaría, 'La reconquista de las vías marítimas,' *Actas
del I° Congreso internacional de História mediterranea*, in the *Anuario de Estudios medievales*, 10
(1980), 55–7; C.E. Dufourcq, 'Aspects internationaux de Majorque durant les derniers
siècles du Moyen Age,' *Mayurqa*, 11 (1974), 6–7, 13–17.

stimulating an increase in royal income were first revealed in the fine study by Durliat and Pons of the revenues received from the *ancoratge* tax, levied on ships coming into port in the early fourteenth century; more of this later.[63] Other sources are even more eloquent: the *Reebudes* and *Dades*, receipts and outgoings of the Majorcan crown, analysed by present-day Mallorcan historians.[64] However, the profitability of the mainland territories is another question; the sources are not comparable, and only guesswork can be applied. Sastre Moll is able to provide the total income received by the crown from each of the main Balearic islands, as well as material on the expenses incurred by the crown in maintaining its administration. He concludes that the monarchy received each year between £20,000 and £22,000 from its island territories, of which £10,000 to £12,000 was required for running expenses. The agricultural and pastoral sectors of the economy produced just over half the income, port revenues about 20 percent, or in good years 25 percent; the major source of agricultural revenue was a tax on grain, the *dret del blat*, though wine and oil also produced a respectable revenue (viticulture was presumably much extended after the Christian conquest).

The *Reebudes*, *Dades* and similar materials also illustrate the overall character of the island economy in the early fourteenth century; they have been used by Santamaría to stress that in the early fourteenth century Mallorca was still concentrating on cereal production, which accounted for 60.24 percent of documented agricultural production in the years 1313 to 1343.[65] Surprising is the relatively small pastoral sector, which at this stage produced only about one-third of the taxes rendered by viticulture, and less than those rendered by the cultivation of olives. Wine production in fact increased slightly from 1313 to 1340, while oil production increased quite sharply, almost by a factor of four, between 1317 and 1342.[66] This arguably may reflect a trend towards local specialisation in the early fourteenth century observable elsewhere in Europe too, but particularly in areas such as Mallorca which were able to draw in grain and other essential commodities from outside: this, after all, is the period of the expansion of Catalan trade in Sicily, and of new opportunities for grain merchants arising from the Aragonese invasion of Sardinia in 1323. It is not impossible, too, that James II's new agro-towns were having

---

[63] Durliat and Pons, 'Recerques sobre el moviment del port de Mallorca', 345–63.
[64] Sastre Moll, *Economía y sociedad*; Santamaría, *Ejecutoria*.
[65] Santamaría, *Ejecutoria*, 378.   [66] Santamaría, *Ejecutoria*, 380–1, 386–7.

an effect on patterns of production. But another factor is the observable decline in Mallorca's population after about 1329, a picture not greatly at odds with that of western Europe in the years either side of 1300: in some parts of Italy (such as rural Pistoia) decline is visible even before the start of the fourteenth century; in areas of northern Europe the great famine of 1315–17 seems to mark a dramatic downturn, followed in some cases by slow recovery up to the Black Death.[67] A particular factor in Mallorcan demography must be the high proportion, approaching one half, of the population that lived in towns, especially in the swollen capital city. If it is true that medieval cities could not reproduce themselves, then a slight tailing off of immigration from outside the island, which had been of such formidable proportions after the Catalan conquest, accompanied by a steady trickle of migration from the countryside to the capital, would result in gradual urban and rural depopulation. It has to be said that this phenomenon needs fuller thought, in the wider context of western Mediterranean demographic trends.

What is more surprising is the decline in pastoral revenues from £658 in 1329–33 to £555 in 1339–43.[68] After the Black Death, Mallorca, and even more Menorca, became important sources of raw wool both for a burgeoning local textile industry and for export by international merchants, notably Francesco Datini of Prato. Although there was a small base on which this wool trade could grow, it clearly was only of modest significance in the wider Mallorcan economy of the early fourteenth century. As in other parts of Europe, the economy of the islands underwent dramatic modifications after the sudden loss of population in the middle of the fourteenth century: it is not so much a question of whether the economy declined into depression or expanded in a new age of growth, as a question how the economy experienced radical restructuring following a major shift in patterns of supply and demand.[69]

---

[67] D. Herlihy, 'Population, plague and social change in rural Pistoia', *Economic History Review*, ser. 2, 18 (1965).   [68] Santamaría, *Ejecutoria*, 395.
[69] Further discussion of trends after about 1350 will be found in chapter 11.

CHAPTER 9

The trade of the autonomous kingdom in its last two decades

I

Unfortunately, the trade of the first two decades of the fourteenth century is poorly documented, and so the main lines of Balearic trade after the settlement of the Vespers conflict cannot be drawn with certainty. The survival of registers of the tax known as *ancoratge*, levied on incoming ships at Ciutat de Mallorca and at La Porassa, a station near the capital, enables a clearer picture to be provided for 1321–2, 1324–5, 1330–3 and 1340–1.[1] Even so, the *ancoratge* documents generally give no information about the route traversed by the ships coming into port. They identify the captain, and his origin, but this information cannot be used to map the route followed by a ship. It is likely that the vessels of P. Hombert of Barcelona, a regular visitor to Mallorca in this period, travelled back and forth to Barcelona, as well as to north Africa, but this is no more than an assumption.[2] Occasionally we learn that a ship is bound for a particular destination, but the information is provided gratuitously. Thus the first entry in the oldest register states that the son of En Terasa of Barcelona paid three *solidi* and that the ship was bound for Menorca.[3]

In analysing this material, emphasis is placed here on the entries revealing intra-Majorcan trade between Mallorca itself and the mainland territories or the other islands, in the hope of identifying signs of the integration of these territories into a single market. Some evidence for trade within the Majorcan realm can be gleaned from

---

[1] ARM, RP 1097 (1321); RP 1098 (1324); RP 1099 (1331); RP 1100 (1332); RP 1101 (1340); RP 1102 (1330). Most of the examples cited here are from the earliest register, but the conclusions are drawn from my study of all six. The major discussion is that of Marcel Durliat and Joan Pons i Marquès, 'Recerques sobre el moviment del port de Mallorca', CHCA VI, 345–63. [2] ARM, RP 1097, f.IV, no. I; see note 12.
[3] ARM, RP 1097, f.Ir, no. I.

the numbers of ships that were owned or operated by captains from Collioure in Roussillon, Agde, near Montpellier, and other ports that could be used to bond together the territories of the kingdom. For example:

> *Anselm Rebugassa de cocljure entra vij yorns d'abril. Leny ... viij ss.*[4]
>
> *A. Sabater de cocljure entra xxij yorns d'abril. Leny. Es nou et no paga ancoratge.*[5]
>
> *R. Baus de cocljure entra xxvij yorns d'abril. Leny ... viij ss.*[6]
>
> *Andreu de Codolet de cocljure entra vij yorns de mag. Leny. Ay v setzenes d'omens de maylorca. v ss. vi [d.]*[7]
>
> *Johan Marty d'acde entra vij yorns de mag. Barca descuberta ... ij ss.*[8]
>
> *Johan Baus de cocljure entra vij yorns de mag. Leny ... viij ss.*[9]

In the period 7 April 1321 to 7 May 1321 seven ships with masters who hailed from Collioure entered the port of Ciutat de Mallorca, and two ships with masters from Agde.[10] However, a total of sixty-nine non-Mallorcan ships are listed over this period. The great majority of these ships were operated by men of Barcelona and Valencia. Tortosa and Tarragona also appear in the records. Collioure was the point of origin of only about 5 percent of the recorded ships.[11]

Yet what is striking is that Collioure appears at all in the list of taxed ships. It was the custom not to levy *ancoratge* on ships of Mallorca itself, unless the crews were partly non-Mallorcan. Equally, non-Mallorcan ships could claim a tax reduction if they carried a partly Mallorcan crew. This applied to the ship of Andreu de Codolet which has just been cited: five-sixteenths of the crew were men of Mallorca. P. Hombert of Barcelona operated a *leny* that normally would have paid four *solidi* on entry, but since half his crew was from Mallorca, he only paid two.[12] In other words, ships of Collioure, or nearby towns, did not count as Mallorcan vessels. The fact that they were under the same ruler did not exempt them from commercial

---

[4] ARM, RP 1097, f.1v, no. 5.

[5] ARM, RP 1097, f.4r, no. 4.

[6] ARM, RP 1097, f.5r, no. 1.

[7] ARM, RP 1097, f.7r, no. 4.

[8] ARM, RP 1097, f.5r, no. 5.

[9] ARM, RP 1097, f.7v, no. 1.

[10] Cases other than those already cited are: ARM, RP 1097, f.1v, no. 5; f.2r, no. 3; f.4r, no. 6 (all for Collioure); f.4r, no. 2 (for Agde).

[11] Durliat and Pons, 'Recerques sobre el moviment del port de Mallorca', 350.

[12] ARM, RP 1097, f.1v, no. 1; 7v, no. 2; f.12v, no. 5, etc. The absences of a few weeks at a time suggest that he was passing to and fro to Catalonia or north Africa or both. His type of ship, a small *lignum* or *leny*, was often used in Mallorcan trade with the Maghrib: RP 1105, Llicències per a barques.

taxes in the Balearics. As if to rub the point in, ships of Barcelona, but not of the rest of Catalonia nor of Valencia, were allowed a 50 per cent reduction in the *ancoratge* from the standard tax of eight *solidi* per *leny*. However, ships on their maiden voyage were exempt from the payment of *ancoratge*, and one of the vessels from Collioure thus had nothing to pay. This measure may have been devised to attract new shipping to the Balearics, in the hope of winning the long-term loyalty of the shipowners. The evidence cited here does not suggest that attempts to permit mariners of all the Majorcan territories to trade under similarly privileged conditions were pressed very far.

Fortunately the keepers of the *ancoratge* records were punctilious enough to list separately the Mallorcan ships that came into port, even though they paid no tax.[13] Twenty-five arrived in the period 7 April 1321 to 7 May 1321, including 2 *lenys* operated by an Ibizan master. Over the whole recorded period from 4 April 1321 to 15 March 1322 we find references to the arrival of 25 Ibizan vessels and 14 Menorcan ones, out of 301 arrivals of ships of Balearic ownership (this figure includes some ships several times, if they commuted back and forth from Mallorca).[14] Durliat and Pons identified broadly similar numbers of Ibizan and Menorcan vessels in subsequent years.[15] The number of Mallorcan ships arriving in port remained fairly stable throughout the year; in 1330–1 they were, month by month from April, 36, 42, 39, 30, 41, 21, 30, 39, 30, 34, 20, 40. It is known that in 1320 plans were being advanced at the royal court for a radical reshaping of the Balearic fleet; large numbers of heavier *naus* and *cocas* were to be built in place of the smaller *lenys* and *barques* that were the mainstay of the Mallorcan fleet in the early fourteenth century.[16] One motive was commercial, to prise mastery of the trade routes from the Italians, who utilised such ships on the long-distance routes and on the most profitable short-distance routes, for instance from Mallorca to Tunis. They were the 747s and 767s of the fourteenth century.[17] But the plans apparently had little effect, since

[13] Cf. the insistence (p. 157) that even when the Mallorcan *lezda* is not charged, the *leudarii* should record the movement of traffic in their books. Record-keeping was nothing if not punctilious; such practices inspire confidence in the documents that survive.
[14] ARM, RP 1097, ff.57r-74v.
[15] Durliat and Pons, 'Recerques sobre el moviment del port de Mallorca', 354.
[16] Durliat, *Art*, 33–4.
[17] The comparison is not fanciful. Travellers in the late twentieth century are likely to board a wide-bodied jet either to go a very long distance, say Washington to London, or to be ferried in company with hundreds of other people over quite a short distance, say Milan to London.

rather few of the Mallorcan-owned vessels in the *ancoratge* registers were *cocas* or other large ships.[18] It is likely that a severe limitation on these schemes arose from the lack of suitable wood on the Balearic islands; the comparison with Catalonia, well-endowed with timber, is a telling one. Moreover, it has been suggested already that there was considerable diffusion of resources among a great many small shipowners. Unlike Venice, Mallorca simply did not have an overweening patrician élite able to organise the production of galley fleets and the management of convoys.

A striking feature of the *ancoratge* records is the consistency of movement through Mallorca all through the year. The seasons had little effect on the rate of arrival of ships, and almost any month could rate as a busy one. Thus in the fiscal year 1321/2 there was a high of 82 arrivals in May 1321 and a low of 33 arrivals in January and February 1322; in 1324/5 there was a high of 55 in August 1324 and a low of 27 in April 1324 (which had the second highest number of arrivals, 56, in 1321/2). In 1340/1 figures oscillated between 40 (November 1340) and 74 (March 1341). The total figures (excluding the fragmentary year 1331–2) are:

1321–2	871
1324–5	957
1332–3	745
1340–1	1094[19]

It is also possible to gain some idea of the range of foreign contacts of the Balearic islands from the same records. The arrival of ships from Sérignan (near Béziers) and Frontignan (in Aumelas), as well as Agde, makes it plain that several ports which provided access to Montpellier were utilised. Larger vessels, galleys and tarides rather than *lenys*, came occasionally from Marseilles. The Italian ships that reached Mallorca originated in Genoa, Pisa, Venice, Gaeta, Sicily and Sardinia, and included Flanders galleys; the Flanders ships were worthy enough of note to have their destination occasionally listed.[20] The Genoese appeared even when their republic was in conflict with the Aragonese (from 1330 to 1335), but they became more enthusiastic by 1340, when the war had come to an end; it will be seen shortly how conflict between the Majorcans and the Genoese

---

[18] Durliat, *Art*, 34, n.31.
[19] Durliat and Pons, 'Recerques sobre el moviment del port de Mallorca', 349 and figure 1; see chapter 7 for a comparison with the evidence from the 1284 licences.
[20] RP 1097, f.17v, f.34v; RP 1098, f.5v, f.6r.

complicated the affairs of Mallorcan businessmen trading in Granada.[21]

However, another important link in the chain of routes tying Italy and Mallorca to Flanders and England was the shipping of northern Spain; cogs of Santander and Castro Urdiales arrived each year in Mallorca, while visits by shipping from the Basque country (San Sebastian, Fuentarrabía, Bayonne and other ports) were generally slightly more frequent. The total numbers of northern Spanish ships each year are as follows:

1321–2	2
1324–5	12
1330–1	15
1332–3	17
1340–1	2[22]

Mallorca's own ships also headed out of the Straits of Gibraltar southwards to the western coast of Morocco, and several trips to Anfa (modern Casablanca) can be identified in the early fourteenth century;[23] by the 1340s they were visiting the Canaries, though not in the first instance for trade.[24] Smaller ships could be used on the Moroccan routes, and it is likely that this was a more intensive trade than the risky Flanders connection, which suffered seriously from the interference of hostile fleets during the Hundred Years War and during the naval conflicts between Genoa and its Catalan and Venetian foes.[25]

The *ancoratge* records are naturally silent about what was in some respects the most important trade route to Mallorca, that linking it to the Maghrib. So well represented in the licences of 1284, this trade disappears from view in the *ancoratge* registers, since the shipping was all, or at least predominantly, Christian; Muslim-owned barques from Bougie simply never appear in the records, and destinations are rarely recorded. The *guiatge* records of 1341/2, listing licences to trade in strategic goods such as iron, make abundantly plain the continuing vitality of Mallorcan-controlled commerce with north Africa and Muslim Spain.[26] In 1341/2 38 out of 87 licences were for

[21] Durliat, *Art*, 39–40, for trouble with Genoa.
[22] Durliat and Pons, 'Recerques sobre el moviment del port de Mallorca', 353–4.
[23] Dufourcq, *Espagne catalane*, 596–7.   [24] See chapter 11.   [25] See chapter 10.
[26] ARM, AH 4390, *Llicències i guiatges*, 1341–2; the most recent study is Pau Cateura Bennàsser, 'El comercio del reino de Mallorca con Cerdeña a traves de los guiatges', *XIV Congresso di Storia della Corona d'Aragona, Sassari-Alghero 19–24 maggio 1990*, vol. I, *Il 'Regnum Sardiniae et*

trade with north Africa; Italy and Catalonia came some way behind with 11 licences each; Valencia and southern France had 9; Sardinia 6; but there were only 2 for Sicily and 1 for Castile.[27]

These records were compiled with care, and there is no reason to suppose a very large number of ships failed to be registered. On the other hand, local shippers from Menorca and Ibiza are almost certainly under-represented, since much of their trade passed through lesser ports along the coasts of Mallorca, such as Alcudia (for Menorca).[28] Others have shown more confidence in the completeness of these records. For Durliat, Dufourcq and others these documents can be used to show that the years around 1330 were the high point of Mallorca's medieval trade. This is certainly a dangerous assumption, since so many factors, notably the recurrent political crises in the western Mediterranean, as well as the constant scourge of piracy, resulted in sharp fluctuations in trade and the deflection of trade routes away from traditional destinations; moreover, there were significant changes in shipping capacity after the arrival in the Mediterranean of the Atlantic cog and its imitations. The *ancoratge* records have no late fourteenth-century or fifteenth-century counterparts in Mallorca, and, unfortunately, they therefore have to be used in isolation.[29]

II

Pisa is less well represented in the *ancoratge* records, but a separate collection of tax documents proves that Pisan shipping made intensive use of the harbour of Mallorca in some years at least.[30] These records show that Tuscan merchants were interested in figs, sweet raisins (*atzebib* or zibibbo, a type of muscat grape), honey, oil, almonds and a few other commodities that are likely to have originated in Mallorca, as well as several items, such as mastic, sulphur, African

Corsicae' nell'espansione mediterranea della Corona d'Aragona (secc. XIV–XVIII) (Sassari, 1990), 169–90.   [27] Sevillano, 'Mercaderes', 33.

[28] A number of Ibizan and Menorcan captains do appear, all the same, among the Mallorcans, notably in winter time when navigation between the islands may have seemed the safest option: see, e.g., ARM, RP 1099 (1331), f.42r, for the *barca* of P. Gitart D'Ivissa, f.42v for the *leny* of P. Sinta de Manorca, etc., in December 1331.

[29] A reference to the accounts of a collector of *ancoratge*, based at Porto Pí in 1276, is found in Santamaría, *Ejecutoria*, 644–5, no. 55; no details of the actual income are supplied.

[30] T. Antoni, *I 'partitari' maiorchini del Lou dels Pisans relativi al commercio dei Pisani nelle Baleari (1304–1322 e 1353–1355)*, (Biblioteca del Bollettino storico pisano, Collana storica, Pisa, 1977), 10–26; also Dufourcq, 'Aspects internationaux', 13–16; S. Petrucci, 'Tra Pisa e Maiorca: avvenimenti politici e rapporti commerciali nella prima metà del XIV secolo', CHCA XIII, vol. II, 137–46.

wool, pepper and sugar among commodities trans-shipped through the Balearic islands. Evidence already examined suggests that significant quantities of these goods arrived from Sicily; commodities were hawked around the western Mediterranean, and low-bulk, high-value items could be sent on to wherever the latest news indicated demand was greatest and prices were highest.[31] Textiles arrived from Italy, and the Pisans also brought alum, which was essential for the Catalan and Mallorcan cloth industries. Ibizan salt appears to have been a major attraction for Pisan merchants only after 1322.[32]

Another source for the same period has recently come to light in the archives of the Cathedral of Palma. A notarial register of 1340, of nearly 170 folios, is almost completely taken up with shipping contracts, *commenda* agreements and other port business.[33] What is striking is, first, the importance of links to Cagliari and to the ports of western Sardinia (Oristano, Bosa and Alghero, a major source of coral).[34] The king of Majorca had supplied ships for the Aragonese invasion of Sardinia, and his subjects were rewarded with a commercial privilege.[35] It looks very much as if they seized the chance to intensify their trade with Sardinia therafter, though there are some scattered records of such trade before then too.[36] Trade with Calabria reflects the closeness of ties with Naples, whose queen was a Majorcan princess; a route from Mallorca to Cagliari and then on to Calabria was sometimes used.[37] In 1325 King Robert confirmed the

---

[31] Compare Zeno, *Documenti*, no. 152. The Datini letters, discussed below, provide good evidence for the hawking of goods.

[32] Antoni, *I 'partitari' maiorchini*, 13–14, 20–23.

[33] Archivo Capitular, Palma de Mallorca (hereafter: ACP), 14564 (Francesc Batlle). On this see Durliat, *Art*, 363. I should like to record my special thanks to Professor Jocelyn Hillgarth and to the Cathedral Chapter of Palma for arranging for the microfilming of the entire document. There are interesting points of comparison with contemporary documents of the notary Rustico de Rusticis, a Pisan working in Palermo, some of whose acts concern Mallorca or the Mallorcans: Zeno, *Documenti*, nos. 179, 182, 186–8.

[34] ACP, 14564, f.23v: 'apud Rosas et abinde ad Caucum Liberum redendo inde ad Rosas et de Rosis in alterum dictorum cuique locorum Oristagni, Bose vel de Alguerio Insule Sardinie et abinde redendo Maioricas vel quicunque aliud locum Catalonie'. Coral was also collected by Marseilles merchants and brought to Mallorca: ACP, 14564, f.35v for a 'barcham ad portandum et colligendum corallum'. For Sicilian evidence of trade towards Cagliari and then Mallorca, see Zeno, *Documenti*, no. 179, of 1340.

[35] Archives Départementales des Pyrénées Orientales, Perpignan, section des Archives de la ville de Perpignan (hereafter: ADP), AA3, f.192v-196r; see Appendix I.

[36] *Assegurances*, vol. II, 335–6, no. 25, describes a complex but not unusual tour of the western Mediterranean, involving Mallorca, Cagliari, Valencia and Murviedro, by *leny* in 1301.

[37] For Calabria generally, see ACP, 14564, f.4r, f.4v; for Mallorca–Cagliari–Calabria, see ACP, 14564, f.69v; cf. f.45v for a Neapolitan businessman trading in Mallorca.

commercial and legal privileges of the merchants of the Majorcan kingdom.[38] But, as ever, north Africa appears to dominate traffic out of Mallorca. There are signs of trouble in the Maghrib in the documents that refer to the redemption of captive Mallorcans in the Maghrib.[39] Overall, the range of ports visited occasions few surprises: they are mostly those of the Abdalwahidid state around Tlemcen, though Morocco is represented with a voyage to Arzila.[40] Mallorcan merchants fostered ties with Granada too; they installed themselves at Almería, where they had a base by 1334 from which they occasionally penetrated into the Granadan interior.[41] Trade to the Levant and Byzantium is much thinner; a *cocha* is recorded bound for Cyprus, and there is a reference to a past trip to *Romania*.[42] It is also striking how many ships are called *cocha bayonesca*, a title which explicitly recognises the Basque derivation of this type of vessel.[43] The patrons of these ships no doubt took greater care to register their business partnerships than the masters of the small *lenys*; local trade is thus poorly represented in these contracts, and here the *ancoratge* records are more suggestive, with their constant references to ships of Barcelona in port in Mallorca. But there are frequent allusions in the notarial register to visits to Valencia, Tarragona, Barcelona and the mainland Mallorcan port of Collioure.[44] The Italian connection is recorded both through the presence of Italian merchants in Mallorca and through contracts for commercial expeditions to Genoa, Pisa and Venice.[45]

[38] ADP, AA3, f.128v. Trade with Aragonese Sicily was also promoted through treaty arrangements: ADP, AA1, Livre vert majeur, f.107v-108r; and AA3, Livre vert mineur, f.98r-v, f.99r-100r; also *Documenta regni Majoricarum*, 99–100 (for a Mallorcan text of the 1305 privilege).

[39] ACP, 14564, f.31r, f.73r; cf. f.64r for a Muslim seeking redemption in Mallorca.

[40] Much of the business recorded in these acts is for Honein: ACP, 14564, f.55v, 56r; Arzila: f.25v.

[41] M. Sánchez Martínez, 'Mallorquines y Genovesos en Almería durante el primer tercio del siglo XIV: el proceso contra Jaume Manfré (1334)', *Miscellània de textos medievals*, vol. IV, *La frontera terrestre i marítima amb l'Islam* (Barcelona, 1988), 102–62, including most of the text of the document preserved in the Arxiu del Regne de Mallorca, Suplicacions, 9, ff.271r-317v and 324v-325r.

[42] ACP, 14564, f.54v, 70r-v.   [43] E.g. ACP, 14564, f.69v.

[44] E.g. ACP, 14564, f.2v and f.20v (Valencia), f.16r (Tarragona and Pisa or Genoa), f.32r (Barcelona), f.59r-v and f.76v (Collioure).

[45] ACP, 14564, f.18v (apud Januam vel Pisas), f.19v (ad partes Venecie), f.26v (illam galeam Januensium), f.44v (Carratus Salvatge Januensis: a *cambium* contract for Flanders), f.45v (Paganino de Butzuhel Januensis de riparia Janue).

III

At the same time, trading enterprises easily found themselves trapped within the political jigsaw puzzle of Mediterranean politics. It has been seen that the years after 1330 were marked by war between the Aragonese and the Majorcans on one side and the Genoese on the other: Sardinia, invaded by James II of Aragon in 1323/4, was one issue. At the same time, the Aragonese, under the new king, Alfonso IV, and the Castilians, under Alfonso XI, were planning a crusade against Almería. In December 1330 the bishop of Barcelona appeared before James III of Majorca to request his collaboration in the holy war against Muhammad IV of Granada, but the Majorcan king appears to have demurred, presumably to the intense irritation of the Aragonese, who always resented any show of independence by their Majorcan vassals. There was in fact a tradition of co-operation between Majorca and Granada; at the time of an earlier crisis in Aragonese–Granadan relations, in April 1309, James II of Majorca had insisted that if he were to join his nephew's crusade against Granada, it would pose too great a threat to the safety of his subjects trading in al-Andalus.[46] Later he offered some naval aid; but he seems to have been only too glad when peace initiatives were made towards Granada the next month by James of Aragon, whom he allowed to act on his behalf.[47] It was only in 1332 that the king of Majorca was levered out of his neutrality as a result of the close ties between the Genoese and the Granadans; Mallorca and Menorca were raided in the summer by a Genoese fleet, and Mallorcan ships suffered from attacks by Genoese privateers. James III was thus sucked into a conflict in which, really, he preferred not to be involved: when the king of Castile requested him to break off the grain trade through Mallorca to the Maghrib, he declined to do so, only agreeing to prohibit such traffic if it was ultimately destined to be carried by Mallorcans to Granada. James also expressed a reluctance formally to defy the king of Granada, since, he said, it was not Majorcan practice to issue a written declaration of war. He explained that relations with the Muslims were always tenuous, and when there was no peace, there was war. Such a truism could not

---

[46] A. Masià de Ros, *Jaume II: Aragó, Granada i Marroc* (Barcelona, 1989), 356–7: 'quod nos sumus in convencionibus cum Rege Granate de non faciendo malum alter alteri sine diffidacione quod feceremus propter securitatem gentium nostrarum que in terris ipsius regis Granate frequenter et multum mercantur'.   [47] Masià, *Jaume II*, 357–8, 363.

mask the continued determination of the Majorcan kings to protect
the interests of their merchants, who had built so heavily on trade
between Europe and north Africa; in a sense James was saying that
the best interests of the kingdom of Majorca were served by a
watchful neutrality. It was only after the Granadans had sought the
aid of Marinid Morocco, and a new large-scale invasion of Spain had
begun to move out of Africa, that frantic diplomatic negotiations
produced peace between the Catalans and the Genoese in 1335, and
agreements were also signed putting to an end the conflict between
Granada (now under a new, more pliant, king) and Aragon.[48]

In September 1334, Jaume Manfré was accused by fellow
merchants of Mallorca of buying a cog in the island in order to sell it
to the Genoese or the Granadans, who were still at war with the king
of Majorca (and of Aragon). Pere Armengol, Jaume de Coromines,
Simó de Boví and Nicolau Guiot denounced Manfré to the royal
lieutenant in Mallorca on behalf of all the merchants who traded in
the Maghrib, in order to show that Manfré had dealings with the
qa'id Ridwan (*alcayt Rodoano*), effectively the prime minister of
Granada, and Nicoloso da Camogli (*Camuja*), a Genoese, to the
dishonour not merely of the interests of Ciutat de Mallorca, but of
those of the entire Catalan nation (*dampnum et lesionem et eversionem
tocius cathalanice nacionis et signanter universitatis Majoricarum*). The
result, the plaintiffs stated in somewhat apocalyptic language, would
be that Mallorcan ships could not sail to the far west, and that
Mallorcan ships such as the *cocha de la Companyia* returning from there
would fall prey to Genoese and Muslim piracy.[49] Manfré's accusers
insisted that the defendant's treachery was regarded as *veritas et
publica vox et fama in regno Majoricarum*: he had had the effrontery to
buy his cog in Mallorca itself from Bernat Anselmi.[50]

Manfré emerges from the extensive documentation that his case
generated as a specialist in trade with the Nasrid kingdom of
Granada, and to some extent Seville.[51] He had modest beginnings,
setting himself up as an independent merchant from October 1332,
and no doubt this was something his rivals continued to hold against

---

[48] N. Housley, *The later crusades. From Lyons to Alcazar, 1274–1580* (Oxford, 1992), 279; L. P.
Harvey, *Islamic Spain, 1250–1500* (Chicago, 1990), 197–9; and, especially, Sánchez Martínez,
'Mallorquines y Genovesos en Almería', 112–6.
[49] Sánchez Martínez, 'Mallorquines y Genovesos en Almería', 147.
[50] Sánchez Martínez, 'Mallorquines y Genovesos en Almería', 148, 151–2.
[51] Sánchez Martínez, 'Mallorquines y Genovesos en Almería', 103–4, 116–37.

him; but he never became a merchant millionaire. They summarised his career in dismissive terms: he had been a mere *mancipium* and *factor* working on behalf of other people's partnerships, and then all of a sudden he began to make money, until he became worth £250.[52] In Seville he was said to have refused to appear before the Catalan consul, on the grounds that he was Genoese, a statement that bears comparison with the attempts of Pere de Grau in 1299 to avoid Catalan jurisdiction in Palermo:

Once upon a time the said Jaume Manfré was summoned before the consul of the Catalans in Seville and the same Jaume, having appeared before him, said and replied that he did not recognise his jurisdiction but only that of the consul of the Genoese who was there in Seville, because he was not regarded as a Catalan but as one of the Genoese.[53]

Indeed, he preferred to spend his time eating with and talking to the Genoese rather than the Catalans.[54] Another witness offered rather different testimony: Jaume Bória had certainly seen Manfré in the Genoese fonduk at Almería, before war broke out with Genoa; but there was no public Catalan or Genoese fonduk in Seville (though there was a Catalan consul), and so traders simply set up their own private *hospicium seu domum*; in fact, Jaume Manfré had always presented himself as a Catalan in Seville, Almería and back home in Mallorca: *viderit ipsum Jacobum indutum sicud catalanum et comportar-se sicut catalanum*.[55] This witness further confused the case by stating, when his evidence was read back to him, that in fact the person he had seen was Pere Manfré, Jaume's brother. On the other hand, he did know about Jaume Manfré's plans to hire a ship, for the accused told him that it would be a most profitable enterprise, and that some Moors had hired space on board at Málaga and Almería, with a view

---

[52] Sánchez Martínez, 'Mallorquines y Genovesos en Almería', 148.

[53] 'Quod quadam vice dictus Jacobus Manfré fuit citatus in Xibilia ante consulem catalanorum in Xibilia et quod ipse Jacobus, constitutus coram eo, dixerat et responderat quod non faceret jus coram eo nisi dumtaxat coram consule januensium qui ibi erat in Xibilia quare ipse non se reputabat esse catalanum set januensium: Sánchez Martínez, 'Mallorquines y Genovesos en Almería', 121, 151–2.

[54] Sánchez Martínez, 'Mallorquines y Genovesos en Almería', 151.

[55] Sánchez Martínez, 'Mallorquines y Genovesos en Almería', 158. This is a curious statement, as Prof. Blanca Garí has kindly indicated to me, because the Genoese were granted a right to a fonduk in Seville in 1251; in 1289 they were said to have 'barrio e alfondiga e forno e baño'; their rights were reconfirmed in 1330, and throughout the fourteenth century they were insisting on their rights to property in Seville! See M. González Jiménez, 'Genovesos en Sevilla (siglos xiii-xv)', in *Presencia italiana en Andalucia, siglos XIV—XVII. Actas del I Coloquio hispano—italiano* (Seville, 1985).

to a passage to Tunis and back to Spain: *nós som noliejats de moros que devem carregar a Màliqua e Almeria per anar a Tonis e devem tornar en Espanya.*[56] Manfré was tarred with the accusation of charging interest at five *solidi* in the pound, as if it is likely his accusers never made money this way.[57] What he was able to offer in return for his interest rate was, it was said, a guarantee of security from interference by either the Genoese or the Saracens.[58] Thus he said, according to the witness Jaume de Canelles: 'si ell era ab la cocha fora les puntes de Mallorques, que eyl assegurava tots quants n'agués en la sua nau de sarreyns e de genoveses.'[59]

The king's lieutenant was not in fact convinced by the evidence, some of which, such as dismissive references to Manfré's lack of means, was circumstantial, an attempt, it may have seemed, to smear the character of someone who had indeed been loyal to the crown, was a citizen and inhabitant of Mallorca, and, above all, was of old Catalan stock: who *traxisse de Catalonia originem ab antiquo.*[60] It would be sufficient for Jaume Manfré to promise that he would not offer aid to the enemies of the Catalans, and more particularly of the king of Majorca, to whose court he must offer an oath and an act of homage.[61] The attempt of the accusers to present Manfré as a foe not merely of Majorcan interests but of Catalan had clearly backfired. The reference by both the accusers and the judge to the 'Catalan nation' is most interesting, suggesting how, even under an autonomous king, the inhabitants of Mallorca did not forget that they were by and large of Catalan origin.

There has been a tendency to think of Granada as effectively a Genoese domain, as it certainly became by the fifteenth century, but the evidence from the trial of Jaume Manfré indicates how regularly Mallorcan merchants visited Almería, Granada and Málaga.[62] From 1351 until 1334 seventeen different merchants trading to Almería (sometimes in conjunction with Seville) can be identified in Manfré's

---

[56] Sánchez Martínez, 'Mallorquines y Genovesos en Almería', 158.
[57] Sánchez Martínez, 'Mallorquines y Genovesos en Almería', 149.
[58] Sánchez Martínez, 'Mallorquines y Genovesos en Almería', 150, and 154 for words attributed to Manfré: 'mas bé creu que la li asseguraré de sarreyns, mas de genoveses'.
[59] Sánchez Martínez, 'Mallorquines y Genovesos en Almería', 157.
[60] Sánchez Martínez, 'Mallorquines y Genovesos en Almería', 162.
[61] Sánchez Martínez, 'Mallorquines y Genovesos en Almería', 162.
[62] For a powerful demonstration of Genoese interests in Granada, see J. Heers, 'Le royaume de Grenade et la politique marchande de Gênes en Occident (xve siècle)', *Le Moyen Age*, 63 (1957), 87–121, repr. in J. Heers, *Société et Economie à Gênes (XIVe-XVe siècles)* (London, 1979), essay VII.

trial record; there are six visitors to Málaga and five to Granada.[63] However, this is the tip of the iceberg: there were twenty Mallorcans in the Granadan kingdom in 1334, half in Almería, six in Málaga and four in the capital, and clearly the outbreak of war did not totally destroy business.[64] The central point here is that Mallorca derived its commercial importance from its function as an intermediary not on one but on several trade routes. It was a safe base from which southern French, Catalan and Italian ships could penetrate north Africa, bringing western woollen and linen cloth through the Balearics to the Muslim countries. It was a safe harbour on the rapid route tying the Tyrrhenian ports of Italy to eastern Spain, much favoured by the Genoese and the Pisans. It was a bridge between al-Andalus and the western Mediterranean. Finally, it was a much-valued staging post for ships on their way to and from the Atlantic, the majority of which did not sail directly to Flanders and England but only as far as Seville, where ocean-going vessels assured the connection to the far north.

IV

The intermediary role of the Balearics on the medieval trade routes was shared by the mainland territories of the kingdom of Majorca. The major city in the rough triangle Roussillon–Cerdagne–Conflent was Perpignan, a relatively young centre of trade and industry which (despite the establishment of a consulate as early as 1197) began to flourish only in the mid-thirteenth century, when it came under the rule of James I of Aragon. Notarial records preserved in Perpignan reveal how the town became a centre for the redistribution of Flemish and northern French cloth brought south by road, often by merchants of Saint-Antonin in south-western France, sometimes by merchants of Perpignan who had reached Flanders.[65] Its position as the last staging post before the Pyrenees, offering a bridge over the River Têt, provided its natives with an opportunity to develop a

[63] For the role of Almería as an outport of Granada, see Blanca Garí, 'Why Almería? An Islamic port in the compass of Genoa', in the special issue on *Aspects of medieval Spain, 711–1492* of the *Journal of Medieval History*, 18 (1992), 211–31.

[64] Sánchez Martínez, 'Mallorquines y Genoveses en Almería', 139–40.

[65] R. W. Emery, 'Flemish cloth and Flemish merchants in Perpignan in the thirteenth century', *Essays in medieval life and thought in honor of A. P. Evans*, ed. R. W. Emery, J. H. Mundy and B. N. Nelson (New York, 1955), 153–65. For Perpignan merchants in Flanders, see ADP, notarial register 3E1, f.31r; Reg. 3E1, f.39v; Emery, 'Flemish merchants', 155 and docs. 7 and 8, 164.

carrying trade across the Pyrenees towards nearby Girona, Ripoll and Vic. By the early fourteenth century this carrying trade was greatly extended and enhanced, reaching as far south as Valencia, and using as means of transport not so much the ships of Collioure and Port-Vendres as overland mule trains.[66] A similar picture, but on a smaller scale, can be drawn for Puigcerdà, the major centre in the mountainous hinterland of Cerdagne.[67]

The expansion of Perpignan's trade and industry is visible in the ground plan of the town itself.[68] As early as 1249 James I was issuing letters of protection to Perpignan cloth workshops, and industrial areas were laid out: a *paratoria vetus*, alongside a new zone of workshops. The leather industry was highly developed, with secondary industries such as shoe-making, parchment preparation and glove-making.[69] But it was the textile industry that remained the special pride of the city, with which its prosperity was identified; it was *lo millor e pus principal membre de la vila*; it was *la cosa per la qual la dita vila ha pres creximent e poblacio*.[70] King Sanç intervened in 1317 to regroup textile workers in their own suburbs, and provided capital for programmes to build workshops. (The same year he confiscated the promissory notes of the Perpignan Jews, whose funds he may have hoped to redirect to these new industrial enterprises.[71]) There are striking parallels here to the slightly earlier intervention by the Aragonese kings in the textile industry of Barcelona. Once again, Puigcerdà provides another parallel; it too switched from an emphasis on the transmission of Flemish cloths into Spain to an emphasis on the sale of its own cloths. Among its cloth merchants were both Jews and Christians. In the third Pyrenean area under Majorcan rule, Conflent, the small but flourishing centre at Villefranche developed its own cloth trade with the help of royal privileges that boosted its fifteen-day fair. In 1327/8 cloth of Villefranche was being exported to Mallorca.[72]

---

[66] G. Romestan, 'Draperie roussillonnaise et draperie languedocienne dans la première moitié du xivᵉ siècle', *52° Congrès de la Fédération historique du Languedoc méditerranéen et du Roussillon*, (Montpellier, 1970) 31–59. Emery, 'Flemish cloth', 162, surmises that the routes carrying cloth south shifted towards Perpignan and away from Montpellier by the end of the thirteenth century, in reaction to French fiscal policies. This would accord with some of the arguments presented in chapter 8 supra.

[67] Durliat, *Art*, 54–6. For the history of Puigcerdà, see *Iᵒ Congrès Internacional d'Història: 8ᵒ Centenari de la Fundació de Puigcerdà (1177–1977)*, Institut d'Estudis Ceretans (Puigcerdà, 1983).   [68] The role of the Jews has already been addressed in chapter 5.

[69] Durliat, *Art*, 44; Alomar, *Urbanismo regional*, 96–100.

[70] Cited by Durliat, *Art*, 48 from a text of 1417.

[71] For Sanç's anti-Jewish measures, see chapter 5.   [72] Durliat, *Art*, 56, n.154.

A further common feature between Roussillon–Cerdagne and Barcelona is the stimulus to the development of a local cloth industry provided by the decline of the north French and Flemish centres of cloth production during the early fourteenth century. Despite the friendly attitude of the Majorcan kings to their overweening French neighbours, French and Majorcan tariff barriers also helped reduce the supply of northern cloths to Roussillon; this prompted the cloth producers of Perpignan to develop their own woollen cloths in imitation of what was traditionally imported from Flanders and England.[73] Such plans might have had scant chance of success but for the growing ease of access to English wool, which arrived both by land and sea from the late thirteenth century onwards; as well as a land route by way of Montpellier and the Rhône, northward links were secured through English-owned Gascony and the sea passage round Brittany to the English Channel. However, the Mallorcan role in opening the Atlantic routes to Mediterranean shipping cannot be ignored. Perpignan and Collioure did not send their own vessels to obtain northern wool, but fellow-subjects of the king of Majorca could obtain it for them through the Straits of Gibraltar. The result of bulk purchases of raw wool was that the Perpignan merchants were able to undercut the cost of Flemish woollen cloth in Mediterranean markets. Perpignan gained a good reputation for its cloths, even if they never achieved the glamorous reputation of those of Flanders; in the early fourteenth century, *pirpignani* were mentioned by Francesco Pegolotti in his *Pratica della Mercatura*.[74]

It can be seen that the kings of Majorca did not confine their patronage to the new economic initiatives of their Balearic subjects. On their mainland territories, there was the same interest in the foundation and expansion of towns, the protection of local industry and (by way of tariff barriers at Collioure and elsewhere) the favouring of local merchants over those of Catalonia proper. The economic success of the Roussillon–Cerdagne region derived from its advantageous position on the trade routes as well as from royal

[73] G. Romestan, 'A propos du commerce des draps dans la Péninsule Ibérique au Moyen Age: les marchands languedociens dans le royaume de Valence pendant la première moitié du xivᵉ siècle', *Bulletin Philologique et Historique (jusqu'à 1610) du Comité des Travaux historiques et scientifiques, 1969, Actes du 94ᵉ Congrès des Sociétés savantes tenu à Pau,* vol. i, *Les relations franco-espagnols jusqu'au XVIIᵉ siècle* (Paris, 1972), 115–92.
[74] Allan Evans, *The Pratica della Mercatura of Francesco Pegolotti* (Cambridge, MA, 1936), 55, 58; also, 425, where it is suggested that by the mid-fourteenth century some *pirpignani* were in fact being made in Florence in imitation of the original: surely a further tribute to Perpignan's success, despite the threat such imitations posed.

patronage, and here the development of Balearic trade was of some importance; supplies of northern wool could often be guaranteed by sea when the land routes were inaccessible. On the other hand, there is little evidence that the merchants of Perpignan and its neighbours were heavily involved in trade across the Mediterranean. It seems that – notwithstanding the respectable role of the Collioure fleet – it was the Balearic subjects of the kings of Majorca who dominated the kingdom's trade with the Maghrib, even when the goods they were carrying were of Roussillonnais origin. There is some evidence for Perpignanais merchants trading in early fourteenth-century Sicily, but the evidence for Mallorcans is far more plentiful.[75] Even the intra-Majorcan trade routes linking the islands to Collioure were dominated by Mallorcan shipping, as the *ancoratge* documents make plain.

To some extent there was a differentiation of function; the mainland territories had a more obviously industrial profile, while the islands flourished as entrepôts. Even so, there was an overlap, as Mallorca's cloth production took off and as merchants of Perpignan used the land routes to reach into Spain. Privileges for Mallorcan merchants in Sicily and Sardinia also attracted merchants of Roussillon, since they were issued in favour of all the king's subjects. Yet one group that had some difficulty in convincing the royal court of its right to enjoy such privileges was the merchant community of Montpellier, the third major economic centre in the kingdom.

v

Not merely did the king of Majorca share his authority in Montpellier with the king of France, especially after 1293, when Philip IV bought the small area of the town controlled by the bishop of Maguelonne.[76] In addition, Montpellier was closely tied to the economy of French Languedoc, and could be squeezed in a vice by the French king if this served his political and financial ends; lacking a good port of its own, it came increasingly to depend on a French trade outlet at Aigues-Mortes. The city was a major centre of banking, but there were also

[75] H. Bresc, 'Marchands de Narbonne et du Midi en Sicile (1300–1460)', *Narbonne. Archéologie et Histoire*, vol. II, *Narbonne au Moyen Age. 65° Congrès de la Fédération historique du Languedoc méditerranéen et du Roussillon* (Montpellier, 1973), 93–9, which also deals with some merchants of Perpignan; Durliat, *Art*, 51; C. Trasselli, 'Prezzi dei panni a Palermo nel XIV secolo', *Economia e Storia*, 1 (1954), 88–90.

[76] J. Strayer, *The Reign of Philip the Fair* (Princeton, NJ, 1980), 53, 106–7, 408.

cloth workshops, both for production from scratch and for the finishing of imported textiles by *tenheyres* (dyers) and other specialists.[77] The city did not earn as fine a reputation for its cloth as did Perpignan, despite some encouragement by the Majorcan king; like Mallorca, its main contribution to the flow of international trade was as a service centre, where goods were collected for trans-shipment and where finance could be arranged for new enterprises.

The links to Mallorca and Menorca were strong. The earliest commercial contracts from Montpellier give a clear idea of the role of Montpelliérain finance along the trade route tying the city to the Balearics and beyond.[78] In January 1294 Pere Calvini and Pere Burgues, merchants of Mallorca, stated their debt to Pere Turasie and his brother Arnaud, merchants of Narbonne, incurred as the result of the purchase in Montpellier of white woollen cloth of Narbonne (the original 'blankets' of Narbonne) worth £90 in money of Melgueil.[79] The Mallorcan merchant Pere Burgues was also the creditor of a Genoese merchant trading through Montpellier, Girardino Cervelas.[80] In March 1294 a merchant of Montpellier, Hugo de Casa, invested £652 of Melgueil with Raffino Dales, who came from Alessandria in Piedmont, for trade in cloths and other goods *per mare et terram in insula maioricarum*.[81]

It is the co-operative nature of trade through Montpellier that is most striking: merchants of Mallorca, Menorca, Montpellier, Barcelona, Marseilles, Genoa, Narbonne and many other towns came together in business here; Montpellier's trade with Mallorca was not exclusively in the hands of subjects of the king of Majorca. This is suggested by the fragmentary acts of 1293–4, and confirmed by the more plentiful notarial acts of 1327–43; much further back in time, it

---

[77] For textiles: L.J. Thomas, *Montpellier ville marchande. Histoire économique et sociale de Montpellier des origines à 1870* (Montpellier, 1936), 37–66. For banking: K. Reyerson, *Business, banking and finance in medieval Montpellier* (Toronto, 1985). For the economy as a whole, see Germain, *Histoire du commerce de Montpellier.*

[78] The first study of the notarial documents cited here was that in the Yale doctoral thesis of K. Reyerson, *Commerce and society in Montpellier, 1250–1350,* 2 vols. (University Microfilms International, 1974); my own archive researches were guided by her invaluable tables, vol. II, 115–278.

[79] Archives Municipales de Montpellier, BB1, f.63v, no. 1; *Archives de la ville de Montpellier,* vol. XIII, *Inventaire analytique série BB (Notaires et greffiers du consolat 1293–1387),* ed. M. de Dainville, M. Gouron and L. Valls (Montpellier, 1984), 28.

[80] BB1, f.79r, no. 5; *Inventaire analytique,* 33.

[81] BB1, f.83v-r, no. 4; *Inventaire analytique,* 35. Interestingly, the additional words *et alibi ubi ut mihi videbitur* appear in the text but were then deleted by the notary. This was to be a trip to Mallorca only.

is obvious that ties between Montpellier and Barcelona had been close under James I, when important local businessmen such as Joan Hom-de-Deu had intimate ties to leading Catalan traders.[82] In Montpellier during November 1327 Michael Macellarius of Barcelona appointed a Mallorcan as his factor in business to be conducted in Mallorca; he was to travel by one of two *linhs* (*lenys*), one at least of which hailed from Barcelona.[83] In October 1340 Montpellier merchants were planning to use a cog from Perpignan to send Autun linens to the Byzantine Empire.[84] A few months later it was a Mallorcan cog that was to take scarlet French woollen cloth to the same destination on behalf of merchants of Montpellier; like many ships cited in these acts, it lay at Aigues-Mortes, the major seaport near Montpellier.[85] The function of Montpellier as a point of transmission southwards of north French and Flemish cloth is thus clear; as the Catalan–Aragonese area of influence expanded, so too did that of Montpellier. Several cloth-bearing expeditions towards Valencia are recorded in the period from 1327 to 1342.[86] Although a vigorous trade in cloth towards Romania, Cyprus and Armenia is documented, the Montpelliérains generally left north African trade to the merchants of Mallorca. Equally, the Mallorcans left the overland trade with Champagne in Montpelliérain hands, and the captain-general of the French merchants at the Champagne fairs was normally from Montpellier. Some leading Montpellier families, such as the Cruzols, had especially close ties to Champagne; in this case, there were also links as far east as Cyprus.

Evidence for trade between Montpellier and the other Majorcan lands is reasonably good. Money was frequently advanced in Montpellier for repayment in the Balearic islands, though once again non-Majorcan subjects are as common as Majorcan ones in such transactions. In July 1327 £238 6s 8d were promised in repayment of a debt incurred at Montpellier by merchants of Narbonne; the amount of the original advance is not stated, to avoid accusations of

---

[82] Abulafia, 'Catalan merchants', 217–18.

[83] Archives Départementales de l'Hérault, Montpellier, II E95/368, f.78v. Reyerson gives the date wrongly as May 1327.

[84] II E95/374, no. 268. Goods also arrived from the Levant on their way to Perpignan: II E95/375, f.5r, 29 May 1339.

[85] II E95/374, no. 275. As a result of the rebinding of this register, this document has disappeared from view.

[86] G. Romestan, 'Les relations commerciales entre Montpellier et Valence dans la première moitié du XIVe siècle', *VIII Congreso de História de la Corona de Aragón, Valencia 1967*, Section 2, *La Corona de Aragón en el siglo XIV*, vol. III (Valencia, 1973), 243–53.

usury. The creditors were from Mallorca, Collioure and Empuries (in Catalonia), and the money was to be repaid in Mallorca within five weeks.[87] In September 1327 a Menorcan merchant advanced money to a Barcelona merchant, to be repaid in one month in Barcelona, in the form of £400 of Barcelona money.[88] Menorcan creditors helped to finance trade as far away as Bruges, and Menorcan debtors received funds from Leridan creditors in their trade with their home island.[89] The evidence for direct links between Menorca and Montpellier is perhaps not surprising, given Menorca's position astride the sea route from Aigues-Mortes to Mallorca and its usefulness as a supplier of dairy goods and livestock, notably mules.[90]

Under pressure from French royal officials at Carcassonne, Béziers, Beaucaire and Nîmes, Montpellier was drawn increasingly into the French political sphere.[91] Some of the ways this was achieved have been observed in earlier chapters; but an overview of the problem may be worthwhile. It is noticeable that the early fourteenth-century notaries were expected to date their documents by the regnal year of the king of France, and not his vassal the king of Majorca. French interference in the economy of Montpellier was felt most acutely by the Italians, who were expelled from the city by Philip III as early as 1278 and were permitted a limited existence at Nîmes before their eventual return in 1314; under James I, the Sienese, Piacenzans and others had been a significant force in the city economy.[92] Similarly the Jews of Montpellier suffered in the wake of the expulsion from Capetian France in 1306, just when the king of Majorça decided not to follow Philip the Fair's lead; indeed, many southern French Jews moved to Majorcan Roussillon. It has been seen already that Montpellier came under pressure of a different sort as the French kings developed Louis IX's new port at Aigues-Mortes as a rival trade centre to Montpellier. Narbonne apart (and Narbonne had a long tradition of virtual autonomy) Aigues-Mortes was the first truly French trading station on the Mediterranean, and the French kings sought either to channel goods through it past Montpellier, or at least

[87] II E95/368, f.11v.   [88] II E95/368, f.39r (not 39v as stated by Reyerson in her tables).
[89] II E95/369, f.70r, 1333; II E95/369, f.83v, 1333; II E95/369, f. 84r, 1333. The appearance in these documents of several members of the Amargos family of Menorca may indicate that this family had a special role in Menorcan trade with Montpellier.
[90] In 1328 a Menorcan sold a mule at Montpellier to a carrier from Perpignan: II E95/368, f.104v.
[91] T. N. Bisson, *Assemblies and representation in Languedoc in the thirteenth century* (Princeton, NJ, 1964), 259–62..   [92] Reyerson, *Business, banking and finance*, 12.

to make it a staple port through which Montpellier's Mediterranean trade would be obliged to pass.[93] The inadequate facilities at the outports of Montpellier within the Majorcan barony of Aumelas in any case stimulated merchants to use Aigues-Mortes. Lattes and Frontignan thus never established themselves as viable rivals to their all-French neighbour. As Riera Melis has shown, French pressure was maintained even when the kings of Majorca were close allies of France during the War of the Sicilian Vespers.[94] It was in fact in the middle of the war that Philip bought the bishop's share of Montpellier.

Maybe it was because the French had been so successful that Montpellier merchants did not secure the favours that the kings of Majorca bestowed on all their other subjects. The Majorcan kings may also have resented the dominating role of the consuls within Montpellier, where even under James I royal power had been greatly circumscribed. The right of its citizens to the same exemption from trade taxes as other Majorcans was in dispute around 1338/9. Since the massive document originally preserved in the Montpellier city archive that reports the arguments for and against Montpellier has disappeared from view, it is hard to be sure whether there was ever any lengthy period when Montpelliérains were treated as full Majorcans.[95] What does survive is the set of instructions for the commission of inquiry, and a helpful seventeenth-century summary of the main text under the heading *Procedure faite à Perpignan pour vérifier les concessions faites par les Seigneurs de Montpellier aux consuls de Montpellier pour raison de l'immunité à eux accordée de leudes, piages et costumes par mer et par terre.*[96] These documents reveal that it was in March 1338 that King James III of Majorca decided to establish the commission to examine Montpelliérain grievances.[97]

---

[93] For a general account, see G. Jehel, *Aigues-Mortes. Un port pour un roi. Les Capétiens et la Méditerrannée* (Roanne, 1985).   [94] Riera Melis, *La Corona de Aragón*, 99–102.

[95] The archive reference is Arm. A, Cassette XVII, Louvet no. 324, and the document contained 360 folios; see *Archives de la ville de Montpellier. Inventaires et documents publiés par les soins de l'administration municipale.* vol. I, *Notice sur les anciens inventaires. Inventaire du Grand Chartrier*, part. 2, *Inventaire du 'Grand Chartrier' rédigé par Pierre Louvet en 1662–1663 publié avec des notes et une table*, ed. J. Berthelé (Montpellier, 1896), 44. The only study of the MS is the brief but valuable notice by G. Romestan, 'Les marchands de Montpellier et la leude de Majorque pendant la première moitié du XIVe siècle', *Majorque, Languedoc et Roussillon de l'Antiquité à nos jours. 53° Congrès de la Fédération historique du Languedoc méditerranéen et du Roussillon*, (Montpellier, 1982), 53–60.

[96] Arm. A, Cass. XVII, no. 324bis, f.1r; Arm. A, Cass XVII, no. 325. For a fuller discussion and for the text of these two documents, see appendix II.

[97] Arm. A, Cass. XVII, no. 324bis, f.1r, referring to Arm. A, Cass. XVII, no. 324, f.1r.

The Montpellier merchants were able to lay before the commision documents dating back as far as Peter II of Aragon in 1204 that apparently demonstrated the special rights of the city's merchants;[98] confirmed by James I, these privileges were renewed (most importantly) under the kings of independent Majorca, for instance by James II and by Sanç in 1298 and 1311.[99] In addition, witnesses were summoned to testify to practice since 1300.[100] As far as can be seen, many of the royal privileges were simply blanket confirmations of past *loix municipales, statuts, libertés, compositions, privilèges et ordonnances*. It is certain that a particular concern of the procurators who examined these claims was the right to exemption from trade taxes at Ciutat de Mallorca and at Collioure, since a separate quire was set aside for an enquiry *sur la franchise des leudes, péages et coustumes, tant par terre que par mer, à ceux de Mompelier qui trafiqueront à Majorque et Collieure*.[101]

A description of Montpellier at this time insists that the city was half full of Italians, Catalans and other foreign residents: *plus des deux parties des habitants sont d'estranges parties, les uns Cathalans, les autres Espaignols, Jennevois, Lombards, Venessiens, Chiprois, Provensals, Alamans et d'autres plusieurs estranges nacions*.[102] While the Catalans of Barcelona were only too glad to see the back of Italian competitors, the banishment of Italians from Montpellier under Philip III of France was probably intended to damage the city's economy. The problem was that there were as many advantages as disadvantages in owing allegiance to the king of Majorca as well as the king of France. Occasionally, the city suffered double taxation.[103] The final sale to France in 1349 was in a sense a formality, for by now the town was under very powerful French influence.[104] On the other hand, the peculiar status of the city may have strengthened economic ties with such valuable non-French trading partners as Barcelona, Valencia and the Balearic islands, and have allowed, via the Balearics, indirect

---

[98] Arm. A, Cass. XVII, no. 324bis, f.1r, referring to Arm. A, Cass. XVII, no. 324, f.8v.

[99] Arm. A, Cass. XVII, no. 324bis, f.1r-2v, referring to Arm. A, Cass. XVII, no. 324, f.11r-12v, 17r-60v.

[100] Arm. A, Cass. XVII, no. 324bis, f.2v-3r, referring to Arm. A, Cass. XVII, no. 324, ff.61r-304r.

[101] The words are those of Louvet in the seventeenth century: *Inventaire du Grand Chartrier*, p. 44. The document, no. 325, resurfaced while this book was nearing completion. A fuller discussion is offered in Appendix II.

[102] Thomas, 'Montpellier', 36; Germain, *Commerce*, vol. I, ii.

[103] Rogozinski, *Power, caste and law*, 142–5.

[104] It is therefore strange that not long after the king of France granted Montpellier to Charles the Bad of Navarre.

access to African markets which were not actively penetrated by the city's own merchants.

VI

The commercial links between Mallorca and other parts of the western Mediterranean were strengthened in the early fourteenth century by a series of trade privileges that reflected the political and family bonds tying together the kings of Majorca, Sicily, Naples, Aragon and Castile. In 1305 and 1313 Mallorcan merchants visiting Sicily were granted a reduction in taxes to the same level as the merchants of Barcelona.[105] Another target was Naples, whose king had a Mallorcan wife; in 1325 King Robert confirmed their commercial and legal privileges.[106] The chain of links to Naples was made secure by events a couple of years earlier; the Catalan invasion of Sardinia in 1323 was the start of a long and painful imperial adventure, but for the Mallorcans, who gave the king of Aragon naval help, it was a chance to gain a commercial privilege that once again placed the Mallorcan merchants on an equal footing with Catalan businessmen.[107] Looking west, the Mallorcans strengthened their links to north-west Africa and the Atlantic by winning promises of protection from several Castilian kings: Alfonso X in 1284, Ferdinand IV in 1310, Alfonso XI in 1334 (at the end of the war with Granada); it has been seen that there was a Majorcan consul in Seville from 1308.[108] Durliat has pointed out that such frequency of confirmation suggests that Mallorcan rights were probably being ignored for long periods, rather than respected; however, the fragile political relationships of the westernmost corner of the Mediterranean, where Muslim fleets were reasserting themselves in defence of Islamic Granada, not just in 1330 but also at the end of the decade, were another motive for constant approaches by the Castilians to the royal court of Majorca.[109]

The economic vitality of the Majorcan territories owed much to the excellent geographical position of Montpellier, Perpignan and the Balearics on the trade routes linking not merely Mediterranean Europe but northern Europe too to Africa, Italy and the Levant. In

---

[105] Archives Départementales des Pyrénées Orientales, Perpignan, Archives de la ville de Perpignan, AA1, Livre vert majeur, f.107v-108r; and AA3, Livre vert mineur, f.98r-v, ff.99r-100r; also *Documenta regni Majoricarum*, 99–100 (for a Mallorcan text of the 1305 privilege).
[106] ADP, AA3, f.128v.
[107] See appendix 1; ADP, AA3, ff.192v-196r.   [108] Durliat, *Art*, 34–5.
[109] Robson, 'Catalan fleet and Moorish sea-power (1337–1344)', 386–408.

other words, Montpellier, Perpignan and Mallorca were all gateways to the Atlantic as well as to the Mediterranean. Even when the merchants of these areas were not very active in the transport of locally produced industrial goods, they found business colleagues, in many cases Majorcan subjects, otherwise Catalans and Italians, to carry their produce across the Mediterranean.

The central question is what influence the creation of the kingdom of Majorca had on their joint and separate fortunes. Royal encouragement to textile producers, tax reductions for Mallorcan and Roussillonnais merchants, the patronage overseas of Majorcan consulates: these are some of the key indications that the monarchy sought to foster the prosperity of its subjects. Favours to Majorcan merchants did not significantly damage royal revenues, since the Balearics attracted so many non-native ships. Elaborate tariff lists from Collioure and elsewhere testify to the efficiency of the kingdom's customs collectors. A reduction of dependence on foreign grain imports might be achieved if the new agro-towns in the Balearics proved a success; but the agrarian sector remained poorly developed. Attempts at integration appear to have been made, notably around 1300. But they were partial and short-term. The economic success of the kingdom was not determined by the monarchy; but it was an objective the monarchy actively sought, with the aim of achieving political and financial security while under constant threat from both France and Aragon.

CHAPTER 10

From the Mediterranean to the Atlantic

I

It has been seen that in the late Middle Ages Mallorca occupied a strategic position in the commercial networks of the Catalan and Italian merchants within the Mediterranean; but the Atlantic also increasingly entered into the calculations of Mallorcan businessmen and their colleagues, and by the late thirteenth century sea links were established as far afield as England and Flanders. These consisted in part, and at first, of indirect links, via Seville, which acted as a terminus for Genoese, Catalan and Mallorcan ships coming out of the Mediterranean, and for Basque and Cantabrian vessels coming from northern Spain and beyond. But penetration of the Atlantic was also directed south-westwards, down the coast of Atlantic Morocco, which features prominently in the *Dret de exida* documents for Mallorcan Muslims in the early fourteenth century.[1] Sailings to Anfa and other ports nearby may long have been more numerous and profitable than those to England or Flanders; but they are also less well documented. Sailings further south as far as the Canaries were certainly a much greater rarity, but have attracted a considerable modern literature. Some shipping from Atlantic ports also penetrated through Gibraltar into the western Mediterranean, as the *ancoratge* records confirm, with their references to boats from northern Spain. Indeed, both Seville and Mallorca became interchange points for goods moving from the Atlantic to the Mediterranean and vice versa in the early fourteenth century.

The first part of this chapter concerns the attempts by Mallorcan ships to penetrate beyond the Mediterranean, on the route to Flanders and England. A second theme of the chapter is an aspect of

---

[1] Sastre Moll, *Economía y sociedad*, 53, 55.

Mallorcan penetration into the Atlantic that has been discussed more fully than the trade to Flanders or England, but which is much more poorly documented, the Mallorcan rôle in the discovery and early settlement of the Canary islands. This subject raises important questions about the activities of the famous Mallorcan cartographers, and their knowledge of what lay beyond the straits of Gibraltar, so a look at their surviving work is also necessary.

The direct sea links between England and Flanders on the one hand and Mallorca on the other had a prehistory in overland trade, mainly through the southern French ports, and then across Langue-doc to Bordeaux or the westernmost Basque ports, above all Bayonne, but also largely overland along the Rhône route favoured by Italian and Provençal merchants bound for Champagne and Flanders. Montpellier was one channel through which this trade passed; but, particularly in northern Europe, the merchants of Montpellier seem disconnected from the Mallorcans and other Catalans. The Mont-pelliérains were reasonably well known in England: in 1294 they received a safe-conduct to trade in England, on the grounds that they were subjects of the king of Majorca; this occurred a year after the acquisition by King Philip IV of France of the bishop of Mague-lonne's rights in Montpellier, and just as England and France were going to war over Gascony. Edward I that year renounced French overlordship in the duchy. Thus the merchants of Montpellier needed to show that they were a neutral party, loyal not to France but to the king of Majorca, who at this stage was himself unable to control the island from which he drew his title. The Montpelliérains were active in the export of wool from England via Gascony to the Mediterranean (probably to Italy in the main); they were pressed to make loans to the English crown, notably a loan of 500 marks in 1277; they traded out of Lynn in Norfolk to and from Norway, using Norwegian ships to convey falcons to England and, it seems, spices towards Scandinavia.[2] Some Montpelliérains may be concealed under the heading of 'merchants of Provence', and many did business alongside or in partnership with other southern French merchants, notably those of Cahors.[3] What is most striking is the part they played in the transport of wool, using the partly overland route that cut across southern France from Bordeaux; it may be significant

[2] T. H. Lloyd, *The English wool trade in the Middle Ages* (Cambridge, 1977), 45–6; T. H. Lloyd, *Alien merchants in England in the High Middle Ages* (Hassocks, Sussex, 1982), 94.
[3] Lloyd, *Alien merchants*, 94.

that they are most active in the export of wool to the Mediterranean before the opening of the route through the Straits of Gibraltar. By 1300 it was the Balearic section of the kingdom of Majorca rather than Montpellier that was becoming the nodal point on the route carrying English wool to Italy: the two routes in a sense competed, and, while the Gascony–Languedoc route never lost its importance entirely, the sea route gained primacy in the long term. An important factor here was surely the competition between England and France for control of Gascony, and the disruption to trade caused by the wars of Philip IV and VI against the English in Aquitaine. Thus in what follows attention concentrates on Mallorcan merchants known or believed to have originated in the Balearic islands; some may in fact have hailed from the Majorcan-owned towns of Collioure and Perpignan, or even Montpellier, but the merchants of Montpellier were generally distinguished quite clearly in the English documents from those of Mallorca itself.

One essential prerequisite of the creation of direct links between the Mediterranean and the Atlantic was technological: sailing through the Straits demanded great skill, because the Atlantic waters migrate at a speed of about six knots into the Mediterranean, which stands at a lower level than the Ocean.[4] Careful management of tricky winds makes the journey possible in the right conditions, though recourse to oars might be necessary. Entry is easier; Sigurð of Norway and his Viking ancestors have already been found raiding the Balearics in earlier centuries. Nevertheless, there was clearly some traffic from the Mediterranean to the Atlantic; movements from Italy to Seville are recorded in the Genoese notarial registers of the twelfth century.[5] In the event of difficulty, Ceuta served as a point of trans-shipment.[6] It is striking how often the city appears in Genoese and Mallorcan commercial documentation of the early to mid-thirteenth century.

Another essential pre-requisite of the creation of Mediterranean–Atlantic trade was the clearance of the seas around Gibraltar. The Christian advances in Spain, and the winning of general control of the Mediterranean by the Italians and (later) the Catalans in the

---

[4] John H. Pryor, *Geography, technology and war. Studies in the maritime history of the Mediterranean, 649–1571* (Cambridge, 1988), 13.

[5] See R. Constable, *At the edge of the west: international trade and traders in Muslim Spain (1000–1250)*, (Columbia University Ph.D. thesis; University Microfilms International, 1989), 54–8.

[6] On Ceuta, see C. E. Dufourcq, 'La question de Ceuta au XIIIe siècle', *Hespéris*, 42 (1955).

course of the twelfth and thirteenth centuries made passage through the far west of the Mediterranean much safer by the 1270s.[7] The conquest of Murcia in 1265 was perhaps especially important, since it brought the Castilians a Mediterranean coast, and brought also an interest in securing the seas to which Christian ships had access either side of Granada. Granada itself now possessed only a single land frontier, with Castile, and occasionally found itself forced to pay *parias* (tribute) to Castile.[8] Almería remained a Muslim port of some repute, giving access to Granada City, and Málaga also gained in significance as a port of call for Italians and Catalans; Catalans and Castilians nurtured plans for the conquest of Almería at the start of the fourteenth century.[9] However, the threat from Muslim piracy was reduced; the way to the Atlantic was effectively open. The danger of a resurgence of Muslim sea-power remained, however; in 1338 Abu'l Hasan Ali I, sultan of Morocco, despatched sixteen galleys to the Balearics, and in 1340 he embarked on an invasion of Spain, in league with the king of Granada, which resulted in the launching of a massive fleet of sixty galleys and nearly two hundred support ships. The threat to Castile and Aragon was felt acutely.[10] However, this only accentuated the need for careful policing of the Mediterranean exit.

II

The Catalan – let alone the Mallorcan – presence in late medieval England has received little attention from historians, despite the existence of good studies of the Castilian ties to England in the same period by Teófilo Ruiz and by Wendy Childs.[11] The reason seems obvious: the volume of English trade both to Atlantic Spain and to Andalucia greatly surpassed that to Catalonia, and the primary Mediterranean customer for English goods was surely Italy, above all Florence. Yet the picture is not so simple. Florence, lacking a fleet of its own until the conquest of Pisa in 1406, had to rely on the use of

---

[7] A. Lewis, 'Northern European sea-power and the Straits of Gibraltar, 1031–1350', in *Order and Innovation in the Middle Ages. Essays in honor of Joseph R. Strayer*, ed. W. C. Jordan, B. McNab and T. F. Ruiz (Princeton, NJ, 1976), 139–64.
[8] Harvey, *Islamic Spain*, 26–8, 191–2, 198. [9] Gari, 'Why Almería?', 226–8.
[10] See the fundamental article by Robson, 'The Catalan fleet and Moorish sea-power', 386–408; also, Pryor, *Geography*, 144.
[11] Wendy Childs, *Anglo-Castilian trade in the later Middle Ages* (Manchester, 1978); T. F. Ruiz, 'Castilian merchants in England, 1248–1350', in *Order and innovation in the Middle Ages*, repr. in Castilian as 'Mercaderes castellanos en Inglaterra, 1248–1350', in T. F. Ruiz, *Sociedad y poder real en Castilla en la Baja Edad Media* (Barcelona, 1981), 201–24.

ships of other cities; Genoese trade with England satisfied the industrial needs not of Genoa, which were slight, but of Florence and other inland centres. The Catalans had an important rôle in the maintenance of contact between England and the Mediterranean, since there were periods when Genoa was unable to trade freely with England; its links to France during the Hundred Years War led to its exclusion from Southampton and London. Other merchants seized the chance to carry English wool to the Mediterranean in their place: among them, the Catalans, including some Mallorcans, who supplied both Florence and the lands of the Crown of Aragon, and who received the financial backing of the great Florentine banks – the Bardi, Peruzzi and Acciaiuoli. Alongside them, often, indeed, in partnership with them, there worked merchants of Andalucia, for the merchants and shippers of all the coastlands of Spain were in an ideal geographical position, midway between the markets of the Atlantic and those of the Mediterranean.

This is to suggest a rather different view of the Mallorcan penetration of England to that offered by Roberto Lopez in his controversial article on 'Majorcans and Genoese on the North Sea route in the thirteenth century'.[12] Although himself a Genoese, he came to the surprising conclusion that 'the Majorcans originally led and the Genoese followed' in the opening of the sea-passage linking the Mediterranean to the North Sea around 1277. His argument was that Mallorca was greatly inferior to Genoa 'in population, capital, business connections and sea-power'; surely, then, if the Genoese had been first on the route to England they would have brooked no competitors, and have excluded Mallorca from the start? Lopez insisted that, within a few decades of the Genoese arrival in England, the Mallorcans were indeed excluded. Genoa had benefited from its own close contacts with Mallorca to steal the secrets of navigation to England; evidence of this rivalry is already visible in a Genoese *commenda* contract of 1274, where members of the de Mari, di Negro and Zaccaria families – all later active in the North Sea trade – propose an expedition to Mallorca and wherever beyond God may lead.[13]

In fact, the evidence suggests that Mallorcans and Genoese opened up access to the North Sea together, not in rivalry. The first reference

---

[12] R. S. Lopez, 'Majorcans and Genoese on the North Sea route in the thirteenth century', *Revue belge de philologie et d'histoire*, 29 (1951), 1163–79; cf. Lewis, 'Northern European sea-power', 139–64.   [13] Lopez, 'Majorcans and Genoese', 1175–6.

to a Mallorcan ship in London dates to 1281, and concerns the galley of William de Bone *de Mayhorke*; yet aboard his ship was the Genoese Bernardus *de Genne*, while there also passed through the port of London that summer two ships, one nef and one galley, of undoubted Genoese ownership.[14] William de Bone carried more than 267 sacks of wool, destined possibly for Italy, though possibly too for Flanders. In the late thirteenth and early fourteenth centuries Mediterranean traders in England acted as carriers between there and Flanders, and it is possible that the Catalans imitated the Genoese by ferrying the prized wools of England to the Flemish towns, where their presence is, as will be seen, clearly documented.

The fact is that around 1280 the Catalans, including the Mallorcans, were providing shipping services for other trading nations in the Mediterranean, and it is no surprise to find that – with their great navigational expertise – they should be doing so beyond the Straits of Gibraltar. Now that Christian rule extended into Andalucia, access to the North Sea was at last much easier, and the Mallorcans would continue to provide shipping services whenever others, notably the Genoese, lacked the vessels required, or were tainted by their links to the kingdom of France.[15] There are useful analogies with the provision of Catalan shipping services in Sicily during the same period. Here too the Mallorcans formed an important group within the Catalan trading community; and (despite Lopez' affirmation to the contrary) it appears that the Mallorcans were very fast in establishing themselves at the hub of the west Mediterranean trade routes in the late thirteenth century; they took good advantage of the superb position of the Balearic islands on the routes from Latin Europe to north Africa and beyond the Straits of Gibraltar.[16]

Lopez found a second reference to a ship of Mallorca, from the summer of 1304.[17] Here again there are two Genoese ships in the port of London, as well as the galley of Pere Berge *Mayoricarum*, carrying more than 328 sacks of wool. The owners of the wool came from Genoa, Piacenza, probably from Venice and maybe from Catalonia or Provence. Pere Berge is perhaps the same person as the Petrus

[14] London Public Record Office (hereafter PRO), E 122, 68/2. The date of departure from London was 25 August, and not as stated by Lopez, 'Majorcans and Genoese', 1173.
[15] Lewis, 'Northern European sea-power', 152–4.
[16] For Sicily, see chapter 7; also Abulafia, 'Catalan merchants'.
[17] PRO, E 122, 68/14; my own examination of this document did not reveal the references Lopez found there, but the condition is poor.

Burget who owned wool aboard one of the Genoese galleys; in any case, the identity of purpose of the Genoese and Mallorcan visitors to England is clear: the carriage of wool out of England. Imports into England aboard these ships included alum, pepper, saffron and leather. It is the classic picture of English trade with the Mediterranean merchants. Lopez pointed out that there were no further references to Mallorcan ships for some time after 1304 in his sources, the Customs Accounts preserved in the Public Record Office in London. However, other English sources from the same archive are, in fact, more forthcoming. The Patent Rolls and Close Rolls reveal several visits to England by Mallorcan ships in the early fourteenth century – beginning, indeed, with documents of the same year, 1304.[18] In fact, as early as 1237 Mallorcan goods may have been reaching England, for in that year the Close Rolls refer to a thousand coney skins *de Meligres*, of Mallorca, brought to London by Spanish and French merchants, and supplied to the royal court.[19] Such goods would probably have travelled overland across southern France before being trans-shipped at Bordeaux.

Edward I of England guaranteed the liberties of foreign merchants trading in England in 1303, and his privilege was re-issued when the rights of Catalans, Majorcans, Castilians, Bardi, Peruzzi or others were in need of repetition.[20] But the king's subjects were often more negligent of Majorcan rights. In October 1304 the crown issued a safe-conduct, valid for one year, to William Pierre, merchant of Mallorca, who had arrived by sea in England seeking justice for a robbery committed against him at sea, near the port of St Mathieu in Brittany.[21] No less a figure than John, duke of Brittany, issued letters in the merchant's favour. William Pierre had started out not from

---

[18] In citing material in the Close Rolls and Patent Rolls, reference will be made both to their location in the Public Record Office, London and to their location in the series of calendars published at the start of the twentieth century: *CCR* for the *Calendar of Close Rolls*; *CPR* for the *Calendar of Patent Rolls*, followed by the name of the reigning king, the years that the individual volume covers and the page reference for the particular document. The intention is to provide an archive reference for each document; a few errors in the otherwise excellent calendars are indicated. In addition, selective references have been given to the compendium by Thomas Rymer, *Foedera, conventiones, literæ, et cujuscunque generis acta publica inter reges Angliæ et alios quosvis imperatores, reges, pontifices, principes, vel communitates*, vol. II (Hagæ Comitis, 1739; repr. Farnborough, 1967).   [19] PRO, c. 54/48 = *CCR* Henry III, 1234–7, 479.

[20] PRO, c. 53/89 = *Calendar of Charter Rolls*, vol. III, 1300–26, 33; and PRO, c. 53/115 = *Calendar of Charter Rolls*, vol. IV, 1327–41, 89; cf. c. 66/170 = *CPR* Edward III, 1327–30, 305 (*Foedera*, vol. II, part 3, 15–17), confirming the document of 1303, and specifically referring, at the end, to merchants of Mallorca.

[21] PRO, c. 66/124 = *CPR* Edward I, 1301–7, 261.

Mallorca but from Seville, where he was in partnership with a local merchant, Domingus Peris (Domingo Pérez); the ship they loaded is described in the Patent Roll as a 'ship of Seville', laden in that city with goods to the value of 4,200 *livres tournois*; its destination was England. But before it was able to cross from Brittany, the ship was pounced upon by no less than eight English ships, some from Bristol, some from East Anglia or elsewhere, and stripped of its ropes, anchors and equipment, taken to England and unloaded. The goods on board were sent all over southern England, the West Country and East Anglia. The crown ordered therefore that a jury be established, with the duty of compensating the two Spanish merchants for their losses.[22] The problem of piracy was exacerbated by the growing conflicts between the English and French kings over control of Gascony. It seems that the ship of Seville was innocently caught up in a conflict that constantly threatened to undermine the trade of England with the Mediterranean, by making the sea-passages impossibly unsafe for trade. It is likely that it was assumed to be a ship friendly to Philip the Fair of France, and thus liable to seizure. It is therefore no coincidence that the Patent Rolls and Close Rolls contain frequent safe-conducts for Majorcan and other merchants at precisely the period when complaints about piracy against Majorcan merchants or ships are most frequent.

But it was not merely Mallorcan trade with England that suffered interference. English ships preyed on foreign ships running between Flanders and the Mediterranean. A particularly severe case occurred on 20 October 1322. Two Mallorcan galleys set out from Flanders for Valencia and Mallorca; the masters were Angelinus Escot and William Bona, and the second name is, of course, reminiscent of that of the first Mallorcan captain to visit England, in 1281; maybe this is a member of the same family.[23] On board the ships were cloths, wool, silver, copper, tin, skins and other goods, under conveyance to merchants based in several different Spanish towns – to Francis Marrades, citizen of Valencia and brother of one of the plaintiffs, to Berengar Letonis, citizen of Manresa, and to unnamed merchants of Mallorca itself. But as the galleys approached the Straits of Dover they were attacked by ships of the Cinque Ports, the privileged ports of south-eastern England; one Mallorcan galley was taken off Calais,

---

[22] PRO, c. 66/124 = *CPR* Edward I, 1301–7, 286.
[23] PRO, c. 66/157 = *CPR* Edward II, 1321–4, 259; PRO, c. 66/158 = *CPR* Edward II, 1321–4, 317.

but the other, somehow separated, was seized at Sandwich, an outport of London. Both galleys were then brought to the Kent coast at the Isle of Thanet, despoiled there and again at Sandwich, and finally allowed to depart, with their crews stripped naked. Probably what appears at first sight a third galley, reportedly carrying the property of a merchant of Bayonne (in English Gascony) is in fact the same ship as the ship seized off Sandwich; this too was a ship of *Malogret* or Mallorca, and its goods were taken away at Sandwich; and the merchant of Bayonne, Bertrand de Vylar, may have been a relative of the Bernard Vylar of *Barselon* who appears trading to England in 1344: in other words, 'Bayonne' may conceivably be an error for '*Barselon*'.[24]

The kings of Aragon and of Majorca expressed deep concern at these events. James of Aragon requested that restitution to the tune of £400 be made to one of the merchants who had been despoiled, Berengar Letonis of Manresa.[25] Edward II's court replied that the English king would be only too glad to provide speedy justice; however, the court was unaware who had committed the trespass and, therefore, according to English law, immediate restitution could not be made. But the English king would be prepared as a favour to establish a special commission to identify the malefactors and to secure restitution. Berengar, however, left the English court without waiting to give evidence to the proposed commission. The case therefore lapsed. It was Berengar's carelessness that denied him justice, according to the English king. The Aragonese king, on the other hand, argued that letters of marque should be issued, permitting the confiscation by his agents of English goods of similar value, from whichever English merchant they could be obtained, without further adjudication. This was, of course, widespread practice where offences of this type had been committed, but the English king again refused to co-operate. He insisted that it was Berengar's failure to wait for justice, not his failure to offer it, that had deprived Berengar of the chance to win restitution. King James replied that Edward's reasons were not sufficient to prevent the issue of letters of marque: the practice in Aragon was that offences of this order were settled by impounding goods of merchants of the offending nation to the value of the lost merchandise. But Edward wrote again, insisting that English law only recognised the right to impound goods

<hr />

[24] PRO, c. 66/159, membrane 8*d*, has *Baionio*, i.e. Bayonne, however; = *CPR* Edward II, 1321–4, 385.　　　[25] PRO, c. 54/173 = *CCR* Edward II, 1323–7, 135.

where the lord of the land had failed to give justice.[26] It was not his business if the laws of the kingdom of Aragon differed from those of England.

Altogether, then, it was an unsatisfactory correspondence. But the king of Majorca, Sanç, was also busily pursuing the interests of his subjects who had suffered in the attack on the two galleys. Sanç took the matter seriously enough to send envoys to Edward II, for whom the king issued a safe-conduct in September 1324.[27] It was now nearly two years since the seizure, but the Majorcan envoy (Peter Jacobi) was urged to stay within England while a commission of enquiry set to work. Edward promised indeed to do justice to all Sanç's subjects who came to England and to favour them in every way possible. By July 1325 there were still no results: the English jury had failed to discover who was responsible for the crime, and the English king repeatedly insisted that he would provide justice if and when the names of the perpetrators were known.[28] Then, indeed, the Aragonese or Majorcan plaintiffs could bring action themselves.

In the light of these replies it is striking that Bertrand de Vylar of Bayonne (or Barcelona), whose goods had also been placed on one of the Mallorcan ships, actually did name the pirates in a petition to the crown: he provided a list of men of Dover and of Winchelsea.[29] Quite possibly, then, the crown and its commissioners were simply making little effort to identify the criminals to the kings of Aragon and Majorca. The English king did, however, have political interests in south-western France that were pushing him closer to the Aragonese court. In September 1324 Edward II wrote to James of Aragon yet again, this time to complain at the attempted seizure of Aquitaine by Charles, king of France and Navarre.[30] Edward complained that he had been denied justice by the French king, and urged James to send an army in defence of English interests in Gascony. A similar letter was sent to the king of Castile and to the Infante Don Juan.[31] It is hard to say whether Edward's dilatory conduct over the Mallorcan ships had any influence on the attitude of the Aragonese king; but the English crown again and again approached the Aragonese or

---

[26] PRO, c. 54/142 = *CCR* Edward II, 1323–7, 312.
[27] PRO, c. 54/140 = *CCR* Edward II, 1318–23, 714; c. 54/142 = *CCR* Edward II, 1323–7, 312; c. 66/161 = *CPR* Edward II, 1324–7, 22.
[28] PRO, c. 54/143 = *CCR* Edward II, 1323–7, 491.
[29] PRO, c. 66/159 = *CPR* Edward II, 1321–4, 385.
[30] PRO, c. 54/142 = *CCR* Edward II, 1323–7, 313–4.
[31] PRO, c. 54/142 = *CCR* Edward II, 1323–7, 314.

Majorcan kings, hoping to find in them suitable allies against French power in southern France. One lure to friendship was promises of aid against the Moors of Granada, as in 1330 when the English king sent an ambassador with secret messages to the king of Aragon, in reply to that king's entreaties.[32] Another lure was the issue of letters of protection in favour of all Aragonese or Majorcan merchants trading between Gascony, Brabant, Ireland and other territories friendly to Edward II or III, and the Spanish ports: such letters were issued in 1336, repeated within a year, as if the initial issue of letters had been of all too little effect, and yet again in 1338.[33] Occasionally individual merchants were named, too: Peter de Touse of Aragon and Salvator Ferer of Mallorca, masters of two Catalan ships, were assured in 1337 that the privilege in favour of foreign merchants issued by Edward I in 1303 applied to them;[34] and Peter de Vilardell, another Mallorcan, was given a safe-conduct for a year from 12 October 1337, after his arrival on his ship *La Seinte Marie* at Southampton.[35] In 1338 Peter de Ceseres and Benedict Ferrandes, cloth-merchants, were allowed to export 87 cloths from Southampton but were made to promise not to sell the goods in lands at war with the English king – that is to say, France – nor to communicate with the king's enemies.[36] The cloth was to be exported free of taxes, for it had already been seized once at sea and taken to London; and among the partners of the two plaintiffs were Aragonese, Majorcan, Lombard and Castilian merchants. It is possible that these merchants were in fact sending Flemish cloth to Spain when it was once again intercepted by English ships, so this evidence seems to point to a Mallorcan presence in Flanders rather than England. The two merchants named are most likely Castilian, since the crown cites as its reason for generosity the affection of the English king for the 'king of Spain', that is, the king of Castile. In other words, once again the co-operation of Castilians, Catalans and (not least) Italians on the sea route linking the North Sea to the Mediterranean is clearly demonstrated.

The question of Flanders and the activities of the Florentine

---

[32] PRO, c. 54/149 = *CCR* Edward III, 1330–3, 137 (*Foedera*, vol. II, part 3, 45²); cf. c. 54/150 = *CCR* Edward III, 1330–3, 331 (Foedera, vol. II, part 3, 68¹). For Aragonese-Granadan relations at this time, see chapter 9.

[33] PRO, c. 66/188 = *CPR* Edward III, 1334–8, 324; c. 66/190 = *CPR* Edward III, 1334–8, 463; c. 66/193 = *CPR* Edward III, 1338–40, 126.

[34] PRO, c. 66/190 = *CPR* Edward III, 1334–7, 464.

[35] PRO, c. 66/191 = *CPR* Edward III, 1334–8, 541.

[36] PRO, c. 54/160 = *CCR* Edward III, 1337–9, 326.

bankers are the two issues that dominate references to Mallorcan merchants in the next few years. Flanders and Florence cannot be disentangled: it was with vast Florentine subventions that Edward III invaded Flanders, becoming literally bogged down in a war that neither he nor the Italian bankers could afford. Documents of 1339 show the English crown making restitution to Spanish merchants whose goods were lost in the fighting off the coast of Flanders. Raymund Leuces of Barcelona and Bartholomew de Spyn of Mallorca, as well as other Catalan and Mallorcan merchants, were offered £2,173 6s 0d in *gros tournois* as a consequence of damage to a great ship called *La Crake*. Aboard the same ship was Henry Benentendi of Florence, who lost a more modest £148 7s 0d[37] And the inhabitants of those Flemish towns that recognised Edward as lawful king of France petitioned the crown to offer protection to merchants of *Catilon* and *Meorke* coming to Ghent, Bruges, Ypres and other Flemish towns by sea.[38] Thus the English king briefly found himself providing the Flemish towns with access to the shipping services they needed if they were to sell their goods in Mediterranean markets. In view of the friendship between the Genoese and the French, and in view of the reluctance of the Venetians to trade in the western Mediterranean and North Sea at this time, the Catalans and Mallorcans were a major means of contact between Flanders and Spain or Italy. Edward III's privilege of 1339 to the Catalans in Flanders was reissued in 1340, including now the Castilians as well: the maritime conflict between England and France was now at its peak, and promises of protection had become essential if trade through the English Channel were to be maintained.[39]

The influence of the Bardi and Peruzzi is visible in a royal letter of 1 June 1339: here Edward III recalls the services of these bankers, and states that he has already granted them the right to export wool from Bristol to Lombardy, only to find that his own officials have become obstructive and have prevented the despatch of this wool.[40] Since ships of Mallorca have been commissioned by the Florentines, and have just arrived or will shortly arrive at Bristol, the king appoints Master Henry de Stretford to supervise the loading of the wool and the unloading of whatever goods arrive on the Mallorcan

[37] PRO, c. 66/201 = *CPR* Edward III, 1338–40, 373–4.
[38] PRO, c. 66/201 = *CPR* Edward III, 1338–40, 396–7.
[39] PRO, c. 54/160 = *CCR* Edward III, 1338–40, 379; c. 66/197 = *CPR* Edward III, 1338–40, 464 (*Foedera*, vol. II, part 4, 72²).
[40] PRO, c. 66/195 = *CPR* Edward III, 1338–40, 285.

ships. Edward reminds his officials that failure to act as promised towards the Bardi and Peruzzi will have severe effects on his interests, for he depends on the Italians for a 'great subsidy'. So once again it is Mallorcans who provide vital shipping services when the Genoese or other Italians are prevented from doing so.

Over the next few years the links between the Florentines and Catalonia or Mallorca remained strong. In August 1341 several leading Florentines, including one of the Bardi, were permitted to purchase 787 sacks of wool and to export them from Southampton and Bristol, paying half a mark per sack; they were to take the wool to Catalonia or Mallorca and nowhere else.[41] At the same time the merchants and mariners, Florentine and Catalan, aboard two ships from Catalonia due in England, were promised royal protection: these were evidently the ships on which the wool was to be exported.[42] In April 1342 the range of destinations where the wool could be carried was extended to Flanders too, as a favour for a loan of £300 made to the king to cover expenses incurred in Bordeaux.[43] As ever, the Florentines were able to use credit to secure extraordinary favours from the crown.

Ships from Mallorca appear several times over the following years, the period of the break-up of the independent Majorcan kingdom. In March 1342 Peter Otly 'of the land of Mallorca', master of the *Seinte Marie*, was given royal protection; his ship stood at Bristol, bound for Lombardy with wool and other goods, property of the third great Florentine bank, the Acciaiuoli (*Achioles*).[44] But in any case the king reiterated his protection over all Majorcans in October 1341, out of regard for his kinsman the king of Majorca.[45] On 12 December 1343 the royal court expressed its concern over an attack on a ship of *Mailogre* driven ashore apparently while trying to reach Bristol; men of the Forest of Dean had plundered the ship and attacked those placed on guard to protect it – this too at a time of general truce between England, France and all other interests.[46] In February 1344 Beringer Kalderere and Bernard Burrell, masters of the *Seint Johan of Aragon*, men of the kingdom of Majorca, were offered a safe-conduct

[41] PRO, c. 66/204 = *CPR* Edward III, 1340–3, 275; c. 54/169 (membrane 5, and not 6 as stated in *CCR*) = *CCR* Edward III, 1341–3, 229–30.
[42] PRO, c. 66/204 = *CPR* Edward III, 1340–3, 275.
[43] PRO, c. 54/171 = *CCR* Edward III, 1341–3, 418.
[44] PRO, c. 66/206 = *CPR* Edward III, 1340–3, 398.
[45] PRO, c. 66/204 = *CPR* Edward III, 1340–3, 293 (*Foedera*, vol. II, part 4, 114^1).
[46] PRO, c. 66/210 = *CPR* Edward III, 1343–5, 186.

while they were in England to trade; and so was Bernard Vylar of Barcelona.[47]

The last years of the kingdom of Majorca saw attempts by Edward III to create an alliance with Majorca that would help him to strengthen English interests in southern France. Edward was interested less in the existence of trade between England and the Balearic islands than in the hold of the Majorcan king on Roussillon, Cerdagne and part of Montpellier. Such contacts also have to be placed in the context of a long tradition of English approaches to each of the Spanish kings, which, as Peter Russell has insisted, showed scant regard for the complex diplomatic realities of the Iberian peninsula at the time of the Hundred Years War.[48] In February 1342 Edward wrote to James III of Majorca, following past exchanges of ambassadors and letters, to say that he would like to seal a marriage alliance between their children, but the dowry proposed for James' daughter seemed excessive; James was, of course, increasingly short of funds, and no doubt he saw the marriage alliance as a financial as much as a political opportunity. Edward said he hoped that negotiations would continue, but he was distracted by his own Scottish war; besides, he wished to consult his own counsellors.[49] Meanwhile, Edward was also writing to a baron of Peter IV of Aragon, soon to conquer Majorca, urging that Peter should be discouraged from giving any help to the king of France.[50] In fact, the English approaches to James of Majorca irritated the Aragonese king who, fearful of the effects of Majorcan political meddling, was only encouraged to put a more rapid end to the independence of the Majorcan territories.[51] Indeed, even the loss of their territories did not prevent the Majorcan kings from taking sides in the Anglo-French conflict: in 1346 James III appeared alongside Philip VI of France at the battle of Crécy, but in 1366–7 his son James IV was with the Black Prince, campaigning in Spain; he (with the titular king of Armenia) was godfather to the Prince of Wales' second son.[52] And after his death the crown of Majorca remained a

---

[47] PRO, c. 66/211 = *CPR* Edward III, 1343–5, 197.
[48] P. Russell, *The English intervention in Spain and Portugal in the time of Edward III and Richard II* (Oxford, 1955), 6n., 15.
[49] PRO, c. 54/171 = *CCR* Edward III, 1341–3, 478 (*Foedera*, vol. II, part 4, 118–19).
[50] PRO, c. 54/171 = *CCR* Edward III, 1341–3, 478 (*Foedera*, vol. II, part 4, 119¹).
[51] Russell, *English intervention*, 6n.
[52] R. Barber, *Edward, Prince of Wales and Aquitaine. A biography of the Black Prince* (London, 1978), 59, 66, 193, 196, 200. For an earlier appearance (1329) see J. Favier, *La Guerre de Cent Ans* (Paris, 1980), 16–17.

live issue in Anglo-French politics, since Duke Louis of Anjou asserted a claim to the Majorcan lands.[53]

Following the incorporation of the Majorcan crown into Aragon, there was no break in trade with England. Bernard Vylar of Barcelona reappears in documents of 1344 and 1345, trading from Bristol to Marseilles and Pisa, and carrying the goods of Lucchesi and of a merchant of Arezzo on his ship the *Seint Vincent*; but the vessel was attacked off Mallorca and the wool of Italian merchants domiciled in London was seized, causing a loss of at least £346.[54] Clearer evidence of attempts to trade with Mallorca comes from the experience of John Joly, citizen of Mallorca and owner of one quarter part of a two-decked cog, *St John the Evangelist*.[55] This was travelling from Flanders to Mallorca, but put in at Dartmouth on the English coast; men of Dartmouth and elsewhere broke up the ship, carried off his goods, and inflicted damage to the value of £1,000; John Joly secured from Peter, king of Aragon, support in the case, and Peter complained to his kinsman Edward, requesting justice to be done to his subject. Not surprisingly, other Mallorcan merchants passing from Flanders to the Mediterranean requested royal protection: in October 1346, as the king was outside Calais, a safe-conduct was issued in favour of Peter de Valle, master of the *Ship of St Anne* of the city of Mallorca, who had loaded his ship at Zwijn in Flanders and was now bound for home; so too for the *Ship of St Julian*, William Porret master, and the *Ship of St John*, Arnold Fresch master, both also of Mallorca.[56] Since at precisely this time Edward III was working hard to re-establish English control in the Pas de Calais, shipping from Flanders to the Mediterranean had to pass through English lines, and presumably paid Edward III handsomely for the favour of passage as well as protection. In August 1347 some Mallorcans actually arrived in England; Edward III issued a letter protecting Raymond Safforteyse, Nicholas Suriani and Raymond Roy of *Malyogres* until the coming Christmas.[57] If anything, the evidence suggests more Mallorcans were arriving around 1340 than at the start of the century: hardly the picture Lopez would have predicted.

[53] Russell, *English intervention*, 221, 249–52.
[54] PRO, c. 54/176 = *CCR Edward III, 1343–6*, 483; c. 66/211 = *CPR Edward III, 1343–5*, 197.
[55] PRO, c. 54/178 = *CCR Edward III, 1343–6*, 628; c. 66/212 = *CPR Edward III, 1343–5*, 426.   [56] PRO, c. 66/219 = *CPR Edward III, 1345–8*, 517.
[57] PRO, c. 66/221 = *CPR Edward III, 1345–8*, 369.

There was still a Mallorcan presence on the route to England in the fifteenth century. An important article by W. B. Watson has illustrated the last phase of Catalan trade in England and has stressed two principal features: the primacy of Catalan interests in Flanders and (by the 1440s) a strong Catalan predilection for English cloth.[58] But such cloth was mainly purchased for consumption in Barcelona, Mallorca or Perpignan and not widely redistributed: even allowing for the researches of del Treppo, Trasselli and Bresc on the presence of English cloth in Sicily, it appears that the main carriers to Sicily were in fact Genoese rather than Catalan, let alone Mallorcan.[59] In any case, by the 1440s Italian trade with England was far more elaborate than it had been even in the days of the Bardi and the Peruzzi. Evidently, there are features of the mid-fifteenth-century trade that simply do not apply a century earlier: under the three Edwards, there was a very limited cloth export trade but a very substantial wool export trade; in the fifteenth century the emphasis was on exports of cloths rather than of raw wool. But, even around 1320, it is probably right to see in the trade of the Mallorcans in England – and that of the Catalans as a whole – a commercial link that always took second place to Mallorcan interests in Flanders. And around 1320 the Mallorcans were important not so much because of their imports from the Mediterranean (for although the pottery named after the island, *maiolica*, was much admired it was actually made in Valencia and Andalucia), nor because of exports directed at the Mallorcan lands, but because they provided carrying facilities for the north Italians. They were agile in taking advantage of the quarrels between the Genoese or other Italians and the English crown; but they never sought to provide banking services, nor did they depend (as did Florence) on regular supplies of English wool for their own cloth industry, which was slowly developing in the early fourteenth century. Because they were far less dependent than the north Italians on trade in England, because they were not creditors of the English crown, they continued throughout the early fourteenth century to provide the same service, shipping and freighting, while

---

[58] W. B. Watson, 'Catalans in the markets of northern Europe during the fifteenth century', *Homenaje a Jaime Vicens Vives* (Barcelona, 1967), vol. II, 787–813.

[59] See *inter alia* C. Trasselli, 'Frumento e panni inglesi nella Sicilia del xv secolo', *Annali della Facoltà di Economia e Commercio dell'Università di Palermo*, 9 (1955), repr. in C. Trasselli, *Mediterraneo e Sicilia all'inizio dell'epoca moderna* (Cosenza, 1980); cf. Watson, 'Catalans', 791. More generally, see M. del Treppo, *I mercanti catalani e l'espansione della Corona d'Aragona nel secolo XV* (Naples, 1972).

the Italians constructed a coherent commercial and industrial system based on their links to England and Flanders. And the Mallorcans and other Catalans were themselves drawn into this system, providing basic facilities to Italian textile cities in danger of being starved of raw materials. Put simply, Mallorcan trade with England was generated and sustained by Italian no less than Catalan interests.

III

The Mallorcans acquired detailed knowledge of the coasts of Atlantic Europe and of north-west Africa, partly as a result of the fact that their sailors travelled along those shores. Something of this knowledge can be recovered from an analysis of the Mallorcan maps that survive in considerable quantity.[60] For among notable exports from Mallorca in the fourteenth and fifteenth centuries were the portolan charts and atlases, which continue to arouse lively debate: Venice and Mallorca appear to have been the two major centres of map production, at least for export, in the late Middle Ages.[61] In 1960 Rey Pastor and Garcia Camareno published a list of thirty Mallorcan charts, including several that are known only from documentary sources; for the fifteenth century the list is much longer. A number of difficult questions arise. Were the portolan charts that survive actually used as sailing charts? What rôle did Jewish cartographers play in the formation of a Mallorcan school of cartographers, and was the success of this school based in part on their specialist knowledge of Arab maps and geographical works? What were the links between Italian and Mallorcan cartography in the early fourteenth century?

---

[60] In preparing this section, particular attention has been paid to British Library Additional MS 25691; but a great many other portolan charts have also been examined in the original, thanks to the excellent displays at the Genoese Esposizione in honour of Christopher Columbus, held in 1992, and at the restored Palazzo Ducale in Genoa.

[61] T. Campbell, 'Portolan charts from the late thirteenth century to 1500', *The history of cartography*, vol. I, *Cartography in Prehistoric, Ancient and Medieval Europe and the Mediterranean*, ed. J. B. Harley and D. Woodward (Chicago, 1987), 371–463 is the best guide; see also the work of Y. Fall mentioned in the following note. The literature is vast. Some clues to its size can be found in J. Rey Pastor and E. Garcia Camareno, *La Cartografía mallorquina* (Madrid, 1960). Other works used here include: A. R. Hinks, *Portolan chart of Angellino de Dalorto of 1325 in the collection of Prince Corsini at Florence* (London, 1929); Y. Kamal, *Monumenta cartographica Africæ et Ægypti*, 5 vols. in 16 parts (Cairo, 1926–51); A. E. Nordenskjöld, *Periplus* (Stockholm, 1897); G. de Reparaz, *Catalunya a les mars: navegants, mercaders i cartògrafs catalans de l'Edat Mitjana i del Renaixement* (Barcelona, 1930), and an article by the same author, 'L'activité maritime et commerciale du Royaume d'Aragon au XIIIe siècle', *Bulletin hispanique*, 49 (1947), 422–51; H. Winter, 'Catalan portolan maps and their place in the total view of cartographic development', *Imago Mundi*, 11 (1954), 1–12.

What if anything be deduced from the detailed portrayal of the coasts of Europe and Africa concerning trade routes, knowledge of the politics of the time, awareness of the Atlantic islands, and so on?

It is possible that virtually all the surviving maps were luxury versions made to satisfy demand at princely courts; this certainly applies to one of the most famous examples, the Catalan atlas attributed to Abraham Cresques, sent to King Charles VI of France and preserved in the Bibliothèque Nationale. New techniques for the analysis of this material have been adopted by the African scholar Yoro K. Fall, who argues that 'toute la perception de l'Afrique, politique, géographique et économique est une tentative en acte de partage de l'Afrique entre musulmans et chrétiens'.[62] The maps define the Christian space, but place it in relationship with Muslim space, and thereby raise questions about the political and religious relationships as well. It is certainly the case that information about the coasts of Africa was understood in Mallorca to have other uses than merely commercial; it was the last king of Majorca, James III, who initiated attempts to conquer, colonise and convert the Canaries in 1342; these grand plans had as their aim a vast crusade against north Africa, from the Balearics southwards and from the Canaries eastwards. The dream did not die with him, for further expeditions are documented under Peter IV, after Mallorca was reconquered by him, and Peter remained a vigorous patron of Mallorcan cartography. However, it is striking that this lead in Atlantic exploration was not sustained into the fifteenth century, even though the mapmakers were extremely active then.

A useful argument against the view that the surviving maps ever set out to sea is the good state of preservation of so many of them; it has been suggested that the lack of pinholes proves that they were never pinned to a board, as one would expect of navigational charts in regular use on a ship.[63] Against this, it has been solemnly suggested that, since parchment swells when wet, and since the sea is notably wet, all pinholes would disappear with use. Lack of holes proves rather than disproves the functionality of these documents! More to the point, the careful coloured decoration of the Mallorcan maps, especially compared to contemporary Italian portolan charts,

[62] Yoro K. Fall, *L'Afrique à la naissance de la cartographie moderne. Les cartes majorquines, 14ème–15ème siècles* (Paris, 1985).
[63] Campbell, 'Portolan charts', 443–4. Interestingly, Campbell makes use of evidence from the Mallorcan Ramón Llull when discussing navigational tables sometimes incorporated into late medieval portolan atlases.

suggests that the Mallorcans took pride in the production of expensive, fragile charts which are unlikely to have been used at sea, but which most likely served as models for less lavish charts which did wear out on the waves. These are master-copies, and their authors were the master mapmakers not just of Mallorca, but of the Mediterranean, Angelino Dalorto or Dulcert, perhaps of Italian birth, Abraham Cresques and his son Jahuda or Jafuda Cresques (who was later known as Master Jaume of Mallorca), and others. The presence of the Jewish Cresques family has long excited comment, especially since it was they who were given the outstanding commission of preparing an atlas for the king of France. It is generally assumed that their access to Hebrew and Arabic geographical knowledge helped place not merely themselves but the Mallorcan map industry ahead of its rivals. Guillermo Soler of Mallorca, a late-fourteenth-century Christian mapmaker, designed two surviving charts, one (now in Paris) in the traditional decorated Mallorcan style and another (preserved, perhaps significantly, in Florence) in the more arid and unadorned Italian style, particularly uninformative on inland geography; Campbell sees this as evidence for the versatility of the map-makers, but perhaps it indicates that maps looked different when their function was different. One may have been a presentation copy, the other may have been intended for more practical uses.[64]

The portolan charts do not indicate sea-routes; in some, major towns and landmarks are picked out in red, but this cannot be held to indicate regular visits by Mallorcan or Catalan shipping. Little success has been achieved by those who have sought to see reflected in these charts changing patterns in east–west trade; such arguments depend on the fact that some Italian charts lay greater emphasis on areas such as the Levant or the Black Sea than on the western Mediterranean. It is likely that the clients of the Mallorcan map-makers included wealthy merchants, who saw in such charts visual information to accompany such manuals as Francesco Pegolotti's *Pratica della Mercatura*. Some may well have been taken to sea not in the captain's chest but among the business papers of the merchants. The Mallorcan maps lay some emphasis on political geography, attaching distinctive banners to places such as Mallorca, Catalonia and France, as well as the Muslim states, whose rulers it would be

---

[64] Campbell, 'Portolan charts', 393.

useful to identify. Mallorca itself is very commonly picked out in blue or gold, a special status that it sometimes retains even in fifteenth-century maps attributed to Barcelonan ateliers. Catalan maps, including those of Mallorca, are distinguishable from those made in Italy because they often carry discursive notes, 'legends' in both sense of the word, when dealing with Black Africa; but they are informative not merely about events in Catalan maritime history but about the Catalan memory for such events: the expedition of Jaume Ferrer of Mallorca to the Canaries in the 1340s remained a fond theme even in the fifteenth century. As with the special attention given to Mallorca, one can see here the force of tradition in the compilation of these maps; they should not simply be seen as a vehicle for scientific innovation such as the marking and naming of newly discovered islands, though this too could be an important function. Recent political changes, such as the purchase of the remaining Majorcan rights in Montpellier, were recorded, though not necessarily very fast.[65] The Catalan maps, Campbell points out, are 'simultaneously terrestrial maps'.[66] The function of those that survive may have been more similar to that of a modern globe illustrating the countries of the world than to coastal navigation charts.

Here, too, though, they had some use: the small rocks off the coast of Mallorca are well illustrated in one of the earliest of these charts to survive, Additional Manuscript 25691 in the British Library, an anonymous work with similarities to the maps of Dulcert, traditionally dated to about 1327, but redated by Campbell to about 1339.[67] What is also striking is the extraordinary attention to place-names. It is here, as much as in the drawing of coast-lines, that the mapmakers display a tremendously detailed knowledge of maritime geography, though naturally it is the Mediterranean that they know best. Dulcert reveals a knowledge in 1339 of the location of Bilbao, a newish port founded around 1300, and a possible place of call, with its harbour of Portugalete or *Galleto*, for shipping bound from Mallorca to England and Flanders.[68] The late-fourteenth-century Mallorcan maps show a knowledge of the Madeira archipelago and the Azores as well as the Canaries, though the Azores appear strung out across the ocean and notably enlarged. Fernández-Armesto convincingly argues that this is not another example of confabulation

[65] Campbell, 'Portolan charts', 400, though he confuses Montpellier's status, giving 'Aragon' in lieu of Majorca.   [66] Campbell, 'Portolan charts', 394.
[67] Campbell, 'Portolan charts', 418.   [68] Campbell, 'Portolan charts', 426.

concerning the mysterious Atlantic, but real evidence for fourteenth-century geographical knowledge acquired, in his view, around the time of the Mallorcan expeditions to the Canary Islands.[69]

The cartographic evidence thus fits the wider argument that the Catalans, and more particularly the Mallorcans, developed impressive navigational skills in the thirteenth and early fourteenth centuries, on the basis of which they were able to offer efficient carrying services even to the Italians, and, most importantly, to maintain regular communication between the Balearic islands and the neighbouring coasts of Europe and Africa. It is no surprise that the Mallorcans traded and explored beyond the Straits of Gibraltar.

IV

It is now time to turn south out of the Straits, and to look at the involvement of the kingdom of Majorca in the early settlement of the Canary islands. Fernández-Armesto, stressing the importance of the Mallorcans in the early exploration of the eastern Atlantic, argues that 'exploration of the Canaries was, in a sense, a natural extension of existing Majorcan interests in Africa and the Atlantic', mentioning in particular the involvement of the Mallorcans in trade running from the Mediteranean to northern Europe.[70] Now, penetration of the waters south-west of the Straits of Gibraltar was to some extent determined by the prevailing winds and currents. For much of the year, shipping that left the Mediterranean would tend to slew towards the Canaries as a matter of course. And in fact there was a long tradition of visits by other Latin merchants than the Catalans to the Atlantic coast of Morocco, even before the opening of the Straits; presumably not all the Genoese visitors who appeared as far south as Safi in the mid-thirteenth century transferred to other vessels after disembarking at Ceuta and moving a short distance overland beyond Gibraltar, and it has been seen that Seville established itself as a Genoese base beyond the Straits even before it fell to the Castilians in 1248. It is fairly clear, too, that the search for gold was already by the mid-thirteenth century a major motive in the penetration of north-west Africa. The renewal of gold minting in western Europe, at Genoa and Florence in 1252, only stimulated further an existing search for cheap supplies of the yellow metal.

[69] F. Fernández-Armesto, 'Atlantic exploration before Columbus: the evidence of maps', *Renaissance and Modern Studies*, 30 (1986), 1–23; Fernández-Armesto, *Before Columbus*, 159–66.   [70] Fernández-Armesto, *Before Columbus*, 156–7.

By the early fourteenth century, moreover, there existed a growing awareness that the high objective of the recovery of the Holy Land could only be achieved by economic as well as naval warfare against the Mamluks and their allies; the writings of Marino Sanudo emphasised the need to deprive Islam of supplies of western arms, but a corollary was to divert from Islam the gold of the Sahara, which might even in part be used to pay for the great crusade that was required. The famous expedition of the Vivaldi brothers in 1291 had as its declared aims both the creation of a supply line that would bring spices from the Indies and a mission to unconverted peoples; it too must be seen as an attempt to deprive Islam of some of the benefits of being the middleman in trade between the Far East and western Europe.[71] There was a Mallorcan connection here, for the Vivaldis sailed by way of Mallorca, and may in particular have hoped to benefit from the geographical expertise of the Mallorcan cartographers. Mallorca achieved further prominence around 1300 in the planning of such measures as a result of the propagandist efforts of Ramón Llull, whose conception of the battle against Islam in north Africa was of a struggle of the mind rather than of the sword.[72] However, his community of missionaries at Miramar was short-lived, perhaps the victim of the disorders engendered by the War of the Vespers. By the time the Mallorcans reached the Canaries, two themes stand out prominently: the mission to the Infidel, whether Muslims of the Maghrib or pagan Guanches of the Canaries, and the supposed advantage that would accrue from penetration of Atlantic Africa in the struggle for Jerusalem. In other words, pure commercial profit should not be placed too high on the list of priorities.

As for the Mallorcan presence in the Canaries, the facts are reasonably clear.[73] On 15 April 1342 Guillem Pere of Mallorca,

---

[71] On this expedition, see G. Moore, 'La spedizione dei fratelli Vivaldi e nuovi documenti d'archivio', *Atti della Società Ligure di Storia Patria*, n.s., 12 (1972), 387–400; also R. Mauny, *Les navigations médiévales sur les côtes sahariennes* (Lisbon, 1960).

[72] Another example of this approach can be identified in the anti-Jewish polemic of Ramón Martí, *Pugio Fidei*, a point well brought out by R. Chazan, *Daggers of faith. Thirteenth-century Christian missionizing and Jewish response* (Berkeley/Los Angeles, 1989).

[73] The literature on this is considerable. See in the first instance: A. Rumeu de Armas, *El Obispado de Telde. Misioneros mallorquines y catalanes en el Atlántico* (Madrid, 1960); E. Serra Ràfols, *El descubrimiento y los viajes medievales de los catalanes a las islas Afortunadas* (La Laguna, Tenerife, 1926/7); E. Serra Ràfols, 'Els catalans de Mallorca a les illes Canaries', *Homenaje a Rubió i Lluch* (Barcelona, 1936), vol. III, 207–28; E. Serra Ràfols, 'Los Mallorquines en Canarias', *Revista de Historia* (1941), 195–209, 281–7 and 'Más sobre los viajes catalano-mallorquines a Canarias', *Revista de Historia* (1943), 280–92; A. Rumeu de Armas, 'Mallorquines en el Atlántico', *Homenaje a E. Serra Ràfols*, vol. III, 265–76; F. Sevillano

owner of a *cocha* and of a smaller vessel, was granted a licence to travel to the islands recently discovered in the west.[74] On 16 April 1342 three Mallorcans, Francesc Desvalers, Pere Margre and Bartolomeu Giges were given licences to travel to the newly found Canary Islands in the cogs *Santa Creu* and *Santa Magdalena*. The document in question is a royal mandate issued by the king's lieutenant on Mallorca addressed to the eight *patronis et armatoribus* of the two cogs.[75] The destination was to be the 'partes insularum noviter repertarum et vulgariter nominatarum insulas Fortunarum', and the patrons of the expedition were expressly ordered not to cause any harm to the 'friends of the said king' of Majorca on their way. Should it come to pass that any of the islands, or any town, inhabited place, fortress or castle be captured by the Mallorcan expedition, the crew 'are to recognise as prince and lord the said lord our king', and none other; all criminal jurisdiction and all appeals are to be directed to the king, who will possess all regalian rights in the conquered territories. The conquerors will then hold the islands as a *feudum honoratum* of the king of Majorca, who retains civil jurisdiction and *alodio*, that is, the actual right of possession of the land. The *patroni* and *armatores* performed an act of homage to the lieutenant expressing their acceptance of these terms. There can thus be no doubt that the king of Majorca saw the conquest of the Canaries as a chance to create a new allodial holding independent of any other authority, not least his rival Peter of Aragon.

Bernat Desvalls was given a similar licence at the same time, together with Guillem Safont; their ship was a *cocha bayonesca* named the *Santa Barbara*. A few days later, another *cocha bayonesca*, the *Sant Joan*, under Domènec Gual of Mallorca, was licensed.[76] It appears that at least two parallel expeditions were being planned, rather than a single convoy; Francesc Desvalers, was appointed captain of the pair of ships *Santa Creu* and *Santa Magdalena* on 16 April 1342, while

Colom, 'Mallorca y Canarias', *Hispania. Revista Española de Historia*, 120 (1972), 123–48; F. Sevillano Colom, 'Los viajes medievales desde Mallorca a Canarias', *Anuario de estudios atlánticos*, 23 (1978), 27–57; Fernández-Armesto, *Before Columbus*, 156–9, 171; and, for events after the fall of the kingdom of Majorca, see also A. Rumeu de Armas, 'La expedición mallorquina de 1366 a las islas Canarias', *Anuario de estudios atlánticos*, 27 (1981), and M. Mitjà, 'Abandó des Illes Canaries per Joan d'Aragó', *Anuario de estudios atlánticos*, 8 (1962). And there is more.
[74] Sevillano Colom, 'Mallorca y Canarias', 125; Rumeu de Armas, 'Mallorquines en el Atlántico', 272.
[75] The text is printed by Sevillano Colom, 'Mallorca y Canarias', 141, no. 1, from the Arxiu del Regne de Mallorca.
[76] Sevillano Colom, 'Mallorca y Canarias', 125–6, 141 no. 2.

a similar honour befell Bernat Desvalls of the *Santa Barbara*.[77] The powers conferred on the captain during the voyage included the exercise of *omnem jurisdiccionem civilem et criminalem ac mixtum et merum imperium*, to be exercised *extra tamen Regnum Maioricarum*; in effect, the king's lieutenant was confirming the traditional authority of a captain, subject to prevailing maritime law.[78] The expedition certainly set out, too: on 26 October 1342, Guillem Jaffe, from Sineu in Mallorca, who had been aboard a ship bound for the Canaries, appointed a procurator whose duty it was to submit on his behalf a demand to be paid his wages, though one of the ships' masters, Pere Margre, had already died, apparently during the journey. Pere Margre appears in earlier documents as one of the masters of the *Santa Creu* and the *Santa Magdalena*. Jaffe was a young man, less than twenty-five years old, he says, but more than twenty. Guillem Jaffe's claim for payment indicates that the *viatico quod fecit apud insulas vocatas perdudes vel de Canaria* took five and a half months; since the earlier documents are dated mid-April 1342 and Jaffe's claim is dated late October, it is likely that the ships set out in late April or early May.[79] A return in early autumn is of some interest: Fernández-Armesto has pointed out that the prevailing winds made a safe passage from the Canaries northwards along the coast of Africa only possible in the winter; the other route home, which would be most sensible at other times of the year, was northwards to Madeira and even the Azores in search of westerly winds. It is thus likely that Canarian exploration had the necessary result of further discoveries, of the uninhabited Atlantic islands.[80] By whatever route he returned, at the end of October Guillem Jaffe would have been anxious to join the crew of a vessel setting out on an autumn sailing, and he would therefore need to appoint an agent to handle his business while he was away. It is probably excessive for Fernández-Armesto to claim that Jaffe's difficulties prove the expedition was a 'commercial failure': the appointment of a procurator to chase up old debts was far from unusual in the late medieval Mediterranean.[81]

Nor were these ships alone in their attempt to reach the islands. There are even hints that Mallorcan pirates in pursuit of an Aragonese galley or galleys found themselves by chance in the

[77] Sevillano Colom, 'Mallorca y Canarias', 127, 142–3 nos. 3–4.
[78] Sevillano Colom, 'Mallorca y Canarias', 142 no. 3.
[79] Sevillano Colom, 'Mallorca y Canarias', 143 no. 7.
[80] Fernández-Armesto, *Before Columbus*, 166.
[81] Fernández-Armesto, *Before Columbus*, 158.

Canaries, either in the 1340s or perhaps the 1370s. On 10 August 1346 Jaume Ferrer of Mallorca sailed for the Canaries and the River of Gold, supposed to lie on the African mainland nearby; this voyage was commemorated in the legends of later Catalan maps, such as the atlas made by the Cresques for Charles VI of France and the fifteenth-century world map preserved in the Biblioteca Estense at Modena. In 1351 Joan Doria, presumably of Genoese origin, Arnald Roger and Jaume Segarra received licences from both Pope Clement VI and the king of Aragon for an expedition to the Canaries; they were to travel with no less than twelve Guanches who had been brought earlier to the Balearics and instructed in Catalan and in Christianity. Later that year Clement actually established a Canarian bishopric at Telde on Grand Canary, and the bishops of Fortuna were still active as late as 1393. In 1360 we find a joint Catalan and Mallorcan expedition, comprising two ships. On this occasion it is reported that the sailors were captured by the Guanches at Telde on Gran Canaria, but they were well treated and taught them the art of building, as well as basic Christianity. However, they were eventually condemned to death.[82] The presence among this group of two priests (or, in another account, five monks or mendicants) signals yet again the interest of these expeditions in the Christianisation of the peoples of Atlantic Africa and the Canaries. Yet more expeditions are documented in the years up to 1386, including the ships of an Aragonese captain, Joan Mora, who in 1366 was expressly instructed to patrol the Canaries and to ensure that fleets from rival kingdoms could not establish bases there: clearly Portugal and Castile were in mind. Peter of Aragon's war with Castile had created a bitter naval conflict in which the Castilians secured the enthusiastic support of their old allies, and Aragon's old enemies, the Genoese, as well as that of Muslim Granada: Pedro the Cruel took his fleet to Ibiza in 1359 after being chased away from the waters around Barcelona itself, and he attempted, fruitlessly, the conquest of the Balearics. All the seas from the Balearics to the Canaries had become a potential theatre of war for Castile, Aragon and others.

The fear of competitors who might intrude themselves more successfully in the remote and barren islands of the Atlantic was real. Around 1345 the Portuguese appear to have sent their first expedition of substance to the islands, and may have hoped to establish a

---

[82] For the later history, see Rumeu de Armas, *Obispo de Telde*; more briefly, Fernández-Armesto, *Before Columbus*, 158.

permanent settlement. At the same time, the Castilian adventurer Luis de la Cerda was granted the combined domain of 'Fortunia' to comprise the Canaries and Goleta (Jalita), an island in the central Maghrib. It is likely that the pope, a little vague about the geography involved, sought to create for Don Luis two island bases from which he could notionally overwhelm the whole of north-west Africa. The importance of this view will be underlined further in a moment. 'Fortunia' was, of course, to depend on the pope as overlord, and this insistence both reflected papal theories of authority and the attempts of other rulers to claim the islands for themselves.[83] It has been seen that in 1342 Francesc Desvalers and his colleagues received their licence to conquer the Canaries on condition that they recognise the king of Majorca as their overlord; the king of Majorca, certainly not the pope or the king of Aragon, would have the ultimate rights of jurisdiction. In fact the expedition brought no such glory to the royal house of Majorca. It left no permanent settlement. But the involvement of the same pope in 1351 in a Mallorcan expedition to the Canaries, expressed in his willingness to approve the creation of a bishopric of 'Fortunia', indicates that Clement VI was well aware of the pretensions of the Mallorcan explorers, and wished to have some say in their actions.[84]

It is probable that Clement was prepared to give his support to the dubious Castilian prince Luis de la Cerda the more readily once the king of Majorca, soundly defeated by Peter IV, was no longer competing for rights in the Canaries. It makes sense to compare the scheme advanced in Don Luis' case, of a double dominion including both a Mediterranean island and some or all of the Canaries, with the scheme being advanced in Majorca in 1342 of a double dominion, again comprising Mediterranean and Atlantic islands (not to mention Montpellier and Roussillon). Mallorca was still living on the crusading reputation it had obtained for itself in the thirteenth century; the idea of Mallorca leading the assault on Morocco and the western Sahara from bases in the Balearics and the Canaries was surely part of a well-established set of theories about the right way to break the power of Islam. Indeed, the continuing activity of Moorish

[83] A similar papal claim to dominion over islands off the coast of Africa was expressed by Boniface VIII, when he granted Jerba and Kerkennah to Roger de Lauria: see chapter 7.
[84] G. Daumet, 'Louis de la Cerda ou d'Espagne', *Bulletin hispanique*, 15 (1913), 38–67; E. Serra Ràfols and M. G. Martinez, 'Sermón de Clemente VI Papa acerca de la otorgación del Reino de Canarias a Luis de España, 1344', *Revista de historia canaria*, 29 (1963/4); Fernández-Armesto, *Before Columbus*, 171–3.

fleets in the waters off Spain in the fourteenth century was a matter of grave concern to Mallorcans and Catalans. In his classic article, J. A. Robson has shown how ill-prepared the Aragonese were to counter the threat from the rulers of Morocco and Granada between 1337 and 1344. The Castilians were defeated off Gibraltar in 1340; Valencia seemed set to rise against its Christian masters; and in fact the king of Majorca, James III, in the same year offered fifteen extra galleys to help the Catalans hold the Moorish fleet at bay. The Aragonese king stressed in a letter to James that the Castilian defeat had only redoubled the need to destroy the Moorish threat. The next year, Peter of Aragon seems to have obtained ten Mallorcan ships, while his capture of Mallorca two years later resulted in the union of the Mallorcan and the Catalan fleets in the effort against the Moroccans, even if, at the time, the invasion of the Balearics was seen by the hard-pressed Castilians as a luxurious distraction from more urgent business.[85] What is being suggested here is that the expeditions to the Canaries were not a diversion from the war against Morocco; they were seen as part of a longer-term programme which would result in the economic strangulation of Morocco, in its military encirclement, and would end the threat to the stability of southern Spain and to the security of the western Mediterranean.

There were other aspects of the crusading heritage of the Majorcans that drew them towards Atlantic Africa. As Fernández-Armesto strongly emphasises, the heritage of Ramón Llull's missionary school of Oriental Studies at Miramar cannot be ignored. In fact, Fernández-Armesto surely exaggerates when he says that 'it may be that the apparent shift of emphasis in the Mallorcan voyages from commerce and conquest to conversion and pastoral care is connected with the reabsorption of Majorca into the Crown of Aragon in 1343'.[86] He himself notes that the activities of Joan Mora in 1366 reveal that the Aragonese Crown absorbed the Majorcan claim to authority in the Canaries; and in any case the missionary element in the Majorcan expeditions predates 1343. It was simply the case that by 1400 other interests were asserting themselves much more strongly in the Canaries, at a time when the Aragonese found themselves busy settling the affairs of Sicily instead.

---

[85] Robson, 'Catalan fleet', 386–408.   [86] Fernández-Armesto, *Before Columbus*, 158.

V

The history of the Mallorcan presence in England and that of their presence in the Canaries might appear to have few direct links. However, the Mallorcans do seem to have been more active in the exploitation of the Atlantic, both north and south of the Straits of Gibraltar, than Lopez was prepared to admit. But they could never hope to compete in the long term with the larger, better financed, fleets of the Italian maritime republics, which seized a lead on the route to Flanders and England. Nor did the kings of Majorca have the resources to create a strong base in 'Fortunia' for the struggle against Islam. Nonetheless, the Mallorcans played a key rôle in the maintenance of free passage through the western Mediterranean to the Atlantic, acting as middlemen for the Italians when Italian fleets were unwelcome in England, and planning grander schemes which would secure for all time a Latin naval ascendancy in the entire western Mediterranean.

CHAPTER 11

The reshaping of Mallorca's economy, 1343–1500

The century after the final reincorporation of the kingdom of Majorca into the lands of the Crown of Aragon (1343) saw the economy of Mallorca, Menorca and Ibiza develop in new directions. The question that must be posed at the outset is whether it was the change in political régime or the economic crisis induced by the Black Death that engendered these changes. Predictably, the answer is a bit of each, to which must be added a widely observable European phenomenon at this period: new initiatives which had begun to succeed on the eve of the Black Death often succeeded even better in the more diversified economy that developed in late fourteenth-century western Europe; a classic Spanish example is the expansion of the *Mesta* and of wool exports out of Castile. It will be seen that Menorca is another good example. High labour costs and the ready availability of land encouraged the expansion of pastoral activity throughout much of Europe.

The first point to stress is that its good position on the international trade routes, combined with the growing difficulties of woollen-cloth producers in Flanders and Florence, gave new life to the Mallorcan textile industry. It is now clear that this industry took several decades to rival that of Barcelona; Antoni Riera Melis has written of 'el lento despertar de la manufactura lanera en Mallorca'. An early attempt to implant a textile industry *ad consuetudinem Narbone*, in 1257, seems to have failed; the intention was to use the best wool of Bougie in north Africa.[1] The king tried at first to solve the teething troubles of this industry by sending Master Bindo, a draper, to the island in 1303 to give instruction. At this stage the king expected wool to be bought in north Africa: *comendamus deliberacionem per vos habitam de emendo lana de Barbaria mitenda ad partes ista filanda*.[2] However, by the late fifteenth

---

[1] Santamaría, *Ejecutoria*, 403–5.   [2] Riera Melis, *Corona de Aragón*, 130–3.

century Mallorca's textile industry appeared to be more resilient than that of mainland Catalonia. The emphasis was on the production of middling to good cloths, rather as in the Catalan case; and, like Barcelona, Mallorca benefited enormously from the conquests of Alfonso the Magnanimous and his attempts to create a Catalan Common Market in the western Mediterranean.[3] Commercial contracts drawn up at the Salerno fair in 1478 reveal that Mallorcan cloths were a common commodity in the Aragonese kingdom of Naples; the notary Petruccio Pisano records the sale of seventy-four Mallorcan cloths, worth a total of 819 ducats.[4] This is more than twice the number of Barcelonan cloths he mentions. Fifty-six Florentine woollen cloths were traded, with an average price four times that of Mallorcan cloths; but the evidence from fifteenth-century Naples makes clear the difficulties Florence now had in facing cheaper competitors from the Catalan world. Only seventeen cloths of Perpignan, once part of the Majorcan kingdom, are listed by this notary, but the average value approached three times that of Mallorcan cloth.[5] There was also Genoese cloth available *a la maiorchina*, in the style of, and no doubt made from the raw wool of, Mallorca, for significant quantities of Mallorcan wool were exported to Genoa in the first half of the fifteenth century.[6]

This, of course, is the crucial transformation. Whereas there is no hard evidence for a lively export trade in Mallorcan or Menorcan raw wool in the thirteenth and early fourteenth centuries, the evidence becomes abundant by 1400, particularly in the private papers of the Tuscan merchant Francesco di Marco Datini. According to Alvaro Santamaría, writing of the autonomous kingdom

---

[3] This is to accept the broad arguments of del Treppo, *I mercanti catalani e l'espansione della Corona d'Aragona*.

[4] David Abulafia, 'The crown and the economy under Ferrante I of Naples (1458–94)', *City and countryside in late medieval and early Renaissance Italy. Essays presented to Philip Jones*, ed. T. Dean and C. Wickham (London, 1990), 140–5; A. Silvestri, *Il commercio a Salerno nella seconda metà del Quattrocento* (Salerno, 1952), 141–50; A. Sapori, 'La fiera di Salerno del 1478', *Bollettino dell'Archivio storico del Banco di Napoli*, 8 (1954), 51–84, repr. as 'Una fiera in Italia alla fine del Quattrocento: la fiera di Salerno del 1478', in his *Studi di storia economica (secoli XIII-XIV-XV)*, 3rd ed. (Florence, 1967), 443–74; E. Ashtor, 'Catalan cloth on the late medieval Mediterranean markets', *Journal of European Economic History*, 17 (1988), 227–57.

[5] Abulafia, 'Crown and economy', 142. For the parallel problem of the origins of the textile industry in mainland Majorca (Roussillon and Cerdagne), see A. Riera Melis, 'L'Aparició de la draperia urbana als Pireneus orientals', *Annals de la Universitat d'Estiu, Andorra 1982. El sigle XIII* (Andorra la Vella, 1983), 152–78.

[6] Silvestri, *Commercio*, 84, doc. 84; P. Macaire, *Majorque et le commerce international (1400–1450 environ)* (Lille, 1986), 499, table.

of Majorca, 'la ganadería tenía menor incidencia y desarollo cual acaecía en las otras monarquías del Occidente europeo'.[7] Taking the fourteenth century as a whole, he has written elsewhere that 'el principal problema que planteaba la ganadería era el de su insuficiencia'.[8] A study of income from tithes levied on Mallorcan pastoral products suggests that between 1329 and 1343 the pastoral economy accounted for 6.79 percent of agrarian production; the income from this source peaked in 1334–8, declining by 1343 to a point lower than the income in 1329.[9] However, there was a broader decline in agricultural production from the mid-1330s onwards, as in many other areas of western Europe.[10] Something significant clearly happened between 1343 and the arrival of the Datini agents in the 1390s. Especially noticeable by 1400 is the attention paid to wool of Menorca, which had a long tradition of pastoral activity;[11] Datini agents made plain in their letters their attention to instructions to find good wool.[12] Considerable quantities of several qualities of wool were being brought out of the Balearics by Datini's agents around 1400. Whereas in the years around 1300 Mallorca had clearly depended on supplies of north African wool, the situation had been completely transformed by 1400: when non-Balearic wool is mentioned in the Mallorcan letters of the Datini firm, it is generally from mainland Spain and is being trans-shipped through Mallorca or Ibiza. Close attention was paid to the variations from year to year in the quality of wool.[13] On 11 August 1404 the Datini agency in

[7] Santamaría, *Ejecutoria*, 395.
[8] Santamaría, *Reino de Mallorca*, 27; however, he speaks here only of Mallorca proper, and mentions imports from Menorca and the Maghrib, which he sees as crucial to the survival of Mallorca's textile industry in the fifteenth century: Santamaría, *Reino de Mallorca*, 28.
[9] Santamaría, *Ejecutoria*, 396.   [10] Santamaría, *Ejecutoria*, 396–8.
[11] The treaty of 1231 between James the Conqueror and the Menorcan Muslims already indicates the significance of animal raising in the Menorcan economy.
[12] Archivio di Stato di Firenze, sezione di Prato (hereafter ASP), Datini 1073, Carteggio Maiorca, lettere Minorca–Maiorca, no. 801487, 1406 dic. 4, and 801490, 1406 mar. 11, Giovanni Perets to Comp. Francesco di Marco Datini and Cristofano di Bartolo Carocci da Barberino. For general comments on the role of the Mallorca branch of Datini's firm, see E. Bensa, *Francesco di Marco da Prato* (Milan, 1928), 112–13; F. Melis, *Aspetti della vita economica medievale (studi nell'Archivio Datini di Prato)* (Siena/Florence, 1962), 261–5; and (for the early stages) the important study by Bruno Dini, *Una Pratica di Mercatura in formazione* (1394–1395) (Florence/Prato, 1980), 16–30.
[13] ASP, Datini 1073, Carteggio Maiorca, lettere Minorca–Maiorca, no. 119409, 1399 feb. 11, Bernart Portal a Comp. Francesco di Marco Datini e Cristofano di Bartolo Carocci da Barberino: 'ay bona sort de lana e lana bona'; no. 801487, 1406 dic. 4, no. 801494, 1406 lugl. 18, both Giovanni di Perets to Comp. Francesco di Marco Datini e Cristofano di Bartolo Carocci da Barberino; cf. F. Melis, *Documenti per la storia economica dei secoli XIII–XV* (Florence/Prato, 1972), 180–1, for a document of 5 March 1399 from the same file.

Mallorca received a report of a ship bearing 220 sacks of wool which was standing in the port of Maó (Mahón) in Menorca.[14] In 1407 Bernat Portal reported from Maó to Mallorca that 'les lanes son estades est any fort bones mes son poches'.[15] Thus quality and quantity did not coincide: Menorca was not flush with wool every year. There was also some interest in sheepskins and cheeses; what all these products have in common is their basis in the expanded pastoral economy of the Balearic islands.[16] The Italians and Catalans brought both finished cloth and wheat in return; often the imported goods were actually bartered for Balearic products.[17] This may reflect the shortage of specie which some historians have identified in this period, though an increasingly convincing alternative view is that barter became fashionable as a means to reduce overheads and dependence on middlemen.[18] In particular, the food needs of the islands remained pressing: the late fourteenth century saw a decline in agricultural output; there was increasing concern for control of exports of grain from Mallorca.

[14] ASP, Datini 1073, Carteggio Maiorca, lettere Mahón–Maiorca, no. 801679, Miquel Angles to Cristofano di Bartolo Carocci da Barberino. The major study of the handling of Menorcan wool is Melis' 'Sei panni di lana minorchina dalla tosa della pecora alle soglie dell'abbigliamento', in Melis, *Aspetti*, 635–729.

[15] ASP, Datini 1073, Carteggio Maiorca, Mahón–Maiorca, no. 119396, 1407 giu. 30, Bernart Portal to Comp. Francesco di Marco Datini and Cristofano di Bartolo Carocci da Barberino.

[16] ASP, Datini 1084, Carteggio Maiorca, Appendice: Lettere a Giovanni e Tuccio di Gennaio in Ivizza, 1400–04, Maiorca–Iviza, nos. 521054 and 521089, 1400 gen. 25, and 1401 mar. 25, both from Comp. Francesco di Marco Datini e Cristofano di Bartolo Carocci da Barberino to Giovanni di Gennaio, referring in the former case to 'pelle ovine' and in the latter to 56 cheeses weighing on average nearly 1 lb each as well as 'formagio insalato'.

[17] ASP, Datini 1073, Carteggio Maiorca, lettere Mahón–Maiorca, nos. 119402, 119405, 119407, all Bernart Portal to Francesco di Marco Datini and Cristofano di Bartolo Carocci da Barberino; ASP, Datini 1084, Carteggio Maiorca, Appendice: Lettere a Giovanni e Tuccio di Gennaio in Ivizza, 1400–4, Maiorca–Iviza, no. 521053, 1400 sett. 17, Comp. Francesco di Marco Datini e Cristofano di Bartolo Carocci da Barberino to Giovanni di Bartolo: 'Facendo la baratta di iij pani di opere di Barzalona a lana'.

[18] Dini, *Pratica di mercatura*, 19–20, expresses current thinking on this; cf. J. Day, *The medieval market economy* (Oxford, 1987), 11, 13, 57, 89, 95, 120. ASP, Datini 1082, Carteggio Maiorca, lettere Maiorca–Venezia, nos. 119475–8, 1398 maggio, Bindo di Gherardo Piaciti a Comp. Francesco di Marco Datini e Cristofano di Bartolo Carocci da Barberino, reveals barter of cloth for pearls in Venice, with a view to the export of the pearls either to Mallorca or (by preference) to Valencia.

II

It is certainly striking that the Balearic islands were a major base for the operations of the obsessively watchful but very successful 'merchant of Prato' throughout most of Datini's career. Yet they functioned as a source of supply, a market for imported goods, and, not least, as a control centre from which Datini's agents could report on the movement of shipping between Venice and Flanders, Genoa and Valencia, and very many other western Mediterranean routes. Many goods coming into the islands were simply being transferred to other ships or stored temporarily before re-export. Ibiza was especially useful in this regard, and the correspondence with the Datini agents on Ibiza is more concerned with reports on middle- to long-distance trade than with the handling of the island's own produce; others than Datini specialised in Ibizan salt. Letters were received from Bruges and Venice as well as nearby Denia, Valencia and Peñiscola.[19] It was a good command centre from which to compare prices and availability of Mallorcan and mainland wools. It was also a valuable clearing house where mainland commodities such as *grana*, the red insect dye used for prestige cloth manufacture, were available.[20]

The Datini evidence, superabundant as it is, cannot be used with confidence to map out Mallorca's trading links at this period. Francesco Datini had clear priorities, and the wool and cloth trades dominated his business affairs. In particular, he showed rather little interest in north Africa. The surviving correspondence between north African towns and Datini agents in the Balearics makes it plain that direct trade with the Maghrib was of marginal importance to Datini's firm.[21] The crown was concerned that there was so much contraband traffic between the Maghrib and Mallorca: Ambrogio di messer Lorenzo de'Rocchi, who did much to set up Datini operations in Mallorca, noted 'molti merchatanti della villa che mettono in Barberia, molte cose contra diveto, chome fe'ferro, pece e simile

[19] ASP, Datini 1084, Carteggio Maiorca, Appendice: Lettere a Giovanni e Tuccio di Gennaio in Ivizza, 1400–4.

[20] ASP, Datini 1076, Carteggio Maiorca, lettere Pisa–Maiorca, no. 120041, 1400 ott. 12, Comp. Francesco di Marco Datini to Comp. Francesco di Marco Datini and Cristofano di Bartolo Carocci da Barberino.

[21] ASP, Datini 1076, Carteggio Maiorca, contains letters from Tunis and Tédèllis to Mallorca: a dozen for Tunis as opposed to one for Tédèllis. There are thought to be 10,218 letters in the Datini archive sent to recipients in Mallorca: Melis, *Aspetti*, 17–23.

cose'; sometimes these bans on trade with north Africa were supposed to be total.[22] On the other hand, Datini's agents showed a strong interest in African products accessible in Mallorca, notably wax, and also to some degree leather; north African wool was less favoured now that the wools of Mallorca, Menorca and mainland Spain were easily available and of requisite quality.[23] A letter from Savona suggests that the proceeds from the sale of hemp, suitable for the making of sailcloths, can be used to buy wax and *chuoio barbarescho*, north African leather, in Mallorca.[24] In April 1404 a Datini agent in Tunis reported to Mallorca that 'qui cio buona somma di quoia di bue ed vitelli', but this was not a major concern of the Datini companies.[25]

II

It is possible to reach closer to the realities of economic life under Peter IV thanks in part to the survival of a unique curial register covering most of the period of office of Mallorca's ninth bishop (and, perhaps surprisingly, first bishop of native Mallorcan origin), Antonio de Galiano. The 214 documents contained in the register fill in the ecclesiastical history of a neglected period in Balearic history, illustrating the conflicts between the bishop and the royal government, but also illuminate the economic and social conditions of an island still reeling from the impact of the plague.[26] It should be emphasised that the years immediately after the confiscation of James III's lands brought many predictable benefits to Mallorca: the king of Aragon celebrated his arrival with reasonably generous privileges,

---

[22] Dini, *Pratica di mercatura*, 15–16, 22.

[23] ASP, Datini 1076, Carteggio Maiorca, lettere Pisa–Maiorca, no. 120042, 1400 nov. 19 (also mentioning dates), Comp. Francesco di Marco Datini to Comp. Francesco di Marco Datini and Cristofano di Bartolo Carocci da Barberino; see also F. Melis, *Documenti per la storia economica*, 170–1.

[24] ASP, Datini 1076, Carteggio Maiorca, lettere Savona–Maiorca, no. 123023, 1396 mar. 30, Bartolomeo di Barone a Ambrogio di Messer Lorenzo (Lorenzi), for which see also Dini, *Pratica*, tavola 6; cf. ASP, Datini 1076, Carteggio Maiorca, lettere Pisa–Maiorca, no. 124208, lettere Pisa–Maiorca, 1406 (= 1407) gen. 13, Comp. Paolo Biliotti a Comp. Francesco di Marco Datini e Cristofano di Bartolo Carocci da Barberino, for both wool and leather from north Africa, as well as mainland Spanish products ('mandorli di Valenza' and no doubt the saffron also mentioned).

[25] ASP, Datini 1076, Carteggio Maiorca, lettere Tunisi–Maiorca, no. 121236, 1404 apr. 1, Antonio Faulli to Comp. Francesco di Marco Datini and Cristofano di Bartolo Carocci da Barberino.

[26] J. N. Hillgarth and Juan Rosselló Lliteras, *The liber communis curiae of the diocese of Majorca (1364–1374)*. Text with English and Spanish introduction and notes (Publications de l'Institut d'Études Médiévales, vol. XXIV; Montreal/Paris, 1989).

such as franchises for traders towards Catalonia.[27] In 1379 Peter IV wrote to the governor of Mallorca, Francesc Sagarriga, expressing his fears at the depopulation, and indicating that not merely plague but military service was taking away the island's inhabitants, so that conditions seemed to be growing worse.[28] The attack by Pedro the Cruel on the Balearics can have done little to restore the mercantile economy; and there were constant demands for cash from the crown, even though the conquest of James III's kingdom had already brought additional wealth in lands and taxes to Peter of Aragon.[29] The result was that opposition was stimulated, as in the case of the knight Joan Brondo, who found himself in trouble for asking sarcastically *¿qual val més al senyor rei lo regne de Cerdenya o lo regne de Mallorca?*: which is worth more, the kingdom of Mallorca or that of Sardinia?[30] And the cost of suppressing the kings of Arborea in Sardinia and their Genoese rivals was borne in part by the Mallorcans, as many a document reveals; in 1356 the king was looking for £15,000 from the Mallorcans to keep Matteo Doria at bay in Sardinia.[31] The island bore the cost of three hundred lightly armed cavalrymen in the war against the king of Castile.[32] Severe depopulation led the island's widows to marry slaves, which the bishop then forbade in 1362. The long-lasting attempts to encourage resettlement on the island are uncannily reminiscent of events in the thirteenth century, after the Catalan conquest. There were promises of freedom from taxes for merchants and artisans, in 1381; promises of amnesty for crimes, in 1427; there were also freed slaves who formed confraternities of Russians, Greeks, Circassians, Turks; under the Trastámara dynasty in the fifteenth century there were appeals not merely to Christians but Jews, *conversos* and, remarkably, Muslims to come and settle; there were cash offers (£10 for each immigrant) in 1442, so the process of drawing in settlers proved a very slow one.[33] For depopulation also reduced production of staple foodstuffs, with

---

[27] P. Cateura Bennàsser, *Política y finanzas del reino de Mallorca bajo Pedro IV de Aragón* (Palma de Mallorca, 1982), doc. 17, 276; but many of the pre-plague documents printed by Bennàsser point in a similar direction: docs. 1–34, 261–91.

[28] Cateura Bennàsser, *Política y finanzas*, doc. 238, 501.

[29] Cateura Bennàsser, *Política y finanzas*, 11, 126–36.

[30] Cateura Bennàsser, *Política y finanzas*, 129.

[31] Cateura Bennàsser, *Política y finanzas*, doc. 59, 313.

[32] Cateura Bennàsser, *Política y finanzas*, 131.

[33] P. Cateura Benàsser, *Sociedad, jerarquía y poder en la Mallorca medieval* (Fontes rerum Balearium, Estudios y textos, 7, Palma de Mallorca, 1984), 45–6, and 66–72 for the *libertos*; Cateura Bennàsser, *Política y finanzas*, 515, doc. 255; Santamaría, *El reino de Mallorca*, 122.

serious effects on the well-being of those peasants who did survive disease; in 1360 the Mallorcans were able to import grain from Menorca, and in 1364 all grain exports from Mallorca were banned. The capital city, too, suffered from the effects of foreign competition in the textile industry, so that this period sees a ban on the import of foreign cloth in order to stimulate local demand. Tensions over Mallorca's trade are perhaps visible in documents that reveal a Genoese attack on a Mallorcan ship, with the result that its captain was killed and that a Mallorcan cleric had a book of hours, a breviary and documents of value to his cathedral stolen from him.[34] Not that Mallorcans always conducted themselves perfectly at sea, as can be seen from the case of a Mallorcan pirate who stole the cargo of a ship bearing building materials to the monastery of St Victor in Marseilles, and contemptuously tore up a papal flag.[35]

In other ways too this was a period of tension, for the war between the two kings Peter, Pedro the Cruel of Castile and Pere IV of Aragon, III of Catalonia, brought Castilian fleets into Balearic waters around 1360, and Ibiza was raided. As Cateura Bennàsser shows, this also meant that tax demands placed a heavy burden on a population ill-fitted to meet them. A possible indication of the social tensions of the late fourteenth century is the growing hostility towards the Jews, visible even before the horrible pogroms of 1391, which affected Mallorca as well as Castile and the mainland Catalan lands. Bishop Antonio, in common with his king, adopted a cautious, traditional approach to the treatment of the Jews, legislating against hasty baptism.[36] Situated on the frontiers of Christendom, a Mallorcan bishop also had to bear in mind the question of Christians who went to live in north Africa and became Muslims, or cases of Mallorcans enslaved in north Africa whose release he could sometimes help negotiate. He also extended his protection to an adherent of the Armenian church, attesting that, at least in the instance of this eastern rite, its members could not be enslaved.

Although the late fourteenth century brought deep tragedy to the Jewish community of Mallorca and the other lands of the Crown of Aragon, with the pogroms and widespread conversions of 1391, Jewish trade through Mallorca did not cease. Indeed, there even seems to have been some resettlement by Jews in the *Call*, consisting

---

[34] *Liber communis curiae*, doc. 138, doc. 211.   [35] *Liber communis curiae*, doc. 1.
[36] *Liber communis curiae*, doc. 206.

of newly invited Portuguese émigrés. The turmoil of 1391 did not necessarily destroy communities, but it stimulated mobility within Iberia. And in fact the commercial life of the Mallorcan Jews in the period from 1391 to 1435 is recorded in the *teshuvot* (*teshuboth*) or *responsa* of Rabbi Shimeon ben Zemah Duran, one of the refugees who left Mallorca in 1391 to live in Algiers. There he lived among Sephardi exiles, many of whom maintained close business and family ties with Spanish Jews, some of them newly converted to Christianity. What can be seen in the *responsa* is a tight network of business links between Mallorca and such African trade centres as Algiers and Mostaganem. The events of 1391 may even, paradoxically, have strengthened such ties, since there were now many Mallorcan and Catalan refugees in the Maghrib who knew the markets back in the land of their fathers.[37] The existence of the *conversos* in rapidly increasing numbers necessitated rabbinic answers to the widest range of questions: was a Christian marriage between two *conversos* to be recognised as valid in Jewish law when they left Spain and settled safely in north Africa among Jews? Was wine handled by Marranos ritually fit? May a woman apostate give a Torah mantle to the Jewish community of Mostaganem?[38] Shimeon Duran showed a sympathy for the plight of his fellow-Jews who had remained in Mallorca and turned Christian which not all rabbis (including some of his family) shared.[39] He assumed that times would improve, and that the Jews of Mallorca would have the chance to return to the fold before long. His *responsa* concerning business affairs have been analysed by Eliezer Gutwirth.[40] Although the names given in the *responsa* are by and large invented ones, drawn from the names of the tribes of Israel, the documents themselves reflect real circumstances. In one text, dating between 1391 and 1427, Reuben is based in

[37] There is an interesting parallel here in the close commercial contacts between Portuguese or Spanish New Christian businessman and their Marrano brethren, often living openly as Jews, in the Netherlands of the early seventeenth century.

[38] B. Netanyahu, *The Marranos of Spain, from the late fourteenth to the early sixteenth century according to contemporary Hebrew sources* (2nd edn, New York, 1973), 56–7; for the context, and a strong critique of Netanyahu's assumptions, see, however, David Abulafia, *1492: the expulsion from Spain and Jewish identity* (Dorfler Memorial Lecture 1992, published as Leo Baeck College Studies in Judaism, no. 2, London, 1992).

[39] Abulafia, *1492*, 15–16; J. Epstein, *The responsa of Rabbi Simon ben Zemah Duran* (London, 1930); H. J. Zimmels, *Die Marranen in der rabbinischen Literatur* (Berlin, 1930).

[40] E. Gutwirth, 'El comercio hispano-magrebi y los Judíos (1391–1444)', *Hispania*, 45 (1985), 199–205; E. Gutwirth, 'Towards expulsion: 1391–1492', in *Spain and the Jews. The Sephardi experience, 1492 and after*, ed. E. Kedourie (London, 1992), 51–73, especially 66–8; there are also some useful comments in Epstein, *The responsa*.

Mallorca, and Simon is working in Algiers, and they invest capital in a common enterprise; the latter makes a sale to a non-Jew and hands over the record of the sale to Levi, who takes the documents to Mallorca where he places them in the custody of a junior assistant. Meanwhile Simon has set out for Valencia. Reuben then intervenes to request that what is owed him be transferred to another party, Judah. Such complications were the stuff of the rabbinic law courts.[41] Proof of the importance of family ties in the creation and maintenance of these trade links is provided in the *responsa*. One document cited within a *responsum* runs:

I Reuben certify that I have received all that was owed to me by Simon my brother and that all our debts are cancelled, both those which concern the merchandise which he used to send me to Mostaganem as well as that which I used to send him from Mallorca and this document is extended as proof of this.[42]

The *responsa* are particularly informative about imports from north Africa. Gold has an important place, as might be expected at a time when demand for precious metals was high. Moreover, the Jews of Mallorca had a longstanding interest in goldsmithery. There was some interest in the grain trade, too.[43] But the most important commodity moving from the Balearics to the Maghrib appears from these documents to have been wine, and Gutwirth assumes it had first place in the actual export traffic. In fact, the reason wine is so frequently mentioned in the *responsa* is that the rules concerning the production and handling of wine were so strict; to be *kasher* it had to be made and supervised by Jews (or at least by circumcised males) all the way from the vine to the cup.[44] Thus wine sent by a converted relative in Mallorca to Mose Amer, who had left the island for Bougie, was the subject of rabbinic discussion.[45] The Mallorcan converts seem to have assumed that their conversion, in so many cases far from sincere, would not destroy their established trade in wine to the Jewish communities of north Africa, who presumably had only limited local supplies. Not surprisingly, the Jews who imported wine

[41] Gutwirth, 'El comercio hispano-magrebi', 201; Gutwirth, 'Towards expulsion', 66.
[42] Gutwirth, 'El comercio hispano-magrebi', 202; Gutwirth, 'Towards expulsion', 67. These are, of course, a different Reuben and Simon to those mentioned in the document concerning trade with Algiers.
[43] Gutwirth, 'El comercio hispano-magrebi', 203, 205; Gutwirth, 'Towards expulsion', 67.
[44] Gutwirth, 'El comercio hispano-magrebi', 203–5; Gutwirth, 'Towards expulsion', 67–8.
[45] Gutwirth, 'El comercio hispano-magrebi', 204.

from Mallorca sought to sell it to non-Jews as well, especially if it was not actually kosher wine; this aroused the ire of the local ruler, who did not want his Muslim subjects to drink wine, so the Jewish community declared itself even ready to excommunicate Jews who sold wine to Muslims.[46] The wine they sent to the Maghrib was not simply Mallorcan, but also kosher wine of Valencia and other Aragonese lands; wine from a Jewish producer in Murviedro was sent by a Mallorcan *converso* to Ténès, and this was good enough for Rabbi Shimeon Duran, who said: 'this wine assuredly was not produced by the Mallorcan convert, since, as all the world knows, it has the appearance and taste of the wine of the kingdom of Valencia'.[47] Strict rules also applied to cheese, the *kashrut* of which was bound to be in doubt if it was sent by a *converso* to a Jew living in north Africa.[48]

Another sign of continuing international links is the interest shown by the Venetians in the creation and maintenance of a consulate in Mallorca. In April 1358 Peter IV expressed his surprise that the Venetians (old allies, it should be remembered, in the war with Genoa over Sardinia) had no special privileges on the island, and granted them the same rights as the Genoese already possessed.[49] A particular concern was the maintenance of unhindered trade to Flanders, *in eorum passagio flandriarum*.[50] In fact, the permanent Venetian presence in Mallorca seems not to have been large: a decision by the Venetian Senate, dated 13 January 1378, indicates that Antonio de'Canielli (Anthonius de Chagneles), who was a citizen and merchant of Mallorca, was then consul for Venice on the island, and that he had succeeded his father in the office.[51] However, Antonio proved quite unworthy of his post; the Senate looked at his performance seventeen years later and blamed him for maltreating Venetian merchants and for failing to defend their interests. He was even supposed to have encouraged royal officials to oppress the Venetians in Mallorca. Thus he may not any longer be consul of Venice in Mallorca, and Bernardo Bovo, a loyal citizen of Venice who also had the right to trade as a Catalan (*qui est fidelissimus civis dominationis nostre, et catellanus per privilegium*) should replace him

---

[46] Gutwirth, 'El comercio hispano-magrebi', 204.
[47] Gutwirth, 'El comercio hispano-magrebi', 204–5. Who tasted it to find out? It is rather like the problem how kosher food manufacturers know that their smoked goose breast tastes like bacon.   [48] Gutwirth, 'El comercio hispano-magrebi', 203.
[49] Pitzorno, 'Consolato veneziano', docs. 1–2, 18–20.
[50] Pitzorno, 'Consolato veneziano', doc. 3, 20.
[51] Pitzorno, 'Consolato veneziano', doc. 4, 21.

forthwith.[52] It was thus still the rule that the Venetian consul in Mallorca should be drawn from those who were, or had the status of, Catalans of Mallorca.[53]

III

Although it is far from clear how seriously Mallorca's commerce suffered from the depression many economic historians have insisted on identifying in the post-Black Death era, it is at least possible to gauge the range of Mallorca's international trade in the fifteenth century, thanks to a Sorbonne thesis which has now been published.[54] Pierre Macaire's study of Mallorcan trade in the first half of the fifteenth century is based heavily on the registers of the Mallorcan notaries Anthoni and Bernat Costanti, of 1403–38 and 1446–51 respectively, and arguably the work suffers from a lack of wider perspective: it is especially surprising that the voluminous Datini papers in Prato are ignored by the author. Macaire's work confirms the continuing primacy of north Africa in Mallorca's trade, and sheds interesting light on the activities of Christian and Jewish merchants in early fifteenth-century Mallorca, as well as on business methods, the design of ships and the variety of commodities handled.

The evidence from the notarial registers of early-fifteenth-century Mallorca confirms that north Africa had not in fact lost its primary importance in Balearic trade. During the first quarter of the fifteenth century, the Jew Astruch Xibili conducted business in all the significant trading towns of the Maghrib, with the other Balearic islands (17 insurances), with Collioure (16 insurances; it clearly retained its importance in Mallorcan trade even after the extinction of the Majorcan state), with Barcelona (62 insurances), Valencia (33), Sicily (27) and Sardinia (10): almost every recorded year he was involved in business with these lands, and, since his function was generally that of an insurance broker, his business affairs are good evidence for the wider trading network of the Mallorcan merchant

---

[52] Pitzorno, 'Consolato veneziano', doc. 5, 22, of 8 March 1395.

[53] Pitzorno, 'Consolato veneziano', 17. The appointment of consuls who were not necessarily Venetian is not particularly unusual. Indeed, in more modern times Sephardic Jews were often employed as British consuls to represent British interests in the Ottoman lands, the Maghrib and elsewhere.

[54] Pierre Macaire, *Majorque et le commerce international (1400–1450 environ)*, doctoral thesis, University of Paris IV, Sorbonne, 1983 (Lille: Atelier réproduction des thèses, Université de Lille III, 1986). This work consists of an assemblage of information, reasonably well organised, but lacking much depth of analysis; the question of the supposed decline of the Crown of Aragon in the fifteenth century requires a more reflective approach.

élite, Christian and Jewish, whose affairs he helped to organise; he also traded extensively in his own right to north Africa. His business affairs in Venice, Provence, southern Italy and the Levant, and, perhaps surprisingly, Granada, were not unimportant, but were less regular, though on twenty-two occasions between 1419 and 1432 he is found insuring journeys to and from Flanders.[55] A Christian merchant from the same period, Guillerm Bramona, had similar interests in the western Mediterranean, with a greater stress on southern Italy and a much less developed interest in Barcelona; he has been seen as 'un marchand type' of early-fifteenth-century Mallorca, though the spread of Astruch Xibili's interests, if not the man himself, is arguably more representative.[56]

The character of the long distance trade can be established with ease. To Flanders spices, wax and oil were carried; many of these products, such as saffron, dates and *grana* were of western Mediterranean rather than oriental origin. Cloths were brought in return.[57] By contrast, the trade to Alexandria, *Romania*, Cyprus and Rhodes, a jumping-off point into the Levant, was dominated by the export of Catalan cloths (Mallorcan, Barcelonan, Perpignanais) and of olive oil, and the import of spices.[58] The registers of Anthoni Costanti mention about 73 trips to the eastern Mediterranean in the first forty years of the fifteenth century; there are 42 references to exports of cloth and 31 to exports of olive oil.[59] By contrast there are 196 references to cloth being sent to the Maghrib, and cloth was by far and away the most important commodity sent south; wax dominated imports from Africa, but leather and gold were also significant.[60] Between Mallorca and the Maghrib, 391 trips have been identified, of which 311, no less than 80 per cent, were by Balearic ships; Barcelona comes next with a mere 20, Castile has 14, Genoa 18 and Collioure only 7 (however these statistics must be taken with a large pinch of Ibizan salt).[61] Sicilian trade was again dominated by cloth

---

[55] These comments are based on the tables in Macaire, *Majorque*, 81–91.

[56] Macaire, *Majorque*, 60, and 61, table.   [57] Macaire, *Majorque*, 332, table.

[58] Macaire, *Majorque*, 356, 361, 368, 370, 373, 375, tables.

[59] Macaire, *Majorque*, 375, table 3.   [60] Macaire, *Majorque*, 426–7, table.

[61] Macaire, *Majorque*, 411, table 1; Macaire does not indicate the direction of trade, so his figures presumably include a high percentage of return trips. Moreover, the number of Genoese trips from Ibiza to Africa bearing the island's salt was surely very high; salt could be exchanged for gold. Finally, this is merely the evidence from a single notary with a large commercial practice, and it must be assumed that non-Mallorcan merchants frequented their own notaries in their own lonja. The lack of *ancoratge* records for fifteenth-century Mallorca simply forces one to use this questionable evidence.

exports but the major import was, predictably, wheat (much the same applied to Sardinia); some other commodities, such as wax, may have been trans-shipped through Sicily, and have been of Tunisian origin.[62] The constant provision of wax by Mallorcan merchants trading to Barcelona serves as a reminder that Mallorca too was a point of trans-shipment for goods from north-west Africa, and confirms the emphasis on this product in some Datini letters. There was some redistribution of Flemish cloths, Sicilian wheat, Almerian silk and Levantine spices to Barcelona; it is less clear what dominated Barcelona's trade to Mallorca.[63] Trade towards Genoa and Savona was certainly heaviest in raw wool, not merely of Mallorca and Menorca but also of Valencia; however, existing documentation may not give enough attention to the salt of Ibiza, which could be obtained directly from the island by Genoese shippers.[64]

It thus seems that the Balearics did undergo an economic transformation in the late fourteenth and fifteenth centuries. Not merely did Mallorca become the centre of a successful textile industry, aimed at the upper middle part of the market, but Menorca, and to some degree Mallorca, became a major wool-producing region, with surplus raw wool being sold to Italian businessmen for transmission to Florence, Genoa and elsewhere in north-western Italy. Yet it did not lose its function as a transit centre for trade in African goods, above all wax and also, when available, gold. By comparison with Barcelona, the impression is of a quite buoyant economy, though social crises in town and country, notably the pogrom of 1391, indicate that the process of adjustment, here as elsewhere in Europe, was difficult.

While some sectors of the economy appear to have adjusted quite well to the challenge of a sudden drop in population in the middle of the fourteenth century, followed by further onslaughts of plague that prevented population recovery, other sectors clearly reponded less happily. The agricultural crisis was still visible in the late fifteenth century, as a study by Maria Barceló Crespi reveals.[65] The capital city too was affected by repeated onslaughts of plague, in 1467, 1481, 1493, 1510, the second of which is said to have carried off 20,000

---

[62] Macaire, *Majorque*, 449, 457, tables.   [63] Macaire, *Majorque*, 471, table 1.

[64] Macaire, *Majorque*, 499, table 2; 500, table 2; cf. Hocquet, 'Ibiza'.

[65] Maria Barceló Crespi, *Ciutat de Mallorca en el Trànsit a la Modernitat* (Palma de Mallorca, 1988).

people. There was a heavy public debt. The king of Naples banned the import of woollen cloth from the lands of the Crown of Aragon in 1472, in an attempt to stimulate native industry in southern Italy. Since his kingdom had been a major market for Mallorcan cloth, and since Mallorca had developed a substantial cloth industry since the mid-fifteenth century, this arguably had serious effects on the island economy, as well as stimulating social unrest.[66] A particularly heavy expense was the importation of massive amounts of grain, rendered necessary by the repeated failure of the rains. Living as it did by trade, the City of Mallorca could not remain immune from wider changes in the economic structure of the western Mediterranean in the late fifteenth century.

V

The aim here has been to contrast two aspects of Mallorca's trade in the late Middle Ages. First appreciated as a stopping-off point, a command centre, a place for the repair of ships, for the storing of African and Iberian goods, Mallorca never abandoned these functions. What is striking is the success of the Balearics in developing their own textile industry, and then, apparently after that, their own woollen export business, so that Mallorca, by the time of Francesco Datini, was more than one big *fondacho* filled with exotic goods. The mystery is to whom to attribute these initiatives. The Black Death undoubtedly stimulated the expansion of pastoral activities; Menorca was never densely settled, and had a long history of sheep and cattle rearing, but it seems that it was only after the mid-fourteenth century that its export trade in raw wool really took off. Mallorca benefited from these changes, in cheap supplies for its own industry, and it also benefited from the wider, and largely successful, challenge by Catalan cloth producers against those of Flanders and Florence. There are striking similarities between this evidence and that from another of the late medieval lands of the Crown of Aragon, Sicily: in the Val Demone, behind Messina, Stephan Epstein has found evidence for greater specialisation in the post-Black Death era, not merely in the island's sugar industry;[67] and recent research on Malta, an outpost of the Sicilian kingdom, suggests that cotton cultivation

---

[66] On the other hand, there were plenty of Mallorcan cloths on sale at the Salerno fair in 1478: David Abulafia, 'The crown and the economy', 142.

[67] S. R. Epstein, *An island for itself. Economic development and social change in late medieval Sicily* (Cambridge, 1992); I owe my information on Malta to Charles Dalli.

took off in the same period, even though (like Menorca's pastoral sector) it had a long prehistory. These trends recall again Mario del Treppo's picture of an integrated western Mediterranean economy under the benevolent aegis of the fifteenth-century kings of Aragon.

Yet it can also be argued that an important step forward was the reintegration of the Balearic islands into the economic system being built up by Catalan merchants across the Aragonese dominions and in north Africa. Attempts by the three independent kings of Majorca to put up tariff barriers against Catalan merchants, and to bond Mallorca more closely to Roussillon by way of Collioure, rebounded on the Majorcan monarchy and economy in the early fourteenth century, for the result was the avoidance of Mallorca by Catalan merchants. The route to success lay along trade routes to Africa, Sardinia, Calabria, Sicily and elsewhere, which were being opened up by the Catalans as a whole: Barcelonans, Mallorcans, Valencians. The success of Mallorca's trade and industry in the late Middle Ages depended on the involvement of Mallorca in the supply system that linked Barcelona and Valencia to the Mediterranean islands and to the Maghrib. Mallorca, as the popes had recognised from the start, could not survive without trade; but the success of that trade depended to some degree on the success of its integration into the trading world of Catalonia.

Conclusion

The Catalan kingdom of Majorca was a political failure. Its rulers did not manage to keep Aragonese pretensions to overlordship at bay, even though the will of the kingdom's founder, James I of Aragon, had stipulated that Majorca and its continental dependencies were to be independent of Aragon. Within three years of James I's death, the Majorcan king had to acknowledge Aragonese suzerainty. The sole way to hold off the Aragonese was to allow the king of France a degree of influence over the kingdom's external relations that only resulted in an Aragonese counter-attack and the loss (between 1285 and 1298) of the Balearic islands to the king of Aragon. The inability of the kings of Majorca to maintain their independence culminated in the crisis of 1343–9, when Peter IV of Aragon conquered the kingdom and James III of Majorca met his death in a vain attempt to recover the Balearics.

At the same time, the kingdom appeared to have formidable strengths of another sort. It occupied a prime position on the international trade routes, at a time of expanding commerce in the western Mediterranean and of the opening of regular trade routes linking Italy and Catalonia to Atlantic Morocco, Portugal, England and Flanders. Already an important base for Genoese and Pisan businessmen when under Muslim rule, Mallorca became in addition the home of influential communities of Catalan merchants, of naturalised Italians and Provençaux and of Jewish merchants from southern France, Spain and North Africa. Also simultaneously, the expansion of industry in Roussillon and the increasing prominence of Montpellier as a centre of banking and exchange meant that the continental territories of the kings of Majorca were also acquiring a new and valuable role in the European economy. Montpellier and Perpignan sat astride the land routes leading towards the Mediterranean; their own industry flourished alongside an active transit trade tying northern France and Flanders to Mediterranean markets. Thus each of the main Majorcan territories played a significant role in both the land and the sea traffic linking the Flanders cloth towns to the centres of demand in southern Europe and the Maghrib.

The problem was, however, that the Balearics in particular were an emporium: they were a centre for the storage and trans-shipment of goods, for the maintenance of the small craft that carried much of the trade bound for the Maghrib, for the provision of financial services. But the region required substantial grain imports in most years to sustain an urban population that accounted for perhaps half the total inhabitants of Mallorca. Ciutat de Mallorca, Montpellier and Perpignan all depended for their prosperity on keeping open the supply lines; but the late thirteenth and early fourteenth centuries were not times in which commerce could flow unhindered through the Majorcan lands. The crucial links between the Majorcan cities and Barcelona proved far more fragile than James I's last will predicted. The War of the Vespers was immediately succeeded by a trade war with Barcelona; by the 1330s the relationship between the Majorcans and the Genoese had been severely compromised by the Aragonese invasion of Sardinia, an almost unconquerable island that, nonetheless, held out hope of ample grain supplies for Mallorca and Barcelona. It is difficult to escape from the conclusion that the separation of the 'merchants of the Catalan nation' who resided in this kingdom from their brethren in Catalonia proper did not best serve the interests of long-distance trade. But there was little time in which to enjoy the benefits of open markets. The conquest of Mallorca by Peter the Ceremonious was soon followed by the catastrophic arrival of plague, itself carried along the Genoese trade routes through Aragonese Sicily to western Europe. Readjustment proved slow and difficult, but it did provide opportunities for specialised producers, notably the wool farmers of Mallorca and Menorca, to increase their output to satisfy both a local woollen industry and the cloth workshops of Tuscany.

There is, then, a notable paradox. Political weakness was not matched by economic weakness. The kingdom of Majorca consisted of a group of successful trading zones, which, indeed, experienced something of a boom in the late thirteenth and early fourteenth centuries. But long-distance trade is about crossing frontiers, not about creating them. In the long term the merchants of the Balearics, and of the other territories, needed to be part of a wider Catalan common market in the western Mediterranean; Peter IV may already have begun to visualise a single Aragonese empire in the western Mediterranean, but it was arguably in the mid-fifteenth century, with the conquests of Alfonso the Magnanimous, that such a common market was brought into being. In achieving that end, the autonomy of the kings of Majorca was an irrelevance, while the prosperity of their territories acted as a magnet to their kinsmen, the kings of Aragon. No longer a buffer between France and Catalonia, the Balearics and Roussillon became advance posts of assertive Mediterranean emperors seeking to extend their influence beyond Sardinia and Corsica to Sicily, Africa and the Levant.

Mallorca and Sardinia, 1267–1343

I

The subject of this appendix is a series of episodes that have considerable bearing on the evolution of an Aragonese-Catalan *imperium* under Peter IV, within which the kingdom of Majorca had become an enclave blocking the chance to dominate the western Mediterranean. The aim of a western Mediterranean thalassocracy was the more urgent in view of the severe worsening of Catalan–Genoese relations during the early fourteenth century, largely as a result of the Catalan invasion of Sardinia, in which the Genoese possessed such important economic and political interests.

The ties between Mallorca and Sardinia are symbolised by the fact that the closest point between modern Spain and modern Italy is the stretch of water between Maó in eastern Menorca and Alghero or l'Alguer, the Catalan-speaking town in north-western Sardinia. It is thus no accident that it was precisely from Maó that the fleet of the Infant Alfonso left in 1323 for the conquest of Sardinia. However, rather little evidence survives for the relationship between the Majorcan kings and the many rulers of late-thirteenth- and early fourteenth-century Sardinia. The fundamental works of Salavert and Arribas that deal with Aragonese ambitions in Sardinia say little about Mallorca; Salavert does, however, stress the importance of the restoration of the Majorcan monarchy to its Balearic lands in the negotiations that led to the acquisition by James II of Aragon of his title to Sardinia and Corsica, between 1295 and 1298.[1]

Another fundamental observation of Salavert is his emphasis on the strategic importance of Sardinia in the creation of a line of

---

[1] V. Salavert y Roca, *Cerdeña y la expansión mediterránea de la Corona de Aragón 1297–1314*, vol. I (Madrid, 1956), 153–5; A. Arribas Palau, *La conquista de Cerdeña por Jaime II de Aragón* (Barcelona, 1952).

Aragonese bases in the Mediterranean: 'el reino sardo era una base intermedia entre las Baleares y Sicilia, resultando esta última, posiblemente, demasiado distante, y peligrosa su posesión, sin el dominio del primero'.[2] Salavert offers as proof of the Aragonese outlook a statement of James II of Aragon, who spoke in 1311 of the Christian army 'procedendo versus orientem per maritimam, semper adheret insulis christianorum, scilicet Maioricarum, Minoricarum, Sardinie et Sicilie, de quibus haberentur assidue victualia et refrescamenta et gentes ad fortificandum exercitum antedictum et patrias populandas, et demum adquirendo posset ad Terram Sanctam, auxiliando Domino, perveniri'.[3] The same passage is, however, analysed differently by Ciro Manca, who shows that the text refers specifically to a project for a crusade to the Holy Land; the *ruta de las illas* thus has a political or religious rather than commercial significance.[4] Interesting nonetheless is the attempt by Salavert to place Sardinia and the Balearic islands in the same field of vision.

The analysis of Salavert, based on the hypothesis that the Aragonese were aiming at the creation of a coherent empire in the western Mediterranean, forms part of the more general assumption that the Crown of Aragon was guided by imperial dreams from the time of James I right through to that of Peter IV. The concept of a *ruta de las illas* thus needs to be modified in the light of the arguments of Jocelyn Hillgarth to the effect that the concept of a single Aragonese dominion stretching across the seas owes more to the sixteenth-century writer Geronimo Zurita than to reliable contemporary voices; some stirrings of a unified vision of the Catalan lands can be seen under Peter the Ceremonious, but only with Alfonso the Magnanimous does a vigorous policy to create a series of dominions with effective central offices become clearly visible.[5] In Hillgarth's view, Catalan merchants did not initiate the great series of conquests; it would be impossible to set aside the evidence that the conquest of Sicily was in the first instance motivated by dynastic considerations. The Catalan chronicles, especially the book of Bernat Desclot, make it plain that dynastic interests, expressive of the

---

[2] Salavert, *Cerdeña*, vol. i, 126.
[3] Salavert, *Cerdeña*, vol. i, 127; V. Salavert y Roca, 'El problema estratégico del Mediterráneo occidental y la política aragonese (siglos xiv y xv)', CHCA iv vol. i, 219.
[4] C. Manca, *Aspetti dell'espansione catalano-aragonese nel Mediterraneo occidentale. Il commercio internazionale del sale* (Biblioteca della rivista Economia e Storia, Milan, 1966), 9–13; M. Tangheroni, *Aspetti del commercio dei cereali nei paesi della Corona d'Aragona. I. La Sardegna* (Pisa/Cagliari 1981), 54.   [5] J. Hillgarth, *Problem*.

honour of the house of Barcelona, were the main motor of the expansion of Aragon–Catalonia. In particular, Aragonese rivalry with the house of Anjou in the second half of the thirteenth century was a factor of the first moment in the formulation of Aragonese policies not merely towards Provence and Sicily, but also with regard to Tunis, the Levant, even, as will be seen, Sardinia. Sardinia has an additional importance in this debate; unlike the Balearic islands and Sicily, it did not become the seat of a separate kingdom under the control of a cadet dynasty. From 1297 onwards, the kings of Aragon treated the *Regnum Sardinie et Corsice* as a single unit bonded in perpetuity to the king of Aragon and count of Barcelona; and this tight link was further strengthened in the Privilege of Union of 1319.

It is in this light that the early history of Catalan aspirations to rule Sardinia is generally interpreted, for example by Casula in his monumental study of the interplay between Aragonese Sardinia and the independent kingdom of Arborea.[6] But in fact the integration of Sardinia into the complex of lands directly ruled by the king-count was not always the aim of the Aragonese monarch. Historians have ignored the project to offer Sardinia in 1267 to the prospective first king of an independent Majorca, the future James II of Majorca. According to Lecoy de la Marche, who discovered a reference to this plan in the archive of the king of Majorca preserved in Paris, the gift of Sardinia to James was an attempt to give some substance to his new kingdom, 'faible et morcelé, entre deux voisins ambitieux et beaucoup plus forts que lui' – that is, France and Aragon; Lecoy cited a few passages from the Paris document, but did not bother to transcribe it completely in his massive collection of documents, mainly from the same archive, that appeared as an appendix to his work.[7] Some historians have dismissed the project as an unreal dream, or have accidentally confused Peter the Great with his younger brother.[8]

Lecoy's explanation is confirmed by a marginal note in the Parisian text of the donation of Sardinia to James of Majorca by his father; Lecoy did not in fact cite this: 'in quantum desiderabat pater quod iste filius esset rex et quod non debet satis dedisse de regno Maioricarum et comitatibus Rosilionis et Ceritanie';[9] thus the

---

[6] F. C. Casula, *La Sardegna Aragonese*, 2 vols. (Sassari, 1990).

[7] Lecoy de la Marche, *Relations*, vol. I, 120.

[8] Hillgarth, *Problem*, 15: 'in 1267 the papacy refused Jaume's request to proclaim Pere king of Sardinia'.

[9] Paris, AN, Chambre des Comptes, P1354¹, no. 800, f.1r = Appendix I, p. 249.

Balearics, Roussillon and Cerdagne did not add up to a viable
kingdom. All the signs are that this note is in fact a late gloss,
probably dating to the time of Louis I of Anjou; the use of the past
tense for *esset* and *desiderabat*, rather than the present forms *sit* and
desiderat strongly suggests that the author of the note was looking
backwards in time. Moreover, such a document was bound to attract
the close interest of Louis of Anjou, who, as has been seen, sought to
reactivate the supposed rights of the independent kings of Majorca,
and whose ambitions did not stop there, but extended even to claims
to Sardinia; almost any Mediterranean crown, lapsed or in contention, acted as a magnet for the duke's unrelenting ambition to
royal status.[10] However, it would be wrong to conclude that the Paris
text is no more than a fantasy of the late fourteenth century, spun in
the hope of exploiting the deep factional divisions within Sardinia,
and of intruding an Angevin seigneury over the heads of the warring
Arboreans and Aragonese. In fact, papal documentation of the
1260s amply confirms the authenticity of the Paris text, which is no
more a late fourteenth century forgery than the other texts in the
archive of Louis of Anjou concerning the ancient rights of the kings
of Majorca in respect to the Crown of Aragon.[11]

   The plan described in the document is for the donation of Sardinia
by the pope to James I of Aragon, who would hold it *ad interim*, but
who would then designate as his heir his younger son James of
Majorca; the latter would hold Sardinia with full rights of jurisdiction, 'in perpetuum post dies nostros Regnum predictum cum
eiusdem dominio et juribus ac omnibus ad eundem spectantibus
francum et liberum'; but 'toto tempore vite nostre nos illud
habeamus et teneamus et de ipso simus domini et potentes'; and only
'post nostrum obitum vos et vester habeatis illud prout superius
continetur'.[12] One explanation for the decision to make James of
Majorca the heir was the fact that Catalonia is simply further away
from Sardinia than Mallorca, and so it made more sense to attach
Sardinia to the Catalan–Aragonese lands through the future king of
Majorca. But another aspect of this policy was James' determination

---

[10] E. R. Labande, 'La politique méditerranéenne de Louis Ier d'Anjou et le rôle qu'y joua la
   Sardaigne', *Atti del VI Congresso internazionale di studi sardi* (Cagliari, 1957), 3–23, where,
   however, the author expresses important doubts concerning the dreams attributed to Louis
   I by (among others) Lecoy de la Marche, *Relations*, vol. II, 190.
[11] E. Martène and U. Durand, *Thesaurus novus anecdotorum*, vol. II, (Paris 1717), col. 510,
   indicates that the pope was well aware that James I of Aragon wished to present Sardinia
   to James of Majorca: see pp. 240–2   [12] AN, P1354^1, no. 800, f.1r.

to make a reality of the new, separate kingdom of Majorca, independent of Aragon–Catalonia, with its own power base in the Balearics, the Pyrenees, and, conceivably, in Sardinia too.[13] Were Sardinia to fall into the hands of the king of Aragon, as happened in the fourteenth century, the terms of James' will would be under threat, since the Balearic islands would find themselves flanked on both east and west by the lands of the king of Aragon. In this sense, then, the argument deployed by Lecoy and by the marginal note in the Paris manuscript is incomplete; James I was not merely aiming at the doubling of the extent of his younger son's inheritance, but also at the confirmation of the separation between Aragon–Catalonia and a truly viable Majorcan kingdom that would dominate the maritime space of the western Mediterranean.

However, there were yet other reasons why the Aragonese wished to intervene in Sardinia at this juncture. The links between noble families in Catalonia and Sardinia in the twelfth century have been examined already by Francesco Artizzu, and there were also some early commercial contacts.[14] Indeed, the history of the links between Sardinia and the Balearics can be traced back further still, to the attempts by Mujahid, lord of Denia and the Balearics, to install himself in Sardinia at the start of the eleventh century, and to the participation a century later of Sardinian nobles with links to Pisa in the Pisan–Catalan crusade against the Almoravids of Mallorca and Ibiza.[15] Possibly a more important factor in the formulation of Aragonese ambitions than casual ties between noble houses in Catalonia and Sardinia was, however, the rivalry between the house of Barcelona and that of Anjou in the thirteenth-century Mediterranean; this raised the question of the future of Sardinia to the level of an issue of contention between the rival monarchs of the Spanish and Italian shores of the western Mediterranean. Deprived of Provence by Charles of Anjou and by the pope, deprived of their ancient influence in Languedoc by the Treaty of Corbeil, the Aragonese found themselves constantly pushed aside as the interests of the house of Anjou were fostered by the papacy and the king of France; the Infant Peter was the leader of a faction at court that sought to resist French and Angevin pretensions, which culminated in the very years under discussion here in the conquest of Sicily and

[13] See chapter 3.
[14] F. Artizzu, 'Penetrazione catalana in Sardegna nel sec. xii', CHCA vi, 11–23.
[15] See chapter 1.

southern Italy by Charles of Anjou, and in the death in battle of the father-in-law of Peter of Aragon. Thus a fundamental feature of Aragonese interest in Sardinia was the awareness that their Angevin rivals also had ambitions to control the island. However, these fears about the rapid ascent of Charles of Anjou to a position of dominance in the western Mediterranean sphere were fortunately shared by the pope, Clement IV, who feared for the stability of papal interests in Rome and central Italy, and who realised that it would not serve his own interests to enlarge Charles' power still further by a grant of Sardinia as well as of Sicily. The papacy needed to retain some at least of the rights of lordship it claimed in Italy and the islands.[16]

Charles I's plan was to obtain Sardinia for his second son, Philip, who was also being placed in line for the management of Angevin lands in Achaia; how he was expected to cope with both a Greek and a Sardinian dominion remains unclear. It is likely that Charles, as the youngest son of King Louis VIII of France, understood well the dilemma of children not in line to succeed to their father's throne; in this sense at least his outlook converged with James of Aragon's constant wish to look after all his sons. But precisely because the Angevins and the Aragonese were at loggerheads over the Sardinian crown, the pope was able to seize his opportunity to deny both sides their chance of success. A letter of 23 July 1267, sent not just to James of Aragon but 'in eodem modo Jacobo filio suo verbis competenter mutatis', explains Clement IV's position concisely. The reference in the letter to James of Majorca, which is noted only in Martène's eighteenth-century edition, confirms the validity of the Paris text examined earlier. After stating that he has received an Aragonese embassy, consisting of the 'dilectum filium Maioricensem archidia- conum et Vicensem capellanum nostrum', the pope explains that there do in fact exist two other claimants to the Sardinian throne, namely Charles, king of Sicily and the Infante Henry of Castile, a *condottiere* who had come to southern Italy in Charles' conquering army. Moreover, the pope has recently lost control of the judgeship of Torres, that very area of north-western Sardinia which would have provided a springboard for any papal champion seeking to quell the island, 'judicatum videlicet Turritanum, per quem dare poteramus ingressum ei qui conveniret nobiscum'. For these reasons, 'nec tibi

[16] For the papal documentation, see E. Jordan, *Les registres de Clement IV (1265–1268)* (Paris 1893–1912); but the important texts concerning Sardinia appear also *in extenso* in Martène, *Thesaurus*, vol. II.

concedere possemus nec ad presens id dabimus alterutri de predictis, set tenebimus in suspenso negotium'.[17]

Clement IV's letters indicate how and why the pope decided against offering the Sardinian crown to any of the three aspirants. Already in July 1266 Clement was warning the Pisans that they must not try to invade the same area in north-western Sardinia mentioned in his letter to the king of Aragon, 'judicatum seu regnum Turritanum, vel in eo Ecclesie Romane possessionem turbaverint, vel alias partes Sardinie quas ab olim non possederint intraverint'.[18] The problem of the Pisans intensified during 1267, when Ugolino dei Gherardeschi was active in Torres; but it was really after the arrival of Charles of Anjou's foe Conradin in Italy in 1268, and after Pisa accorded him the customary welcome it reserved for its Hohenstaufen friends, that the pope turned decisively against Pisan interests. A letter of 17 May 1268 excommunicated the Pisans, though not solely because of their high-handed behaviour in Sardinia; Pisan lands in Sardinia were actually declared forfeit: 'alioquin ipsos exnunc omni terra et jure, siqua forsan habent in insula Sardinie, vel aliqua parte ipsius, apostolica auctoritate privamus, et manere decrevimus ipso facto privatos'.[19]

At the same time, the pope sought to restrain the enthusiasm of the three princes in search of a Sardinian crown; on 5 January 1267 Clement warned Henry of Castile against any attempt to take over the island. Clement knew that 'ad regnum Sardinie tuos oculos direxisti', but, having examined the state of affairs in Sardinia, the pope had concluded that 'tibi utilius judicamus id non aggredi'. The pope declared he wanted to honour Henry in other ways, by promoting a favourable marriage.[20]

Clement had further doubts about Angevin ambitions in Sardinia. In 1267 the pope was showing some scepticism about Charles of Anjou's financial difficulties; the king of Sicily 'dicat se pauperem', but he has also been responsible for the destruction of the great estates, the 'massarias de quibus vivere poterat abundanter. Hec est enim vita regum Sicilie. Et si hodie haberet Sardiniam, sic eum vivere oporteret.'[21] This burst of sarcasm is aimed at the Angevin appetite for further expansion in the Mediterranean, and at the readiness of

---

[17] Martène, *Thesaurus*, vol. II, coll. 509–10; Jordan, *Registres*, no. 1231; Salavert, *Cerdeña*, 4, no. 3.   [18] Martène, *Thesaurus*, vol. II, coll. 373–4; Jordan, *Registres*, no. 1100.
[19] Jordan, *Registres*, no. 701.
[20] Martène, *Thesaurus*, vol. II, col. 438; Jordan, *Registres*, no. 1165.
[21] Martène, *Thesaurus*, vol. II, coll. 443–4; Jordan, *Registres*, no. 1173.

Charles of Anjou to take vast sums from the papal treasury to finance his schemes to conquer Sicily and much else, without bothering to repay his vast debts.

The pope seems to have known what he was doing when he refused to choose a king for Sardinia. A new pact between Mariano, judge of Arborea, and the Pisans, in 1265, had stimulated a return to disorder, especially in Sassari, where Ugolino dei Gherardeschi and others obtained the capitulation of the town two years later. Besta remarked that the pope reacted to these disturbances by deciding to 'ceder l'isola ad un signor unico, che, estraneo ad essa e fedele alla Santa Sede, fosse di potenza tale da poter troncare una volta per sempre le incessanti gare'.[22] Another interpretation of papal policy, less generous but perhaps more exact, would be that the popes hoped to provide decisive help for the pro-Guelf factions on the island, but that they were restricted in their freedom of action by justifiable fears at the repercussions that Guelf intervention in Sardinia might have on their already delicately balanced policy in Tuscany. Besta in fact admitted that the papacy saw clearly what trouble was bound to result from the imposition of a foreign lord on communities already torn apart by bloody strife; the bitterness of these struggles would only increase further.[23] Thus it was at this period that the Doria and Spinola families were seeking to obtain the office of vicar in the island; they were not placing their hopes in a foreign lord, Aragonese, Angevin or Castilian, but were trying to seize a golden opportunity to consolidate the influence of their mother city of Genoa in Sardinia.[24]

It is clear that the election of an overlord and king at Sassari in August 1269 was the work of only one faction, decidedly pro-Guelf, and that it had little real significance outside the ranks of this group. On 11 August 1269 (1270 *stile pisano*) the bishops of Torres, in conjunction with the representatives of the Commune of Sassari, and acting also on behalf of 'universitate omnium bonorum virorum fidelium ecclesie Romane totius regni Logudorii', gathered in the palace of the bishop of Ploaghe in Sassari, and elected as the king and lord of the entire island Philip of Anjou, the son of the king of Sicily: 'eligimus in postulandum et postulando eligimus in regem et dominum totius insule Sardinie pro sancta Romana ecclesia, cuius predicta insula de iure et facto dignoscitur esse, salvo semper in

[22] E. Besta, *La Sardegna medioevale*, vol. 1 (Bologna 1908), 235.
[23] Besta, *La Sardegna*, vol. 1, 236.   [24] Besta, *La Sardegna*, vol. 1, 237.

omnibus omni iure et ratione et proprietate sancte Romane ecclesie et mandato et voluntate domini pape futuri'. It is perhaps strange that the representatives of Torres and Logudoro assumed this right over the other regions of the island, Gallura nearby to the east, Arborea in the west and centre, and Cagliari in the deep south. In reality, of course, this was a unilateral step, made without papal prompting, let alone the support of other Sards; they expected papal confirmation, but such expectations failed to take into account the increasing prudence of the papacy in its Sardinian policy between 1267 and 1269.[25]

It is worth returning to the point that the electors sought to appoint a king not just for Torres-Logudoro, but for all the island. The papacy was clearly thinking increasingly of a single Sardinian monarchy in lieu of the multiplicity of warring judgeships that had so easily become the playthings of the Pisans and the Genoese; this appears to have been a reversion to the position briefly proclaimed by Frederick I, when, in August 1164, he solemnly crowned Barisone, Judge of Arborea, as *rex Sardinie*. Indeed, the same approach can, perhaps surprisingly, be found in the Ghibelline camp, where the rightful ruler of Sardinia was held to be Frederick II's son Enzo, king of Torres and Gallura, who was, however, a prisoner of the Guelfs in Bologna (and, in any case, his marriage to Adelasia of Torres, which had brought him his crown in the face of bitter Genoese opposition, had been annulled).[26] He died still a prisoner in 1272, and in his testament can be found attempts to confer rights throughout the island, with the Gherardeschi as main beneficiaries.[27] Whether or not Enzo was king over all Sardinia (over which he eventually extended his claims), there was, at any rate, a nominal Ghibelline king of Torres when Philip of Anjou was elected by the Guelfs of Torres. Besta appeared to identify a continuing tradition in the election of Philip, for all its peculiarity; it was conducted, he argued *ut moris erat*, according to some sort of traditional method which presumably went back centuries. Unfortunately, he misinterpreted the document from which he took this phrase. It speaks of the invocation of the Holy Ghost, according to current custom: 'Sancti Spiritus gratia invocata, ut moris est' (not *erat*, as in Besta); it seems unlikely in the extreme

---

[25] E. Winkelmann, *Acta imperii inedita seculi XIII et XIV. Urkunden und Briefe zur Geschichte des Kaiserreichs und des Königreichs Sicilien in den Jahren 1200–1400*, vol. II (Innsbruck, 1885), no. 1053, 737–8. [26] For Enzo's Sardinian marriage, see Abulafia, *Frederick II*, 311–12. [27] Besta, *La Sardegna*, vol. I, 240.

that there existed precedents for the election that took place in Sassari in 1269, considering that an attempt was being made to create a united Sardinian monarchy whose rights over all the judgeships were made far more explicit than those already claimed by Enzo.[28]

In one sense, it is true that the Aragonese lost the struggle for the crown of Sardinia in the 1260s; but in another sense it is clear that 'King' Philip had nothing to offer his kingdom, which he never found time to visit. Indeed, it is not even clear that the Angevins still wanted a Sardinian crown; this kingdom attracted less attention thereafter than some of the other fantastic kingdoms to which the dynasty laid claim, notably that of Albania. Philip had more than enough to do setting up secure bases for the Angevins in Elis, the flat coastline of the western Peloponnese where Chiarenza was to emerge as the great Angevin base. A more concrete result was the deepening dislike of the Pisans for the house of Anjou; they saw in Philip an instrument not merely of Angevin policy but also potentially of Genoese ambitions expressed through allies in the Torres region.[29] From the Aragonese point of view, the affair was irritating because it revealed how ready the Angevins were to stand in their way in every corner of the western Mediterranean. Yet the Aragonese had not sought to establish themselves in Sardinia as a result of grand imperial dreams for the conquest of, and protection of trade through, the *ruta de las illas*; quite simply, the king of Aragon hoped to establish his younger surviving son as king over a land well known for its food resources, lacking secure leadership, and in danger of falling into the sphere of his Angevin rivals. In a certain sense, the kingdom of Majorca was to gain its original meaning from the concept of creating an Aragonese forward base in the Pyrenean foothills, in the islands closest to Languedoc, in Montpellier too, of course; the danger of French threats to the integrity of the Majorcan kingdom was clear, and it was no doubt on this presumption that James I argued that any king of Aragon would be a close ally of his kinsman the king of Majorca.[30] Sardinia too could have a place in this strategy. A multiple kingdom in the Balearics, Roussillon, Montpellier and Sardinia would extend the front line of Catalan–Aragonese influence in a band across the western Mediterranean, and would help hold back the ambitious, expanding power of the Angevins of Provence and Naples. The first attempt by the Aragonese to acquire Sardinia

[28] Besta, *La Sardegna*, vol. I, 238.　　[29] Besta, *La Sardegna*, vol. I, 238.
[30] See chapter 3.

may not have proceeded very far, but it reveals much about James I's aims and about the possible functions of a strengthened, enlarged, Majorcan kingdom. The point was not lost on Duke Louis I of Anjou over a century later, with his own plans, at various times, to add to his possession of Provence the kingdoms of Naples, Sardinia and Majorca.

II

The second phase of the relationship between the kingdom of Majorca and Sardinia commences in 1279 with James II of Majorca's recognition of his state of vassallage to Peter the Great. It has been seen in earlier chapters that the War of the Vespers saw the court of Majorca enter into a complex, but in essence friendly, relationship with the French; and from this followed closer ties with the house of Anjou in Naples and Provence, too. The route from Catalonia to Naples lay through Mallorca and Sardinia; as early as 1284, Peter III wrote to the Judge of Arborea in central Sardinia, hoping to secure his help against Pisan ships which 'did much damage to us' in the waters between Sardinia and Mallorca, and which were quite deliberately trying to break the essential communications link between Catalonia and Sicily.[31]

The granting of rights over Sardinia and Corsica to James II of Aragon, in 1297, automatically resulted in the denial of any residual Majorcan claim to Sardinia, assuming that such claims were even remembered. Indeed, the offer of Sardinia and Corsica to the Aragonese king was an attempt to recompense him for his loss of direct authority over the Majorcan and Sicilian kingdoms.[32] All the same, there remained some political links between Majorca and Sardinia. In 1308 Cristiano Spinola, a Genoese, addressed a letter to James II of Aragon on the problem of how Sardinia could be conquered; he advised him to create an alliance of himself, the king of Majorca, the king of Naples and the king of Trinacria (Sicily), should the pope fail to excommunicate all those who were opposed to an Aragonese takeover of Sicily: he had the Pisans and his fellow-Genoese primarily in mind here.[33] In 1310 James of Aragon wrote to his Majorcan namesake to approve the marriage of the Majorcan Infant Ferran to Giovanna, princess of Gallura; James promised Ferran lands in Sardinia in recognition of his help during the siege of

---

[31] Salavert, *Cerdeña*, vol. II, 6, no. 6.   [32] Salavert, *Cerdeña*, vol. I, 127, 130, 151–5.
[33] Text in Salavert, 'El problema', 215–16, n.41.

Moorish Almería a short time earlier; but such generosity was of no account, given that Sardinia was as yet unconquered, and given that Ferran had his own dangerous ambitions of creating a lordship in Greece.[34] Mallorcan galleys did participate in the invasion of Sardinia in 1323, and were a clear reminder of the vassal relationship between the conciliatory King Sanç of Majorca and his overlord James II of Aragon.[35]

More intense, however, were the commercial ties between Mallorca and Sardinia. Documents in the Pisan archives indicate the presence of Mallorcan merchants at Cagliari in 1315, 1317 and 1319.[36] Riera Melis has noted the presence of Perpignan cloths in Sardinia even before 1315.[37] A major study of the Sardinian grain trade by Marco Tangheroni shows that, at least after the Aragonese invasion, there was an active trade in Sardinian grain towards the Balearic islands, and there is no reason to doubt that its origins go back much further in time;[38] the same can be said, too, for the salt trade of Sardinia, examined by Manca, even though Ibiza too was a major salt exporter;[39] in addition, documents from the last years of Majorcan independence, the *guiatge* registers of 1341–2, indicate that there regularly arrived in Sardinia significant quantities of iron which had been brought from, or through, Ciutat de Mallorca.[40]

It is thus not surprising that immediately before the Aragonese invasion of Sardinia the king of Aragon rewarded the Majorcans with a commercial privilege for Sanç of Majorca's subjects, including the inhabitants of Roussillon, Cerdagne and Conflent.[41] In fact, the privilege offers the Majorcans the same rights as are enjoyed by other Catalans, and it is unclear when an actual exemption from Sardinian commercial taxes was permitted.[42] Received from King James of Aragon at Portfangós, the privilege was then confirmed a few months

---

[34] Salavert, *Cerdeña*, vol. II, 531–2, no. 411; but cf. 528–9, no. 409, and vol. I, 374.

[35] Arribas, *La conquista*, 194, citing the chronicle of Peter the Ceremonious: twenty galleys *que eren armades en las maritimes del dit rey en Sanxo.*

[36] F. Artizzu, *Documenti inediti relativi ai rapporti economici tra la Sardegna e Pisa nel Medioevo* (Padua/Cagliari, 1961–2), vol. I, 47–8, 117–18, nos. 33, 71; vol. II, 30–4, 34–8, 82–4, nos. 11, 12, 35. [37] Riera Melis, *Corona de Aragón*, 152.

[38] Tangheroni, *Aspetti* 84, 85, 92, 94, 112, 174, 183; also 110, with reference to a merchant of Collioure. [39] Manca, *Aspetti*, 161–9.

[40] ARM, AH 4390, Llicències i guiatges 1341–1342, ff.2v, 6r, 15v, 35r, 50r.

[41] ADP, AA I (*Livre vert majeur*, of 1389 onwards), ff.192v–193v (text A), 194r–196r (text B) = Appendix IIA, IIB *infra*.

[42] The lack of any reference to the merchants of Montpellier may reflect the special position of this territory within the Majorcan crown; cf. the evidence that the rights of its merchants had to be investigated in 1339 by royal officials: Appendix II.

later, in Sardinia, by the Infant Alfonso, who was just then at the port of Palma di Sulcis.[43] Among the witnesses to both versions of the privilege were Joan Eiximenis de Urrea and Artau de Luna. In other words, the documents show the gratitude of King James for the help offered in the invasion of Sardinia by his vassal Sanç of Majorca, in the form of twenty galleys and other aid. As far as is known, the privilege was not the result of a specific request by Majorcan merchants already active in Sardinian trade; but the effect was an advantageous position for both island and mainland Majorcans, though probably not the merchants of Montpellier;[44] the response is visible in the presence by 1331 of Perpignan grain merchants;[45] and when in November 1332 the Aragonese imposed a ban on the export of grain from Sardinia, they excluded from the order the lands of the Crown of Aragon, including for this purpose the kingdom of Majorca.[46] It has been seen in an earlier chapter that notarial acts from Mallorca, of 1340, reveal an intense trade to Sardinia, which involved a number of key ports: Alghero and Bosa as well as Cagliari and Oristano; this suggests an extensive penetration of Sardinia by Balearic merchants.[47] There is thus no doubt that the aid proffered to James and Alfonso of Aragon secured valuable advantages for Majorca, not least in a period in which grain supplies were often scarce and costly. It was not just the merchants, but the king of Majorca and all his subjects who benefited.[48]

The privilege for the Majorcan merchants in Sardinia forms part of a wider extension of Majorcan commercial privileges in the 1320's and 1330s, partly in response to the penetration of new markets by these merchants, partly providing opportunities to carve out new markets in the future; these privileges seem to have stimulated a regional expansion of Majorcan trade within the waters around Sardinia and in the Tyrrhenian Sea. In 1325 the Majorcan trade network benefited from the guarantees offered by King Robert the Wise of Naples, husband of a Majorcan princess;[49] having already secured a series of privileges from the Aragonese kings of Sicily, the

---

[43] Portfangós: Document IIA; port of Palma de Sulcis: Document IIB.
[44] But merchants also arrived from Montpellier: ADH, II E 95/372, f.12r-v, where a *linh* of Agde leaves 'in viatgio Sardinie', 1343.   [45] Tangheroni, *Aspetti*, 84.
[46] Tangheroni, *Aspetti*, 85.
[47] See chapter 9 for a discussion of ACP, register 14564 (Francesc Batlle).
[48] A disadvantage for the Majorcan crown was the migration of Balearic Jews to Cagliari in the 1330s: p. 89 above.
[49] ADP, AA 3 (Livre vert mineur), f. 128v.

merchants of Majorca thus enjoyed at this time free access to the major grain depositories of the western Mediterranean[50]; additional privileges, in some cases of long standing, in the Maghrib, further bolstered the success of the subjects of the Majorcan king in areas famous for their supplies of gold, leather and, on occasion, grain too.[51] The Sardinian privilege was thus an opportunity for the extension of Majorcan trade, but the difference between the rights obtained in the Maghrib and those obtained in Sardinia was that the north African privileges were gained often in the teeth of Aragonese–Catalan opposition, but those in Sardinia could never have been obtained without Aragonese–Catalan approval. Thus the Sardinian privilege demonstrates not the political freedom of the king of Majorca, but his state of subordination.

In substance, then, the circumstances of the grant of 1323/4 were very different from those of the 1267 initiative. In the first decade of the fourteenth century the Aragonese kings were able to extend their influence over the Balearic islands, which had ceased to be an obstacle to their Sardinian ambitions; the Majorcan kingdom found itself, after 1323, stuck in the middle of an arc, almost a ring, of lands under the domination or protection of the Aragonese; the Balearics were imprisoned in the middle of a Catalan–Aragonese lake. In 1380 the king of Aragon, now lord also of Mallorca, understood that there existed a tight link between his island territories across the western Mediterranean: 'if Sardinia is lost, it will follow that Mallorca will also be lost, because the food that Mallorca is accustomed to receiving from Sicily and Sardinia will stop arriving, and as a result the land will become depopulated and will be lost'.[52] To be sure, the Aragonese conquest of Sardinia guaranteed the provisioning of Mallorca; but, equally, the conquest of Sardinia was a severe blow to Majorcan independence, denying the king of Majorca the chance to ally himself with other powerful neighbours, such as the king of France, as had occurred during the War of the Vespers. In the long term, the result was the strangulation of the Majorcan state on the part of Peter the Ceremonious.

---

[50] ADP, AA 3, f.98r-v (1303), ff.99r-100r (1305 – printed from a text in the ARM in *Documenta regni Majoricarum*, 99–100, no. 81).
[51] Paris, BN, MS latin 9261, no. 1, 2, 8a, 8b, 29, 37; Mas Latrie, *Traités de paix* 182, 187–8, 192, 280, of 1231, 1235, 1271, 1278, 1313, 1339.
[52] Cited by Salavert, 'El problema', 213–14, n. 37. For the Catalan text, see p. 104 supra.

DOCUMENT I

Donation of Sardinia by James I of Aragon to James, future king of Majorca, XIV Kal. Madii 1267

Paris, Archives Nationales, Chambre des Comptes, P1354[1], no. 800, f.1r.

Donatio facta per dominum Jacobum Aragonum et Maioricarum Regem Infanti Jacobo filio suo de Regno Sardinie Anno Mill°. CC.LX° septimo. Noverint universi quod cum nos Jacobus Dei gracia Rex Aragonum, Maioricarum et Valentie, Comes Barchinone et Urgelli et dominus Montispessulani, confidentes speramus quod summus pontifex nobis conferat et concedat Regnum Sardinie cum dominio eiusdem et juribus ac omnibus spectantibus ad eandem, ideoque per nos et nostros damus et concedimus vobis carissimo filio nostro Infanti Jacobo heredi Maioricarum et Montispessulani ac Rossillionis, Ceritanie et Confluentis et vostris successoribus in perpetuum post dies nostros Regnum predictum cum eiusdem dominio et juribus ac omnibus ad eundem spectantibus francum et liberum prout illud summus pontifex nobis dantes [*marginal note*: in quantum desiderabat pater quod iste filius esset rex et quod non debet satis dedisse de regno Maioricarum et comitatibus Rosilionis et Ceritanie]. Ita tamen quod toto tempore vite nostre nos illud habeamus et teneamus et de ipso simus domini et potentes. Et in omnibus et per omnia in ipso utamur, plene iure. Sed post nostrum obitum vos et vester habeatis illud prout superius continetur. Datum Barchinione, XIIII Kal. Madii, Anno domini Millesimo CC°.LX° septimo. Signum Jacobi Dei gracia Regis Aragonum, Maioricarum et Valentie, Comitisque Barchinone et Urgellensis et domini Montispessulani. Testes etc.

DOCUMENT II

Archives Départementales des Pyrenées-Orientales, AA 1 (*Livre vert majeur*, of 1389 onwards), ff.192v–193v (text A), 194r–196r (text B). (Text A mentioned by Arribas, *La conquista*, 181, without transcription, from documents in the Arxiu de la Corona d'Aragó, Gratiarum, reg. 17 (pars secunda), Jac. II, ann. 1322–3, and Reg. 223, f.267v).

The transcription follows text A, with the addition of notes indicating variants in text B.

A Privilege of King James of Aragon, Portfangós, X. Kal. Iun. 1323

Carta de la franquesa quel Senyor Rey en Jacme darago atorga als homes de perpinya e daltres lochs en la illa de Cerdenya.

Noverint universi quod nos Jacobus Dei gracia Rex Aragonum, Valencie etc., Sardinie et Corsice ac Comes Barchinone meditantes et revolventes[a] intra nos annexum consanguinitatis debitum quo illustris et magnificus princeps Sancius Maioricarum Rex Comes Rossilionis et Ceritanie ac dominus Montispessulani a natura nobis conjungitur ac intime dileccionis affectum sincerum quo unimur ac

---

[a] B: revolvantes

etiam prospicientes sucursum subsidium et juvamen per memoratum regem nobis exhibita et impensa pro presenti adquisicione felici Sardinie et Corsice Regni nostri tam in copioso galearum stolio quam aliter multis modis ob que eum opportuit magnas et multiplices subire expensas ad quam siquidem adquisicionem Deo propicio pagendam inclitum et carissimum primogenitum et generalem procuratorem nostrum Infantem Alfonsum Comitem Urgelli principaliter[b] destinamus, propter hec dignum et congruum vidimus ut ipsius Regis beneplacitis et rogatoriis suis intercessionibus favorabiliter annuamus inducti igitur ex premissis et ex intendivis[c] precibus prefati Maioricarum Regis volentes subscriptos suos subditos gracia prosequi et favoribus specialibus ampliare per nos et omnes heredes et successores nostros gratis et ex certa scientia ac mera et spontanea voluntate emfranquimus et francos[d] liberos exemptos ac immunes facimus probos homines et universitates civitatis seu locorum infrascriptorum videlicet Maioricarum et regni eiusdem et insularum adjacentium eidem regno et villarum etiam Perpiniani Cauquiliberi Podii Ceritani ac Ville Franche Confluentis et omnes et singulos cives incolas et habitatores earumdem Civitatis et Regni Maioricarum et villarum atque locorum predictorum presentes pariter et futuros in perpetuum[e] cum omnibus rebus mercibus et bonis suis in dicto Regno nostro Sardinie et Corsice et insulis sibi adjacentibus et quibuscunque locis dicti Regni et insularum eiusdem ab omni leuda[f] pedagio portatico[g] mensuratico et penso anchorragio travetagio passagio et gabella[h] et ab[i] omni alia quacumque impositione seu consuetudine nova vel veteri statuta et statuenda et alio quolibet[k] seu servitute reali et personali vel mixta que dici nominari vel[l] excogitari possit aliqua ratione sic quod in dicto Sardinie et Corsice Regno nostro vel insulis aut aliis locis adjacentibus eidem dicte universitatis[m] cives incole ac habitatores predictarum civitatis villarum atque locorum presentes[n] et futuri tam in veniendo a quibuscunque partibus[o] [f. 193v] vel per quascunque partes ad dictum Regnum aut insulas seu loca ipsius Regni quia ibidem stando mercando aut inde exeundo seu recedendo pro aliquibus rebus mercibus vel bonis suis quibuscumque ullo unquam tempore nullam letzdam[p] nullumque pedagium portaticum mensuraticum pensum anchoragium passagium[q] seu gabellam vel aliam quamcumque imposicionem seu consuetudinem novam vel veterem statutam vel statuendam aut aliud quidcunque jus seu servitutem realem vel personalem aut mixtam que dici nominari vel excogitari possit nobis vel successoribus nostris aut quibuscunque aliis nomine nostro et nostrorum dare et[r] solvere teneantur ymo[s] ab ipsorum omnium et cuiuslibet eorum prestationibus sint semper in regno predicto et insulis ac locis ei adjacentibus franchi exempti perpetuo liberi et immunes concedentes nichilominus eisdem universitatibus ac civibus et habitatoribus eiusdem civitatis et villarum atque locorum predictorum et singulis eorum presentibus et futuris quod de Regno predicto Sardinie et Corsice et insulis ac locis adjacentibus possint extrahere emere et vendere a quibuscunque franche et[t] absque impedimento et prestacione cuiuslibet servitutis vel juris imposed vel imponendi ibidemque inmittere seu apportare[u] frumentum et omne aliud genus bladi vinum et quascunque victualia et omnes alias res et merces absque impedimento nostro et nostrorum ac officialium nostrorum et successorum nostrorum ipsaque victualia et merces[v]

[b] B: Urgellensem presencialiter	[c] B: intentivis	[d] B: franchos
[e] B: predictorum presentes et futuros imperpetuum	[f] B: letzda	[g] B: portagio
[h] B: anchoragio passagio et gabella	[i] B: *om.* ab	[k] B: alio jure quolibet
[l] B: *om.* vel	[m] B: universitates	[n] B: pariter	[o] A: partitibus
[p] B: leudam	[q] B: anchoragium travacagium passagium		[r] B: aut
[s] B: ymmo	[t] B: *om.* et	[u] B: portare	[v] B: victualia res et merces

carricare et discarricare sine aliquo albarano nec licencia seu mandato nostri vel[w] successorum nostrorum seu ipsorum successorum nostrorum obtenta vel etiam expectata. Volentes eciam civitati et Regno Maioricarum villis ac locis predictis et earum incolis[x] et habitatoribus in perpetuum ampliorem graciam facere concedimus eisdem per nos et nostros quod super rebus seu mercibus quas in insulis seu locis dicti regni nostri Sardinie et Corsice inmiserint seu inde extraxerint per se vel negociatores suos credatur ipsorum civium incolarum et habitatorum vel suorum negociatorum ipsa res seu merces immittencium seu extrahencium[y] vel concivium incolarum aut habitatorum eorumdem locorum et non alterius proprio juramento. Sane cum intelleximus quod[z] in dicto Regno Sardinie et Corsice nostro ante donationem nobis factam de eo post omnes Cathalani in Regno ipso franquitate et immunitate obtinebant quod tamen ignoratur a nobis volumus atque concedimus per nos et nostros quod si fortasse in posterum [f. 194r] universos Cathalanos dominacionis nostre in regno predicto ex causa premissa invenerimus franquitatem habere vel nos contigerit illis graciam super eo facere generalem omnes et singuli subditi[aa] Maioricarum Regis infra dumtaxat Cathaloniam residentes presentes pariter et futuri similibus franquitate libertate et immunitate quibus dicti Cathalani dominacionis nostre generaliter in dicto Regno Sardinie et Corsice utentur et habuerint gaudeant inibi et utantur. Mandantes per presens privilegium nostrum procuratoribus baiulis leudariis pedagiariis et aliis[bb] officialibus nostris quocunque nomine eos nominari contingat quos per nos et nostros[cc] in dicto regno et insulis locis eius proponi seu ordinari contingerit[dd] quatinus dictis civibus incolis et habitatoribus predictarum civitatis villarum atque locorum et singulis eorum ac rebus mercibus et bonis eorum franquitate libertatem et immunitatem predictas teneant inviolabiliter et observent et contra eas vel aliquam earum ipsos vel bona ipsorum nullatenus[ee] impedire molestare seu agravare[ff] presumant sicuti de nostri vel nostrorum gracia confiderint vel mercede. Quod si secus temerarie fecerint iram et indignationem nostram et nostrorum se noverint incursuros. Et nichilominus penam mille morabatinorum auri nostro erario confiscandam absque remedio aliquo punientur. In cuius rei testimonium et memoriam sempiternam presens privilegium nostrum inde fieri[gg] et sigillo plumbee bulle nostre jussimus comuniri. Datum in Castris apud Portum Fangosum decimo kalendis junii. Anno domini millesimo trecentesimo vicesimo tercio. Subscripsi: G.

Signum Jacobi Dei gracia Regis Aragonum Valentie Sardinie et Corsice ac Comitis Barchinone. Testes sunt Infans Raymundus Berengarii dicti domini Regis natus, Petrus archiepiscopus Cesarauguste, Artaldus de Luna, Johannes Eximini de Urrea, Guillelmus de Angularia. Signum mei Bernardi de Aversone dicti domini Regis notarii qui de mandato ipsius domini[hh] Regis hec scribi feci et clausi loco die et anno prefixis.

B *Confirmation by the Infant Alfonso of the privilege of James II of Aragon, Palma di Sulcis, Sardinia, xvi Kal. Iul.* 1323

Cartes de franquesa quel Infant Namfos qui conquista Serdenya atorga en Serdenya als homes de perpinya ed altres lochs.

[w] B: seu   [x] B: ac locis et earum incolis   [y] B: extrahencium que sint sue
[z] B: *om.* quod   [aa] B: subditi dicti   [bb] B: et quibuslibet aliis
[cc] B: *om.* quos per nos et nostros   [dd] B: contigerit   [ee] B: ullatenus
[ff] B: gravare   [gg] B: presens privilegium fieri   [hh] B: ipsius dicti domini

Noverint universi. Quod nos Infans Alfonsus illustrissimi domini Regis Aragonum primogenitus eiusque generalis procurator ac Comes [f.194v] Urgelli viso et plenarie intellecto tenore privilegii per dictum dominum Regem Aragonum genitorem nostrum ad preces magnifici principis domini Sanccii Dei gracia Regis Maioricarum carissimi consanguinei nostri ex causis probabilibus infrascriptis concessis hominibus et universitati civitatis et locorum infra scriptorum videlicet Maioricarum et regni eiusdem et insularum adiacentium eidem regno et villarum etiam Perpiniani Cauquiliberi Podii Ceritani ac Ville franche Confluentis et omnibus et singulis civibus incolis et habitatoribus earundem predictorum presentibus pariter et futuris prout in ipso privilegio latius continetur cuius series sic se habet:

(there follows the text of the privilege of James II, from f.194v to f.196r; vide supra).

[f.196r] Idcirco cupientes sequi sicut convenit vestigia dicti domini genitoris nostri ac beneplacitis prefati domini Regis Maioricarum adherere volentes gratis et ex certa scientia privilegium franquitatis et immunitatis ac libertatis predictarum laudamus approbamus ac per omnia prout melius et plenius per iam dictum regem genitorem nostrum predictis universitatibus civitatis villarum et locorum predictorum et eorum incolis presentibus et futuris latius est concessum, et ut tenor supra insertus indicat privilegia supradicta promittentes per nos et omnes nostros privilegium supradictum et omnia contenta in eo observare perpetuo et facere inviolabiliter observari. Mandamus itaque universis et singulis officialibus et subditis dicti domini regis genitoris nostri et nostris presentibus et futuris quod iam dictum privilegium et omnia et singula in eo contenta observent in concusse et faciant inviolabiliter observare et non contra veniant nec alique contra venire permittant aliqua racione si de nostri confidunt gracia vel amore. In cuius rei testimonium presentem cartam fieri jussimus nostro pendenti sigillo munitam. Datum in Castris apud Portum Palani de Sulcis, sexto decimo kalendis julii anno domini millesimo trecentesimo vicesimo tercio.

Signum Infantis Alfonsi illustrissimi domini Regis Aragonum primogeniti eiusque generalis procuratoris ac Comitis Urgelli. Testes sunt: Guillermus de Angularia, Petrus de Luna, Artaldus de Luna, Johannes Eximini de Urrea, Petrus de Queralto. Signum mei Clementis de Salaviridi scriptoris dicto domini Infantis que de mandato eiusdem domini Infantis hec scripsi et clausi cum litteris suppositis in linea vicesima ubi scribitur subditi.

APPENDIX II

The Montpellier inquest, 1338–1339

In 1338/9 the consuls of Montpellier addressed a supplication to the king of Majorca, in the hope of demonstrating that the merchants of their home town were exempt from the commercial taxes levied by royal officials at Collioure and in Mallorca. The documentation concerning this case has been examined by Guy Romestan, who had the additional advantage of notes left by another distinguished Languedoc historian, Jean Combes; but it was not apparently known to the earlier historians of Montpellier such as Germain, Thomas and Baumel, nor by Lecoy de la Marche.[1] Moreover, the larger of the key documents in this case is no longer accessible, though other important material exists to demonstrate how the supplication was handled at court.

The interest of these documents stems from the practical problem of how Montpellier was to exercise commercial privileges within a kingdom where its own status differed significantly from the other territories such as Roussillon, Cerdagne and the Balearics themselves. It has been seen that in Montpellier the king was *dominus*, under the suzerainty of the king of France, who had bought out the rights of the bishop of Maguelonne in 1293 and who was also direct lord, since then, of the suburb of Montpelliéret; French intervention was expressed in the insistence that notarial acts should be dated by the regnal year of the king of France, not of Majorca, by the presence of a French mint in Montpelliéret, and by the regular attempts of the seneschals of Beaucaire and Carcassonne to intervene in the city's affairs.[2]

The question of the rights of the Montpelliérains in the commerce

---

[1] G. Romestan, 'Les marchands de Montpellier et la leude de Majorque pendant la première moitié du XIVᵉ siècle', *Majorque, Languedoc et Roussillon de l'Antiquité à nos jours. Actes du LIIIᵉ Congrès de la Fédération historique du Languedoc méditerranéen et du Roussillon* (Montpellier, 1982), 53–60.   [2] See chapter 3; Thomas, 'Montpellier entre la France et l'Aragon'.

of the kingdom of Majorca has an additional dimension, provided by their participation on such a significant scale in the conquest of Mallorca by James I; this aid brought them rights within Ciutat de Mallorca, including extensive urban property and the opportunity to set up their own business community under a consul.[3] The claim of the Montpelliérains to privileged status thus cannot be separated from the fact that in Mallorca itself there lived numerous Montpelliérains (or their descendants) who were at the same time citizens of the Mallorcan capital; on the other hand, the intensity of the trade links between Montpellier and Mallorca must not be exaggerated. The conclusion of Guy Romestan, on the basis of lists of tax payments made by Montpellier merchants in Mallorca and copied into the text of the royal inquest on the rights of the Montpelliérains, is that this commerce dealt in 'marchandises variées, mais quantités modestes', worth on average £1,400 per annum; the value reached £2,500 in 1321, 1325, 1328, 1330, £5,000 in 1323, and as much as £8,000 in 1327. He identified more than 250 references to traffic between Montpellier and Mallorca over a period of thirty-eight years; but the amount of visits oscillated greatly, from an apparent zero in 1311 and 1314 to fifteen in 1323, 1327 and 1336.[4] 1327 seems to be the high point of Montpellier's Balearic island commerce. This trade was dominated by the carriage of woollen and linen cloths from Languedoc towards the Balearic islands; in return, the merchants of Montpellier brought leather, wax and other north African produce, as one might expect.[5] It should also be remembered that some business between Montpellier and Mallorca was conducted by Balearic or Roussillonnais merchants, so that a lack of known trips from Montpellier to Mallorca in 1311 does not mean a lack of contact between the two entrepôts.

The fundamental difficulty faced by the Montpelliérains was the insistence, since 1300, of the kings of Majorca on the levying of trade taxes in order to maximise royal revenues; the passage of goods through Mallorca, Collioure and Montpellier had a significant impact on the king's income. So it made sense for the royal councillor Arnau Puig d'Orfila to investigate the claims of the Montpelliérains to exemption from the *leuda*, the more so since his father Guillem, another royal adviser, is mentioned in the document of about 1297

[3] Lecoy de la Marche, *Relations politiques*, vol. 1, 77, 79.
[4] Romestan, 'Les marchands de Montpellier', 58–9.
[5] Romestan, 'Les marchands de Montpellier', 59.

setting out the *lezda* or *leuda* of Collioure.[6] Another official appointed to examine the case was Dalmau Engles, the royal procurator, whose concern lay with the protection of the rights of the royal domain.[7] There are interesting parallels between this contest and the mightier one from 1300 onwards between the kings of Majorca and of Aragon over the entitlement of the Majorcan crown to levy imposts on Catalan merchants trading through Collioure and Mallorca. A complication then was the attempt by the French kings to use Aigues-Mortes as a base from which to tax merchandise moving towards Montpellier and other Languedoc towns.[8]

Another indication of the way trade taxes were being used to bolster royal authority can be found in the many texts of *lezde* from the lands of the Crown of Aragon, and in particular from the Majorcan territories: from Perpignan, Puigcerdà, Val de Querol and Collioure; the last of these provided a model for the *lezda* of Tortosa, which was used to tax traffic between Catalonia and the Balearics.[9] In the Collioure *lezda*, which survives in several versions, there appears merchandise of high value, such as pepper, ginger, cinnamon, brazilwood, coral, sugar, saffron; there are also references to cloths, iron, tin, Mallorcan figs, honey and wheat, indeed to almost any commodity that was regularly traded in these waters. In the Perpignan *lezda* it is, not surprisingly, cloths that have the dominant role; while the *lezde* of Val de Querol and Puigcerdà suggest the importance of livestock, pastel and other characteristic products of a Pyrenean economy. The initiative for the levying of these taxes emanated from the royal court; in the case of Puigcerdà, in 1288, a Templar knight acts as royal procurator, with the aim of drawing up the text of the *memoria et capbreu... de la leuda que'l dit senyor rey pren e pendre ha acostumat en la vila de Peugcerda.*[10] In a late-thirteenth-century version of the *lezda* of Collioure the following rubric appears: *La leuda que'l senyor rey pren a Cobliure, la qual se pren en la forma d'auayl scrita*, and *Aquesta es la hordonacio que'l senyor rey ha feta de la leuda.*[11] In 1284 James

---

[6] Miguel Gual Camarena, *Vocabulario del Comercio medieval* (Tarragona, 1968/Barcelona, 1976), doc. 24, 168.   [7] Romestan, 'Les marchands de Montpellier', 55.

[8] See chapter 8.

[9] Gual, *Vocabulario*, 36–40; doc. 4, 75–80 (Collioure/Tortosa, 1249?); doc. 5, 80–7 (Perpignan, 1250?); doc. 9, 102–7 (Collioure/Tortosa, 1252); doc. 16, 142–7 (Perpignan, 1284); doc. 17, 147–50 (Puigcerdà, 1288); doc. 16, 150–2 (val de Querol, 1288); doc. 24, 161–69 (Collioure, 1297?); doc. 26, 174–5 (Collioure, *lleudes de terra*, 1300?); doc. 27, 175–8 (El Voló, Roussillon, 1310–16?); doc. 28, 178–9 (Perpignan, 1321); doc. 29, 179–83 (Collioure, 1365?).   [10] Gual, *Vocabulario*, doc. 17, 148.

[11] Gual, *Vocabulario*, doc. 24, 162, 167.

II of Majorca established a tariff in Perpignan for cloths and imports; the document makes it quite plain that the *reua* (as the *lezda* is termed) is the result of a royal ordinance.[12] The produce of the Majorcan lands was not automatically exempt from taxes; the level of exemption was determined by the condition of the merchants themselves, whether Mallorcan, Barcelonese, Jewish, Muslim, foreign Christian; and the Montpelliérains were unfortunate enough to be counted among the last.[13] Their own products were also liable for taxes: the coloured cloth known as *porpra de Monpestler* was taxed at the rate of two *diners* per piece.[14]

It is possible to see in these royal attempts to insist on the imposition of commercial taxes a consistent programme of action, common to the Majorcan, French, Aragonese and other rulers: each was anxious to define the frontiers of the kingdom, by placing there royal officials charged with the levying of trade taxes. A feature of the first document printed here is the mention of *leudarii* and other representatives of royal authority in the ports. In other words, the levying of trade taxes was not simply a fiscal decision, but it was also a manifestation of the authority of the state in an age of growing government centralisation. Even the physically fragmented and politically enfeebled kingdom of Majorca was not exempt from this trend; indeed, its rulers were especially well placed to benefit from commercial taxes both on foreign goods passing through the kingdom's ports and on goods moving from one region of the kingdom to another.

Montpellier was thus the loser; its ambiguous political status, under the competing authority of two kings, brought it a heavier, not a lighter, tax burden.[15] The Montpelliérains failed to convince the Majorcan royal officials of their special rights of exemption from trade taxes; the officials were able to lay their hands on the registers of trade taxes levied in Mallorca, which showed conclusively that the merchants of Montpellier were accustomed to pay commercial taxes in the Majorcan kingdom. This was not a matter the Montpelliérains were prepared to forget, however, and as late as 1366 they were again trying to demonstrate their special rights of tax exemption, even

---

[12] Gual, *Vocabulario*, doc. 16, 142.
[13] The only reference to Montpellier in the *lezda* of Collioure of *circa* 1297 refers to a standard measure used in that city, the *quintal*: Gual, *Vocabulario*, doc. 24, 168.
[14] Gual, *Vocabulario*, doc. 16, 144.
[15] Rogozinski, *Power, Caste and Law*, 142–5 for evidence of double taxation.

though the Majorcan kingdom had now vanished and Montpellier had been placed under the lordship of Charles the Bad, king of Navarre; yet again their claims were firmly rebutted.[16]

The detailed record of the investigations conducted by the king's officials can no longer be traced in the Archives Municipales of Montpellier. However, two other documents, which have escaped attention so far, serve as guides to the case. One is the document commissioning the inquest into Montpelliérain rights at Mallorca City and Collioure; the other is a seventeenth-century summary of the results of the inquest, from which it is clear that the Montpelliérains were anxious to present all and every proof of favour by the kings of Aragon and of Majorca, even when such privileges did not really prove their special rights to exemption from trade taxes in Mallorca and Collioure.

DOCUMENT III

Montpellier, Archives Municipales, Grand Chartrier, Armoire A, Cassètte XVII, Louvet no. 325

147x220mm. The document contains 12 folios, of which three are blank.

[f.2r] Jacobus Dei gratia Rex Maioricarum dilecto et fideli auditori et conciliario nostro Arnaldo de Podiorfila legum doctori salutem et dilectionem. Per fideles nostros consules Montispessulani exposita nobis simpliciter continebatur quod per predecessores nostros Reges Maioricarum a tempore citra quo fuerunt domini Montispessulani per eos et successores suos eorum liberalitate fuit concessa hominibus Montispessulani immunitas de leudis, pedagiis et costumarum per terram et mare in omnibus terris suis, quodquam nos omnes consuetudines, usus, libertates, franquesias et immunitates dicte ville confirmamus et iuramus facere observare, et quod homines predicti dicta immunitates et libertate fuerunt usi temporibus retrolapsis. Et cum ut asseruerunt ab aliquo tempore citra contra immunitatem prefatam tam in Maioricis quam Cauquolibero circa quantitas ex(i)gatur ab illis pro rebus eorum et mercibus que per vel ad Maioricas [f.2v] seu Cauquoliberum faciant vehi. Videlicet in Cauquolibero sub nomine leude et in Maioricis pro introhitu et exitu illarum fuit nobis supplicatum quatenus prospecto, quod ad supplicationes illorum predecessores nostri et nos pluries concessimus super eis facere debitam

[16] Romestan, 'Les marchands de Montpellier', 60; for trade between Roussillon and Mallorca after the disappearance of the Majorcan state, see P. Macaire, 'Les relations commerciales entre Majorque, Colliuoure et Perpignan au XVe siècle', *Majorque, Languedoc et Roussillon de l'Antiquité à nos jours. Actes du LIIIe Congrès de la Fédération historique du Languedoc méditerranéen et du Roussillon* (Montpellier, 1982), 77–90. For the rights of the French crown and of Charles of Navarre in Montpellier see *Ordonnances des Rois de France de la Troisième Race*, ed. D. Secousse, vol. v (Paris, 1736), 477–80, referring to the second grant of the city to Charles the Bad (1372).

iustitiam exibere eis immunitatem ac libertatem prefatas feceremus inviolabiliter observare. Cassando omnes impedimentum appositum contra illas et faciendo restituere quod abinde exactum est ab eisdem. Quare mandamus et comitimus vobis quathinus de privilegiis et usus superius allegatis vocatis qui fuerunt evocandi informetis vos summariter et simpliciter et de plano et sine strepitu iudicii et figura. Et que inde reperieritis nobis fideliter refferatis. Datum Perpiniani xiij kalendis aprilis anno domini mcccxxxviij.

Per dominum Regem de eius concilio. Perpiniani Yberti.

[f.3r] Unde Dominus Arnaldus prefatus literas regias cum debita reverencia recipiens dixit se fore paratum in predictis procedere iuxta formam comissionis regie antedicte in omnibus observatam. Hoc ex requirente syndico memorato nomine universitatis predicte et sic dictus dominus comissarius requirente ut premititur sindico antedicto et etiam iustitia exigente prefixit diem martis proximam. Que intitulabitur quanto nonis madii et horam vesperorum eiusdem dicto syndico antedicto, nomine quo supra, ut coram eadem domino comissario compareat in castro regio Perpiniani super predictis legitime processuris ac etiam mandavit per Guillermum Gamosium nuncium Curie Regie citata procuratores domini nostri Regis ut dictis die et loco at hora coram dicto domino comissario compareant super predictas ut agunt processum.

[f.3v] Ad informandum religionem venerabilis et circumspecta viri domini Arnaldi de Podiorfile legum doctoris et conciliarii illustrissimi principis domini Jacobi Dei gracia Maioricarum Regis Comitis Rossillionis Ceretanie et domini Montispessulani eiusdem quam commissarii ad infrascripta deputati dicit et proponit Petrus Texerii syndicus universitatis hominum Ville Montispessulane quod dominus Petrus bone memorie condam Regis Aragonum comes Barchinone et dominus Montispessulani predecessor dicti domini nostri regis per se et per suos successores donavit et concessit per imperpetuum omnibus hominibus de Montepessulano presentibus et futuris immunitatem et franquesiam in tota terra sua et per totam terram suam in toto posse suo et per totum possem suum tam in mari quam in terra de pedagiis lesdis et costumis. Et hec tenere complere et servare promisit et iuravit super sancta quatuor dei evangelia prout de predictis [f.4r] plene constat per publicum instrumentum scriptum ut in eo legitur per Hugonem Laurencii notarium publicum signatum a tergo cum litera .a. quod exibit et producit ad probandum predictam et ad informandum dominum comissarium supradictum de predictis.

Item dicit et proponit dictus Petrus Texerii nomine quo supra, quod post mortem dicti domini Petri bone memorie quondam Regis dominus Jacobus bone memorie filius suus et Rex Aragonum et Regni Maioricarum comes Barchinone et dominus Montispessulani cum carta publica concessit, laudavit et per imperpetuum confirmavit dilectis et fidelibus suis duodecim probis viris electis ad consulendum communitatem Montispessulani per presentis tote Universitatis Montispessulani presentibus et futuris donacionem quam fecerat cum publico suo instrumento dictus [f.4v] dominus Petrus Rex pater suus Universitati Montispessulani. Videlicet quod non teneantur donare leudam, pedagium toltam consuetudinem novam vel veterem statutam vel statuendam de rebus vel mercaturas suis habitis vel habendis per terram vel mare stagnum vel aquam dulce in loco aliquo terrarum vel dominationis dicti domini Jacobi, et mandavit firmiter et distincter officialibus suis in dicto instrumento nominatis leudariis pedageriis et aliis quibuslibet suum locum tenentibus et subditis universis presentibus et futuris quod predictam franquesiam hominibus Montispessulani observent et faciunt observare firmiter et in aliquo non contraveniant si de sua omnia confidant vel amorum prout de predictas plene constat per publicum instrumentum scriptum et signatum per magistrum Guillelmum scribe ut ibi continetur. Qui de mandato dicti domini Regis [f.5r] ut asserit pro Guillelmo de Sala notario dicti domini Regis scripsit dixit cartam signatam a tergo cum litera .b.

Item protestatur dictus Petrus Texerii nomine quo supra quod dictus dominus Jacobus nondum confirmavit concessionem factam per dictum dominum Petrum ymo de novo ipse concessit ut apparet ex tenore instrumenti sue concessionis cum plura privilegia seu immunitates per ipsum data ibi contineantur quia contineantur in instrumento concessionis facte per dictum dominum condam Petrum bone memorie quondam Regem predecessorem suum et etiam idem dominus Jacobus per totam suam dominationem predicta precepit observari.

Item dicit et proponit dictus syndicus quod tam dictus Sanxius bone memorie condam Rex Maioricarum Comes Rossillionis et Ceritanie et dominus Montispessulani qui successit [f.5v] in dicto Regno comitatibus et in Montepessulano dicto domino Jacobo bone memorie condam Regi quia etiam dominus Jacobus Rex odiernus in predicto Regno Maioricarum comitatibus et in Montepessulano dicto domino Saxio successit omnes consuetudines usus libertates franquesias et immunitates dicte ville laudaverunt et confirmaverunt et ea tenere suarum tenere et observare facere promiserunt et etiam ad sancta quatuor Dei evangelia iuraverunt prout de predictis plene constat per publicum instrumentum scriptum et signatum ut in eo legitur per Guillelmum de Pedio notarium publicum Montispessulani signatum a tergo cum litera .C. Que instrumenta inquantum pro parte sua faciunt et aliquid non ad probandum predictam exibet et producit ad informandum dominum comissarium supradictum.

i. Item etiam superhabundanter intendit probus dictus [f.6r] syndicus quod homines Universitatis ville Montispessulani temporibus retroactis cum contingebat eos venire et transitum facere cum eorum mercaturis per mare in iurisdictionem dicti domini Regis Maioricarum et per terram apud [Cataloniam *del.*] Cauquoliberum et apud Maioricas usu fuerunt dicta immunitate et franquesia et quieti erant et fuerunt a solucione leude pedagii et cuiuslibet alterius exactionis pro rebus seu mercibus eorumdem.

ii. Item quod de hiis est vox et fama [publica *del.*] tam in civitate Maioricarum quam in loco de Cauquolibero quam in aliis locis sive terris dicti domini nostri Regis ubi leude et pedagia est levari consuetum.

Non astringens se ad probandum omnia supra dicta sed tamen ad ea que sibi quo supra nomine sufficere videbuntur ad informandum dominum comissarium supradictum.

[f.6v] Item protestatur dicens Petrus Texerii quo supra nomine quod posito sine preiudicio quod homines [Montipessulani *del.*] Universitatis Ville Montispessulani nunquam usu fuissent dicta immunitate hoc non debet eis preiudicens si decetero uti. Veluit ymo dicens dominus noster Rex uti eos permitere debet si veluit uti ea cum prope dominus Rex tentatum servire ut successor privilegia et immunitates per suos predecessores concessa hominibus Universitati dicte Ville maxime ubi iuramentum intervenit et iuramenta sunt roborata sicut hic aparet manifeste.

Requirens vos dictum dominum comissarium dicens Petrus Texerii nomine quo supra ut sibi concedere litteras vestras habeatis dirigendas tam cuilibet de Maioricis quam de Cauquolibero quam de Montepessulano, et cuilibet eorundem ut testes quos pars dictorum consulum Montispessulani producere valeat coram eis supra dictas intentionibus [f.7r] recipere habeant et examinere diligenter vocatis qui fuerunt evocandi et depositiones dictorum testium sub eorum sigillis una cum dictis intentionibus remitere habeant vobis ad expensum consulum predictorum.

Item producit et carta publica instrumenta ut prima facere apparebat in dicta cedula designata quorum tenores inferius sunt conscripti.

Verum ad magis clarifficandum et hostendum de iure prefati domini nostri Regis et ad dictum Petrum Texerii et partis sue et intencionem elidendam et penitus revocandam ponitur idem procurator regius ut sequitur.

Ponit quod ab hominibus [Ville *del.*] Montispessulani pro rebus et mercibus eorum que in Maioricis fecerunt vehi consuevit exigi pro introhitu et exitu illorum quod in dicto loco est exigi et solvi consuetum pro introhitu et exitu mercium.

[f.7v] Ponit quod ab hominibus Ville Montispessulani acthenus facientibus transitum cum eorum mercaturis per Cauquoliberum et per mare domini nostri Regis consuevit leudam et pedagium exigi pro dictis eorum mercibus seu rebus.

Item ponit quod dominus noster Rex est et predecessor eiusdem in dicto Regno Maioricarum et comitatibus eiusdem fuerunt in possessione seu quasi per se et (e)orum officiales leudarios et exactores exigendi levandi recipiendi ab hominibus Ville Montispessulani pro eorum mercibus et mercaturis apud Cauquoliberum leudam et pedagium et apud Maioricas introhitum et exitum prout a ceteris mercatoribus extraneis pro eorum mercaturis et rebus in Maioricis introitus et exitus et in Coquolibero leuda et pedagium consueverunt exigi et levare et hoc per x.xx.xxx.xll. [*sic*] annos et supra et per tanti temporis spacium quod de contrario memoria hominum [f.8r] non existit.

Item ponit quod de predictis est fama.

Ad id quo supra ponit Dalmatius Englesii regius procurator ut sequitur.

i. Ponit quod tempore quo dicta concessio dicitur fuisse facta per dictum dominum Petrum Regem tunc Aragonum Regnum Maioricarum non erat sub eiusdem tunc dominio et potestate nec per eundem adhuc fuit conquistatum.

ii. Item ponit quod tempore quo dicta concessio dicitur fuisse facta et tempore quo dicta concessio dicitur fuisse confirmata per dominum Jacobum Regem Aragonum comitatus predicti Rossillionis et Ceritanie erant extra eorundem dominium et sub [ducat *del.*] dominio domini Rmonis Saxii [*sic*] Comitis Rossillionis et Ceritanie conoscuntur.

iii. Item ponit quod homines predicte Ville Montispessulani cessaru(n)t in dictis locis de Maioricis de Cauquolibero [f. 8v] uti immunitates non solvendi leuda et pedagium per eorum mercaturis in Cauquolibero et introhitu in Maioricis.

v. [*sic*] Item ponit quod de predictis est fama.

Protestatur tamen dicens procurator quod non astringit se probiturum omnia supradicta et singula proposita per eundem sed solum ea que incertam sufficienter probata de premissis.

Intendit probare Petrus Texerii syndicis hominum Universitatis Ville Montispessulani temporibus retroactis cum contingebat eos venire et transitum facere cum eorum mercaturis per mare in iurisdictione domini Regis Maioricarum et per terram quam apud Cauquoliberum et apud Maioricas usi sunt et fuerunt immunitates et franquesia cessandi solvere leudam seu pedagium vel aliqua aliorum exactionem et quieti erant et fuerunt a solucione leude et pedagii et cuiuslibet alterius exactionis, pro [f.9r] rebus seu mercibus eorundem.

Item intendit probare quod de hiis est vox et fama tam in civitate de Maioricis quam in loco de Cauquolibero quam in Montepessulano quam in aliis locis sive terris dicti domini Regis et ubi leudam seu pedagium est levare consuetum.

Et ibidem incontinenti dictus Petrus Texerii ablata cedula nomine quo supra petit sibi concedi literas quas supra aliter petit pro danda probatione intentionis sue.

Dicens vero procurator regius nomine procuratorio predicto obtulit incontinenti quandam papiri cedulam scriptam cuiusque tenor talis est.

i. I(n)tendit probare Dalmacius Englesii regius procurator predictus quod ab hominibus Montispessulani pro rebus et mercibus eorum quas in Maioricas fecerunt vehi consuevit exigi pro introhitu et exitu illarum id quod in dicto loco [f.9v] est exigi et solvi consuetum pro introitu et exitu mercium ibidem dictarum et vehendorum.

ii. Item intendit probare quod ab hominibus Ville Montispessulani actenus facientibus transitum cum eorum mercaturis per Cauquoliberum et per mare domini Regis consuevit leudam et pedagium exigi pro dictas eorum mercibus seu rebus.

iii. Item intendit probare quod dominus noster Rex et predecessores eiusdem in dicto Regno Maioricarum et comitatibus eiusdem fuerunt in possessione seu quasi per se et eorum officiales leudarios et exactores exigendi levandi et recipiendi ab hominibus Ville Montispessulani pro eorum mercibus et mercaturis apud Cauquoliberum leudam et pedagium et apud Maioricas introhitum et exitum prout a ceteris mercatoribus extraneis pro eorum rebus [f. 10r] et mercaturis introhitus et exitus et in Cauquolibero leudam et pedagium consueverunt exhigi et levare et hoc per decem .xx.xxx.xl. annos et per tantum temporis spatium quod de contrario memoria hominum non existit.

iiii. Item intendit probare quod homines Ville Montispessulani cessarunt in dictis locis de Maioricis et de Cauquolibero uti immunitates non solvendi leudam et pedagium per eorum mercaturis in Cauquolibero et introhitum exitum in Maioricis.

v. Item intendit probare quod vox et fama est quod in dictis temporibus videlicet in anno quo computabatur sexto kalendas septembris anno domini millesimo ducentesimo tricesimo primo dictus dominus Nino Sanxius erat comes et dominus comitatus Rossillioni et Ceritanie.

vi. Item intendit probare quod de predictis est [f.10v] fama in locis de Maioricis et de Cauquolibero et locis circumvicinis.

Qua cedula oblata dictus procurator regius petit diem congruam sibi assignare ad facienda interrogatoria super articulis ex adverso traditis et ad repellendum eosdem articulos si sibi videbitur faciendum.

DOCUMENT IV

Montpellier, Archives Municipales, Grand Chartrier, Armoire A, Cassètte XVII, Louvet no. 324bis

Sommaire du livre No. 1 de l'armoire A de la Caisse 17. Procedure faite a Perpignan en 1339 pour verifier les concessions faites par les Seigneurs de Montpellier aux consuls de Montpellier pour raison de l'immunité a eux accordee de leudes, piages et costumes par mer et par terre.

[f.1r] fol. 1 sont les patantes de la R. commission donnees par Jaq. Roy de Majorque le 13 des calendes d'avril 1338.

fol. 8 v°. Confirmation faite au mois de Juin 1204 par Pierre Roy d'Aragon seig^r de Montpellier et Marie fille de Guillaume son eppouse, en faveur de la comunauté dudit Montpellier des bonnes costumes dudit Montpellier, et de tout ce qu'il plairra aux 7. essens d'ajouter et corriger ou statuer de nouveau pour l'utilité de la ville.

Item ledit Roy Pierre donne a la dite comunauté pour l'advenir l'immunité de franchise dans toute la terre tant par mer que par terre, des peages, leudes et costumes. Fait le 17. des calendes de juillet.

fol. 11. Confirmation faite le 6. des calendes de septembre 1231 par Jaq. Roy d'Aragon et de Majorque et seig^r de Montpellier a la comunauté de Montpellier de la concession faite par Roy Pierre d'Aragon pere dudit Jaques a la dite comunauté de l'exemtion de leude piage, tolte, costume nouvelle ou ancienne statuee ou a statuer des marchandises par terre, mer, estary, eau douce de sa jurisdiction *in loco aliquo terrarum vel dominationis.*

[f.1v] fol. 13. Testament fait le 16. avril 1213 par Marie reyne d'Aragon et dame de Montpellier par lequel elle fait son heritier universel Jaques son fils et du Roy d'Aragon, et decedans sans enfans, lui substitue les deux filles Matildes Peyrone quelle a eües du comte de Comenge, et de meme facon substitue lesdites fille l'une a l'autre.

fol. 17. Confirmation fait par Jacques Roy de Majorque seig^r de Montpellier a ladite comunauté de Montpellier de toutes les costumes ou loix municipales, libertes, immunités et bons usages de ladite ville ainsi que Jaques roy de Majorque son ayeul et apres lui Sance son oncle paternel roy de Majorque avoit fait comme il apparait par acte du jour avant les ides de janvier 1311. dont la teneur est telle.

fol. 18. Confirmation faite par Sance roy de Majorque seig^r de Montpellier a ladite comunauté de toutes les costumes ou loix municipales de Montpellier avisis que fait Jaq. roy d'Aragon son ayeul et apres lui Jaques roy de Majorque son oncle paternel par instrument dont la teneur est telle.

fol. 18 v°. Confirmation faite par Jacques roy de Majorque seigneur de Montpellier a ladite comunauté, de toutes les costumes ou loix municipales de la ville de Montpellier ainsi que Jaques roy d'Aragon son pere les a confirmées, ensemble toutes les libertes et immunités et bons usances de ladite ville. La teneur de laquelle confirmacion dudit Roy Jaques pere est telle.

fol. 19v°. Confirmation faite le 4 des ides de decembre 1298 par Jaques roy de Aragon seigneur de Montpellier des costumes [f.2r] et loix municipales libertés et bons usages de ladite ville, dans laquelle confirmation sont inserés les premiers et derniers mots des articles desdits costumes.

fol. 25v° audits feuillets verso, commencant par le mot *Item. Nos Jacobus* &c. Est que Jaques roy de Majorque susdit seig^r de Montpellier promet a ladite comunauté qu'il ne retenira jamais service in present pour la baylie et la cour de Montpellier et qu'il observera le contenu et carte dudit baille de nomination des officiers di celle cour faite le 5. des ides de feb. 1270.

fol. 27. Audit feuillet comancant par *Rursus nos Idem Sancius* &c. etc. que ledit Sance roy de Majorque et seig^r de Montpellier confirme a ladite comunauté toutes les costumes ou loix municipales et statuts concedés a icelle par le roy de Majorque son pere comme est contenu aux privileges dont les premiers et derniers mots sont inseres – et suite, confirmant aussi toutes les costumes ou loix municipales, statuts, libertes, compositions, privileges, et ordres concedees et confirmees par son dit pere ensemble toutes les libertés et immunités et bons usages de ladite ville fait aux ides de janvier 1311.

fol. 29. Audits feuillets comancant par *Rursus nos Idem Jacobus* &c. Est que ledit Jaques roy de Majorque et seig^r de Montpellier confirme a ladite comunauté toutes les costumes ou loix municipales et statuts ensemble toutes les libertés, immunités et bons usances de ladite ville concedees par ledit Sance roy de [f.2v] Majorque son oncle paternel conformemant aux actes des privileges dont les premiers et derniers mots des articles sont inseres ensuite. Plus loue et continue ledit Roy Jaques toutes les autres costumes ou loix municipales, statuts, libertes, compositions, privileges et ordonnances concedees et confirmees par Sanch son oncle, ensemble toutes les libertés, immunités et bons usages de ladite ville fait le 3. des calendes de juin 1301.

fol. 61. Comancent les articles du procureur du Roy de Majorque par lesquels les temoins fairont leurs depositions par le fait de la leude.

fol. 67. Lettres du Roy Jaques de Majorque sur le sujet de la justification de l'octroi de leude, &c.

fol. 76. Autres dudit Roy Jaque com dessus.

fol. 81. Autres lettres dudit Roy Jaques sur le mesme sujet.

fol. 105v°. Icy comancent les depositions des tesmoins produit de la part du procureur du Roy de Majorque sur le sujet de ladite leude.

fol. 128. Autres lettres dudit Roy Jaques sur le mesme sujet scavoir pour informer desdit privileges datees de 1300.

fol. 145v°. Icy comancent les depositions des tesmoins produit de la par du procureur desdits Sieurs Consuls justifiant ladite immunité de leude et peage.

fol. 192. Autres lettres dudit Roy Jaques de 1338. sur le subjet de ladite leude quedessus.

[f.3r] fol. 197. Autres depositions de tesmoins de la part du procureur dudit Roy de Majorque.

fol. 252. Icy finissent les depositions.

fol. 255. Autres lettres de Commission dudit Roy Jaques de 1308.

fol. 262v°. Continuation des depositions des tesmoins produits de la part dudit Roy de Maiorque.

fol. 304. Icy finissent lesdits depositions.

fol. 312. Extrait des rolles des debiteurs de la leude jusques au dernier feuillet cotte 363.

[ff.3v, 4r-v blank].

Bibliography

MANUSCRIPT SOURCES

FRANCE

Montpellier

Archives Départementales de l'Hérault
  Fonds des Consuls de Mer
    8 B 11 (formerly B.47)
  Notarial registers
    II E 95/368, Jean Holanie
    II E 95/369, Jean Holanie
    II E 95/370, Jean Holanie
    II E 95/371, Jean Holanie
    II E 93/372, Jean Holanie, Perier and Lafon
    II E 95/374, G. Nogaret
    II E 95/375, Pierre Pena
Archives Municipales
  Notarial registers
    BB1, Jean Grimaud
    BB2, Jean Laurens
  Other documentation
    Arm. A, Cassette XVII, Louvet 324bis, 325

Paris

Archives Nationales
  Chambre des Comptes
    KK 1413
    P1353
    P1354^1
    P1354^2
Bibliothèque Nationale
  MS français 3884
  MS latin 9261

Perpignan

Archives Départementales des Pyrénées Orientales
Archives de la ville de Perpignan
  AA1 Livre vert majeur
  AA3 Livre vert mineur
Notarial registers
  3 E 1, 1 (1261)
  3 E 1, 2 (1266)
  3 E 1, 3 (1272-3)
  3 E 1, 4 (1273)
  3 E 1, 5 (1274-5; 1278)
  3 E 1, 6 (1276-7)
Registres de la Procuración Real
  I B 69 (Leuda de Collioure)
  I B 70 (1336)
  I B 94 (Leuda de pizans, 1321, in Registre XVII, 1257-1335, f.74v)
  I B 95 (1233-1341)

ITALY

Genoa

Archivio di Stato
  Cartolare Notarile 2

Prato

Archivio di Stato di Firenze, Sezione di Prato
  Archivio Datini, Carteggio Maiorca
  1073, 1076, 1082, 1084

SPAIN

Palma de Mallorca

Archivo Capitular
  14564 Francesc Batlle
Arxiu del Regne de Mallorca
  Escribanía de Cartas Reales, Series Civitatis et Partis Foraneæ
    Prot. 341
    Prot. 342
    Prot. 343
  Gobernación
    AH 4390: Llicències i guiatges, 1341-2
  Real Patrimonio
    1097: *ancoratge* of 1321
    1098: *ancoratge* of 1324
    1099: *ancoratge* of 1331

1100: *ancoratge* of 1332
1101: *ancoratge* of 1340
1102: *ancoratge* of 1330
1105/1: Libro de licencias para barcas

UNITED KINGDOM

London

British Library
    Additional MS 25691
Public Record Office
    R 122, 68: London port records
    Close Rolls, Edward II–III
    Patent Rolls, Edward II–III

PRINTED PRIMARY SOURCES

Aguiló, E. K. 'Capbreu ordenat l'any 1304 dels establiments y donacions fets per Don Nunyo Sanç, de la seu porció', *Bolletí de la Societat arqueológica Luliana*, 14 (1913), 209–24, 241–56, 273–85.

Annali Genovesi di Caffaro e de'suoi Continuatori, ed. L. T. Belgrano and C. Imperiale di Sant'Angelo, 5 vols. (Fonti per la Storia d'Italia, Roma, 1890–1929).

Archives de la ville de Montpellier. Inventaires et documents publiés par les soins de l'administration municipale. Vol. I. *Notice sur les anciens inventaires. Inventaire du Grand Chartrier*, part 2, *Inventaire du 'Grand Chartrier' rédigé par Pierre Louvet en 1662–1663 publié avec des notes et une table*, ed. J. Berthelé (Montpellier, 1896).

Archives de la ville de Montpellier, vol. XIII, *Inventaire analytique série BB (Notaires et greffiers du consolat 1293–1387)*, ed. M. de Dainville, M. Gouron and L. Valls (Montpellier, 1984).

Artizzu, F. *Documenti inediti relativi ai rapporti economici tra la Sardegna e Pisa nel Medioevo*, 2 vols. (Padua/Cagliari, 1961–2).

Baer, F. (later known as Y.), *Die Juden im Christlichen Spanien. Erster Teil: Urkunden und Regesten*, vol. I. *Aragonien und Navarra* (Berlin, 1929; repr. with additional material by H. Beinart, Farnborough, 1970).

Blancard, L. (ed), *Documents inédits sur le commerce de Marseille au Moyen Age*, 2 vols. (Marseilles, 1884–5).

Bonner, A. (ed.), *Selected Works of Ramón Llull (1232–1316)*, 2 vols. (Princeton, NJ, 1985).

Calendar of Charter Rolls.

Calendar of Close Rolls.

Calendar of Patent Rolls.

de Capmany y de Monpalau, A., *Memorias sobre la marina, comercio y artes de la antigua ciudad de Barcelona*, ed. with annotations by E. Giralt y Raventos and C. Batlle y Gallart (Barcelona, 1962).

Chronicle of James I king of Aragon, The, transl. J. Forster, 2 vols. (London, 1883).

Chronicle of Muntaner, The, transl. Lady Goodenough, 2 vols. (Hakluyt Society, London, 1920–1).

Chronicle of the reign of King Pedro III, The, by Bernat Desclot, transl. F. L. Critchlow, 2 vols. (Princeton, NJ, 1928–34).

Chronicle of San Juan de la Peña. The. A fourteenth-century official history of the Crown of Aragon, transl. Lynn H. Nelson (Philadelphia, 1991).

Consulate of the Sea and related documents, The, transl. S. S. Jados (Alabama, 1975).

Desclot, Bernat, *Llibre del rey en Pere,* in *Les quatre grans cròniques,* ed. F. Soldevila (Barcelona, 1971).

Dini, Bruno, *Una pratica di mercatura in formazione (1394–1395)* (Florence/Prato, 1980).

Documenta regni Majoricarum (Miscelanea), ed. J. Vich y Salom and J. Muntaner y Bujosa (Palma de Mallorca, 1945).

Evans, Allan (ed.), *The Pratica della Mercatura of Francesco Pegolotti* (Cambridge, MA, 1936).

Fita, F. 'Los Judíos mallorquines y el Concilio de Viena', *Boletín de la Real Academia de la Historia,* 36 (1900).

'Privilegios de los Hebreos mallorquines en el Códice Pueyo', *Boletín de la Real Academia de la Historia,* 36 (1900).

García Sanz, A. and Ferrer i Mallol, M. T., *Assegurances i Canvis marítims medievals a Barcelona,* 2 vols. (Barcelona, 1983).

García Sanz, A. and Madurell i Marimón, J. M., *Societats mercantils medievals a Barcelona,* 2 vols. (Barcelona, 1986).

Guichard, P., *L'Espagne et la Sicile musulmanes aux XIᵉ et XIIᵉ siècles* (Lyons, 1990).

Gulotta, P., *Le imbreviature del notaio Adamo de Citella a Palermo (2° Registro: 1298–1299)* (Fonti e studi del Corpus membranarum italicarum, ser. 3, Imbreviature matricole statuti e formulari notarili medievali 2, Rome, 1982).

Hillgarth, J. N. and Rosselló, Juan, *The liber communis curiae of the diocese of Majorca (1364–1374).* Text with English and Spanish introduction and notes (Publications de l'Institut d'Études Médiévales, vol. XXIV; Montreal/Paris, 1989).

Hinks, A. R., *Portolan chart of Angellino de Dalorto of 1325 in the collection of Prince Corsini at Florence* (London, 1929).

James I, *Crònica o Llibre des Feits,* in *Les quatre grans cròniques,* ed. F. Soldevila (Barcelona, 1971).

Jordan, E., *Les registres de Clement IV (1265–1268)* (Paris, 1893–1912).

La Mantia, G., *Codice diplomatico dei re aragonesi di Sicilia Pietro I, Giacomo, Federico II, Pietro II e Ludovico, dalla rivoluzione siciliana del 1282 sino al 1355,* vol. I (1282–90), (Palermo, 1917).

Layettes du trésor des Chartes, 3 vols, ed. J. B. A. T. Teulet (Paris, 1863–75).

Liber iurium reipublicae Genuensis, in Historiae Monumenta Patriae, *Chartarum*, vol. I (Turin, 1836–54).

Liber Maiolichinus de gestis Pisanorum illustribus, ed. C. Calisse (Fonti per la Storia d'Italia, Rome, 1904).

Llull, Ramón, *Blanquerna*, transl. E. A. Peers and ed. R. Irwin (London, 1987).

Madurell Marimón, J. M. and García Sanz, A., *Comandas comerciales barcelonesas de la baja edad media* (Barcelona, 1973).

Martène, E., and Durand, U., *Thesaurus novus anecdotorum*, vol. II (Paris, 1717).

de Mas Latrie, L., *Traités de paix et de commerce et documents divers concernant les relations des Chrétiens avec les Arabes de l'Afrique septentrionale au Moyen Age* (Paris, 1866).

Masià de Ros, A., *Jaume II: Aragó, Granada i Marroc* (Barcelona, 1989).

Melis, F., *Documenti per la storia economica dei secoli XIII–XV* (Florence/Prato, 1972).

Muntaner, Ramòn, *Crònica*, in *Les quatres grans cròniques*, ed. F. Soldevila (Barcelona, 1971).

Ollich i Castanyer, I. and Casas i Nadal, M., *Miscellània de Textos Medievals*, vol. III, *Els 'Libri Iudeorum' de Vic i de Cardona* (Barcelona, 1985).

Pere III of Catalonia (Peter IV of Aragon), *Chronicle*, transl. Mary Hillgarth, ed. J. Hillgarth, 2 vols. (Toronto, 1980).

Peter the Ceremonious, *Crònica*, in *Les quatre grans cròniques*, ed. F. Soldevila (Barcelona, 1971).

Régné, J., *History of the Jews of Aragon. Regesta and documents*, ed. Y. T. Assis from the original publication in separate parts of the *Revue des Études juives* (Hispania Judaica, 1, Jerusalem, 1986).

Registro del notaio ericino Giovanni Maiorana (1297–1300), *Il*, ed. A. Sparti, 2 vols. (Palermo, 1982).

Registro notarile di Giovanni Maiorana (1297–1300), *Il*, ed. A. de Stefano (Memorie e documenti di storia siciliana, 2, Documenti 2, Palermo, 1943).

Riera, A., 'La Llicència per a barques de 1284. Una font important per a l'estudi del commerç exterior mallorquí del darrer quart del segle XIII', *Faventia*, 2 (1980), 53–73, published also in *Fontes Rerum Balearium*, 3 (1979–80), 121–40.

Riera Melis, A., *La Corona de Aragón y el reino de Mallorca en el primer cuarto del siglo XIV*. Vol. I, *Las repercussiones arancelarias de la autonomía balear (1298–1311)* (Barcelona, 1986): Appendix of documents.

Rymer, Thomas, *Foedera, conventiones, literæ, et cujuscunque generis acta publica inter reges Angliæ et alios quosvis imperatores, reges, pontifices, principes, vel communitates*, vol. II (Hagæ Comitis, 1739; repr. Farnborough, 1967).

Sánchez Martínez, 'Mallorquines y Genovesos en Almería durante el primer tercio del siglo XIV: el proceso contra Jaume Manfré (1334)', *Miscellània de textos medievals*, vol. IV, *La frontera terrestre i marítima amb l'Islam* (Barcelona, 1988).

Santamaría, A., *Ejecutoria del Reino de Mallorca* (Palma de Mallorca, 1990): Appendix of documents.

Soldevila F. (ed.), *Les quatre grans cròniques* (Barcelona, 1971).

Soto Company, R., *L'ordenació de l'espai i les relacions socials a Mallorca en el segle XIII (1229–1301)* (doctoral thesis of the Autonomous University of Barcelona, published in microfiche, Bellaterra, 1992): Appendix of documents.

Travels of ibn Jubayr, The, ed. and transl. R. J. C. Broadhurst (London, 1952).

Villanueva, J. L. *Viage literario a las Iglesias de España*, tomos XXI–XXII, *Viage a Mallorca* (Madrid, 1851–2).

Winkelmann, E., *Acta imperii inedita seculi XIII et XIV. Urkunden und Briefe zur Geschichte des Kaiserreichs und des Königreichs Sicilien in den Jahren 1200–1400*, vol. II (Innsbruck, 1885).

Zeno, R. *Documenti per la storia del diritto marittimo nei secoli XIII e XIV* (Documenti e studi per la storia del commercio e del diritto commerciale italiana 6, Turin, 1936).

SECONDARY SOURCES

This list does not aim to provide a list of all the literature on the Majorcan realm, but to indicate which works have been used most intensively in the preparation of this book; a few items mentioned only in passing in the footnotes are omitted, and several items that do not appear in the notes are added. Particular attention is drawn to the numerous items containing often large amounts of source material, indicated by *.

CHCA indicates the various Congresses of the History of the Crown of Aragon: these are listed in chronological order under *Congreso* below.

Abulafia, David, 'Le attività economiche degli Ebrei siciliani attorno al 1300', *Convegno internazionale di Studi Italia Judaica*, 5, Palermo, June 1992 (1995).

'Catalan merchants and the western Mediterranean, 1236–1300: studies in the notarial acts of Barcelona and Sicily', *Viator*, 16 (1985); repr. in *Italy, Sicily and the Mediterranean*.

Commerce and conquest in the Mediterranean, 1100–1500 (Aldershot, 1993).

'The commerce of medieval Majorca, 1150–1450', *Medieval Spain and the western Mediterranean. Studies in honor of Robert I. Burns*, ed. Donald Kagay et al. (Berkeley/Los Angeles, 1994).

'Una comunità ebraica della Sicilia occidentale: Erice 1298–1304', *Archivio storico per la Sicilia orientale*, 80 (1984); repr. in *Commerce and conquest*, and published in Hebrew in *Zion*, 51 (1986).

'The crown and the economy under Ferrante I of Naples (1458–94)', in *City and countryside in late medieval and early Renaissance Italy. Essays presented to Philip Jones*, ed. T. Dean and C. Wickham (London, 1990); repr. in *Commerce and conquest*.

'The end of Muslim Sicily', in *Muslims under Latin rule, 1100–1300*, ed. J. M. Powell (Princeton, NJ, 1990); reprinted in *Commerce and conquest.*

Frederick II. A medieval emperor (London, 1988).

'From privilege to persecution: crown, church and synagogue in the city of Majorca, 1229–1343', in *Church and city, 1000–1500. Essays in honour of Christopher Brooke*, ed. D. Abulafia, M. Franklin and M. Rubin (Cambridge, 1992).

Italy, Sicily and the Mediterranean, 1100–1400 (London, 1987).

'Jews, Christians and Muslims in the Catalan kingdom of Majorca', in *Relationships between Jews, Christians and Muslims*, ed. J. Irmscher (Amsterdam/Las Palmas de Gran Canaria, 1993).

'The Levant trade of the minor cities in the thirteenth and fourteenth centuries: strengths and weaknesses', in *The Medieval Levant. Studies in memory of Eliyahu Ashtor (1914–1984)*, ed. B. Z. Kedar and A. Udovitch, *Asian and African Studies*, 22 (1988); repr. in *Commerce and conquest.*

'Les Llicències per a barques et le commerce de Majorque en 1284', *Les Catalans et la Mer. Mélanges C.-E. Dufourcq*, ed. H. Bresc, Paris, 1994.

'Marseilles, Acre and the Mediterranean, 1200–1291', in *Coinage in the Latin East: the fourth Oxford Symposium on Coinage and Monetary History*, ed. P. W. Edbury and D. M. Metcalf (British Archaeological Reports, International Series, vol. LXXVII, Oxford, 1980).

'The Mediterranean islands in the Middle Ages. 1. The Balearic islands', *Medieval History*, 1 (1991).

'The merchants of Messina: Levant trade and domestic economy', *Papers of the British School at Rome*, 54 (1986); repr. in *Commerce and conquest.*

'Monarchs and minorities in the Mediterranean around 1300: Lucera and its analogues', in *Christendom and its discontents*, ed. Scott L. Waugh (Berkeley/Los Angeles, 1994).

'Narbonne, the lands of the Crown of Aragon and the Levant trade 1187–1400', *Montpellier, la Couronne d'Aragon et les pays de Langue d'Oc (1204–1349). Actes du XII⁰ Congrès d'Histoire de la Couronne d'Aragon, Montpellier, 26–29 septembre 1985 = Mémoires de la Société archéologique de Montpellier*, 15 (1987); repr. in *Commerce and conquest.*

'The Norman kingdom of Africa and the Norman expeditions to Majorca and the Muslim Mediterranean', *Anglo-Norman Studies*, 7 (1985); repr. in *Italy, Sicily and the Mediterranean.*

'The problem of the kingdom of Majorca. 1: Political identity', *Mediterranean Historical Review*, 5 (1990).

'The problem of the kingdom of Majorca. 2: Economic identity', *Mediterranean Historical Review*, 6 (1991).

'Les relacions comercials i polítiques entre el regne de Mallorca i l'Anglaterra, segons fonts documentals angleses', CHCA XIII (1989–90), vol. IV.

'Le relazioni fra il regno di Maiorca e la Sardegna, 1267–1324', CHCA XIV (1990), vol. I.

'A settler society: the Catalan kingdom of Majorca', historiographical essay, *Aspects of medieval Spain, 711–1492*, special issue of the *Journal of Medieval History*, 18 (1992).

Spain and 1492. Unity and uniformity under Ferdinand and Isabella (Bangor, 1992).

'Sul commercio del grano siciliano nel tardo Duecento', CHCA XII (1983–4) vol. II; repr. in *Italy, Sicily and the Mediterranean.*

The two Italies. Economic relations between the Norman kingdom of Sicily and the northern communes (Cambridge, 1977); Italian edn, with additional chapter: *Le Due Italie: relazioni economiche fra il Regno normanno di Sicilia e i comuni settentrionali* (Naples, 1991).

'A Tyrrhenian triangle: Tuscany, Sicily, Tunis, 1277–1300', *Studi di storia economica toscana nel Medioevo e nel Rinascimento in memoria di Federigo Melis*, ed. C. Violante, Biblioteca del Bollettino Storico Pisano, Collana storica, Pisa, 1987); repr. in *Commerce and conquest.*

Alomar Esteve, G., *Cataros y occitanos en el reino de Mallorca* (Palma de Mallorca, 1978).

Urbanismo regional en la edad media: las 'Ordinacions' de Jaime II (1300) en el reino de Mallorca (Barcelona, 1976).*

Amengual i Batle, Josep, *Els origens del Cristianisme a les Balears*, 2 vols. (Palma de Mallorca, 1991–2).*

Antoni, T., *I 'partitari' maiorchini del Lou dels Pisans relativi al commercio dei Pisani nelle Baleari (1304–1322 e 1353–1355)* (Biblioteca del Bollettino Storico Pisano, Collana storica, Pisa, 1977).*

Arribas Palau, A., *La conquista de Cerdeña por Jaime II de Aragón* (Barcelona, 1952).*

Artizzu, F. 'Penetrazione catalana in Sardegna nel sec. XII', CHCA VI; repr. in F. Artizzu, *Pisani e Catalani nella Sardegna medioevale* (Padua/Cagliari, 1973).

Ashtor, E., 'Catalan cloth on the late medieval Mediterranean markets', *Journal of European Economic History*, 17 (1988).

Assis, Y. T., *The Jews of Santa Coloma de Queralt* (Jerusalem, 1988).*

Bach, E., *La Cité de Gênes au XII⁰ siècle* (Copenhagen, 1955).

Barceló Crespi, M., *Ciutat de Mallorca en el Trànsit a la Modernitat* (Palma de Mallorca, 1988).

'Promoción del area rural de Mallorca: adquisiciones territoriales de Jaime II', CHCA XI, vol. II.

Batlle, C., Busqueta, J. and Cuadrada, C., 'Notes sobre l'eix comercial Barcelona–Mallorca–Barbaria, a la meitat del s.XIII', CHCA XIII, vol. II.

Baumel, J., *Histoire d'une seigneurie du Midi de la France*, vols I–III (Montpellier, 1969–73).

Beinart, H., 'Perpignan', in *Encyclopaedia Judaica*, s.v.

Bel, A., *Les Benou Ghânya, derniers représentants de l'empire almoravide et leur lutte contre l'empire almohade* (Paris/Algiers, 1903).

Bensa, E. *Francesco di Marco da Prato* (Milan, 1928).*

Berner, L., 'On the western shores: the Jews of Barcelona during the reign of Jaume I, "*el Conqueridor*", 1213–1276' (University of California, Los Angeles, Ph.D. thesis, University Microfilms International, 1986).*

Berti, G., Rosselló Bordoy, G. and Tongiorgi, E., *Alcuni bacini ceramici di Pisa e la corrispondente produzione di Mallorca nel secolo XI*, Trabajos del Museo de Mallorca (Palma de Mallorca, 1987).

Besta, E., *La Sardegna medioevale*, vol. i (Bologna, 1908).

Bisson, T. N., *Assemblies and representation in Languedoc in the thirteenth century* (Princeton, NJ, 1964).

The medieval Crown of Aragon. A short history (Oxford, 1986).

Boswell, J., *The royal treasure. Muslim communities under the Crown of Aragon in the fourteenth century* (New Haven, 1977).

Braunstein, B., *The Chuetas of Majorca. Conversos and the inquisition of Majorca* (New York, 1936).

Bresc, H., 'L'esclavage dans le monde méditerranéen des XIVᵉ et XVᵉ siècles: problèmes politiques, réligieux et morales', CHCA XIII, vol. i.

'Marchands de Narbonne et du Midi en Sicile (1300–1460)', *Narbonne. Archéologie et histoire*, vol. II, *Narbonne au Moyen-Age. 65° Congrès de la Fédération historique du Languedoc méditerranéen et du Roussillon* (Montpellier, 1973).

Politique et société en Sicile, XIIᵉ–XVᵉ (Aldershot, 1991).

Un monde méditerranéen. Économie et société en Sicile, 1300–1450, 2 vols. (Rome/Palermo, 1986).

Burns, R. I., *Muslims, Christians and Jews in the crusader kingdom of Valencia* (Cambridge, 1984).

'Muslims in the thirteenth-century realms of Aragon: interaction and reaction', in *Muslims under Latin rule, 1100–1300*, ed. J. M. Powell (Princeton, NJ, 1990).

Burns, R. I., (ed.) *The worlds of Alfonso the Learned and James the Conqueror* (Princeton, NJ, 1985).

Calmette, J., *La question des Pyrénées et la marche d'Espagne au Moyen Age* (9th edn, Paris, 1947).

Campbell, T., 'Portolan charts from the late thirteenth century to 1500', *The history of cartography*, vol. i, *Cartography in prehistoric, ancient and medieval Europe and the Mediterranean*, ed. J. B. Harley and D. Woodward (Chicago, 1987).

Carrère, C., *Barcelone centre économique à l'époque des difficultés, 1380–1462*, 2 vols. (Paris/ The Hague, 1967).

Casula, F. C., *La Sardegna Aragonese*, 2 vols. (Sassari, 1990).

Cateura Bennàsser, P., 'El comercio del reino de Mallorca con Cerdeña a traves de los guiatges', CHCA XIV, vol. i.

Politica y finanzas del reino de Mallorca bajo Pedro IV de Aragon (Palma de Mallorca, 1982).*

'La repoblació nobiliària de Mallorca per Nuno Sans', CHCA XII, vol. II.

Sociedad, jerarquia y poder en la Mallorca medieval (Fontes rerum Balearium, Estudios y textos, vol. VII, Palma de Mallorca, 1984).

'Urbanismo y finanzas: adquisiciones de propriedades urbanas por Jaime II de Mallorca', CHCA xi, vol. ii.

Cazenave, A., 'L'échec de la régence de Philippe de Majorque', CHCA xii, vol. ii.

Caucanas, S., *Introduction à l'histoire du Moyen Age en Roussillon* (Direction des Services des Archives, Perpignan, 1985).*

Chazan, R., *Daggers of faith. Thirteenth-century Christian missionizing and Jewish response* (Berkeley/Los Angeles, 1989).

Childs, Wendy, *Anglo-Castilian trade in the later Middle Ages* (Manchester, 1978).

Cipollone, G. 'L'ordo Trinitatis et Captivorum. Il suo insediamento nelle Baleari', CHCA xiii, vols. ii and iii.

Cohen, J., *The friars and the Jews* (Ithaca, NY, 1982).

IV° Congreso de la História de la Corona de Aragón, published as a series of monographs (Palma de Mallorca, 1955).

VI° Congreso de História de la Corona de Aragón, Cerdeña 8–14 diciembre 1957 (Madrid, 1959).

X° Congreso de la História de la Corona de Aragón: Jaime I y su Epoca, 3 vols. (Saragossa, 1979–80).

XI° Congresso della Corona d'Aragona/VII Centenario del Vespro Siciliano: La società mediterranea all'epoca del Vespro, 4 vols. (Palermo, 1983–4).

XII° Congrès d'Histoire de la Couronne d'Aragon: Montpellier, la Couronne d'Aragon et les pays de Langue d'Oc (1204–1349). Actes du XII° Congrès d'Histoire de la Couronne d'Aragon, Montpellier, 26–29 septembre 1985, 3 vols. = *Mémoires de la Société archéologique de Montpellier*, 15–17 (1987–9).

XIII° Congrés d'Història de la Corona d'Aragó, Palma de Mallorca, septembre 1987, 4 vols. (Institut d'Estudis Baleàrics, Palma de Mallorca, 1989–90).

XIV° Congresso di Storia della Corona d'Aragona, devoted to *La Corona d'Aragona in Italia nei secoli XIII–XVIII*, Sassari/Alghero/Nuoro, Sardinia, 19–24 May 1990, 5 vols. (pre-print edition) (Sassari/Alghero, 1990); definitive edition (Cagliari, 1993–4).

Constable, R., 'At the edge of the west: international trade and traders in Muslim Spain (1000–1250)' (Columbia University Ph.D. thesis; University Microfilms International, 1989).

Coville, A., *La vie intellectuelle dans les domaines d'Anjou–Provence de 1380 à 1435* (Paris, 1941).

Day, J., *The medieval market economy* (Oxford, 1987).

La Sardegna sotto la dominazione pisano-genovese (Storia degli Stati italiani dal Medioevo all'Unità, ed. G. Galasso, Turin, 1987).

Delcor, M., 'Les Juifs de Puigcerdà au xiii° siècle', *Sefarad*, 26 (1966).

del Treppo, M., *I mercanti catalani e l'espansione della Corona d'Aragona nel secolo XV* (Naples, 1972).

Doxey, G. B., 'Christian attempts to conquer the Balearic islands, 1015–1229' (Ph.D thesis, Cambridge University, 1991).

Dufourcq, C. E., 'Aspects internationaux de Majorque durant les derniers siècles du Moyen Age', *Mayurqa*, 11 (1974).

L'Espagne catalane et le Maghrib au XIIIe et XIVe siècles. De la bataille de Las Navas de Tolosa (1212) à l'avènement du sultan mérinide Aboul-Hasan (1331) (Bibliothèque de l'École des Hautes Études Hispaniques, 37, Paris, 1966).

L'Ibérie chrétienne et le Maghreb (XIIe–XVe siècles), (Aldershot, 1990).

'La question de Ceuta au xiiie siècle', *Hespéris*, 42 (1955); repr. in *L'Ibérie chrétienne et le Maghreb*.

La vie quotidienne dans les ports méditerranéens au Moyen Age (Provence/ Languedoc/Catalogne) (Paris, 1975).

Durliat, M., *L'art dans le royaume de Majorque* (Toulouse, 1962; Catalan edn: *L'art en el regne de Mallorca*, Palma de Mallorca, 1989).

Durliat, M. and Pons i Marquès, J., 'Recerques sobre el moviment del port de Mallorca en la primera meitat del segle xiv', CHCA vi.

Eberenz, R., *Schiffe an den Küsten der Pyrenäenhalbinsel. Ein kulturgeschichtliche Untersuchung zur Schiffstypologie und terminologie der iberoromanischen Sprachen bis 1600* (Europäische Hochschulschriften, Iberoromanische Sprachen und Literaturen, series 24, no. 6, Bern/Frankfurt-am-Main, 1975).

Egidi, P., *La colonia saracena di Lucera e la sua distruzione* (Naples, 1915).

Emery, R. W., 'Flemish cloth and Flemish merchants in Perpignan in the thirteenth century', *Essays in medieval life and thought in honor of A.P. Evans*, ed. R. W. Emery, J. H. Mundy and B. N. Nelson (New York, 1955).

The Jews of Perpignan in the thirteenth century (New York, 1959).

'Les juifs en Conflent et en Vallespir', *Conflent, Vallespir et Montagnes Catalanes. 53° Congrès de la Fédération historique du Languedoc méditerranéen et du Roussillon* (Montpellier, 1980).

'The wealth of the Perpignan Jewry in the early fifteenth century', *Les Juifs dans l'histoire de la France* (Haifa, 1980).

Ensenyat Pujol, G., 'El "lon" dels genovesos: els canvis operats després de l'annexió de Mallorca', CHCA xiii, vol. ii.

Epstein, J., *The responsa of Rabbi Simon ben Zemah Duran* (London, 1930).

Epstein, S. R., *An Island for Itself. Economic development and social change in late medieval Sicily* (Cambridge, 1992).

Fall, Yoro K., *L'Afrique à la naissance de la cartographie moderne. Les cartes majorquines, 14ème–15ème siècles* (Paris, 1985).

Fernández-Armesto, F., 'Atlantic exploration before Columbus: the evidence of maps', *Renaissance and Modern Studies*, 30 (1986).

Barcelona. A thousand years of the city's past (London, 1991).

Before Columbus. Exploration and colonisation from the Mediterranean to the Atlantic, 1229–1492 (London, 1987).

Ferrer i Mallol, M. T., 'Els italians a terres catalanes (segles xiii–xv)' *Actas del I° Congreso international de História mediterranea*, in *Anuario de Estudios medievales*, 19 (1980).

Gais, N. E., 'Aperçu sur la population musulmane de Majorque au xıv^e siècle', *Revue d'histoire et civilisation du Maghreb*, 9 (1970).

Galasso, G., *Il regno di Napoli Angioino e Aragonese 1266–1494* (Storia d'Italia UTET, Turin, 1992).

García de la Torre, J. 'La Orden del Temple como ejemplo de atipismo social de la Edad Media en Mallorca medieval', CHCA, xııı, vol. ıı.

Garí, Blanca, 'Why Almería? An Islamic port in the compass of Genoa', *Aspects of medieval Spain, 711–1492*, special issue of the *Journal of Medieval History*, 18 (1992).

Germain, A. *Histoire du commerce de Montpellier*, 2 vols. (Montpellier, 1861).*

Gual Camarena, M., *Vocabulario del comercio medieval* (Tarragona, 1968/ Barcelona, 1976).*

Guichard, P., *Les musulmans de Valence et la reconquête, XIe–XIIIe siècles*, 2 vols. (Damascus, 1990–1).

Gutwirth, E., 'El comercio hispano-magrebi y los Judíos (1391–1444)' *Hispania*, 45 (1985).*

'Towards expulsion: 1391–1492', in *Spain and the Jews. The Sephardi experience, 1492 and after*, ed. E. Kedourie (London, 1992).*

Harvey, L. P., *Islamic Spain, 1250–1500* (Chicago, 1990).

Haywood, J., *Dark Age naval power. A reassessment of Frankish and Anglo-Saxon seafaring activity* (London, 1991).

Heers, J., 'Le royaume de Grenade et la politique marchande de Gênes en Occident (xve siècle)' *Le Moyen Age*, 63 (1957); repr. in J. Heers, *Société et Economie à Gênes (XIVe–XVe siècles)* (London, 1979).

Herde, Peter, *Karl I. von Anjou* (Stuttgart, 1979).

Herlihy, D., 'Population, plague and social change in rural Pistoia', *Economic History Review*, ser. 2, 18 (1965).

Hibbert, A. B., 'Catalan consulates in the thirteenth century', *Cambridge Historical Journal*, 9 (1949), 352–8.

Hillgarth, J. N., *The problem of a Catalan Mediterranean Empire, 1229–1323* (English Historical Review, supplement no. 8, London, 1975).

Ramon Lull and Lullism in fourteenth-century France (Oxford, 1971).

Readers and books in Majorca, 1229–1550, 2 vols. (Paris, 1992).

The Spanish kingdoms, 1250–1500, 2 vols. (Oxford, 1975–8).

História de Mallorca, ed. J. Mascaró Pasarius, vol. ııı (Palma de Mallorca, 1978).

Hocquet, J. C., 'Ibiza, carrefour du commerce maritime et témoin d'une conjoncture méditerranéenne (1250–1650 env.)', *Studi in memoria di Federigo Melis*, vol. ı (Naples, 1978).

Hogendorn, J. and Johnson, M., *The shell money of the slave trade* (Cambridge, 1986).

Housley, N., *The later crusades. From Lyons to Alcazar, 1274–1580* (Oxford, 1992).

Hunt, Edwin, S., *The medieval super-companies: a study of the Peruzzi Company of Florence* (Cambridge, 1994).

Isaacs, A. L., *The Jews of Mallorca* (London, 1936; Catalan translation as *Els jueus de Mallorca*, Palma de Mallorca, 1986).*

Jacoby, D., 'Crusader Acre in the thirteenth century: urban layout and topography', *Studi medievali*, ser. 3, 20 (1979); repr. in D. Jacoby, *Studies on the crusader states and on Venetian expansion* (Northampton, 1989).

Jehel, G., *Aigues-Mortes. Un port pour un roi. Les Capétiens et la Méditerranée* (Roanne, 1985).

'La place de Majorque dans la stratégie économique de Gênes aux xiie et xiiie sièles', CHCA xiii, vol. ii.

Jordan, W. C., *The French monarchy and the Jews. From Philip Augustus to the last of the Capetians* (Philadelphia, 1989).

Kamal, Y., *Monumenta cartographica Africæ et Ægypti*, 5 vols. in 16 parts (Cairo, 1926–51).*

Labande, E. R., 'La politique méditerranéenne de Louis 1er d'Anjou et le rôle qu'y joua la Sardaigne', *Atti del VI Congresso internazionale di studi sardi* (Cagliari 1957); repr. in E. R. Labande, *Histoire de l'Europe occidentale, XIe–XIVe siècle* (London, 1973).

Lacarra, J. *História del reino de Navarra en la edad media* (Pamplona, 1976).

Lacave, M. and M., *Bourgeois et marchands en Provence et en Languedoc* (Avignon, 1977).

Lalinde Abadía, J., 'El desarollo político e institucional del Reino Privado de Mallorca', CHCA xiii, vol. i.

Lecoy de la Marche, A., *Les relations politiques de la France avec le royaume de Majorque*, 2 vols. (Paris, 1892).*

Le roi René, 2 vols. (Paris, 1875).

Léonard, E., *Les Angevins de Naples* (Paris, 1954).

Leroy, B., *La Navarre au Moyen Age* (Paris, 1984).

Lewis, A., 'Northern European sea-power and the straits of Gibraltar, 1031–1350', *Order and innovation in the Middle Ages. Essays in honor of Joseph R. Strayer*, ed. W. C. Jordan, B. McNab and T. F. Ruiz (Princeton, NJ, 1976).

Lewis, A. R., 'James the Conqueror, Montpellier and southern France', in A. R. Lewis, *Medieval society in southern France and Catalonia* (London, 1984); and in R. I. Burns (ed.), *The worlds of Alfonso the Learned and James the Conqueror* (Princeton, NJ, 1985).

Limor, O., *Vikuah Mayurqa*, offset edn, with introduction in Hebrew, 2 vols. (Hebrew University of Jerusalem, Jerusalem, 1985).*

Lionti, F., 'Le società dei Bardi, dei Peruzzi e degli Acciaiuoli in Sicilia', *Archivio storico siciliano*, n.s. 14 (1908).

Lloyd, T. H., *Alien merchants in England in the High Middle Ages* (Hassocks, Sussex, 1982).

The English wool trade in the Middle Ages (Cambridge, 1977).

Loeb, I., 'Histoire d'une taille levée sur les Juifs de Perpignan en 1413–1414', *Revue des Études juives* (1887).

Lopez, R. S., 'Majorcans and Genoese on the North Sea route in the thirteenth century', *Revue belge de philologie et d'histoire*, 29 (1951).

Lourie, E., 'Anatomy of ambivalence: Muslims under the Crown of Aragon in the late thirteenth century,' in Lourie, *Crusade and colonisation*.

'La colonización cristiana de Menorca durante el reinado de Alfonso III "el Liberal", rey de Aragón', *Analecta sacra Tarraconensia*, 53/4 (1983); repr. in Lourie, *Crusade and colonisation*.*

Crusade and colonisation. Muslims, Christians and Jews in medieval Aragon (Aldershot, 1990).

'Free Moslems in the Balearics under Christian rule in the thirteenth century', *Speculum*, 45 (1970), 624–49, repr. in Lourie, *Crusade and colonisation*.

'A plot which failed? The case of the corpse found in the Jewish *Call* of Barcelona (1301)', *Mediterranean Historical Review*, 1 (1986), repr. in Lourie, *Crusade and colonisation*.

Macaire, P., *Majorque et le commerce international (1400–1450 environ)* (doctoral thesis, University of Paris IV, Sorbonne, 1983; Atelier réproduction des thèses, University of Lille III, Lille, 1986).

McVaugh, M., *Medicine before the plague. Practitioners and their patients in the Crown of Aragon, 1285–1345* (Cambridge, 1993).

Manca, C., *Aspetti dell'espansione catalano-aragonese nel Mediterraneo occidentale. Il commercio internazionale del sale* (Biblioteca della rivista Economia e Storia, Milano, 1966).

Martinez Ferrando, J. E., *La tràgica història dels reis de Mallorca* (Barcelona, 1960).

Masía de Ros, A., *La Corona de Aragòn y los Estados del Norte de Africa. Política de Jaime II y Alfonso IV en Egipto, Ifriquía y Tremecén* (Barcelona, 1951).*

Massip, J., 'Les franqueres dels ciutadans de Tortosa al regne de Mallorca', CHCA XIII, vol. II.

Mata, M., *Conquests and reconquests of Menorca* (Barcelona, 1984).

Mauny, R., *Les navigations médiévales sur les côtes sahariennes* (Lisbon, 1960).

Melis, F., *Aspetti della vita economia medievale (studi nell'Archivio Datini di Prato)* (Siena/Florence, 1962).*

Meyerson, M., *The Muslims of Valencia in the age of Fernando and Isabel* (Berkeley/Los Angeles, 1991).

Moore, G., 'La spedizione dei fratelli Vivaldi e nuovi documenti d'archivio', *Atti della Società Ligure di Storia Patria*, n.s. 12 (1972).*

Moore, K., *Those of the street. The Catholic Jews of Mallorca* (Notre Dame, IN, 1976).

Murillo i Tuduri, A., *Documentaciò medieval menorquina. El llibre de la Cort Reial de Ciutadella. Index de cartes registrades de 1350 a 1403, segons còpia conservada a l'arxiu del regne de Mallorca* (Ciutadella, 1981).*

Musto, R. G., 'Queen Sancia of Naples (1286–1345) and the spiritual Franciscans', in *Women of the medieval world. Essays in honor of John H. Mundy*, ed. J. Kirshner and S. F. Wemple (Oxford, 1985).

Mut Calafell, A., 'La documentación del Archivo del Reino de Mallorca en la época de las Vísperas Sicilianas', CHCA XI, vol. III.

Nordenskjöld, A. E., *Periplus* (Stockholm, 1897).

Otis, L. L., 'Prostitution and repentance in late medieval Perpignan', *Women of the medieval world*, ed. J. Kirshner and S. F. Wemple (Oxford, 1985).

Prostitution in medieval society. The history of an urban institution in Languedoc (Chicago, 1985).

Parpal, C., *La conquista de Menorca en 1287 por Alfonso III de Aragòn* (Barcelona, 1901; Catalan edn, Barcelona, 1964).

Peláez, M., *Cambios y seguros marítimos en derecho catalan y balear*, Studia Albornotiana, Real Colegio de España (Bologna, 1984).

Catalunya després de la guerra civil del segle XV (Barcelona, 1981).

Perelló i Mas, Maria, *Menorca a l'epoca de Pere el Cerimoniós* (Ciutadella, 1986).*

Perez, L., 'Documentos conservados en los archivos vaticanos relativos al primer episcopado de Mallorca', *Boletí de la Societat Arqueològica llulliana*, 32 (1961/2).*

Petrucci, S., 'Tra Pisa e Maiorca: avvenimenti politici e rapporti commerciali nella prima metà del xiv secolo', CHCA xiii, vol. ii.

Piña (Pinya) Homs, R., *El consolat de Mar. Mallorca 1326–1800* (Palma de Mallorca, 1985).

Els reis de la casa de Mallorca (Palma de Mallorca, 1982).

Piponnier, F., *Costume et vie sociale. La cour d'Anjou, XIVᵉ–XVᵉ siècle* (Paris, 1970).

Pitzorno, B., 'Il consolato veneziano di Maiorca', *Studi nelle scienze guiridiche e sociali della Facoltà di Giurisprudenza della R. Università di Pavia*, 22 (1938).*

Pons, A., *Los Judíos de Mallorca durante los siglos XIII y XIV*, 2 vols. (Palma de Mallorca, 1957–60).*

'El reino privativo de Mallorca. Jaume II', in *História de Mallorca*, ed. J. Mascaró Pasarius, vol. iii (Palma de Mallorca, 1978).

Porcel, B., *Los Chuetas mallorquines. Quince siglos de racismo* (6th edn, Palma de Mallorca, 1986).

Primer Congrès Internacional d'Història: *8° Centenari de la Fundaciò de Puigcerdà (1177–1977)*, Institut d'Estudis Ceretans (Puigcerdà, 1983).

Pryor, J. H., *Business contracts of medieval Provence. Selected notulae from the cartulary of Giraud Amalric of Marseilles, 1248* (Toronto, 1981).*

Commerce, shipping and naval warfare in the medieval Mediterranean (London, 1987).

Geography, technology and war. Studies in the maritime history of the Mediterranean, 649–1571 (Cambridge, 1988).

Raynaud-Nguyen, I., 'Les Portulans: texte et iconographie', *Iconographie médiévale. Image, texte, contexte*, ed. G. Duchet-Suchaux (Paris, 1990).

Reglà Campistol, J., *Francia, la Corona de Aragón y la frontera pirenaica. La lucha por el Valle de Arán, siglos XIII–XIV*, 2 vols. (Madrid/Barcelona, 1951).*

de Reparaz, G., 'L'activité maritime et commerciale du Royaume d'Aragon au xiiᵉ siècle', *Bulletin hispanique*, 49 (1947).

Catalunya a les mars: navegants, mercaders i cartògrafs catalans de l'Edat Mitjana i del Renaixement (Barcelona, 1930).

Rey, E. G., *Les colonies franques de Syrie aux XII*ᵉ *et XIII*ᵉ *siècles* (Paris, 1883).

Rey Pastor, J. and Garcia Camareno, E., *La cartografia mallorquina* (Madrid, 1960).

Reyerson, K., *Business, banking and finance in medieval Montpellier* (Toronto, 1985).*

Commerce and society in Montpellier, 1250–1350, 2 vols. (Yale University Ph.D. thesis; University Microfilms International, 1974).*

'Flight from prosecution: the search for religious asylum in medieval Montpellier', *French Historical Studies*, 17 (1992).

'Montpellier and the Byzantine Empire: commercial interaction in the Mediterranean world before 1350', *Byzantion*, 48 (1978).

Riera Melis, A., 'L'Aparició de la draperia urbana als Pireneus orientals', *Annals de la Universitat d'Estiu, Andorra 1982. El sigle XIII* (Andorra la Vella, 1983).

La Corona de Aragón y el reino de Mallorca en el primer cuarto del siglo XIV. Vol. I, *Las repercussiones arancelarias de la autonomía balear (1298–1311)* (Madrid/Barcelona, 1986).*

'Mallorca 1298–1311, un ejemplo de "planificación económica" en la época de plena expansión', *Miscellanea en honor de Josep Maria Madurell i Marimón*, in *Estudios Históricos y Documentos de los Archivos de Protocolos*, 5 (1977).

'El regne de Mallorca en el context internacional de la primera meitat del segle XIV', *Homenatge a la memòria del Prof. Dr Emilio Sáez* (Barcelona, 1989).

Riu, M., 'Algunes fonts i bibliografia dels darrers anys sobre el Regne privatiu de Mallorca', CHCA XIII, vol. I.

Robson, J. A., 'The Catalan Fleet and Moorish sea-power (1337–1344)' *English Historical Review*, 74 (1959), 386–408.

Rogozinski, J., *Power, caste and law. Social conflict in fourteenth-century Montpellier* (Cambridge, MA, 1982).

Romestan, G., 'A propos du commerce des draps dans la Péninsule Ibérique au Moyen Age: les marchands languedociens dans le royaume de Valence pendant la première moitié du XIVᵉ siècle', *Bulletin Philologique et Historique (jusqu'à 1610) du Comité des Travaux historiques et scientifiques*, 1969, *Actes du 94ᵉ Congrès des Sociétés savantes tenu à Pau*, vol. I, *Les relations franco-espagnols jusqu'au XVIIᵉ siècle* (Paris, 1972).

'Draperie roussillonnaise et draperie languedocien dans la première moitié du XIVᵉ siècle', *51º Congrès de la Fédération historique du Languedoc méditerranéen et du Roussillon* (Montpellier, 1970).

'Les marchands de Montpellier et la leude de Majorque pendant la première moitié du XIVᵉ siècle', *Majorque, Languedoc et Roussillon de l'Antiquité à nos jours. 53º Congrès de la Fédération historique du Languedoc méditerranéen et du Roussillon* (Montpellier, 1982).

'Les relations commerciales entre Montpellier et Valence dans la première moitié du xive siècle', *VIII Congreso de História de la Corona de Aragón, Valencia 1967*, Section 2, *La Corona de Aragón en el siglo XIV*, vol. III (Valencia, 1973).

Rosselló Bordoy, G., *Notas para un estudio de Ibiza musulmana*, Trabajos del Museo arqueológico de Ibiza (Ibiza, 1985).

Rosselló Bordoy, G. (ed.), *Les illes orientals d'al-Andalus i les seves relacions amb Sharq al-Andalus, Magrib i Europa cristiana (ss. VIII–XIII)*. *V Jornades d'Estudis històrics locals* (Palma de Mallorca, 1987).

Rosselló Vaquer, Ramón, *Aportació a la història medieval de Menorca. El segle XIII* (Ciutadella, 1980).*

Aportació a la història medieval de Menorca. Segle XIV (Reis de Mallorques i Pere el Cerimoniós) (Ciutadella, 1985).*

Aportació a la història medieval de Menorca. El segle XV (Ciutadella, 1982).*

Libre del notari de Ciutadella Jaume Riudavets 1450–1453 (Ciutadella, 1982).*

La revolta menorquina contra Joan II (1463–1472). Aportació documental a la història medieval de Menorca (Ciutadella, 1981).*

Ruiz, T. F., 'Castilian merchants in England, 1248–1350', in *Order and innovation in the Middle Ages. Essays in honor of Joseph R. Strayer*, ed. W. C. Jordan, B. McNab and T. F. Ruiz (Princeton, NJ, 1976); repr. in Castilian as 'Mercaderes castellanos en Inglaterra, 1248–1350', in T. F. Ruiz, *Sociedad y poder real en Castilla en la Baja Edad Media* (Barcelona, 1981).

Rumeu de Armas, A., *El Obispado de Telde. Misioneros mallorquines y catalanes en el Atlántico* (Madrid, 1960).*

Runciman, Steven, *The Sicilian Vespers. A history of the Mediterranean world in the later thirteenth century* (Cambridge, 1958).

Russell, P., *The English intervention in Spain and Portugal in the time of Edward III and Richard II* (Oxford, 1955).

Sahlins, P., *Boundaries. The making of France and Spain in the Pyrenees* (Berkeley/Los Angeles, 1989).

Salavert y Roca, V., *Cerdeña y la expansión mediterránea de la Corona de Aragón 1297–1314*, 2 vols. (Madrid 1956).*

'El problema estratégico del Mediterráneo occidental y la política aragonese (siglos xiv y xv)', *IV Congreso de História de la Corona de Aragón, Mallorca 25 septembre–2 octobre 1995, Actas y Comunicaciones*, vol. 1 (Palma de Mallorca, 1959).

Sánchez Martínez M., 'Mallorquines y Genovesos en Almería durante el primer tercio del siglo xiv: el proceso contra Jaume Manfré (1334)', *Miscellània de textos medievals*, vol. iv, *La frontera terrestre i marítima amb l'Islam* (Barcelona, 1988).*

Santamaría, A., 'Communidades occitanes en la conquista y repoblación de Mallorca', in *El regne de Mallorca i el Sud Francès. IV Jornades d'Estudis històrics locals* (Palma de Mallorca, 1986).

Ejecutoria del Reino de Mallorca (Palma de Mallorca, 1990).*

'Enfeudación de la Corona de Mallorca a la Corona de Aragón', CHCA xi, vol. iv.

'El patrimonio de los communidades de Marsella y de Montpeller en el Repartimento de Mallorca', CHCA xii, vol. i.

'La reconquista de las vías marítimas', *Actas del I° Congreso internacional de História mediterranea*, in the *Anuario de Estudios medievales*, 10 (1980).

El reino de Mallorca en la primera mitad del siglo XV, monograph of *IV Congreso de la História de la Corona de Aragón* (Palma de Mallorca, 1955).

Sapori, A., 'La fiera di Salerno del 1478', *Bollettino dell'Archivio storico del Banco di Napoli*, 8 (1954), 51–84, repr. as 'Una fiera in Italia alla fine del Quattrocento: la fiera di Salerno del 1478', in his *Studi di storia economica (secoli XIII–XIV–XV)*, 3rd edn (Florence, 1967).

Sastre Moll, J., *Economía y sociedad del reino de Mallorca. Primer tercio del siglo XIV*, Trabajos del Museo de Mallorca (Palma de Mallorca, 1986).

'La salida de los Musulmanes menorquines tras la conquista de la isla por Alfonso III (1287)', CHCA xiii, vol. iii.

'Notas sobre la población musulmana a Menorca (1287)', in G. Rosselló Bordoy (ed.), *Les illes orientals d'al-Andalus* (Palma de Mallorca, 1987).

'Relaciones politico-comerciales entre Mallorca y el Rosellón en el primer tercio del siglo xiv', CHCA xii, vol. i.*

Sastre Portella, F., 'La conquista de Menorca en 1287: estado de la cuestion y perspectivas de futuro', CHCA xiii, vol. i.

'Sobre la repoblación de Menorca en la época de las Visperas Sicilianas', CHCA xi, vol. iv.

Sayous, A. E., *Commerce et finance en Méditerranée au Moyen Age* (London, 1988).

Selke, A. S., *The Conversos of Majorca. Life and death in a crypto-Jewish community in seventeenth-century Spain* (Hispania Judaica, 5, Jerusalem, 1986).

Serra Ràfols, E., 'Els catalans de Mallorca a les illes Canaries', *Homenaje a Rubió i Lluch* (Barcelona, 1936), vol. iii.*

'Los Mallorquines en Canarias', *Revista de Historia* (1941).*

'Mas sobre los viajes catalano-mallorquines a Canarias', *Revista de Historia* (1943).

Sevillano Colom, 'Mallorca y Canarias', *Hispania. Revista Española de Historia*, 120 (1972).

'Mercaderes y navegantes mallorquines. Siglos xiii–xv', in the *História de Mallorca*, ed. J. Mascaró Pasarius, vol. viii (Palma de Mallorca, 1978).

'Los viajes medievales desde Mallorca a Canarias', *Anuario de estudios atlánticos*, 23 (1978).

Sevillano Colom, F. and Pou Muntaner, J., *História del puerto de Palma de Mallorca* (Palma de Mallorca, 1974).*

Shatzmiller, J., *Shylock reconsidered* (Berkeley/Los Angeles, 1990).*

Shneidman, J. L., *The rise of the Aragonese–Catalan Empire, 1200–1350*, 2 vols. (New York, 1970).

Silvestri, A., *Il commercio a Salerno nella seconda metà del Quattrocento* (Salerno, 1952).*

Simon, L., 'The friars of the sack in Majorca', *Aspects of medieval Spain, 711–1492*, special issue of the *Journal of Medieval History*, 18 (1992).

'Society and religion in the kingdom of Majorca, 1229–c. 1300' (Ph.D. thesis, University of California, Los Angeles, 1989).

Smith, R. S., *The Spanish gild merchant. A history of the consulado, 1250–1700* (Durham, NC 1940).

Soto Company, R., *L'ordenació de l'espai i les relacions socials a Mallorca en el segle XIII (1229–1301)* (doctoral thesis of the Autonomous University of Barcelona, published in microfiche, Bellaterra, 1992).*

'La población musulmana de Mallorca bajo el dominio cristiano (1240–1276)', *Fontes Rerum Balearium* (Palma de Mallorca, 1978–80), vols. II–III.*

'Sobre mudèixars a Mallorca fins a finals del segle XIII', *Estudis d'història de Mayurqa i d'història de Mallorca dedicats a Guillem Rosselló i Bordoy* (Palma de Mallorca, 1982).

Störmann, Auguste, *Studien zur Geschichte des Königreichs Mallorka* (Abhandlungen zur mittleren und neueren Geschichte, 66, Berlin/Leipzig, 1918).

Strayer, J., *The reign of Philip the Fair* (Princeton, NJ, 1980).

Tangheroni, M., *Aspetti del commercio dei cereali nei paesi della Corona d'Aragona.* Vol. I, *La Sardegna* (Pisa/Cagliari, 1981).

Thomas, L. J., 'Montpellier entre la France et l'Aragon pendant la première moitié du XIVᵉ, siècle', *Monspeliensia. Mémoires et documents relatifs à Montpellier et à la région montpelliéraine publiés par la Société archéologique de Montpellier*, 1 (1928/9).*

Montpellier ville marchande. Histoire économique et sociale de Montpellier des origines à 1870 (Montpellier, 1936).

Trasselli, C. 'Frumento e panni inglesi nella Sicilia del xv secolo', *Annali della Facoltà di Economia e Commercio dell'Università di Palermo*, 9 (1955), repr. in C. Trasselli, *Mediterraneo e Sicilia all'inzio dell'epoca moderna* (Cosenza, 1980).

'Nuovi documenti sui Peruzzi, Bardi e Acciaiuoli in Sicilia', *Economia e Storia*, 3 (1956).

'Prezzi dei panni a Palermo nel xiv secolo', *Economia e Storia*, 1 (1954), 88–90.

Ullmann, W., 'The development of the medieval idea of sovereignty', *English Historical Review*, 64 (1949).

Urgell Hernández, R., 'Proceso entre Sancho de Mallorca y la Iglesia de Tarragona por derechos de jurisdicción en Ibiza y Formentera', CHCA XIII, vol. II.

Vale, M. G. A., *The Angevin Legacy and the Hundred Years War, 1250–1340* (Oxford, 1990).

Watson, W. B., 'Catalans in the markets of northern Europe during the fifteenth century', *Homenaje a Jaime Vicens Vives* (Barcelona, 1967), vol. II.

Wolff, P., 'Un grand centre économique et social', in *Histoire de Perpignan*, ed. P. Wolff (Pays et villes de France, Toulouse, 1985).

Willemsen, C. A., 'Jakob II. von Mallorka und Peter IV. von Aragon (1336–1349)', *Gesammelte Aufsätze zur Kulturgeschichte Spaniens*, 8 (1940).

'Der Untergang des Königreiches Mallorka und das Ende des Mallorkinischen Dynastie', *Gesammelte Aufsätze zur Kulturgeschichte Spaniens*, 5 (1935).

Winter, H., 'Catalan portolan maps and their place in the total view of cartographic development', *Imago Mundi*, 11 (1954).

Yates, F., 'Ramon Lull and John Scotus Erigena', *Journal of the Warburg and Courtauld Institutes*, 17 (1954), 1–44.

Zimmels, H. J., *Ashkenazim and Sephardim : their relations, differences and problems as reflected in the rabbinical responsa* (London, 1958).

Die Marranen in der rabbinischen Literatur (Berlin, 1930).

Index

For the kingdom of Majorca, see under individual kings (James II of Majorca, Sanç, James III of Majorca); for the Balearic islands see under Formentera, Ibiza, Mallorca (island), Menorca; for Mallorca (island) see also under Mallorca City.